PoetryFocus

2024

Leaving Certificate poems and notes for **English Higher Level**

Martin Kieran & Frances Rocks

Gill Education
Hume Avenue
Park West
Dublin 12
www.gilleducation.ie

Gill Education is an imprint of M.H. Gill & Co.

ISBN: 978-0-7171-93714

Design: Graham Thew
Print origination: Carole Lynch

At the time of going to press, all web addresses were active and contained information relevant to the topics in this book. Gill Education does not, however, accept responsibility for the content or views contained on these websites. Content, views and addresses may change beyond the publisher or author's control. Students should always be supervised when reviewing websites.

For permission to reproduce photographs, the authors and publisher gratefully acknowledge the following:

© Alamy: 2, 8, 11, 12, 15, 19, 20, 23, 32, 35, 36, 46, 98, 100, 103, 109, 112, 114, 130, 133, 141, 160, 180, 183, 191, 195, 198, 208, 211, 214, 227, 229, 235, 239, 242, 287, 288, 297, 334, 337, 340, 342, 349, 352, 362, 366, 368, 376, 378, 385, 388, 389, 392, 398, 400, 401, 411, 414, 421, 424; © Bridgeman Images: 58, 62, 71, 73, 79, 312, 315, 316, 320; © Collins Agency: 302; © Derek Speirs: 223; © Getty Images: 4, 7, 75, 77, 83, 84, 85, 87, 145, 147, 230, 232, 266, 268, 271, 275, 277, 292, 295, 328, 381, 382, 395, 407, 410; © iStock/Getty Premium: 16, 18, 26, 29, 49, 51, 53, 56, 67, 69, 105, 122, 137, 140, 162, 165, 166, 170, 172, 173, 177, 178, 184, 186, 187, 190, 249, 279, 282, 306, 308, 331, 332, 354, 357, 360, 403, 425; © Livioandronico2013/Wikimedia Commons: 283, 285; © PD Smith: 418, 420; © Rolling News: 244; © RTÉ Archives: 264; © Saint Patrick's Cathedral: 215; © Shutterstock: 134, 136; © Stephanie Joy: 206; © Topfoto: 118, 126, 127, 149.

The authors and publisher have made every effort to trace all copyright holders. If, however, any have been inadvertently overlooked, we would be pleased to make the necessary arrangement at the first opportunity.

The paper used in this book is made from the wood pulp of managed forests. For every tree felled, at least one tree is planted, thereby renewing natural resources.

Contents

(OL) indicates poems that are also prescribed for the Ordinary Level course.

(OL) indicates poems that are also
prescribed for the Ordinary Level course.

Introduction

Poetry Focus is a modern poetry textbook for Leaving Certificate Higher Level English. It includes all the prescribed poems for the 2024 exam as well as succinct commentaries on each one. Well-organised study notes allow students to develop their own individual responses and enhance their skills in critical literacy. **There is no single 'correct' approach to answering the poetry question.** Candidates are free to respond in any appropriate way that shows good knowledge of and engagement with the prescribed poems.

- **Concise poet biographies** provide context for the poems.
- **List of prescribed poems** gives a brief introduction to each poem.
- **Personal response** questions follow the text of each poem. These allow students to consider their first impressions before any in-depth study or analysis. These questions provide a good opportunity for written and/or oral exercises.
- **Critical literacy** highlights the main features of the poet's subject matter and style. These discussion notes will enhance the student's own critical appreciation through focused group work and/or written exercises. Analytical skills are developed in a coherent, practical way to give students confidence in articulating their own personal responses.
- **Analysis (writing about the poem) is provided using graded sample paragraphs** which aid students in fluently structuring and developing valid points, using fresh and varied expression. These model paragraphs also illustrate effective use of relevant quotations and reference.
- **Class/homework exercises** for each poem provide focused practice in writing personal responses to examination-style questions.
- **Points to consider** provide a memorable snapshot of the key aspects to remember about each poem.
- **Full sample Leaving Certificate essays** are accompanied by marking-scheme guidelines and examiner's comments. These show the student exactly what is required to achieve a successful top grade in the Leaving Cert. The examiner's comments illustrate the use of the PCLM marking scheme and are an invaluable aid for the ambitious student.
- **Sample essay plans** on each poet's work illustrate how to interpret a question and recognise the particular nuances of key words in examination questions. Student evaluation of these essay plans increase confidence in developing and organising clear response to exam questions.
- **Sample Leaving Cert questions** on each poet are given at the end of their particular section.
- **Revision Overviews** provide a concise and visual summary of each poet's work, through highlighting and interlinking relevant themes.
- **Unseen Poetry** provides guidelines for this 20-mark section of the paper. Included are numerous sample questions and answers, which allow students to practise exam-style answers.

The FREE eBook contains:

- **Investigate Further** sections, which contain **useful weblinks** should you want to learn more.
- **Pop-up key quotes** to encourage students to select their own individual combination of references from a poem and to write brief commentaries on specific quotations.
- Additional sample graded paragraphs called '**Developing your personal response**'.
- Audio of a selection of the poetry read by the poets, including audio of all Paula Meehan poetry.

Further material can also be found on GillExplore.ie:

- **A glossary of common literary terms** provides an easy reference when answering questions.
- **A critical analysis checklist** offers useful hints and tips on how to show genuine engagement with the poetry.

How is the Prescribed Poetry Question Marked?

The Prescribed Poetry Question is marked out of 50 marks by reference to the PCLM assessment criteria:

- Clarity of purpose (P): 30% of the total (15 marks)
- Coherence of delivery (C): 30% of the total (15 marks)
- Efficiency of language use (L): 30% of the total (15 marks)
- Accuracy of mechanics (M): 10% of the total (5 marks)

Each answer will be in the form of a response to a specific task requiring candidates to:

- Display a clear and purposeful engagement with the set task (P)
- Sustain the response in an appropriate manner over the entire answer (C)
- Manage and control language appropriate to the task (L)
- Display levels of accuracy in spelling and grammar appropriate to the required/chosen register (M)

General

'Students at Higher Level will be required to study a representative selection from the work of eight poets: a representative selection would seek to reflect the range of a poet's themes and interests and exhibit his/her characteristic style and viewpoint. Normally the study of at least six poems by each poet would be expected.' (DES English Syllabus, 6.3)

The marking scheme guidelines from the State Examinations Commission state that in the case of each poet, the candidates have **freedom of choice** in relation to the poems studied. In addition, there is **not a finite list of any 'poet's themes and interests'**.

Note that in responding to the question set on any given poet, the candidates must refer to the poem(s) they have studied but are not required to refer to **any specific poem(s), nor are they expected to discuss or refer to all the poems they have chosen to study**.

In each of the questions in **Prescribed Poetry**, the underlying nature of the task is the invitation to the candidates to **engage with the poems themselves**.

Exam Advice

- **You are not expected to write about any set number of poems** in the examination. You might decide to focus in detail on a small number of poems, or you could choose to write in a more general way on several poems.

- Most candidates write one or two well-developed **paragraphs** on each of the poems they have chosen for discussion. In other cases, a paragraph will focus on one specific aspect of the poet's work. When discussing recurring themes or features of style, appropriate cross-references to other poems may be useful.

- Reflect on central **themes** and viewpoints in the poems you discuss. Comment also on the use of language and the poet's distinctive **style**. Examine imagery, tone, structure, rhythm and rhyme. Be careful not to simply list aspects of style, such as alliteration or repetition. There's little point in mentioning that a poet uses sound effects or metaphors without discussing the effectiveness of such characteristics.

- Focus on **the task** you have been given in the poetry question. Identify the key terms in the wording of the question and think of similar words for these terms. This will help you develop a relevant and coherent personal response in keeping with the PCLM marking scheme criteria.

- Always root your answers in the text of the poems. Support the points you make with **relevant reference and quotation**. Make sure your own expression is fresh and lively. Avoid awkward expressions, such as 'It says in the poem that …'. Look for alternatives: 'There is a sense of …', 'The tone seems to suggest …', 'It's evident that …', etc.

- Neat, **legible handwriting** will help to make a positive impression on examiners. Corrections should be made by simply drawing a line through the mistake. Scored-out words distract attention from the content of your work.

- Keep the emphasis on why particular poets **appeal to you**. Consider the continuing relevance or significance of a poet's work. Perhaps you have shared some of the feelings or experiences expressed in the poems. Avoid starting answers with prepared biographical sketches. Brief reference to a poet's life are better used when discussing how the poems themselves were shaped by their experiences.

- Remember that the examination encourages **individual engagement** with the prescribed poems. Poetry can make us think and feel and imagine. It opens our minds to the wonderful possibilities of language and ideas. Your interaction with the poems is what matters most. **Commentary notes and critical interpretations are all there to be challenged.** Read the poems carefully and have confidence in expressing your own personal response.

Emily Dickinson

1830–1886

'Forever is composed of nows.'

Emily Dickinson was born on 10 December 1830 in Amherst, Massachusetts. Widely regarded as one of America's greatest poets, she is also known for her unusual life of self-imposed social seclusion. An enigmatic figure with a fondness for the macabre, she was a prolific letter-writer and private poet, though fewer than a dozen of her poems were published during her lifetime. It was only after her death in 1886 that her work was discovered. It is estimated that she wrote about 1,770 poems, many of which explored the nature of immortality and death, with an almost mantric quality at times. Ultimately, however, she is remembered for her distinctive style, which was unique for the era in which she wrote. Her poems contain short lines, typically lack titles and often ignore the rules of grammar, syntax and punctuation, yet she expressed far-reaching ideas in compact phrases. Amidst paradox and uncertainty, her poetry has an undeniable capacity to move and provoke.

Investigate Further

To find out more about Emily Dickinson, or to hear readings of her poems, you could do a search of some of the useful websites available such as YouTube, BBC Poetry, poetryfoundation.org and poetryarchive.org, or access additional material on this page of your eBook.

Prescribed Poems

(OL) indicates poems that are also prescribed for the Ordinary Level course.

POETRY FOCUS

1

'Hope' is the thing with feathers

'Hope' is the thing with feathers—
That perches in the soul—
And sings the tune without the words—
And never stops—at all—

And sweetest—in the Gale—is heard—   5
And sore must be the storm—
That could abash the little Bird
That kept so many warm—

I've heard it in the chillest land—
And on the strangest Sea—   10
Yet, never, in Extremity,
It asked a crumb—of Me.

And sweetest—in the Gale—is heard: hope is most comforting in times of trouble.
abash: embarrass; defeat.

in Extremity: in terrible times.

'And sweetest—in the Gale—is heard—'

👤 Personal Response

1. What are the main characteristics of the bird admired by Dickinson?
2. Dickinson uses an extended metaphor to explore her theme of hope. Comment on the effectiveness of this technique in the poem.
3. In your view, what is the purpose of the poem – to instruct, to explain, to express a feeling? Support your response by reference to the text.

👁 Critical Literacy

Few of Emily Dickinson's poems were published during her lifetime and it was not until 1955, 69 years after her death, that an accurate edition of her poems was published, with the original punctuation and words. This instructive poem explores an abstraction: hope. It is one of her 'definition' poems, wherein she compares hope to a little bird, offering comfort to all.

In stanza one, Dickinson explores hope by using the **metaphor of a little bird** whose qualities are similar to those of hope: non-threatening, calm and powerful. Just like the bird, hope can rise above the earth with all its troubles and desperate times. Raised in the Puritan tradition, Dickinson, although rejecting formal religion, would have been aware of the religious symbolism of the dove and its connection with divine inspiration and the Holy Spirit or Holy Ghost, as well as the reference to doves in the story of Noah's Ark and the Flood. Hope appears against all odds and 'perches in the soul'. But this hope is not easily defined, so she refers to it as 'the thing', an inanimate object.

Hope's silent presence is able to **communicate** beyond reason and logic and far **beyond the limitations of language**: 'sings the tune without the words'. Hope's permanence is highlighted by the unusual use of dashes in the punctuation: 'never-stops-at-all', suggesting its continuity and endurance.

Stanza two focuses on the tangible qualities of hope (sweetness and warmth) and shows the spiritual, emotional and psychological **comfort found in hope**. The 'Gale' could refer to the inner state of confusion felt in the agony of despair. The little bird that comforts and shelters its young offers protection to 'so many'. The energy of the word 'abash' suggests the buffeting wind of the storm against which the little bird survives. The last two run-on lines convey the protective, welcoming circle of the 'little bird's wing'.

Stanza three refers to a personal experience of hope in times of anguish ('I've heard'). Extreme circumstances are cleverly expressed in the phrases 'chillest land' and 'strangest Sea'. This reclusive poet spent most of her life indoors in her father's house. She then explains that hope is not demanding in bad times; it is generous, giving rather than taking: 'Yet, never, in Extremity,/It asked a crumb—of Me.' The central paradox of hope is expressed in the metaphor of the bird, delicate and fragile, yet strong and unbeatable. The tiny bird is an effective image for the first stirring of hope in a time of despair. The solemn ending gives hope its deserved dignified celebration.

Dickinson was a unique and original talent. She used the regular rhythm of hymns. She also used their form of the four-line verse. Yet this is not conventional poetry, due to Dickinson's use of the dash to slow the line and make the reader pause and consider. Ordinary words like 'at all' and 'is heard' assume a tremendous importance and their position is to be considered and savoured. **Her unusual punctuation has the same effect, as it highlights the dangers ('Gale', 'Sea')**. The alliteration of 's' in 'strangest Sea' and the run-on line to suggest the circling comfort of the little bird all add to the curious music of Dickinson's poems. The uplifting, self-confident tone of the poem is in direct contrast to the strict Puritanical tradition of a severe, righteous God, with which she would have been familiar in her youth and which she rejected, preferring to keep her Sabbath 'staying at home'.

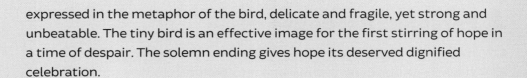

✒ Writing About the Poem

'Emily Dickinson's poetry contains an intense awareness of the private, inner self.' Discuss this view with particular reference to '"Hope" is the thing with feathers'.

Sample Paragraph

Everyone has experienced moments of depression when it seems that nothing is ever going to go right again. Dickinson, with her simple image of the bird singing, provides an optimistic response to this dark state of mind. She develops this metaphor, comforting us with the thought that the bird (symbolising hope) can communicate with us without the need for language, 'sings the tune without words'. Dickinson understands the darkness of despair, 'in the Gale', 'the strangest Sea'. But the bird of hope provides comfort ('sweetest'). The poet uses enjambment effectively in the lines 'That could abash the little Bird/That kept so many warm'. The run-on rhythm suggests the protection of hope encircling us, just as the wing of the bird protects her young in the nest. The phrase 'perches in the soul' suggests to me that the poet regards hope as coming of its own choice.

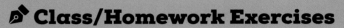
🖊 Class/Homework Exercises

1. 'Dickinson is a wholly new and original poetic genius.' Do you agree or disagree with this statement? Support your response with reference to '"Hope" is the thing with feathers'.

2. 'Emily Dickinson often uses concrete language to communicate abstract ideas in her unusual poems.' Discuss this view, with reference to '"Hope" is the thing with feathers'.

◉ Points to Consider

• The poem explores the concept of hope and its impact on human life.

• Effective use of the extended metaphor of 'the little Bird'.

• Symbols represent the challenges people face in life.

• Variety of tones: assured, personal, reflective, optimistic, etc.

2 There's a certain Slant of light

There's a certain Slant of light,
Winter Afternoons—
That oppresses, like the Heft
Of Cathedral Tunes—

Heavenly Hurt, it gives us—   5
We can find no scar,
But internal difference,
Where the Meanings, are—

None may teach it—Any—
'Tis the Seal Despair—   10
An imperial affliction
Sent us of the Air—

When it comes, the Landscape listens—
Shadows—hold their breath—
When it goes, 'tis like the Distance   15
On the look of Death—

Slant: incline; fall;
interpretation.

oppresses: feels heavy;
overwhelms.
Heft: strength; weight;
influence.

Any: anything.

Seal Despair: sign or
symbol of hopelessness.
imperial affliction: God's
will for mortal human
beings.

'Heavenly Hurt, it gives us—'

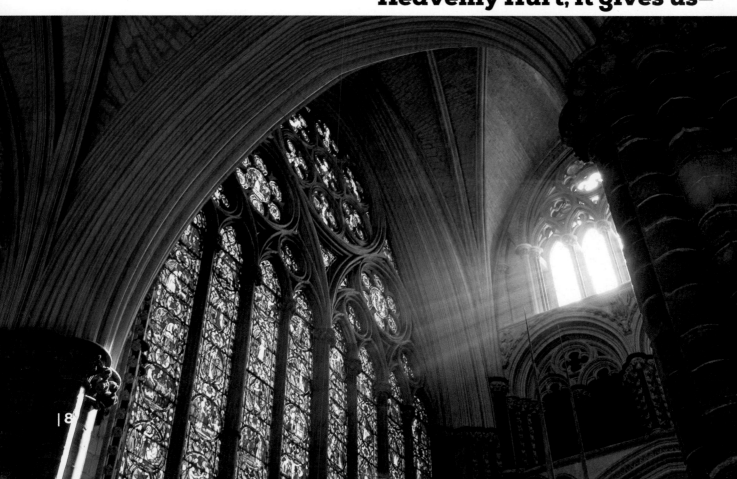

👤 Personal Response

1. Describe the mood and atmosphere created by the poet in the opening stanza.
2. Comment on Dickinson's use of personification in the poem.
3. Write your own personal response to the poem, supporting your views with reference or quotation.

👁 Critical Literacy

Dickinson was a keen observer of her environment, often dramatising her observations in poems. In this case, a particular beam of winter light puts the poet into a mood of depression as the slanting sunlight communicates a sense of despair. The poem illustrates her creeping fascination with mortality. But although the poet's subject matter is intricate and disturbing, her own views are more difficult to determine. Ironically, this exploration of light and its effects seems to suggest a great deal about Dickinson's own dark consciousness.

From the outset, Dickinson creates an uneasy atmosphere. The setting ('Winter Afternoons') is dreary and aimless. Throughout stanza one, there is an underlying sense of time weighing heavily, especially when the light is compared to solemn cathedral music ('Cathedral Tunes'). We usually expect church music to be inspirational, but in this case, its 'Heft' simply 'oppresses' and adds to the **downcast mood**.

In stanza two, the poet considers the significance of the sunlight. For her, its effects are negative, causing pain to the world: 'Heavenly Hurt, it gives us.' The paradoxical language appears to reflect Dickinson's ironic attitude that **human beings live in great fear of God's power**. Is there a sense that deep down in their souls ('Where the Meanings, are'), people struggle under the weight of God's will, fearing death and judgement?

This feeling of humanity's helplessness is highlighted in stanza three: 'None may teach it' sums up the predicament of our limitations. Life and death can never be fully understood. Perhaps this is our tragic fate – our 'Seal Despair'. Dickinson presents **God as an all-powerful royal figure** associated with suffering and punishment ('An imperial affliction'). Is the poet's tone critical and accusatory? Or is she simply expressing the reality of human experience?

Stanza four is highly dramatic. **Dickinson personifies a terrified world** where 'the Landscape listens'. The earlier sombre light is now replaced by 'Shadows' that 'hold their breath' in the silence. The poet imagines the shocking moment of death and the mystery of time ('the Distance'). While the poem's ending is open to speculation, it seems clear that Dickinson is exploring the transition from life into eternity, a subject that is central to her writing. The only certain conclusion is an obvious one – that death is an inescapable reality beyond human understanding, as mysterious as it is natural. The poet's final tone is resigned, almost relieved. The 'Slant of light' offers no definitive answers to life's questions and the human condition is as inexplicable as death itself.

Throughout the poem, Dickinson's fragmented style is characterised by her **erratic punctuation and repeated use of capital letters**. She uses the dash to create suspense and drama. For the poet, the winter light is seen as an important sign from God, disturbing the inner 'Landscape' of her soul. In the end, the light (a likely metaphor for truth) causes Dickinson to experience an inner sadness and a deep sense of spiritual longing.

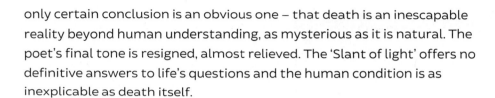

Writing About the Poem

In your view, what is the central theme in 'There's a certain Slant of light'? Support the points you make with suitable reference to the text.

Sample Paragraph

EXAMINER'S COMMENT

A well-written, top-grade response that shows good engagement with both the poem and the question. References and succinct quotations used effectively to illustrate the poet's startling consideration of death. Confident and varied discussion of the poet's style throughout.

I think that death is the main theme in Dickinson's poems. The poem is atmospheric, but the light coming through the window can be interpreted as a symbol of hope. However, Dickinson's language is quite negative and it could be argued that our lives are under pressure and that fear of eternal damnation is also part of life. 'Heavenly Hurt' and 'imperial affliction' suggest that we are trying to avoid sin in this life in order to find salvation after death. I believe that the central message is that death comes to us all and we must accept it. The mood is oppressive, just like the sunlight coming in through the church window and the depressing 'Cathedral Tunes'. Dickinson's theme is distressing and images such as 'Seal Despair' and 'Shadows' add to the uneasiness of the reality that death is unavoidable.

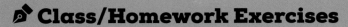

🖊 Class/Homework Exercises

1. How would you describe the dominant mood of the poem? Is it positive in any way? Explain your response, supporting the points you make with suitable reference to the text.
2. Identify the dramatic elements of 'There's a certain Slant of light', commenting on their impact.

☉ Points to Consider

- **The relationship between God and human beings is a central theme.**

- **Dickinson also explores the mystery of death.**

- **Dramatic atmosphere created by dynamic imagery and fragmented rhythm.**

- **Variety of moods – unease, fear, pessimism, etc.**

3

I felt a Funeral, in my Brain

I felt a Funeral, in my Brain,
And Mourners to and fro
Kept treading—treading—till it seemed
That Sense was breaking through—

And when they all were seated,   5
A Service, like a Drum—
Kept beating—beating—till I thought
My Mind was going numb—

And then I heard them lift a Box
And creak across my Soul   10
With those same Boots of Lead, again,
Then Space—began to toll,

As all the Heavens were a Bell,
And Being, but an Ear,
And I, and Silence, some strange Race   15
Wrecked, solitary, here—

And then a Plank in Reason, broke,
And I dropped down, and down—
And hit a World, at every plunge,
And Finished knowing—then—   20

treading: crush by walking on.
Sense: faculty of perception; the senses (seeing, hearing, touching, tasting, smelling); sound, practical judgement.

toll: ring slowly and steadily, especially to announce a death.
As all: as if all.

And Being, but an Ear: all senses, except hearing, are now useless.

'And then a Plank in Reason, broke'

👤 Personal Response

1. Do you find the images in this poem frightening, gruesome or coldly realistic? Give reasons for your answer, supported by textual reference.
2. Where is the climax of the poem, in your opinion? Refer to the text in your answer.
3. Write a short personal response to the poem, highlighting the impact it made on you.

👁 Critical Literacy

This poem is thought to have been written in 1861, at a time of turbulence in Dickinson's life. She was having religious and artistic doubts and had experienced an unhappy time in a personal relationship. This interior landscape paints a dark picture of something falling apart. It is for the reader to decide whether it is a fainting spell, a mental breakdown or a funeral. That is the mystery of Dickinson.

The startling perspective of this poem in stanza one can be seen as the view experienced by a person in a coffin, if the poem is read as an **account of the poet imagining her death**. Alternatively, it could refer to the suffocating feeling of the breakdown of consciousness, either through fainting or a mental breakdown. Perhaps it is the death of artistic activity. Whichever reading is chosen, and maybe all co-exist, the **interior landscape of awareness is being explored**. The use of the personal pronoun 'I' shows that this is a unique experience, although it has relevance for all. The relentless pounding of the mourners walking is reminiscent of a blinding migraine headache. The repetition of the hard-sounding 't' in the verb 'treading—treading' evocatively describes this terrible experience. The 'I' is undergoing an intense trauma beyond understanding: 'Sense was breaking through.' This repetition and disorientation are closely associated with psychological breakdown.

Stanza two gives a **first person account of a funeral**. The mourners are seated and the service has begun. Hearing ('an Ear') is the only sense that is functioning. All the verbs refer to sound: 'tread', 'beat', 'heard', 'creak', 'toll'. The passive 'I' receives the experience, hearing, not actively listening. The experience is so overwhelming that 'I' thought the 'Mind was going numb', unable to endure any more. The use of the past tense reminds the reader that the experience is over, so is the first-person narrative told from beyond the grave? Is this the voice of someone who has died? Or is it the voice of someone in the throes of a desperate personal experience? The reader must decide.

The reference to 'Soul' in stanza three suggests a **spiritual dimension** to the experience. The 'I' has started to become disoriented as the line dividing an external experience and an internal one is breaking. The mourners 'creak across my Soul'. The oppressive, almost suffocating experience is captured in the onomatopoeic phrase 'Boots of Lead' and space becomes filled with the tolling bell. Existence in stanza four is reduced totally to hearing. The fearful transitory experience of crossing from awareness to unconsciousness, from life to death, is being imagined. The 'I' in stanza four is now stranded, 'Wrecked', cut off from life. The person is in a comatose state, unable to communicate: 'solitary, here'. The word 'here' makes the reader feel present at this awful drama.

Finally, in stanza five, a new sensation takes over, **the sense of falling uncontrollably**. The 'I' has finished knowing and is now no longer aware of their surroundings. Is this the descent into the hell of the angels in 'Paradise Lost'? Is it the descent of the coffin into the grave? Or is it the descent into madness or oblivion? The 'I' has learned something, but it is not revealed. The repetition of 'And' advances the movement of the poem in an almost uncontrollable way, mimicking the final descent. The 'I' is powerless under the repetitive verbs and the incessant rhythm punctuated by the ever-present dash. This poem is extraordinary, because before the study of psychology had defined it, it is a step-by-step description of mental collapse. Here is 'the drama of process'.

✒ Writing About the Poem

'"I felt a Funeral, in my Brain" is a detailed and intense exploration of the experience of death.' Discuss this statement, using references from the text to support your views.

Sample Paragraph

Dickinson's imagined funeral suggests the losing of the grip on life by the individual 'I'. The noise ('treading', 'beating') induces an almost trance-like state as the brain becomes numb. The poet suggests that awareness is reduced to a single sense – hearing – 'an Ear'. I also find the poetic voice chilling. But the most compelling line in the poem is 'And then a Plank in Reason, broke'. This conveys the end of reason as the 'I' loses consciousness, hurtling away into another dimension. Even the punctuation, with the use of commas, conveys this reality. But the most unnerving word is yet to come – 'then'. What exactly does the poet know? Dickinson leaves us with unanswered questions.

EXAMINER'S COMMENT

A sustained personal response which attempts to stay focused throughout. The intensity within the poem is conveyed through a variety of expressions ('compelling', 'unnerving') and there is some worthwhile discussion on how features of the poet's style advance the theme of death. A solid high-grade answer.

✒ Class/Homework Exercises

1. 'She seems as close to touching bottom here as she ever got.' Discuss this view of Emily Dickinson with reference to the poem 'I felt a Funeral, in my Brain'.
2. Comment on the conclusion of the poem. Did you think it is satisfactory? Or does it leave unanswered questions?

⊙ Points to Consider

- Themes include the imagined experience of loss of control and death.
- Vivid imagery depicts funeral scene.
- Introspective tones of uncertainty, shock and terror.
- Insistent rhythms, anguished tone, abrupt syntax all create dramatic impact.
- Striking use of onomatopoeia, assonance, repetition, etc.

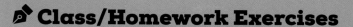

4

A Bird came down the Walk

A Bird came down the Walk—
He did not know I saw—
He bit an Angleworm in halves
And ate the fellow, raw,

And then he drank a Dew   5
From a convenient Grass—
And then hopped sidewise to the Wall
To let a Beetle pass—

He glanced with rapid eyes
That hurried all around—   10
They looked like frightened Beads, I thought—
He stirred his Velvet Head

Like one in danger, Cautious,
I offered him a Crumb
And he unrolled his feathers   15
And rowed him softer home—

Than Oars divide the Ocean,
Too silver for a seam—
Or Butterflies, off Banks of Noon
Leap, plashless as they swim.   20

Angleworm: small worm used as fish bait by anglers.

the Ocean: Dickinson compares the blue sky to the sea.
silver: the sea's surface looks like solid silver.
a seam: opening; division.
plashless: splashless; undisturbed.

'He glanced with rapid eyes'

👤 Personal Response

1. In your view, what does the poem suggest about the relationship between human beings and nature?

2. What is the effect of Dickinson's use of humour in the poem? Does it let you see nature in a different way? Support the points you make with reference to the text.

3. 'Emily Dickinson expresses her admiration for nature through evocative sound effects.' To what extent do you agree with this statement? Support your answer with reference to the poem.

👁 Critical Literacy

In this short descriptive poem, Dickinson celebrates the beauty and wonder of animals. While the bird is seen as a wild creature at times, other details present its behaviour and appearance in human terms. The poem also illustrates Dickinson's quirky sense of humour as well as offering interesting insights into nature and the exclusion of human beings from that world.

The poem opens with an everyday scene. Because the bird is unaware of the poet's presence, it behaves naturally. Stanza one demonstrates the **competition and danger of nature**: 'He bit an Angleworm in halves.' Although Dickinson imagines the bird within a human context, casually coming 'down the Walk' and suddenly eating 'the fellow, raw', she is amused by the uncivilised reality of the animal kingdom. The word 'raw' echoes her self-critical sense of shock. Despite its initial elegance, the predatory bird could hardly have been expected to cook the worm.

The poet's comic portrayal continues in stanza two. She gives the bird certain social qualities, drinking from a 'Grass' and politely allowing a hurrying beetle to pass. The tone is relaxed and playful. The slender vowel sounds ('convenient') and soft sibilance ('sidewise', 'pass') add to the seemingly refined atmosphere. However, the mood changes in stanza three, reflecting the bird's cautious fear. Dickinson observes the rapid eye movement, 'like frightened Beads'. Such **precise detail increases the drama of the moment**. The details of the bird's prim movement and beautiful texture are wonderfully accurate: 'He stirred his Velvet Head.' The simile is highly effective, suggesting the creature's natural grace.

The danger becomes more explicit in stanza four. Both the spectator and the observed bird are 'Cautious'. The crumb offered to the bird by the poet is rejected, highlighting the **gulf between their two separate worlds**. The description of the bird taking flight evokes the delicacy and fluidity of its movement: 'And he unrolled his feathers/And rowed him softer home.' The confident rhythm and emphatic alliteration enrich our understanding of the harmony between the creature and its natural environment. The sensual imagery captures the magnificence of the bird, compared to a rower moving with ease across placid water.

Stanza five develops the metaphorical description further, conveying the bird's poise and mystery: 'Too silver for a seam.' Not only was its flying seamless, it was smoother than that of butterflies leaping 'off Banks of Noon' and splashlessly swimming through the sky. The **breathtaking image and onomatopoeic language** remind us of Dickinson's admiration for nature in all its impressive beauty and is one of the most memorable descriptions in Dickinson's writing.

✍ Writing About the Poem

In your view, does Dickinson have a sense of empathy with the bird? Support your response with reference to the poem.

Sample Paragraph

Dickinson is both fascinated and amused by the small bird in her garden. She seems honoured that out of nowhere 'A Bird came down the Walk'. When it swallows a worm 'raw', she becomes even more interested. The fact that she admits 'He did not know I saw' tells me that she really has empathy for the bird. Her tone suggests she feels privileged to watch and she certainly doesn't want to disturb it in its own world. The poet also finds the bird's antics funny. Although it devours the worm, it behaves very mannerly towards the beetle. Dickinson shows her feelings for the bird when it becomes frightened and she notices it is 'in danger'. At the very end, she expresses her admiration for the beauty of the bird as it flies off to freedom – to its 'softer home'. The descriptions of it like a rower or a butterfly suggest that she admires its grace.

EXAMINER'S COMMENT

Apt references and short quotations are effectively used to illustrate the poet's regard for the bird. The answer ranges well over much of the poem and considers various tones (including fascination, amusement, reverence, concern and admiration). A confident top-grade response.

✒ Class/Homework Exercises

1. Comment on Dickinson's use of imagery in 'A Bird came down the Walk'. Support the points you make with the aid of suitable reference.

2. In your opinion, what does the poem suggest about the differences (or similarities) between animals and humans? Support your response with reference to the text.

◎ Points to Consider

- **Exploration of the wonder of nature.**

- **Interesting use of personification gives the bird social graces.**

- **Impact of sensuous imagery, metaphorical language, sibilant effects.**

- **Contrasting tones – bemused, concerned, surprised, upbeat, etc.**

5 I heard a Fly buzz— when I died

EMILY DICKINSON

I heard a Fly buzz—when I died—
The Stillness in the Room
Was like the Stillness in the Air—
Between the Heaves of Storm—

Heaves: lift with effort.

The Eyes around—had wrung them dry—   5
And Breaths were gathering firm
For that last Onset—when the King
Be witnessed—in the Room—

Onset: beginning.
the King: God.

I willed my Keepsakes—Signed away
What portion of me be   10
Assignable—and then it was
There interposed a Fly—

Keepsakes: gifts treasured for the sake of the giver.

interposed: inserted between or among things.

With Blue—uncertain stumbling Buzz—
Between the light—and me—
And then the Windows failed—and then   15
I could not see to see—

'And then the Windows failed–'

👤 Personal Response

1. How would you describe the atmosphere in the poem? Pick out two phrases which, in your opinion, are especially descriptive and explain why you chose them.
2. Do you think Dickinson uses contrast effectively in this poem? Discuss one contrast you found particularly striking.
3. Write a brief personal response to the poem, highlighting its impact on you.

 Critical Literacy

Dickinson was fascinated by death. This poem examines the moment between life and death. At that time, it was common for family and friends to be present at deathbed vigils. It was thought that the way a person behaved or looked at the moment of death gave an indication of the soul's fate.

The last moment of a person's life is a solemn and often sad occasion. The perspective of the poem is that of the person dying and this significant moment is dominated by the buzzing of a fly in the room in the first stanza. This is **absurdly comic and strangely distorts** this moment into something strange. Surely the person dying should be concerned with more important matters than an insignificant fly: 'I heard a Fly buzz—when I died.' The room is still and expectant as last breaths are drawn. The word 'Heaves' suggests the force of the storm that is about to break.

In the second stanza, the mourners no longer cry but hold their breath, steadfast ('firm') in their religious belief as they await the entrance of God ('King'). 'Be witnessed' refers to both the mourners and the dying person, conjuring up the deep solemnity of a court. The word 'firm' also suggests these people's steadfast religious beliefs. The third stanza is concerned with putting matters right. The dying person has made a will – 'What portion of me be/Assignable' – and what is not assignable belongs to God. The person is awaiting the coming of his/her Maker, 'and then it was/There interposed a Fly' – the symbol of decay and corruption appeared. Human affairs cannot be managed; real life intervenes. The **fly comes between ('interposed') the dying person and the moment of death, which trivialises** the event.

The fractured syntax of the last stanza shows the **breakdown of the senses** at the moment of death: 'Between the light—and me.' Sight and sound are blurring. The presence of the fly is completely inappropriate, like a drunken person at a solemn ceremony, disturbing and embarrassing and interrupting proceedings. The fly is now between the dying person and the source of light. Does this suggest that the person has lost concentration on higher things, distracted by the buzzing fly? The sense of sight then fails: 'And then the Windows failed.' The moment of death has come and gone, dominated by the noisy fly. Has the fly prevented the person from reaching another dimension? Is death emptiness, just human decay, as signified by the presence of the fly, or is there something more? Do we need comic relief at overwhelming occasions? Is the poet signalling her own lack of belief in an afterlife with God? Dickinson, as usual, intrigues, **leaving the reader with more questions than answers**, so that the reader, like the dying person, is struggling to 'see to see'.

✒ Writing About the Poem

'Dickinson's poems on mortality often lead to uncertainty or despair.'
Discuss this statement with particular reference to 'I heard a Fly
buzz—when I died'.

Sample Paragraph

The view of this deathbed scene is from the dying person's perspective.
Dickinson seems to be saying that life and death are random –
and this goes against the human desire for order, 'Signed
away/What portion of me be/Assignable'. I feel the poet
may be suggesting that the dying person, distracted by
the fly is, therefore, cheated. The occasion has passed,
dominated by a buzzing fly. Dickinson's voice is far
from reassuring. Instead, she draws a deathbed scene
and lets us 'see to see'. The divided voice, that of the
person dying and that of the person after death
leaves us with a question – is death just the final stage
in the meaningless cycle of life? In the end, this poem
leaves me with uncertainties about the human condition
and our ability to exercise control.

EXAMINER'S COMMENT

*This solid, high-grade
response includes interesting
and thought-provoking ideas on a
challenging question. Comments
show some good personal
engagement with the poem and the
issues raised by Dickinson. Expression
is impressive and apt quotations are
used effectively throughout the
answer. References to the
dramatic style and tone
would have improved
the standard.*

✑ Class/Homework Exercises

1. Comment on how Dickinson's style contributes to the theme or
   message in this poem. Refer closely to the text in your response.
2. Is there any suggestion that the speaker in this poem believes in a
   spiritual afterlife? Give a reason for your response, supporting your
   views with reference to the text.

⊙ Points to Consider

- **Dickinson raises questions about death and the possibility of an afterlife.**
- **Surreal sense of the absurd throughout.**
- **Dramatic elements – the deathbed scene, still atmosphere, observers,
  noises, etc.**
- **Contrasting tones include disbelief, confusion, resignation and
  helplessness.**
- **Effective use of contrast and symbols (light, the fly) and repetition.**

The Soul has Bandaged moments

The Soul has Bandaged moments—
When too appalled to stir—
She feels some ghastly Fright come up
And stop to look at her—

Salute her—with long fingers—   5
Caress her freezing hair—
Sip, Goblin, from the very lips
The Lover—hovered—o'er—
Unworthy, that a thought so mean
Accost a Theme—so—fair—   10

The soul has moments of Escape—
When bursting all the doors—
She dances like a Bomb, abroad,
And swings upon the Hours,

As do the Bee—delirious borne—   15
Long Dungeoned from his Rose—
Touch Liberty—then know no more,
But Noon, and Paradise—

The Soul's retaken moments—
When, Felon led along,   20
With shackles on the plumed feet,
And staples, in the Song,

The Horror welcomes her, again,
These, are not brayed of Tongue—

Bandaged moments: painful experiences.
appalled: shocked, horrified.
stir: act; retaliate.

Accost: address.

Escape: freedom.

like a Bomb: dramatically.
abroad: in unusual directions.

Dungeoned: imprisoned in the hive.

Felon: criminal.

shackles: chains, ropes.
plumed: decorated.
staples: fastenings.

brayed of Tongue: spoken of.

👤 Personal Response

1. What details in the poem evoke the feelings of 'ghastly Fright' experienced by the soul? Support your answer with quotation or reference.
2. Choose one comparison from the poem that you find particularly effective. Explain your choice.
3. Comment on Dickinson's use of dashes in this poem, briefly explaining their effectiveness.

👁 Critical Literacy

In much of her poetry, Dickinson focuses on the nature of consciousness and the experience of being alive. She was constantly searching for meaning, particularly of transient moments or changing moods. This search is central to 'The Soul has Bandaged moments', where the poet takes us through a series of dramatic images contrasting the extremes of the spirit and the conscious self.

Stanza one introduces the soul as being fearful and vulnerable, personified as a terrified female who 'feels some ghastly Fright', with the poem's stark

'As do the Bee—delirious borne—'

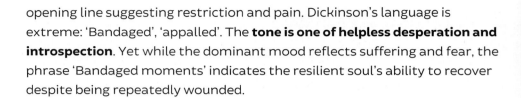

opening line suggesting restriction and pain. Dickinson's language is extreme: 'Bandaged', 'appalled'. The **tone is one of helpless desperation and introspection**. Yet while the dominant mood reflects suffering and fear, the phrase 'Bandaged moments' indicates the resilient soul's ability to recover despite being repeatedly wounded.

Stanza two is unnervingly dramatic. The poet creates a mock-romantic scene between the victimised soul and the 'ghastly Fright' figure, now portrayed as a hideous goblin and her would-be lover, their encounter depicted in terms of gothic horror. The soul experiences terrifying fantasies as the **surreal sequence becomes increasingly menacing** and the goblin's long fingers 'Caress her freezing hair'. The appearance of an unidentified shadowy 'Lover' is unexpected. There is a sense of the indecisive soul being caught between two states, represented by the malevolent goblin and the deserving lover. It is unclear whether Dickinson is writing about the choices involved in romantic love or the relationship between herself and God.

The stanza ends inconclusively, juxtaposing two opposites: the 'Unworthy' or undeserving 'thought' and the 'fair' (worthy) 'Theme'. The latter might well refer to the ideal of romantic love. If so, it is confronted by erotic desire (the 'thought'). Dickinson's disjointed style, especially her frequent use of dashes within stanzas, isolates key words and intensifies the overwhelmingly **nightmarish atmosphere**.

The feeling of confused terror is replaced with ecstatic 'moments of Escape' in stanzas three and four. The soul recovers in triumph, 'bursting all the doors'. This **explosion of energy** ('She dances like a Bomb') evokes a rising mood of riotous freedom. Explosive verbs ('bursting', 'dances', 'swings') and robust rhythms add to the sense of uncontrollable excitement. Dickinson compares the soul to a 'Bee—delirious borne'. After being 'Long Dungeoned' in its hive, this bee can now enjoy the sensuous delights of 'his Rose'.

The mood is short-lived, however, and in stanzas five and six, 'The Horror' returns. The soul becomes depressed again, feeling bound and shackled, like a 'Felon led along'. **Dickinson develops this criminal metaphor** – 'With shackles on the plumed feet' – leaving us with an ultimate sense of loss as 'The Horror welcomes her, again'. Is this the soul's inevitable fate? The final line is unsettling. Whatever horrible experiences confront the soul, they are simply unspeakable: 'not brayed of Tongue.'

As always, Dickinson's poem is open to many interpretations. Critics have suggested that the poet is dramatising the turmoil of dealing with the loss of creativity. Some view the poem's central conflict as the tension between romantic love and sexual desire. Others believe that the poet was exploring the theme of depression and mental instability. In the end, readers must find their own meaning and decide for themselves.

🖋 Writing About the Poem

Comment on the dramatic elements that are present in the poem, supporting the points you make with reference to the text.

Sample Paragraph

'The Soul has Bandaged moments' is built around a conflict between the 'Soul', or spirit, and its great enemy, 'Fright'. Dickinson sets the dramatic scene with the Soul still recovering – presumably from the last battle. It is 'Bandaged' after the fight with its arch enemy. The descriptions of the soul's opponent are startling. Fright is 'ghastly', a 'Horror' who is trying to seduce the innocent soul. Dickinson's images add to the tension. In the seduction scene, the goblin is described as having 'long fingers'. The goblin uses its bony claws to 'Caress her freezing hair'. The drama continues right to the end. The soul is compared to a 'Felon' being led away in 'shackles'. Finally, Dickinson's stop-and-start style is unsettling. Broken rhythms and condensed language increase the edgy atmosphere throughout this highly dramatic poem.

EXAMINER'S COMMENT

An assured and focused top-grade response, showing a clear understanding of the poem's dramatic features. The answer addressed both subject matter and style, using back-up illustration and integrated quotes successfully. Expression throughout was also excellent.

🖋 Class/Homework Exercises

1. How would you describe the dominant tone of 'The Soul has Bandaged moments'? Use reference to the text to show how the tone is effectively conveyed.
2. Identify the poem's surreal aspects and comment on their impact.

⊙ Points to Consider

- **An intense exploration of the nature of spiritual awareness.**

- **Dickinson focuses on a series of traumatic experiences.**

- **Effective use of dramatic verbs and vivid imagery.**

- **The soul is personified to convey various states – fear, joy, terror, etc.**

7 I could bring You Jewels—had I a mind to

I could bring You Jewels—had I a mind to—
But You have enough—of those—
I could bring You Odors from St. Domingo—
Colors—from Vera Cruz—

Berries of the Bahamas—have I—   5
But this little Blaze
Flickering to itself—in the Meadow—
Suits Me—more than those—

Never a Fellow matched this Topaz—
And his Emerald Swing—   10
Dower itself—for Bobadilo—
Better—Could I bring?

Odors: fragrances, perfumes.
St. Domingo: Santo Domingo (now the Dominican Republic) in the Caribbean.
Vera Cruz: city on the east coast of Mexico.

Bahamas: group of islands south-east of Florida.
Blaze: strong fire or flame; very bright light.

Dower: part of her husband's estate allotted to a widow by law.
Bobadilo: braggart; someone who speaks arrogantly or boastfully.

'Never a Fellow matched this Topaz—'

👤 Personal Response

1. Does the poet value exotic or homely gifts? Briefly explain your answer.
2. How effective, in your opinion, is Dickinson's use of visual imagery in her celebration of nature? Support your views with reference to the poem.
3. What is the tone in this poem: arrogant, humble, gentle, strident, confident? Quote in support of your opinion.

👁 Critical Literacy

Although described as a recluse, Dickinson had a wide circle of friends. She wrote letter-poems to them, often representing them as flowers, 'things of nature which had come with no practice at all'. This poem is one without shadows, celebratory and happy, focusing out rather than in as she concentrates on a relationship.

In the first stanza, the poem opens with the speaker **considering the gift she will give** her beloved, 'You'. The 'You' is very much admired, and is wealthy ('You have enough'), so the gift of jewels is dismissed. The phrase 'had I a mind to' playfully suggests that maybe the 'I' doesn't necessarily wish to present anything. There is a certain flirtatious air evident here. A world of privilege and plenty is shown as, one after another, expensively exotic gifts are considered and dismissed. These include perfumes and vibrant colours from faraway locations, conjuring up images of romance and adventure: 'Odors from St. Domingo.'

The second stanza continues the list, with 'Berries of the Bahamas' being considered as an option for this special gift, but they are not quite right either. The tense changes to 'have I' and the laconic listing and dismissing stops. A small wildflower 'in the Meadow', 'this little Blaze', is chosen instead. This 'Suits Me'. Notice that it is not that this suits the other person. **This gift is a reflection of her own unshowy personality**. The long lines of considering exotic gifts have now given way to shorter, more decisive lines.

In the third stanza, 'the speaker's strength of feeling is evident, as she confidently states that 'Never a Fellow matched' this shining gift of hers. No alluring, foreign gemstone, be it a brilliant topaz or emerald, shines as this 'little Blaze' in the meadow. The gift glows with colour; it is natural, inexpensive and accessible. The reference to a dower might suggest a gift given by a woman to a prospective husband. This **gift is suitable** for a Spanish adventurer, a 'Bobadilo'. The assured tone is clear in the word 'Never' and the jaunty rhyme 'Swing' and 'bring'. The final rhetorical question suggests that this is the best gift she could give. The poem shows that **the true value of a present cannot be measured in a material way**.

✒ Writing About the Poem

'Dickinson is fascinated by moments of change.' Discuss this statement with reference to 'I could bring You Jewels—had I a mind to'.

Sample Paragraph

In this lively poem, the speaker considers what present would be most suitable to give to her arrogant lover. The first change occurs when this confident woman dismisses expensive, exotic gifts, 'But You have enough' and chooses something which is natural – and, more importantly – which is to her liking: 'Suits Me –' The simple flower she offers is unexpectedly beautiful – this 'little Blaze' suggests the hidden passion of the woman herself. The changing breathless tone reflects the love she feels. The flower is brighter than any precious stone of 'Topaz' or 'Emerald'. Short lines express the self-belief of a woman who knows best. Even the rhyme changes from where she is considering her options ('those'/'Cruz') in the first stanza, to the more definite jaunty rhyme of 'Swing' and 'bring' in the final stanza. Dickinson is fascinated by the spontaneity of life.

EXAMINER'S COMMENT

A confident top-grade response to the question, backed up with a convincing use of quotation. Good discussion about changes in thought and tone. The point about the change in line length was particularly interesting. Assured, varied vocabulary is controlled throughout and the paragraph is rounded off impressively.

🖋 Class/Homework Exercises

1. 'Dickinson disrupts and transforms our accepted view of things.' What is your opinion of this statement? Refer to 'I could bring You Jewels—had I a mind to' in support of your response.
2. Comment on the impact of Dickinson's use of sound effects in the poem.

⊙ Points to Consider

- **Central themes include the wonder and beauty of nature.**

- **Celebratory mood conveyed by powerful visual imagery and lively rhythm.**

- **Simplicity of the wildflower contrasted with extravagant glamour.**

- **Confident, optimistic tone contrasts with the poet's downbeat poems.**

8 A narrow Fellow in the Grass

A narrow Fellow in the Grass
Occasionally rides—
You may have met Him—did you not
His notice sudden is—

The Grass divides as with a Comb—   5
A spotted shaft is seen—
And then it closes at your feet
And opens further on—

He likes a Boggy Acre
A Floor too cool for Corn—   10
Yet when a Boy, and Barefoot—
I more than once at Noon
Have passed, I thought, a Whip lash
Unbraiding in the Sun
When stooping to secure it   15
It wrinkled, and was gone—

Several of Nature's People
I know, and they know me—
I feel for them a transport
Of cordiality—   20

But never met this Fellow
Attended, or alone
Without a tighter breathing
And Zero at the Bone—

a spotted shaft: patterned skin of the darting snake.

Whip lash: sudden, violent movement.
Unbraiding: straightening out, uncoiling.

transport: heightened emotion.

cordiality: civility, welcome.

Zero at the Bone: cold terror.

👤 Personal Response

1. Select two images from the poem that suggest evil or menace. Comment briefly on the effectiveness of each.
2. How successful is the poet in conveying the snake's erratic movement? Refer to the text in your answer.
3. Outline your own feelings in response to the poem.

'His notice sudden is—'

29 |

👁 Critical Literacy

In this poem, one of the few published during her lifetime, Dickinson adopts a male persona remembering an incident from his boyhood. Snakes have traditionally been seen as symbols of evil. We still use the expression 'snake in the grass' to describe someone who cannot be trusted. Central to this poem is Dickinson's own portrayal of nature – beautiful, brutal and lyrical. She seems fascinated by the endless mystery, danger and unpredictability of the natural world.

The opening lines of stanza one casually introduce a 'Fellow in the Grass'. (Dickinson never refers explicitly to the snake.) The **conversational tone immediately involves readers** who may already 'have met Him'. However, there is more than a hint of warning in the postscript: 'His notice sudden is.' The menacing adjective 'narrow', and the disjointed rhythm foreshadow an underlying sense of caution.

Dickinson focuses on the volatile snake's dramatic movements in stanza two. The verbs 'divide', 'closes' and 'opens' emphasise its dynamic energy. The snake suddenly emerges like a 'spotted shaft'. The poet's **comparisons are particularly effective**, suggesting a lightning bolt or a camouflaged weapon. Run-on lines, a forceful rhythm and the repetition of 'And' contribute to the vivid image of the snake as a powerful presence to be treated with caution.

Stanza three reveals even more about the snake's natural habitat: 'He likes a Boggy Acre.' It also divulges the speaker's identity – an adult male remembering his failed boyhood efforts to capture snakes. The memory conveys something of the intensity of childhood experiences, especially of dangerous encounters with nature. The boy's innocence and vulnerability ('Barefoot') contrasts with the 'Whip lash' violence of the wild snake. **Dickinson's attitude to nature is open to interpretation**. Does the threat come from the animal or the boy? Did the adult speaker regard the snake differently when he was young? The poet herself clearly appreciates the complexities found within the natural world and her precisely observed descriptions ('Unbraiding', 'It wrinkled') provide ample evidence of her interest.

From the speaker's viewpoint in stanza four, nature is generally friendly. This positive image is conveyed by the affectionate tribute to 'Nature's People'. The familiar personification and personal tone underline the mutual 'cordiality' that exists between nature and human nature. Despite this, **divisions between the two worlds cannot be ignored**. Indeed, the focus in stanza five is on the sheer horror people experience when confronted by 'this Fellow'. The poet's sparse and chilling descriptions – 'tighter breathing', 'Zero at the Bone' – are startling expressions of stunned terror.

As in other poems, Dickinson attributes human characteristics to nature – the snake 'Occasionally rides', 'The Grass divides' and the bogland has a 'Floor'. One effect of this is to highlight the **variety and mystery of the natural environment**, which can only ever be glimpsed within limited human terms. The snake remains unknowable to the end, dependent on a chance encounter, a fleeting glance or a trick of light.

✒ Writing About the Poem

Comment on the effectiveness of Dickinson's use of the male persona voice in 'A narrow Fellow in the Grass'. Support the points you make with reference to the poem.

Sample Paragraph

In some poems, Dickinson chose to substitute her own voice with a fictional narrator. This is the case in 'A narrow Fellow in the Grass', where she uses a country boy to tell the story of his experiences trying to catch snakes. It is obvious that he has a great love for nature, but neither is he blind to the fear he felt when he came face to face with the 'spotted shaft'. Dickinson's language emphasises terror. The images are disturbing: 'a tighter breathing.' The boy remembers shuddering with fright, 'Zero at the Bone'. The poem is all the more effective for being centred around one terrified character, the young boy. I can visualise the child in his bare feet trying to catch a frightened snake in the grass. By using another persona, Dickinson explores the excitement and danger of nature in a wider way.

EXAMINER'S COMMENT

A sustained response that includes some good personal engagement and a great deal of insightful discussion – particularly regarding the conflict between the boy and the snake. References and quotations are well used throughout the answer to provide a very interesting high-grade standard.

✒ Class/Homework Exercises

1. In your opinion, how does Dickinson portray nature in 'A narrow Fellow in the Grass'? Support your points with reference to the poem.
2. Identify the dramatic moments in this poem and comment on their impact.

⊙ Points to Consider

- **Dickinson explores contrasting aspects of the natural world.**
- **Effective use of everyday conversational language.**
- **The poet adopts the persona of a young boy who encounters a snake.**
- **Dramatic atmosphere concludes on a note of terror.**

9 I taste a liquor never brewed

I taste a liquor never brewed—
From Tankards scooped in Pearl—
Not all the Vats upon the Rhine
Yield such an Alcohol!

Inebriate of Air—am I—   5
And Debauchee of Dew—
Reeling—thro endless summer days—
From inns of Molten Blue—

When 'Landlords' turn the drunken Bee
Out of the Foxglove's door—   10
When Butterflies—renounce their 'drams'—
I shall but drink the more!

Till Seraphs swing their snowy Hats—
And Saints—to windows run—
To see the little Tippler   15
Leaning against the—Sun—

Tankards: one-handled mugs, usually made of pewter, used for drinking beer.
Vats: large vessels used for making alcohol.

Debauchee: someone who has overindulged and neglected duty.

Seraphs: angels who are of the highest spiritual level.

Tippler: a person who drinks often, but does not get drunk.

**'Not all the Vats upon the Rhine/
Yield such an Alcohol!'**

👤 Personal Response

1. What is the mood in this poem? Does it intensify or change? Use references from the text in your response.
2. Which stanza appeals to you most? Discuss both the poet's style and the poem's content in your answer.
3. Dickinson creates a slapstick cartoon-like scene in this poem. Why, in your opinion, does the poet use this technique to convey the exuberance of summer?

👁 Critical Literacy

This 'rapturous poem about summer' uses the metaphor of intoxication to capture the essence of this wonderful season. Dickinson's family were strict Calvinists, a religion that emphasised damnation as the consequence of sin. Her father supported the Temperance League, an organisation that warned against the dangers of drink.

This poem is written as a **joyful appreciation of this wonderful life**. The tone is playful and exaggerated from the beginning, as the poet declares this drink was never 'brewed'. The reference to 'scooped in Pearl' could refer to the great, white frothing heads of beer in the 'Tankards'. The poet certainly conveys the merriment of intoxication, as the poem reels along its happy way. The explanation for all this drunkenness is that the poet is drunk on life ('Inebriate', 'Debauchee'). The pubs are the inns of 'Molten Blue', i.e. the sky (stanza two). It is like a cartoon, with little drunken bees being shown the door by the pub owners as they lurch about in delirious ecstasy. The drinkers of the natural world are the bees and butterflies, but she can drink more than these: 'I shall but drink the more!' This roots the poem in reality, as drunken people always feel they can manage more.

But this has caused uproar in the heavens, as the angels and saints run to look out at this little drunk, 'the little Tippler'. She stands drunkenly leaning against the 'Sun', a celestial lamppost. The final dash suggests the crooked stance of the little drunken one. **There is no heavy moral at the end of this poem. In fact, there seems to be a slight note of envy for the freedom and happiness being experienced by the intoxicated poet**. Are the angels swinging their hats to cheer her on in her drunken rebellion? Is this poem celebrating the reckless indulgence of excess? Or is the final metaphor of the sun referring to Christ or to the poet's own arrival in heaven after she self-indulgently enjoys the beauty of the natural world?

Nature is seen as the spur for high jinks and good humour. The riddle of the first line starts it off: how was the alcohol 'never brewed'? The exaggerated imagery, such as the metaphor of the flower as a pub and the bee as the drunk, all add to the fantasy-land atmosphere. The words 'Inebriate',

'Debauchee' and 'renounce' are reminiscent of the language that those who disapprove of the consumption of alcohol might use for those who do indulge. Is the poet having a sly laugh at the serious Temperance League to which her father belonged? The ridiculous costumes, 'snowy Hats', and the uproar in heaven ('swing' and 'run') all add to the impression of this land of merriment. The juxtaposition of the sacred ('Seraphs') and the irreverent ('Tippler') in stanza four also adds to the comic effect. However, it is the verbs that carry the sense of mad fun most effectively: 'scooped', 'Reeling', 'drink', 'swing', 'run' and 'Leaning'. The poem lurches and flows in an almost uncontrollable way as the ecstasy of overindulging in the delirious pleasure of nature is vividly conveyed.

There are two different types of humour present in this irrepressible poem – the broad humour of farce and the more **subversive humour of irony**. The poet even uses the steady metre of a hymn, with eight syllables in lines one and three and six syllables in lines two and four. Dickinson seems to be standing at a distance, smiling wryly, as she gently deflates.

✒ Writing About the Poem

'Dickinson was always careful to avoid expressing excessive emotion, even of joy.' Discuss this statement with reference to 'I taste a liquor never brewed'.

Sample Paragraph

This is a funny poem and the poet is enjoying herself. She is drunk on nature and it is humourous when the angels are waving their caps, egging her on. I think this is really a happy poem, unlike Dickenson's disturbing poems we studied about funerals and souls. It goes to show she also writes happier poetry when she wants. Dickenson hardly ever uses normal punctuation. Her poems are hard as they don't have normal sentences but use capital letters. There is a comparison for drinking all through to describe being drunk on nature. The poem is definately full of joy, eg the story about the bee. The lines describing the tippler are joyful. I think everyone should be able to enjoy Emily's brilliant poem as it has happy images.

EXAMINER'S COMMENT

This note-like answer shows limited engagement with the poem. While there is a recognition of the poem's joyful tone and some supportive reference, the lack of substantial analysis is noticeable. Language use is repetitive, expression is flawed and there are several mechanical mistakes. The over-enthusiastic ending is not convincing. Closer study of the poem and greater care in writing the response would raise the standard from a basic grade.

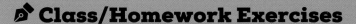

✒ Class/Homework Exercises

1. 'Hypersensitivity to natural beauty produced Dickinson's poetry.'
   Do you agree or disagree with this statement? Refer to the poem 'I
   taste a liquor never brewed' in your response.
2. Identify the childlike elements of the poem and comment on their
   impact.

⊙ Points to Consider

- The poem highlights Dickinson's close relationship with nature.

- Exuberant mood conveyed by sibilant sounds, vivid images,
  lively rhythm, etc.

- Extended metaphor of intoxication used effectively throughout.

- Dominant sense of delight, celebration and good humour.

10 After great pain, a formal feeling comes

After great pain, a formal feeling comes—
The Nerves sit ceremonious, like Tombs—
The stiff Heart questions was it He, that bore,
And Yesterday, or Centuries before?

The Feet, mechanical, go round—   5
Of Ground, or Air, or Ought—
A Wooden way
Regardless grown,
A Quartz contentment, like a stone—

This is the Hour of Lead—   10
Remembered, if outlived,
As Freezing persons, recollect the Snow—
First—Chill—then Stupor—then the letting go—

formal: serious; exact.

ceremonious: on show.

He: the stiff Heart, or possibly Christ.
bore: endured; intruded.

Ought: anything.

Quartz: basic rock mineral.

Hour of Lead: traumatic experience.

Stupor: numbness; disorientation.

👤 Personal Response

1. Comment on the poet's use of personification in the opening stanza. Does it add drama?
2. How does the language used in the second stanza convey the condition of the victim in pain?
3. How, in your opinion, does Dickinson's use of punctuation in the last line of the poem heighten the sense of descending into nothingness?

'First—Chill—then Stupor'

 Critical Literacy

Dickinson wrote 'After great pain, a formal feeling comes' in 1862, at a time when she was thought to have been experiencing severe psychological difficulties. The poet addresses the effects of isolation and anguish on the individual. Ironically, the absence of the personal pronoun 'I' gives the poem a universal significance. The 'great pain' itself is never fully explained and the final lines are ambiguous. Like so much of Dickinson's work, this dramatic poem raises many questions for consideration.

From the outset, Dickinson is concerned with the emotional numbness ('a formal feeling') that follows the experience of 'great pain'. The poet's authoritative tone in stanza one reflects a first-hand knowledge of trauma, with the adjective 'formal' suggesting self-conscious recovery from some earlier distress. Dickinson personifies the physical response as order returns to body and mind: 'The Nerves sit ceremonious, like Tombs'. The severe pain has also shocked the 'stiff Heart', which has become confused by the experience. Is the poet also drawing a parallel with the life and death of Jesus Christ (the Sacred Heart), crucified 'Centuries before'? The images certainly suggest timeless suffering and endurance. This **sombre sense of loss** is further enhanced by the broad vowel assonance of the opening lines.

The feeling of being in a dazed standstill continues into stanza two. In reacting to intense pain, 'The Feet, mechanical, go round'. It is as if the response is unfocused and indifferent, lacking any real purpose. Dickinson uses two **analogies to emphasise the sense of pointless alienation**. The reference to the 'Wooden way' might be interpreted as a fragile bridge between reason and insanity, or this metaphor could be associated with Christ's suffering as he carried his cross to Calvary. The level of consciousness at such times is described as 'Regardless grown', or beyond caring. Dickinson's second comparison is equally innovative: 'A Quartz contentment' underpins the feeling of complete apathy that makes the victims of pain behave 'like a stone'. Is she being ironic by suggesting that the post-traumatic state is an escape, a 'contentment' of sorts?

There is a disturbing sense of resignation at the start of stanza three: 'This is the Hour of Lead'. The dull weight of depression is reinforced by the insistent monosyllables and solemn rhythm, but the devastating experience is not 'outlived' by everyone. Dickinson defines the aftermath of suffering by using one final comparison: 'As Freezing persons.' This shocking simile evokes the unimaginable hopelessness of the victim stranded in a vast wasteland of snow. The poem's last line traces the tragic stages leading to oblivion: 'First—Chill—then Stupor—then the letting go—.' The inclusion of the dash at the end might indicate a possibility of relief, though whether it is through rescue or death is not revealed. In either case, **readers are left with an acute awareness of an extremely distraught voice**.

✒ Writing About the Poem

One of Dickinson's great achievements is her ability to explore the experience of deep depression. To what extent is this true of her poem 'After great pain, a formal feeling comes'? Refer closely to the text in your answer.

Sample Paragraph

'After great pain, a formal feeling comes' is a good example of Dickinson's skill in addressing distressing subjects. Although she never explains the 'pain' in the first line, she deals with the after-effects of suffering. What Dickinson does well is to explain how depression can lead to people becoming numb, beyond all emotion. I believe this is what she means by 'a formal feeling'. She uses an interesting image of a sufferer's nerves sitting quietly at a funeral service. This same idea is used to describe the mourners – 'Feet mechanical'. I get the impression that grief can destroy people's confidence. Dickinson's images suggest the coldness experienced by patients who have depression. The best description is when she compares sufferers to being lost in the snow. They will slowly fade into a 'stupor' or death wish. Dickinson is very good at using images and moods to explore depression.

🔍 Class/Homework Exercises

1. In your opinion, what is the dominant mood in 'After great pain, a formal feeling comes'? Is it one of depression, sadness or acceptance? Refer closely to the text in your answer.
2. In your view, which metaphor in the poem best conveys a sense of deep depression? Briefly explain your choice.

⊙ Points to Consider

- Intense exploration of depression and psychological suffering.

- Effective use of vivid imagery, personification and serious tone.

- Disturbing mood throughout is solemn and sombre.

- Ambiguous, open-ended conclusion.

Sample Leaving Cert Questions on Dickinson's Poetry

1. 'Emily Dickinson's unique poetic style is perfectly suited to the extraordinary themes which she explores in her poems.' Do you agree with this assessment of Dickinson's poetry? Develop your answer with suitable reference to the poems by Dickinson on your course.

2. 'Dickinson's exploration of profound life experiences is effectively conveyed through her innovative style.' Discuss this statement, supporting your answer with reference to the poetry of Emily Dickinson on your course.

3. 'A dark, eccentric vision is at the heart of Emily Dickinson's most dramatic poems.' Discuss this view, supporting the points you make with reference to the poems by Dickinson on your course.

Understanding the Prescribed Poetry Question

Marks are awarded using the PCLM Marking Scheme: P = 15; C = 15; L = 15; M = 5 Total = 50

- **P** (Purpose = 15 marks) refers to the set question and is the launch pad for the answer. This involves engaging with all aspects of the question. Both theme and language must be addressed, although not necessarily equally.
- **C** (Coherence = 15 marks) refers to the organisation of the developed response and the use of accurate, relevant quotation. Paragraphing is essential.
- **L** (Language = 15 marks) refers to the student's skill in controlling language throughout the answer.
- **M** (Mechanics = 5 marks) refers to spelling and grammar.
- Although no specific number of poems is required, students usually discuss at least 3 or 4 in their written responses.
- Aim for at least 800 words, to be completed within 45–50 minutes.

How do I organise my answer?

(Sample question 1)

'Emily Dickinson's unique poetic style is perfectly suited to the extraordinary themes which she explores in her poems.' Do you agree with this assessment of Dickinson's poetry? Develop your answer with suitable reference to the poems by Dickinson on your course.

Sample Plan 1

Intro: *(Stance: agree with viewpoint in the question)* Dickinson is an original voice who addresses abstract subject matter, such as states of consciousness, hope, death and the relationship between nature and human nature. Her energetic style is in keeping with the intense approach to her extraordinary themes.

Point 1: *(Positive approach in keeping with spontaneous enthusiastic tone)* '"Hope" is the thing with feathers' – metaphorical language reflects the small bird's presence to illustrate and highlight various aspects of hope and human resilience.

Point 2: *(Evocative language matches startling sense of self-awareness)* Dramatic atmospheres in 'I felt a Funeral, in my Brain' and 'I Heard a Fly buzz—when I died'. Surreal imagery, haunting aural effects and fragmented rhythms effectively convey disorientation and powerlessness.

NOTE

In keeping with the PCLM approach, the student has to take a stance by agreeing, disagreeing or partially agreeing with the statement that:

– **Dickinson's unique poetic style** (condensed poetic forms, compressed language, unconventional punctuation, broken rhythms, haunting aural effects, unsettling humour, intriguing perspectives, insightful reflection, vivid dramatisation, surreal imagery, quirky precise details, etc.)

… is perfectly suited to the exploration of:

– **her extraordinary themes** (hope/despair, loss, death/afterlife, consciousness/disorientation, the natural world, etc.)

Point 3: *(Unusual view of the natural world in line with off-beat dramatisation)* The poet's strangely realistic view of nature evident in 'A Bird came down the Walk'. Use of odd, precise details, onomatopoeic language and comic moments enhance the reader's understanding of Dickinson's attitude.

Point 4: *(Playful poetic voice enhances the ecstatic portrayal of nature)* Extended metaphor of drunkenness to reflect the poet's celebration of nature in 'I taste a liquor never brewed' reveals an idiosyncratic sense of humour. Strikingly imaginative images, forceful rhythms and enthusiastic tones all echo the poet's response to natural beauty.

Conclusion: Condensed poetic forms, compressed syntax and daring language use is entirely appropriate to Dickinson's insightful reflections and themes. Readers can engage more immediately with the intensity of the poet's heightened experiences.

Sample Paragraph: Point 2

In both 'I felt a Funeral, in my Brain' and 'I heard a Fly buzz—when I died', Dickinson creates a disturbing account of the sensation of dying. The two poems are dramatic, with terrifying images. I thought the poet's style is in keeping with this alarming subject in 'I felt a Funeral', especially her presentation of the 'Mourners' who keep 'treading' as the coffin is lowered – 'I dropped down, and down'. Repetition – the drum 'beating—beating' – and broken phrasing emphasised the feeling of helplessness. Dickinson's vivid imagery and sounds add to the feeling of being overpowered. There is a more absurd atmosphere in 'I heard a Fly buzz'. The exaggerated scene seems distorted, particularly when the insect became the centre of attention, an 'uncertain stumbling Buzz'. The ending stops abruptly, 'I could not see to see', a line suggesting the dreadful frustration and struggle for clarity.

EXAMINER'S COMMENT

As part of a full examination essay, this is a clear personal response that addresses the question directly. The sustained focus on Dickinson's language use is aptly supported with effective use of quotation. Both poems were treated succinctly and included some thoughtful discussion. Well-controlled expression added to the quality of the response. Top-grade answer.

(Sample question 2)

'Dickinson's exploration of profound life experiences is effectively conveyed through her innovative style.' Discuss this statement, supporting your answer with reference to the poetry of Emily Dickinson on your course.

NOTE

In keeping with the PCLM approach, the student has to take a stance by agreeing, disagreeing or partially agreeing with the statement that:

– **Dickinson's exploration of profound life experiences** (loneliness/depression, death, mental anguish, joy, appreciation of life/relationships, deep response to the world of nature, etc.)

... is conveyed through:

– **her innovative style** (disruptive perspectives, innovative syntax, surreal sequences, dynamic verbs, colloquial language, memorable sound effects, unusual imagery, extended metaphor, dramatic personification, subversive humour.)

Sample Plan 2

Intro: *(Stance: agree with viewpoint in the question)* Dickinson looks to understand death, mental anguish and intensely vivid moments of joy. Through her inventive approach to language, she invites readers to join her as she tells 'the truth, but tells it slant'.

Point 1: *(The shock of intense self-consciousness – powerful language use)* 'After great pain, a formal feeling comes' – surreal sequence, alliteration, unusual syntax and monosyllabic words create a vivid exploration of disorientation.

Point 2: *(Original, vibrant poetic voice – deep appreciation of nature)* 'I could bring You Jewels—had I a mind to' – unusual appreciation of nature's simple joys. Chooses a simple, modest meadow flower ('But this little Blaze/Flickering to itself'). Alliteration, onomatopoeia, a run-on line and the monosyllabic broad vowel sound describe the strong impact of the flower. The dynamic verb 'Flickering' suggests its lively movement.

Point 3: *(Intensity of emotion – fresh comparative effects)* 'I taste a liquor never brewed' – another poem delighting in the natural world's everyday delights. Startling extended metaphor of stages of intoxication irrepressibly conveys the delirious pleasures of nature ('When landlords turn the drunken Bee/out of the Foxglove's door'). Unconventional use of capital letters evokes a fantastical landscape.

Point 4: *(Unique poetic style – confronting fear and intrigue)* 'A narrow Fellow in the Grass' – contrasting description of the brutal, unpredictable aspects of nature. Personification increases the surreal unnerving quality, 'the Grass divides', the bogland has a 'Floor'. The discomfiting experience and extreme fright conveyed in the cryptic phrase 'Zero at the Bone' alarms readers.

Conclusion: Dickinson's disconcerting use of humour, unconventional punctuation, dramatic use of personification coupled with unusual imagery disrupt the reader's conventional awareness of life experiences.

Sample Paragraph: Point 1

Dickinson's poem, 'After great pain, a formal feeling comes', uses surreal images to examine how emotional numbness, 'a formal feeling', often follows a difficult experience, 'great pain'. Emphatic alliteration ('formal feeling') underlines the constrictive paralysis of emotion into which a person sinks after trauma. There is a sense of losing control as the 'Feet, mechanical, go round'. The line suggests a lack of purpose in the body's movements. The bridge between sanity and insanity, 'A Wooden way', is breaking, leaving the helpless individual incapable of rational thought – 'regardless grown'. Monosyllables describe this nightmarish experience of sinking into inertia, 'First— Chill'. The final dash marks the disorientating awareness of the swirling 'Snow'. By this stage, all sense of direction has been lost. Dickinson is exploring the numbing effects of tragedy.

EXAMINER'S COMMENT

As part of a full essay answer to question 2, this is an impressive top-grade standard that shows close engagement with Dickinson's poetry. Incisive discussion of the poet's curious style (sound effects, syntax, punctuation, etc.) is also commendable. Excellent use of quotations and the expression is exceptionally good throughout (e.g. 'the constrictive paralysis of emotion', 'disorientating awareness').

EXAM FOCUS

- As you may not be familiar with some of the poems referred to in the sample plans, substitute poems that you have studied closely.
- Key points about a particular poem can be developed over more than one paragraph.
- Paragraphs may also include cross-referencing and discussion of more than one poem.
- Remember that there is no single 'correct' answer to poetry questions, so always be confident in expressing your own considered response.

Leaving Cert Sample Essay

'Emily Dickinson's distinctly eccentric poems explore intense emotions that range from stark desolation to giddy delight.' Discuss this view, supporting your answer with reference to the poetry of Dickinson on your course.

Sample Essay

1. Emily Dickinson writes poems about intense emotions that everyone has. These can go from stark desolation to giddy delight. She always uses language in a strange way, especially using capital letters, personification and a weird order of words. Her poems can be very eccentric and depressing, but she also writes with a giddy sense of humour. I will examine four poems, 'There's a certain Slant of light', 'I felt a Funeral, in my Brain', '"Hope" is the thing with feathers' and 'A narrow Fellow in the Grass'.

2. In writing 'There's a certain Slant of light' she uses a capital letter to draw attention to the word 'Slant'. Dickinson sets the scene in a church in wintertime which is dramatic in itself. Their's a religious setting immediately and this sets the scene for being mainly about death and how we all have a relationship with God. The low angle of the winter's afternoon sunlight is like a warning from God. It 'oppresses' her just like the 'Cathedral Tunes' (which is also written in capital letters). This is unusual because light and hymns can normally be expected to lift people up, they do not depress them. But Dickinson is really pointing out the fear people sometimes have because God has great power over them, 'Heavenly Hurt'. God punishes. 'An imperial affliction' means the whole world is afraid, so 'The Landscape listens'. In this poem Dickinson presents a very original way of looking at life. She uses dashes to make the poem extremely dramatic and full of dread.

3. 'I felt a Funeral, in my Brain' also deals with terror. Dickinson uses nightmarish images in which she imagines the experience of her own burial, 'mourners to and fro'. She shows her helplessness by making references to their feet, 'threading, threading'. This is a haunting sound affect. She also imagines hearing a funeral drum 'beating, beating'. This is a continuous sound – like a pounding beat. It's also a very sad scene of desolation with the rhythms of sorrowful mourners which just adds to the poet's panic. A stark image of a coffin being put into a grave is described. 'And I dropped down'. The poet writes in short bursts of a fragmented style bringing out the nightmare atmosphere. She creates fear, the feeling of being a victim confined in the coffin, 'solitary', lowered down into her own grave. This surreal scene is dramatic. It sends shock waves when we imagine what is happening as Dickinson describes the traumatic protrayal of an actual burial.

4. '"Hope" is the thing with feathers' is a poem full of giddy delight. The bird suggests hope, as a positive symbol high above the world's stark desolation. This is another of Dickinson's eccentric poems. It is like the dove in the bible story of Noah's Ark and the Flood. In this bible story, a dove let Noah know that the waters were going down and people would be able to survive. Therefore, the bird is 'sweetest' because it would of always brought good news.

5. In 'A Narrow Fellow in the Grass', Dickinson uses the voice of a young boy to tell a story of surprise and fear. She mixes up the order of words in a very eccentric way, 'His sudden notice is'. This shows the effect the unexpected snake had on the boy. This event is dramaticed. The setting is the strange field, the event is the meeting of the snake and the 'Barefoot' boy, the action is the snake 'Unbraiding in the sun'. The boy is 'stooping to secure it'. I thought the image of the snake as 'A spotted shaft' was

INDICATIVE MATERIAL

- **Dickinson's distinctly eccentric poems** (inventive style, vivid/surreal imagery, dramatic personification, fragmented syntax, unconventional punctuation, unusual settings, unnerving sense of humour, etc.)

... explore:

- **intense emotions from stark desolation to giddy delight** (mental anguish, death, loneliness and depression, moments of surprise and joy, love and loss, profound reactions to the natural world, etc.)

unusual. It suggested a bolt of lightning or a hidden weapon, both conveying danger. Nature is filled with mystery. I also thought the personification in the line 'The Grass divides as with a Comb' was very unusual. I could imagine the snake slithering along, the only movement is the grass parting as if someone was combing their hair. I thought this was surreal but Dickinson is also celebrating nature.

6. Dickinson's poems vary from terror of dying to intense feelings about the natural world. She looks at everything 'Slant', whether it is winter sunshine, hymns, a little bird or a snake. She made me think twice about nature and death. She also writes about the beauty and mystery of nature. Dickinson's language is eccentric. She is by far the most unusual of the poets we have studied.

(750 words)

EXAMINER'S COMMENT

A solid mid-grade standard, with reasonably focused engagement and analysis – particularly in paragraphs 2, 3 and 5. More emphasis on the element of 'giddy delight' would be expected. Paragraph 4 is particularly slight and lacking in developed discussion. Expression varies greatly from fluent to awkward and the essay included several mechanical errors ('Their's', 'affect', 'protrayal', 'would of', 'dramaticed'). Some personal engagement evident at times and the essay was rounded off well in the concluding paragraph.

GRADE: H3
P = 11/15
C = 11/15
L = 10/15
M = 4/5
Total = 36/50

Revision Overview

'"Hope" is the thing with feathers'
Theme of hope, extended metaphor, unusual punctuation, reflective, optimistic tones.

'There's a certain Slant of light'
Reflection on human mortality and our relationship with God, personification, fragmented rhythm and style add to unease and pessimism.

'I felt a Funeral, in my Brain' (OL)
Shocking introspection on loss and death, first-person perspective, onomatopoeia and repetition.

'A Bird came down the Walk'
Bemused observation of nature, personification, rich imagery and sound effects.

'I heard a Fly buzz–when I died' (OL)
Dramatic exploration of death and the afterlife, surreal, use of contrast and symbols add to feeling of helplessness.

'The Soul has Bandaged moments'
Unsettling examination of nature of consciousness, central conflict, changing moods.

'I could bring You Jewels–had I a mind to'
Treatment of relationship, celebration of nature, vivid imagery, optimistic tone.

'A narrow Fellow in the Grass'
Danger and beauty in nature, use of persona, colloquial language, concluding tone of terror.

'I taste a liquor never brewed'
Joyful celebration of nature, extended metaphor, subversive humour.

'After great pain, a formal feeling comes'
Disquieting exploration of depression, rich imagery, sombre tone, ambiguous ending.

Last Words

'The Dickinson dashes are an integral part of her method and style … and cannot be translated … without deadening the wonderful naked voltage of the poems.'
Ted Hughes

(On her determination to hide secrets) 'The price she paid was that of appearing to posterity as perpetually unfinished and wilfully eccentric.'
Philip Larkin

'The Brain–is wider than the Sky–
The Brain is deeper than the sea–'
Emily Dickinson

JOY/HOPE

NATURE

RELIGION/
SPIRITUALITY

SUFFERING

DEATH

MEANING
OF LIFE

John Donne
1572–1631

*'Be thine own palace,
or the world's thy jail.'*

John Donne was born in London in 1572 into a prominent Roman Catholic family (his mother was a relation of the martyr Sir Thomas More). Donne was educated at home by Catholic tutors before attending university, where he trained as a lawyer. He converted to the Church of England during the 1590s.

After several appointments and trips abroad, he secretly married seventeen-year-old Anne More in 1601 and was briefly imprisoned as a result of her father's objection. The poet once wrote about the experience: 'John Donne – Anne Donne – Undone'. However, the marriage was a happy one, although the family struggled financially at times. His wife died in 1617 aged thirty-three after giving birth to their twelfth child.

In 1615, Donne had been ordained as an Anglican priest and was later appointed Dean of St Paul's Cathedral, where he became famous for his spellbinding sermons. He also made his name as a highly original love poet. In his later years, Donne turned his talents to religious poetry, hymns and sermons.

Whatever the subject, his writing reveals the same characteristics that typified the work of the greatest metaphysical poets: dazzling wordplay; subtle argument; surprising contrasts; intricate analysis; and striking imagery selected from law, medicine, geography, science and mathematics. His most prominent themes include love – romantic and spiritual – time, and death. Donne is now considered the most outstanding of all the English metaphysical poets.

Investigate Further

To find out more about John Donne, or to hear readings of his poems, you could search some useful websites, such as YouTube, BBC Poetry, poetryfoundation.org and poetryarchive.org, or access additional material on this page of your eBook.

Prescribed Poems

(OL) indicates poems that are also prescribed for the Ordinary Level course.

A Note on Metaphysical Poetry

Metaphysics is usually defined as a branch of philosophy concerned with explaining **the fundamental nature of existence**. 'Meta' means beyond, so metaphysical poems deal with philsophical subjects, such as religion, love and beauty.

Metaphysical poetry is a term used to describe the work of a group of British lyric poets who lived in England between 1590 and 1680. Among them were John Donne, George Herbert and Andrew Marvell. They did not call themselves Metaphysicals but were given this name by later writers because their poetry dealt with **philosophical speculation and abstract ideas**.

Their work was characterised by inventiveness of metaphor (often involving unusual and dissimilar images known as conceits). Such **witty and complex poetry** was influenced greatly by the changing times, new sciences and the newfound liberal behaviour of the 17th century.

Intellect and wit blending with strong feelings typify metaphysical poetry, especially that of John Donne. Indeed, Donne represents very well the school of poetry which is still somewhat vaguely called 'Metaphysical'. He brought the **whole of his experience** into his poetry.

Donne's writing is full of far-fetched imagery and allusions borrowed from various branches of learning. He often makes use of ideas and experience – and the most startling connections are discovered between them. The hallmark of Donne's metaphysical poetry is **passionate feeling and forceful argument**.

During the 18th century, many critics believed that the metaphysical poets only wanted to show off their learning. However, their work had a significant influence on leading 20th-century poets, such as T. S. Eliot, who promoted its **innovative and intellectual qualities**, and helped bring the poetry of John Donne back into favour with readers.

1 The Sun Rising

　　Busy old fool, unruly sun,
　　　Why dost thou thus,
Through windows, and through curtains call on us?
Must to thy motions lovers' seasons run?
　　　Saucy pedantic wretch, go chide　　　　　5
　　　Late school boys and sour prentices,
　　Go tell court huntsmen that the King will ride,
　　Call country ants to harvest offices;
Love, all alike, no season knows nor clime,
Nor hours, days, months, which are the rags of time.　　10

　　Thy beams, so reverend and strong
　　　Why shouldst thou think?
I could eclipse and cloud them with a wink,
But that I would not lose her sight so long;
　　　If her eyes have not blinded thine,　　　　　15
　　　Look, and tomorrow late, tell me,
　　Whether both th' Indias of spice and mine
　　Be where thou leftst them, or lie here with me.
Ask for those kings whom thou saw'st yesterday,
And thou shalt hear, All here in one bed lay.　　　　20

　　She's all states, and all princes, I,
　　　Nothing else is.
Princes do but play us; compared to this,
All honour's mimic, all wealth alchemy.
　　　Thou, Sun, art half as happy as we,　　　　　25
　　　In that the world's contracted thus.
　　Thine age asks ease, and since thy duties be
　　To warm the world, that's done in warming us.
Shine here to us, and thou art everywhere;
This bed thy centre is, these walls thy sphere.　　　30

Saucy: impertinent, brazen.
pedantic: particular, fussy.
chide: scold.

court huntsmen: opportunistic courtiers.
country ants/harvest offices: probably a comic reference to farmers, telling them to get on with their work.
clime: climate.
rags: divisions.

eclipse and cloud: blot out, hide.

both th' Indias: East Indies (South Asia) and West Indies, famous respectively for spice and gold.

play: imitate.

all honour's mimic: everything which is held in high esteem is only an impersonation of the lovers.
alchemy: false gold, pretence.

sphere: world, universe.

'so reverend and strong'

👤 Personal Response

1. Describe Donne's attitude to the sun in the opening four lines of this poem. How is this reaction established?
2. Describe the poet's tone throughout stanza two. Is it respectful and realistic? Or exaggerated and mocking? Briefly explain your response.
3. Based on your reading of the poem, has Donne convinced you that true love is an all-conquering power? Give a reason for your answer.

👁 Critical Literacy

'The Sun Rising' (written in 1605) is one of Donne's most charming and successful metaphysical love poems. Although the title suggests an aubade (a song sung by lovers who must part at dawn), the poet has actually written a parody making fun of such tender declarations of love. Indeed, this humorous, exuberant poem cheekily scolds the sun for waking Donne and his lover. He is so irritated that he firmly instructs the interfering sun to go off and annoy others.

The opening lines dramatically convey the intimate scene of an irritated lover woken up too soon by a busybody sun. Donne personifies the sun and in a half-serious, petulant tone, he reprimands this 'Busy old fool' for intruding. He does not see why he and his lover should live their lives according to the dictates of the sun: 'Must to thy motion lovers' seasons run?' Throughout this first stanza, **the poet mocks the sun** ('Saucy pedantic wretch') and is highly dismissive of its power. Such lively personification of the sun gives great energy to the poem's opening. Donne goes on to instruct the sun to pester others, repeating the verb 'Go'. As far as he is concerned, lovers should define their own seasons and the sun should do trivial things like 'chide/Late school boys' and other people who have to get up early.

Donne argues that the sun would be better advised to concentrate on sycophantic courtiers and hard-working farmers who are struggling to survive. This is in contrast to the timeless world of true love, which is more important than anything else. Perhaps Donne is protesting too much because he really knows that the sun reminds lovers how their exhilarated state may change over time. However, he concludes confidently with an emphatic rhyme ('clime' and 'time') insisting that **love transcends time**: 'Love, all alike, no season knows nor clime,/Nor hours, days, months, which are the rags of time.'

Mischievously, in stanza two, Donne boasts that he can shut out the power of the sun's rays 'with a wink'. He merely has to close his eyes to 'eclipse and cloud' the sun. But he does not want to be parted from his lover ('would not lose her sight so long') for even that small measure of time. In fact, he believes her beautiful eyes are so bright that they could blind the sun. **In**

a clever conceit, the poet shrinks the huge expanse of the world, its exotic destinations and far–off islands ('both th' Indias') and even the magnificence of the King's court into one little room. He tells the sun that the world's real treasures are contained right there in the bedroom, which is now the centre of the universe, 'All here in one bed lay'. As far as Donne is concerned, his lover is worth more than anything the sun can ever find outside their bedroom. The monosyllabic phrasing asserts that their bed contains the whole world, not only for the lovers but also for the sun. Again, the forceful rhyme ('yesterday' and 'lay') emphasises how love has altered space. For lovers, the universe is contracted into their own enclosed private space: 'All here in one bed lay'.

The third stanza begins with Donne dramatically dismissing the external world, 'Nothing else is'. With typically playful reasoning, he exaggerates the power of love: 'She is all states, and all princes, I'. Reality is subverted as real princes are seen as mere actors pretending to be lovers, 'Princes do but play us'. Riches are dismissed as 'alchemy' (or illusion), a poor substitute for true feeling. The poet then realises that the sun – which is a single star – is only half as happy as the lovers who have created their own romantic kingdom. His **tone becomes gentle and more respectful** as he acknowledges that the sun is old, 'Thine age asks ease'. In contrast to the earlier disquiet, the mood has now become much more relaxed and assured.

Donne suggests that since the sun's function is to 'warm the world' and since the lovers encapsulate the whole world, the sun will do his duty if he shines on them. So the poet invites the sun to remain: 'Shine here to us'. **The lovers' bed is the centre of the universe**, their walls its borders. This world of love contains everything of value; it is the only one worth exploring and possessing. The final rhyme ('everywhere' and 'sphere') shows how love overcomes all boundaries with its limitless power. In the end, the sun is seen as a satellite encircling the lovers. 'The Sun Rising' demonstrates many of the qualities of metaphysical poetry. Donne's characteristic use of figurative and rhetorical techniques presents readers with a wonderfully conversational and witty poem, celebrating love and transcending the centuries with its lively energy.

✒ Writing About the Poem

'Donne's original approach to poetry results in lively ideas and ingenious language.' Give your opinion on this statement in relation to the poem 'The Sun Rising'. Use references from the poem to support your views.

Sample Paragraph

It is astonishing to me how Donne in 'The Sun Rising' plays with time, space and location, almost as if none of the physical rules of the world matter. In the early 17th century, the discovery of new lands was the exciting news of the day. Donne uses this contemporary image to great effect. In this unusual love poem, he asks the 'Busy old fool', the sun, to let him know if exotic places like 'both th' Indias of spice and mine' are still where they were when the sun orbited past or whether they now 'lie here with me'. The poet uses this image to show that everything of importance is now contained in the lovers' room. I think this unique idea is wittily expressed by the poet's use of personification of the sun as an interfering intruder. Donne is cleverly showing that love transcends the physical world. This 17th-century poet has transcended time.

EXAMINER'S COMMENT

As part of a full essay, this is a thoughtful response that attempts to address the question directly, using reference to both content and style. There is also some good personal interaction with the poem and points are clearly expressed throughout. Top-grade standard.

✒ Class/Homework Exercises

1. 'John Donne's love poetry is dramatic, conversational and intimate.' Is this a valid statement in relation to 'The Sun Rising'? Use quotation from the poem in your response.
2. The effective use of striking rhetorical features – particularly repetition and questions – reinforces Donne's assured tone throughout the poem. Discuss this view with particular reference to 'The Sun Rising'.

⊙ Points to Consider

- **Donne celebrates the joys of love and romance.**
- **Poet apostrophises (i.e. addresses the sun in a rhetorical fashion).**
- **Characteristically witty wordplay.**
- **Contrasting tones – playful, loving, comic, dismissive, logical.**
- **Effective developed conceit of the lovers' special world.**
- **Language varies from conversational to dramatic.**

2 Song (Go, And Catch A Falling Star)

Go, and catch a falling star,
Get with child a mandrake root,
Tell me, where all past years are,
   Or who cleft the Devil's foot,
Teach me to hear mermaids singing,   5
Or to keep off envy's stinging,
     And find
     What wind
Serves to advance an honest mind.

If thou be'est born to strange sights,   10
   Things invisible to see,
Ride ten thousand days and nights,
   Till age snow white hairs on thee,
Thou, when thou return'st, wilt tell me,
All strange wonders that befell thee,   15
     And swear
     No where
Lives a woman true, and fair.

If thou find'st one, let me know,
   Such a pilgrimage were sweet,   20
Yet do not, I would not go,
   Though at next door we might meet,
Though she were true, when you met her,
And last, till you write your letter,
     Yet she   25
     Will be
False, ere I come, to two, or three.

mandrake: a poisonous plant with a forked root.

cleft: split in two.

mermaids singing: when a traveller heard the song of the mermaids, it was an omen of disaster.
envy's stinging: jealous insults and attacks.

be'est born: are destined.

that befell thee: that you experienced.

true, and fair: honest and beautiful.

false: unfaithful.
ere: before.
two, or three: other lovers.

'a falling star'

👤 Personal Response

1. Describe the mood of the first stanza and show how the poet's use of verbs contributes to that mood.
2. Donne uses sound effects throughout the poem – mainly for emphasis. Choose one interesting example and comment briefly on its effectiveness.
3. From reading the poem, what is your initial impression of Donne? Is he a bitter misogynist who has no respect for women? Or is he simply being mischievous? Briefly explain your response.

👁 Critical Literacy

Written by Donne in his youth, when he had seen a good deal of London life (he was a 'great visitor of ladies'), 'Song (Go, And Catch A Falling Star)' is a humorous example of his early work. A woman's faithlessness was a conventional subject of Elizabethan poetry, but Donne's cunning line of argument leaves us wondering. Is he mocking the standard Petrarchan love poem in which a woman is seen as an object of adoration, when he cynically sets out to prove that it is impossible to find a really beautiful and loyal woman?

Stanza one includes a list of sharp commands ('Go', 'Get', 'Tell', 'Teach', 'find') as Donne demands a series of impossible tasks. The comma after 'Go' establishes the curt, almost overbearing tone of the poet. These unachievable tasks range from the magical first line, 'Go, and catch a falling star', to the nightmarish reference to conceiving a child with a poisonous plant. He also wants to know where the past has gone and he wishes to learn how to hear the unworldly music of the 'mermaids singing'. In line 6, Donne returns to the real world, as he seeks to find out how to change human nature so that it will not become jealous or bitter. The poet ends his wish list with another request – that everyone could be totally honest. The regular line length has now shortened, highlighting his frustration. Indeed, Donne's exasperation is vigorously expressed in rhyme ('wind', 'mind') as he struggles to comprehend why life does not encourage honesty. It is typical of his wry humour that his series of impossible demands will lead to his playful views on just **how hard it is to find a beautiful woman who will stay true to her husband**.

The first appearance of emphatic alliteration occurs in the second stanza ('If thou be'est born to strange sights') as the poet introduces an imaginary traveller, one who was destined to see strange and perplexing scenes. The **disquieting world of nightmare fantasy** is continued in the vivid, dramatic details; 'Things invisible', riding 'ten thousand days and nights', return with hair of snow white, telling tales of 'strange wonders'. Although great distances will have been covered and a long time will have expired, yet the poet confidently declares that 'No where/Lies a woman true, and fair'. Is Donne serious in these lines? Is he suggesting that ugly women will remain true, perhaps due to a lack of offers?

The conditional word 'If', which began the previous stanza, is also used at the beginning of the final stanza. This device of supposition ('if this were the case, then this follows') is a favourite rhetorical technique used by Donne. For a brief moment, **his tone appears to become more hopeful** when he states that if a perfect woman were discovered ('If thou find'st one, let me know'), then he would go on a 'pilgrimage', a holy journey. He thinks this would be delightful, 'sweet'. But he soon challenges the reader with a swift change of heart as he now decides that it would be better not to know. The stanza ends with Donne petulantly declaring that he would not even go next door to meet such an exceptional woman.

Disillusionment dominates the poem's final lines. The poet asserts that even if the ideal female were found, she would have very likely been unfaithful several times before the poet could have met her. The 'pilgrimage' would have been futile. In Donne's cynical view, there is no one to worship. All beautiful women are unreliable. He uses the recurring pattern of two lines of two words and a three-line rhyme, 'Yet she/Will be/False, ere I come, to two or three', to conclude the poem with a masculine swagger. The theory of the falseness of attractive women has been cleverly proved using the conventions of a type of love poetry which puts women on a pedestal. The heavenly body, 'falling star', has been toppled. Donne's satirical 'song' reflects the underlying theme of many of his other poems in which he blames the apparent wickedness of women for his own pain and heartbreak.

✒ Writing About the Poem

'Donne's changing viewpoint and tone challenge the reader.' Discuss this statement in relation to the poem 'Song (Go, And Catch A Falling Star)'. Refer closely to the text in your answer.

Sample Paragraph

Donne begins 'Song (Go, And Catch A Falling Star)' by setting up expectations of romantic love poetry. He quickly undermines these by the brutal image of the 'mandrake root', a poisonous plant, and the reader is taken into a nightmarish scenario. The poet swaps this surreal scene and expresses disgust at the difficulty of finding 'an honest mind'. Donne uses the device of the traveller, who has seen many 'strange wonders' in far-off places, not to celebrate women but to condemn them. This traveller will 'swear' that 'No where/Lives a woman true, and fair'. The reader is likely to be shocked by this attack. Cruelly, he reinforces his cynical view by stating that even if such a perfect creature was discovered, she would be unfaithful before the traveller could even write a letter informing the poet of her existence, 'False, ere I come to two, or three'. Donne uses his changing tone and viewpoint to lead the reader through several twists before his final expression of disillusionment.

✒ Class/Homework Exercises

1. 'Donne's love poetry is energetic, intelligent and engaging.' Discuss this statement with reference to 'Song (Go, And Catch A Falling Star)'.
2. In your opinion, is Donne being at all serious in his poem 'Song (Go, And Catch a Falling Star)'? Support your answer with close reference to the text.

⊙ Points to Consider

- **Central themes include romantic love and the unreliability of women.**
- **Contrasting tones – humorous, demanding, satirical, loving, cynical.**
- **Effective use of a series of impossible demands.**
- **Characteristic stylistic features – rhetoric, repetition, wit, striking imagery.**

The Anniversary

All kings, and all their favourites,
   All glory of honours, beauties, wits,
The sun itself, which makes times, as they pass,
Is elder by a year now, than it was
When thou and I first one another saw.   5
All other things to their destruction draw,
   Only our love hath no decay;
This, no tomorrow hath, nor yesterday;
Running it never runs from us away,
But truly keeps his first, last, everlasting day.   10

Two graves must hide thine and my corse;
   If one might, death were no divorce.
Alas, as well as other princes, we
(Who prince enough in one another be)
Must leave at last in death, these eyes and ears,   15
Oft fed with true oaths, and with sweet salt tears;
   But souls where nothing dwells but love
(All other thoughts being inmates) then shall prove
This, or a love increased there above,
When bodies to their graves, souls from their graves remove.   20

And then we shall be throughly blest,
   But we no more than all the rest;
Here upon earth, we're kings, and none but we
Can be such kings, nor of such subjects be.
Who is so safe as we? where none can do   25
Treason to us, except one of us two.
   True and false fears let us refrain,
Let us love nobly, and live, and add again
Years and years unto years, till we attain
To write threescore; this is the second of our reign.   30

honours: important people of prominence and distinction.
makes times: the sun controls the passing of time.
Is elder: everything in the world is older by a year.

Running it never runs from us away: ongoing love can never cease.

corse: corpse. (In Donne's time, it would have been unacceptable for an unmarried couple to be buried in the same grave.)

sweet salt tears: love can bring both joy and heartbreak.

inmates: temporary occupants.
or a love increased there above: the couple's love will be greater in heaven.

throughly blest: totally blessed.

True and false fears let us refrain: we should put aside both real and imagined misgivings.
the second of our reign: the lovers are now entering the second year of their relationship.

'Who is so safe as we?'

👤 Personal Response

1. What expectations are set up in the opening five lines of this poem? Are they realised or refuted in the remainder of the poem? Refer to the text in your answer.
2. Do you find the ending of the poem convincing or unrealistic? Support your response with close reference to the text.
3. Write a short personal response to this poem, using references to illustrate your views.

👁 Critical Literacy

'The Anniversary' is about a couple celebrating their first year together. Royalty is the underlying conceit of the entire poem, with the speaker addressing his lover as though they were both nobles. Some critics felt that Donne should not irritate women with questions of reason and logic, but should engage their hearts. In fact, he does both. At the age of twenty-seven, he fell in love with sixteen-year-old Anne More. As he was not financially secure, they kept their love and marriage secret. When Donne eventually told her father, he was thrown in prison, and he ended a letter to Anne with the pun, 'John Donne – Anne Donne – Undone'. This type of clever wordplay is a recurring feature of metaphysical poetry.

An anniversary is a useful moment to stand back and reflect. In stanza one, the young lover confidently proclaims that the entire world, 'All kings, and all their favourites ... beauties, wits,/The sun itself', is a year older since he and his beloved first met. Everyone and everything on Donne's magnificent list has been changed over time. All splendour fades. The list is not a fanfare, but a requiem, a funeral song. However, in contrast to this 'destruction', the shared love of the young couple escapes: 'Only our love hath no decay'. This short line stands out in defiance of time. The poet's clever paradox (a comparison of opposites) illustrates how their love survives: 'Running it never runs from us away'. The perpetual, unbroken movement is the rhythm and pulsing beat of their constant love. According to Donne, the lovers are at **the centre of the universe, unaffected by time**. The beautifully balanced final line ('But truly keeps his first, last, everlasting day') ends the opening stanza on an assertive note.

However, in stanza two, the poet faces up to life's stark reality and the inevitability of death. He pictures the lovers' bodies lying in separate graves, 'Two graves must hide thine and my corse'. But the couple's love is so strong that even death cannot separate them on a spiritual level. Donne develops the metaphor of royalty to emphasise how their mutual love sets them apart: 'Who prince enough in one another be'. For a moment, the mood is suddenly regretful at the thought of leaving behind love's 'true oaths, and with sweet salt tears'. The argument soon twists as Donne considers how death will free their loving souls from the prison of physical life. **The couple will then be reunited spiritually** 'where nothing dwells but love'. Indeed, they will find in heaven a much greater happiness, 'love increased there above'.

In the third stanza, Donne imagines the afterlife of the sanctified lovers when they will be 'throughly blest'. Yet he realises that they will be no different in heaven than all other lovers who have died – 'But we no more than all the rest'. It is ironic that they will not be as they are on earth, where they are 'kings'. During their lives, the two of them are royalty and subjects at the same time. Their mutual love is beyond deceit ('Treason'). Any harm which can happen to the couple would be self-destructive, so they can love without fear. Donne confidently dismisses whatever anxiety they might feel, whether real or imagined: 'True and false fears let us refrain'. He encourages them to 'love nobly', so they will enjoy a long life and even celebrate their 60th anniversary ('threescore'). Once more, the royal metaphor (suggested by 'nobly' and 'reign') is used to stress the special status of true love. Donne's final tone is optimistic, with its positive message to live in the moment, to love in this world. **The couple can now look forward to celebrating the second year of their relationship**: 'the second of our reign'.

Throughout this **passionate love poem**, the inward-looking nature of young lovers in the excitement of a new romance is beautifully evoked in the conceit of royalty. Love is an exceptional state, an absorbing experience, incapable of being touched by the outside world. But while there is plenty of passion in 'The Anniversary', Donne also gives readers a somewhat superior view of romantic love. The dominant tone throughout is highly assured, 'Only our love hath no decay', yet intimate, 'Who is so safe as we?' Characteristically, the poet's restless mind searches for far-fetched ideas and extravagant images in order to convey the quality of unconditional love. There is much metaphysical wit in Donne's poetry and he was known for his inventive wordplay, such as the oxymoron (the linking of opposite aspects) 'sweet salt tears'.

🖋 Writing About the Poem

'Donne's love poetry is lively, inventive and highly compelling.'
Discuss this view of the poet's work in relation to the poem 'The
Anniversary'. Quote in support of your response.

Sample Paragraph

'The Anniversary' is another of Donne's love poems. It is the celebration of a relationship that is a year old. Donne uses the extended metaphor of royalty to illustrate the special state of the lovers. The opening which begins with the list, 'All kings, and all their favourites,/All glory of honours, beauties' is in the tradition of courtly love. But it is the ending of the poem which is really creative as the poet reassures his loved one: 'Who is so safe as we?' This is also typically imaginative as Donne suggests that they celebrate while they can, 'Here upon earth we're kings'. Donne's language is energetic, particularly in the paradox, 'Running it never runs from us away'. I thought the unusual idea of movement going nowhere was interesting. The poet uses alliteration, especially the dull 'd' sound in 'destruction draw', to emphasise how everything in the world will change – except for the lovers themselves.

EXAMINER'S COMMENT

As part of a full essay, this is a well-managed paragraph which addresses the question directly and shows good personal interaction with the poem. The focus on Donne's language is clear and supported effectively with suitable reference. Expression is clear, but a little repetitive. Overall, a high-grade standard.

🖋 Class/Homework Exercises

1. In your own words, trace the development of the royalty metaphor throughout 'The Anniversary'.
2. Tensions between love's timelessness and the reality of death are central to Donne's poem 'The Anniversary'. To what extent do you agree with this view? Support your response with reference to the text.

⊙ Points to Consider

- **Donne argues that true love is timeless.**
- **Presents passionate feelings within a logical context.**
- **Typical use of a developed conceit comparing the lovers to royalty.**
- **Contrast between the decaying reality and the lovers' transcendent world.**
- **Effective use of repetition, paradox and changing moods.**

The short fifth line in each stanza also adds drama, particularly 'Then fear not me'. He is reassuring her that he will return quickly. Finally he reminds her that this separation is just a short night's sleep. After all the drama between the lovers, there is a gentle resolution in the end.

EXAMINER'S COMMENT

This high-grade paragraph addresses the question directly and explores key dramatic aspects of the poem both explicitly and implicitly. Expression is varied and well controlled and there is some good personal engagement. Effective use is also made of apt quotation and reference throughout.

✐ Class/Homework Exercises

1. 'John Donne's poetry is intimate and engaging.' Discuss this statement in relation to 'Song (Sweetest Love, I Do Not Go)'. Support the points you make with reference to the poem.
2. Forceful rhythm is one of Donne's most effective stylistic features. Discuss this view with particular reference to 'Song (Sweetest Love, I Do Not Go)'.

⊙ Points to Consider

- **Another of Donne's explorations of ideal love.**

- **Musical sounds, personification, emphatic rhythm, rhyme and repetition.**

- **Language varies – simple, exaggerated, argumentative.**

- **Effective use of contrast.**

- **Ambivalent moods – tender, light-hearted, serious.**

A Valediction: Forbidding Mourning

Title: The title comes from the Latin for a farewell message.

As virtuous men pass mildly away,
    And whisper to their souls, to go,
Whilst some of their sad friends do say,
    The breath goes now, and some say, no:

As virtuous men pass mildly: just as good men die peacefully.

So let us melt, and make no noise,   5
    No tear-floods, nor sigh-tempests move,
'Twere profanation of our joys
    To tell the laity our love.

melt: dissolve and blend together.

profanation: irreverence, offensiveness.
laity: ordinary people.

Moving of th'earth brings harms and fears,
    Men reckon what it did and meant,   10
But trepidation of the spheres
    Though greater far, is innocent.

reckon what it did and meant: try to understand the significance of the turbulence.
trepidation of the spheres: movement of the planets.

Dull sublunary lovers' love
    (Whose soul is sense) cannot admit
Absence, because it doth remove   15
    Those things which elemented it.

sublunary: undependable; mundane.

elemented: formed.

But we by a love so much refined,
    That our selves know not what it is,
Inter-assured of the mind,
    Care less, eyes, lips, and hands to miss.   20

Inter-assured: trusting.

Our two souls therefore, which are one,
    Though I must go, endure not yet
A breach, but an expansion,
    Like gold to airy thinness beat.

breach: separation.

If they be two, they are two so   25
    As stiff twin compasses are two,
Thy soul the fixed foot, makes no show
    To move, but doth, if the other do.

twin compasses: instrument for measuring circles.

And though it in the centre sit,
    Yet when the other far doth roam,   30
It leans, and hearkens after it,
    And grows erect, as that comes home.

Such wilt thou be to me, who must
    Like th' other foot, obliquely run;   **obliquely:** curved.
Thy firmness makes my circle just,   35   **just:** exact.
    And makes me end, where I begun.

'Thy firmness makes my circle just'

👤 Personal Response

1. Trace Donne's line of argument in the poem 'A Valediction: Forbidding Mourning'. Support your answer with suitable reference.
2. Which comparison appeals most to you in this poem? Briefly explain why.
3. In what way does Donne see the parting of lovers as a positive move? Give reasons for your response using reference from the poem.

◉ Critical Literacy

'A Valediction: Forbidding Mourning' dates from 1611 when Donne embarked on a long journey to Europe and wrote this special farewell poem for his wife. The poet explores the familiar theme of separation from a loved one, and claims that the relationship between the lovers is such that physical distance cannot part them. Indeed, he argues, being apart actually strengthens their love. Characteristically, Donne breathes new life into this traditional subject by using a series of ingenious metaphors and comparisons. These provide fresh ways of looking at separation which will help the couple to avoid the mourning forbidden by the poem's title.

Stanza one opens on a reflective note. Donne considers how 'sad friends' grieve for those who are dying. The atmosphere is usually sombre but tranquil as loved ones take comfort that 'virtuous' people 'pass mildly away', confident of a spiritual life hereafter. Soft sibilant 's' sounds ('whisper' and 'souls') create this untroubled mood. The separation of body and soul is so gentle that those surrounding the dying are uncertain about whether they are still alive or not. Donne uses breaks in punctuation to suggest this confusion, 'The breath goes now, and some say, no'. This gives way to a metaphor in the second stanza where the poet makes a suggestion to his lover: 'So let us melt, and make no noise'. For Donne, the couple's separation is like a minor death which should also be treated in a dignified and restrained way. **He ridicules people who cannot control their feelings and resort to 'tear-floods' and 'sigh-tempests'**. Such hyperbole (exaggerated speech) was typical of courtly love. The poet emphasises the sacred nature of true love by asserting that it would be almost blasphemous – a 'profanation of our joys' – to let outsiders ('the laity') know about it.

Donne introduces a further conceit in the third stanza when he tells his loved one that earthquakes and similar disturbances – perhaps a hint at her outpourings of grief – only bring 'harms and fears'. However, a mere earthquake is relatively unimportant compared to the movement of the planet, which ordinary people see as presenting no danger. Therefore, the geographical separation which the couple will experience should not be feared. **This astrological analogy** continues into the fourth stanza where the poet speaks disapprovingly of 'Dull sublunary lovers' love'. Unlike the poet and his lover, other couples cannot tolerate being apart because their inferior type of love is dependent on physical contact. As always, Donne interlinks numerous poetic devices. The assonance of the short 'u' sounds in each word of the first line reinforces the concept of dreariness which he associates with shallow relationships. The term 'sublunary' (literally meaning 'under the moon') suggests that all these other lovers are changeable and unreliable just like the variable moon.

Stanza five continues to focus on the superiority of the couple's shared love. This is the reason why Donne forbade mourning in the title. From his viewpoint, their relationship is purified like precious metal. They both know that each is loyal to the other, 'Inter-assured of the mind', because they share this special love. In contrast to ordinary couples, they are not dependent on the actual presence of the loved one, making each of them 'Care less, eyes, lips and hands to miss'. **Their love is more a union of souls which transcends the physical.** Geographical separation means nothing to two united spirits. The poet's forceful, rhetorical tone is developed in stanza six. Donne argues that since their two souls are 'one', they are not really faced with any 'breach' or division. Indeed, they are experiencing an 'expansion' in much the same way as gold can be stretched to the slender width of paper if it is beaten to 'airy thinness'. Since gold is always associated with beauty and value, this typically inventive simile flatters Donne's lover and celebrates the couple's love.

The final reason for refusing to mourn being separated is presented in stanzas seven and eight when Donne uses compasses as a metaphor to describe the couple's unity. Although lovers retain their souls, they are divided into two parts. When the compasses draw a circle, one point remains stationary in the centre, at a fixed point, which allows the other to complete its circuit. Similarly, if one of the lovers remains at home, it ensures the return of the other. A perfect circle is a symbol of infinity, as there is no apparent beginning or end. This ingenious conceit aptly sums up the couple's spiritual relationship, which is also balanced and mutual. In the final stanzas, their heightened love is seen as serious and beautiful in its simplicity. Yet there is still a human dimension; the fixed foot 'hearkens after' the moving foot. The loved one will always yearn for the one who has gone. Overall, the **poem tenderly comforts both lovers** at this moment of uneasy parting. Donne concludes by offering a firm assurance that the traveller eventually 'comes home'.

✍ Writing About the Poem

'Donne's poetry rarely tells us anything new; rather it reminds us of what we know already.' To what extent is this true of 'A Valediction: Forbidding Mourning'? Support your answer with relevant quotation.

Sample Paragraph

I agree with this view. Donne addresses familiar themes, particularly in his love poetry. However, it is his unique approach which makes him an original poet. He dares to go against conventions and appeals not only to a woman's emotions, but to her intellect through clever comparisons. 'A Valediction: Forbidding Mourning' presents the reader with a sad scene of men accepting death, 'pass mildly away'. The poet is suggesting that this attitude – 'make no noise'– is how he would like himself and his loved one to part, 'So let us melt'. Just as gold expands to 'airy thinness', so their love will bridge the gap of their separation. Finally, Donne compares these two lovers to a mathematical compass, free to move, yet always connected. So the treatment of an ordinary theme – separation – is raised to a new level as readers follow the poet's thought-provoking logic. Donne may not explore new ideas, but he does offer original perspectives.

EXAMINER'S COMMENT

This is a confidently written response to the question and addresses some of Donne's prominent ideas directly. Several suitable references are used effectively to discuss the poet's treatment of recurring themes. Expression is controlled throughout and there is some interesting personal engagement. Impressive top-grade standard.

✒ Class/Homework Exercises

1. 'Donne is an original and thought-provoking poet.' Discuss this statement in relation to the poem, 'A Valediction: Forbidding Mourning'. Use evidence from the poem to support your response.
2. Donne is known for drawing on images from a wide range of sources. To what extent is this true of 'A Valediction: Forbidding Mourning'? Support your answer with reference to the poem.

⊙ Points to Consider

- **Donne focuses on the spiritual nature of true love.**
- **Inventive metaphors and extended image patterns illustrate separation.**
- **Effective use of contrast; varying tones – confident, assuring, loving.**
- **Arguments lead to logical conclusion that genuine lovers are never parted.**

6

The Dream

Dear love, for nothing less than thee
Would I have broke this happy dream,
    It was a theme
For reason, much too strong for fantasy.
Therefore thou waked'st me wisely; yet   5
My dream thou brok'st not, but continued'st it.
Thou art so true that thoughts of thee suffice
To make dreams truths, and fables histories;
Enter these arms, for since thou thought'st it best,
Not to dream all my dream, let's act the rest.   10

As lightning, or a taper's light,
Thine eyes, and not thy noise waked me;
    Yet I thought thee
(For thou lovest truth) an angel, at first sight,
But when I saw thou saw'st my heart,   15
And knew'st my thoughts, beyond an angel's art,
When thou knew'st what I dreamt, when thou knew'st when
Excess of joy would wake me, and cam'st then,
I must confess, it could not choose but be
Profane, to think thee anything but thee.   20

Coming and staying showed thee, thee,
But rising makes me doubt, that now,
    Thou art not thou.
That love is weak where fear's as strong as he;
'Tis not all spirit, pure and brave,   25
If mixture it of fear, shame, honour have;
Perchance as torches which must ready be,
Men light and put out, so thou deal'st with me,
Thou cam'st to kindle, goest to come; then I
Will dream that hope again, but else would die.   30

suffice: are enough.

fables histories: stories become true.

taper's light: bright candlelight.

beyond an angel's art: more than an angel.

it could not choose but be: there was no other option.
Profane: disrespectful.

showed thee, thee: revealed your true self.

Perchance as torches which must ready be: worn torches light up more quickly than new ones.
kindle: re-ignite; awaken.
goest to come: you leave in order to return again.

'this happy dream'

👤 Personal Response

1. In your own words, describe Donne's attitude to his lover in the opening stanza.
2. Choose one image from the poem which you consider particularly effective. Briefly explain your choice.
3. Although John Donne enjoys arguing in his love poetry, he treats women as his intellectual equals. Where is this evident in 'The Dream'? Quote in support of your response.

👁 Critical Literacy

John Donne's love poetry reacted against the courtly love tradition of his time. He did not believe in worshipping an aloof, inaccessible figure. Instead, he wanted a real connection with his loved one. This can be clearly seen in 'The Dream', a sensual love poem which plays with ideas of dreams, desire and truth. Like love itself, the woman Donne addresses is praised in exaggerated terms and acclaimed as someone who is above even the level of angels.

At the start of stanza one, Donne is clearly delighted to have been awoken by the same person he was dreaming about. The poet's engaging tone is evident as he sleepily declares, 'Dear love, for nothing less than thee/Would I have broke this happy dream'. There is an unexpected gentleness in these lines. Using this playfully intimate mood, Donne explains that reality (his lover's physical presence) is stronger than fantasy, 'It was a theme/For reason'. The poet congratulates his lover on waking him, 'Therefore thou waked'st me wisely'. He even suggests that she can alter history, 'Thou art so true, that thoughts of thee suffice,/To make dreams truths'. Donne is implying that women have remarkable power over the perception of reality. **This subtle poem blends dream and reality seamlessly** as the poet declares that his loved one did not ruin his dream, 'My dream thou brok'st not', but by her actual presence, she is continuing it, and so he invites her to 'Enter these arms … let's act the rest'. Donne is clearly not satisfied with any distant adoration of a loved one. Instead, he desires an urgent, passionate connection, 'Not to dream all my dream', but to make his dream come true.

Stanza two begins with a flattering analogy. Donne compares the woman's eyes to a soft light, 'As lightning, or a taper's light,/Thine eyes'. Such characteristic wordplay emphasises her beauty and more than compensates for any interruption which may have disturbed him, 'not thy noise waked me'. For a brief moment, he thought she was an angel, but the bracketed afterthought, '(For thou lovest truth)', removes this romantic poem from the conventional style of Donne's time and gives it a more personal significance. There is no denying the poet's emotional vulnerability. He suddenly realises that his lover 'knew'st my thoughts' – something that makes her more special than any heavenly angel. He imagines that she knew he was dreaming of her and wanted to play out the dream in reality so that they could share the 'Excess of joy'. The **complicated and challenging argument** continues as Donne confesses that it would be 'Profane' or blasphemous to regard his loved one as anyone but herself. From the poet's viewpoint, their relationship is based on mutual empathy, a sharing of thoughts.

Donne continues to applaud his lover in the opening lines of stanza three. By 'Coming and staying', she has revealed her real character, 'showed thee, thee'. He maintains that when she is with him, she is most like her true self. However, there is an **abrupt change of mood** as she attempts to leave, 'rising makes me doubt'. Donne suddenly criticises his companion for not being truly in love with him, 'that now,/ Thou art not thou'. He challenges her feelings towards him in a finely balanced argument, 'love is weak, where fear's as strong as he'. The personification suggests that her fear becomes stronger as her love weakens.

The poet claims that the woman's reluctance to express her love physically is because of various social pressures, especially 'fear, shame, honour'. He bitterly accuses her of taking him for granted, like an old torch. Up until this moment, Donne had been hoping she had come to ignite their love, 'Thou cam'st to kindle'. However, in another startling turn, he uses an oxymoron (a contradictory expression) to reassure himself that his companion only leaves him in order to return, 'goest to come'. She will revisit him and inflame his desires for her even further, just as torches, once lit, are easier to ignite a second time. **The poem ends on an enthusiastic note of expectation**. Donne will 'dream that hope again'. Meantime, he leaves his lover with a parting shot that he 'but else would die' if she does not return to him. Clearly, without the woman of his dreams, he can never be truly satisfied.

🖊 Writing About the Poem

'John Donne develops his poetic themes by means of vigorous and surprising arguments.' Discuss this statement in relation to 'The Dream'. Use close reference to the text to support your points.

Sample Paragraph

With an intimate glimpse of the poet in the unguarded moments between sleep and wakefulness, Donne wakes to find his loved one at his side. In an enthusiastic tone, he aims to pursue in real life what he has been dreaming of. He begins with compliments, telling her she is so real that her very presence turns his imaginings to fact, 'Thou art so true'. The poet was so intensely aware of her in his dream that he does not feel that the spell is broken when he wakes, 'My dream thou brok'st not'. His reasoning develops, particularly in the last stanza, he abruptly changes course because she is leaving, accusing her that 'love is weak'. Unexpectedly, the logic takes a different direction as he consoles himself that she 'cam'st to kindle' and she is only going so that she can come again, 'goest to come'. His argument ends optimistically, that he 'Will dream that hope again' – as a result of his dependency on her.

EXAMINER'S COMMENT

This is a sustained response to a challenging question. There is good engagement with the development of thought in the poem, and supportive reference to the changes in Donne's line of argument. Expression is assured throughout and effective use is made of suitable quotation. Top-grade standard.

✒ Class/Homework Exercises

1. 'The Dream' is a highly passionate and uninhibited love poem.' To what extent would you agree with this view? Support your answer with reference to the text.
2. Witty wordplay is a recurring feature of John Donne's poetry. In your opinion, is this true of 'The Dream'? Refer closely to the poem in your answer.

⊙ Points to Consider

- Positive, sensual love poem exploring aspects of dreams, desire and truth.
- Simple, conversational language adds immediacy and authenticity.
- Varying moods – happiness, misgiving, anticipation.
- Mix of serious and light-hearted tones.
- Characteristic use of strong rhythm, exaggeration, logical argument.

7 The Flea

JOHN DONNE

Mark but this flea, and mark in this,
How little that which thou deny'st me is;
Me it suck'd first, and now sucks thee,
And in this flea, our two bloods mingled be;
Thou know'st that this cannot be said   5
A sin, nor shame, nor loss of maidenhead,
    Yet this enjoys before it woo,
    And pampered swells with one blood made of two,
    And this, alas, is more than we would do.

O stay, three lives in one flea spare,   10
Where we almost, yea more than married are.
This flea is you and I, and this
Our marriage bed, and marriage temple is;
Though parents grudge, and you, w'are met,
And cloistered in these living walls of jet.   15
    Though use make you apt to kill me,
    Let not to that self-murder added be,
    And sacrilege, three sins in killing three.

Cruel and sudden, hast thou since
Purpled thy nail, in blood of innocence?   20
Wherein could this flea guilty be,
Except in that drop which it sucked from thee?
Yet thou triumph'st, and say'st that thou
Find'st not thy self, nor me the weaker now.
    'Tis true, then learn how false, fears be;   25
    Just so much honour, when thou yield'st to me,
    Will waste, as this flea's death took life from thee.

Mark: note.

our two bloods mingled be: intimacy between lovers was believed to result in the mingling together of each partner's blood.
maidenhead: virginity.
this enjoys before it woo: the flea achieves what the poet desires, without the trouble of courtship.

cloistered: enclosed.
jet: shiny black.
apt: ready.

sacrilege: destruction of something holy.

sudden: without warning.

Purpled: stained with the blood of the flea.

Yet thou triumph'st: Donne declares that the woman believes she has defeated his argument.

'our two bloods mingled'

👤 Personal Response

1. In your opinion, what is Donne's attitude to love and romance in this poem? Support your answer by close reference to the text.
2. Choose two lines or phrases which you think would have surprised or shocked Donne's readers in the 1600s. Briefly explain your choice in each case.
3. Write your own personal response to the poem, highlighting its impact on you.

👁 Critical Literacy

Donne's humorous and sensual poem makes use of the conceit (extended image) of a flea to explore his relationship with the woman he loves. However, in associating romantic love with a bloodsucking parasite – rather than something of beauty – the poet expresses his own desire for intimacy in an unexpected way. While many of Donne's poems deal with spiritual love between couples, here it is purely physical.

The reader is immediately plunged into a turbulent scene between two lovers in stanza one. The poet addresses an unnamed woman, insisting that she pay close attention to what he is saying. She is denying him something he craves, which is as yet unspecified, but – according to Donne – is trivial, 'How little that which thou deny'st me is'. He then comments on the actions of the flea, 'it suck'd me first, and now sucks thee'. The poet even uses religious imagery ('sin', 'shame') to add weight to his argument that an intimate physical relationship is not wrong. He complains that **the flea has already enjoyed more intimacy than himself with this woman**, even though it has not had to go through the ritual of courtship.

Unlike Donne, the flea is 'pampered' and satisfied. The monosyllabic verb 'swells' dramatically describes the bloating of the insect with the couple's blood. The peevish complaint, 'Yet this enjoys before it woo', highlights just how frustrated Donne feels. **Although he has played the game of love by the rules**, he is a miserable failure. The punctuation breaks before and after 'alas' emphasise how cruelly he believes he is being treated. Is the tone here mock-dramatic, with the use of the regretful 'alas'? If so, the reader can react with amusement. Or is the tone emotional, verging on petulant blackmail? Then the reader might feel anger at the poet's whining, adolescent behaviour.

In stanza two, Donne's argument switches as he asks his lover to respect the flea and what it represents. His pleading tone is evident when he begs for its life to be spared, 'O, stay'. Such flamboyant exaggeration strikes a note of humour. The poet presents an elaborate explanation outlining why the flea should be allowed to live. Killing it will result not only in the insect's death, but also the symbolic death of the couple, as their bloods are mingled in the body of the flea, 'three lives in one flea spare'. Donne maintains that the couple are even closer than if they were joined together in marriage ('yea, more than married are') since their bloods have now combined. To the poet, this represents a relationship that is blessed in heaven. He argues that even though there are objections to this sacred union from both his loved one herself and her family, 'Though parents grudge, and you', yet the fact remains that **the lovers are already joined together**, 'cloistered in these living walls of jet'. This striking religious image is typical of Donne, who exaggerates how the flea's glossy, black body contains the couple's unified blood.

Donne develops his argument by referring to a major difficulty in their relationship – the woman's coldness towards him. As far as he is concerned, she takes him for granted, 'Though use make you apt to kill me'. **The tone changes from an almost reflective voice to a more impatient one**. But he continues to persuade the woman, urging her to spare the flea and show her love for him. The 'three lives in one' of the flea (her blood, his and its) is a clear reference to the Christian idea of the Trinity. The flea is seen as their marriage 'temple', which it would be 'sacrilege' to destroy. It's interesting that Donne never lets the reader hear the woman speak, yet from the various twists and turns of his argument, there is a real sense of her presence, and the reader is left in no doubt of her negative reaction to the poet's persistent pleas.

The tone becomes increasingly accusatory in stanza three as Donne reacts to his companion's impulsive killing of the flea, 'Cruel and sudden'. But his real resentment is almost certainly because of the woman's forceful rejection of his advances. Like the unfortunate flea, **he sees himself as a victim of her callous behaviour**. The vivid, colloquial language ('hast thou since/Purpl'd thy nail, in blood of innocence?') seems to have a timeless resonance. For a moment, Donne appears to admit defeat ('Yet thou triumph'st') – but is he lulling his lover into a false sense of security before coming up with yet another argument?

In a final flourish, **the poet insists on having the last word by turning the woman's own resistance against her**. He admits that, of course, she is completely right, ''Tis true'. Neither she nor Donne has lost anything by the flea's death, 'not thy self, nor me the weaker now'. Once again, as in the poem's opening lines, he issues instructions to this alluring woman – 'then learn'. What he wants her to believe is that she will lose almost nothing in yielding to his sexual advances. But readers are still left with an unresolved situation. Will the poet ever convince his beloved to put aside her 'fears'? Or will he be forced to accept that he cannot always get what he desires? What is certain, however, is that during the course of this unusual love poem, Donne's dazzling argument has ingeniously explored some of the age-old questions about the games lovers play.

✒ Writing About the Poem

'John Donne's poems can be described as intimate dramas.' Discuss this statement in relation to 'The Flea', using quotations from the text to support your answer.

Sample Paragraph

Donne's erotic poem opens with an emphatic repetition as he instructs his lover to pay more attention to him – 'How little that which thou deny'st me is'. The seduction scene is highly charged as they disagree about committing to a full sexual relationship. The conflict increases when the poet begs her not to kill the flea – 'O, stay'. Detailed, probing argument is used as Donne points out that this flea 'is you and I', since it contains their mixed blood. The poet's annoyance is suggested in the melodramatic third stanza as he calls his beloved 'Cruel' because she has killed the insect. The drama reaches a high point when he tricks her by suddenly agreeing with her cruel decision to refuse him – 'Yet thou triumph'st'. He ends by then reminding her how little she will have lost if she gives in to his advances. The poem is typical of Donne's exaggerated dramas, filled with striking imagery and characteristic playfulness.

EXAMINER'S COMMENT

This is a confident top-grade response which addresses the question directly and includes good engagement with the poem. Suitable quotations illustrate key points, highlighting the various references to drama (in this case, a seduction scene involving conflict and melodramatic dialogue). Expression is varied, fluent and very well controlled throughout.

🖊 Class/Homework Exercises

1. Comment on the effectiveness of Donne's use of imagery in his poem 'The Flea'. Support your answer with suitable reference and quotation.
2. In your opinion, does Donne present an effective and convincing argument to his lover in this poem? Support your answer with reference to the text.

⊙ Points to Consider

- **Light-hearted, erotic love poem exploring aspects of desire.**
- **Effective development of witty, provocative imagery based on the central flea conceit.**
- **Use of dramatic, eloquent and precise language.**
- **Typically argumentative and logical.**

8

At the Round Earth's Imagined Corners

JOHN DONNE

At the round earth's imagined corners, blow
Your trumpets, angels, and arise, arise
From death, you numberless infinities
Of souls, and to your scattered bodies go,
All whom the flood did, and fire shall, o'erthrow,   5
All whom war, dearth, age, agues, tyrannies,
Despair, law, chance, hath slain, and you whose eyes
Shall behold God, and never taste death's woe.
But let them sleep, Lord, and me mourn a space;
For, if above all these, my sins abound,   10
'Tis late to ask abundance of thy grace,
When we are there. Here on this lowly ground,
Teach me how to repent; for that's as good
As if thou hadst sealed my pardon, with thy blood.

the round earth's imagined corners: biblical idea of four corners of earth.
Your trumpets: old maps include illustrations of angels blowing trumpets.
All whom the flood did, and fire shall, o'erthrow: God drowned the world in a great flood. Fire will destroy it in the end.
dearth: scarcity, famine.
agues: sickness, disease.
Shall behold God, and never taste death's woe: those people who are still alive on the Last Day will go straight to judgement.
But let them sleep: Donne asks God to postpone Judgement Day.
a space: for a moment.
abundance of thy grace: God's forgiveness.
lowly ground: here on earth.
repent: ask for God's mercy.
As if thou hadst sealed my pardon: Jesus died for people's sins.

'to your scattered bodies go'

👤 Personal Response

1. What picture of the Last Judgement is given in the poem's opening eight lines? Refer to the text in your answer.
2. The poem changes direction in line 9. Describe this change and explain why you think the poet has switched his line of thought. Support your answer with close reference to the text.
3. In your opinion, is Donne fascinated by death? Choose two lines or phrases from the poem which support your view and discuss their impact.

👁 Critical Literacy

John Donne's famous Holy Sonnet, 'At the Round Earth's Imagined Corners', is set against the dramatic backdrop of the Apocalypse, the final destruction of the world, described in the Bible's Book of Revelations. The poem is divided into two parts: the chaotic tumult of Judgement Day in the octet and the quieter, more meditative sestet. What gives this powerful poem its universal significance is that Donne confronts the certainty of death, which all humans face.

Donne presents the reader with a tantalisingly surreal paradox in line 1. Using the traditional expression, 'the round earth's imagined corners', he visualises what will happen when the dead are resurrected and reunited with their spirits. Broad vowel assonance adds to the **magnificent tension of this imagined scene**. The poet's powerful, visual language has cleverly captured a sense of huge expanse. He quickly introduces an urgent tone with the monosyllabic verb 'blow' which teeters at the end of the opening line. Donne is demanding that the angels signal Judgement Day, almost as if it were a race. He imagines them with bright trumpets sounding a triumphant call, just as a fanfare announces the arrival of a king. The sound is so loud and resonant that it immediately wakens the dead. Is this the sign of triumph over death? Donne heightens the drama as he repeats 'arise, arise', insisting that all the dead souls 'go' to their bodies. The run-on lines (enjambment) accelerate with breathless energy as confusion reigns. Spirits rush around trying to find their 'scattered' bodies. Throughout this first quatrain, the forceful end-of-line verbs ('arise', 'go') emphasise this momentous occasion. With characteristic hyperbole, Donne speaks of 'numberless infinities', successfully reinforcing the scale of the overwhelming numbers involved in this frenzy.

In the second quatrain, Donne reflects on how all these people died. The repetition of the phrase, 'All whom', with its monosyllabic broad vowels, signifies the enormity of these events. Ranging over time, the poet considers great natural disasters, 'All whom the flood did' (a reference to the Great Flood described in the Bible). He then imagines the future, 'and fire shall o'erthrow' (another biblical prophecy about the destruction of the world by fire). Donne sweeps at breathtaking pace through possible causes of death, such as 'war, dearth, age, agues, tyrannies'. His **pounding rhythm is relentless** as he rushes on through his solemn list: 'Despair, law, chance'. The poet then thinks about everyone who will be alive on the Last Day, those who will 'never taste death's woe'. For Donne, these are the fortunate ones who will go straight to God's judgement, having been spared the ordeal of death. The forceful eight lines with their purposeful, regular rhyme form one overwhelming sentence, concluding with triumph over death.

There is a sudden change of tone in line 9. This dramatic turn (volta) diverts the poem from Donne's insistent demand that the world should end now, and allows readers realise that the apocalypse has not yet happened. Indeed, the poet has been imagining the whole panoramic scene. His enthusiasm for the end of the world evaporates and the earlier impassioned conviction gives way to **a mood of self-doubt and contrition**. But as Donne focuses on his own personal relationship with God, we are left wondering whether his apparent concern for the dead is an act of compassion, or just a selfish request for his own spiritual salvation. At any rate, he realises that he needs time to atone for his own sins, 'and me mourn a space'. Donne becomes acutely aware that he was hasty in calling for the Day of Judgement before knowing if he himself had been forgiven. Now he pleads for more time, begging God to be taught 'how to repent'. He realises that it will be too late to seek forgiveness on Judgement Day, 'to ask abundance of thy grace/When we are there'. His submissive tone is plainly evident in the poignant phrase, 'Here on this lowly ground'.

The sonnet's final lines confirm Donne's belief that Christ's death on the cross brought salvation to the world. This paradox shows that although human beings as a group were redeemed, individuals cannot be saved unless they recognise this sacrifice of 'blood'. An individual act of faith is required. Donne's language is dense and legalistic. This conclusion is a plea for 'pardon', a reprieve. Christ's blood is the seal on the poet's 'pardon'. This poem has moved on considerably from the octet, where Donne confidently urged the angels and the dead to prepare for the end of the world. In the sestet, **he has become unsettled, afraid of the consequences of the Apocalypse for himself**. However, the concluding couplet represents a resolution, since the poet now puts his trust in Christ's salvation. Readers are left with their own questions. Is the poem merely a display of arrogant presumption which ends with a servile plea for forgiveness? Or is it a genuine act of repentance?

✒ Writing About the Poem

Donne's sonnet 'At the Round Earth's Imagined Corners' is a private, personal religious meditation which alienates the modern reader. Discuss this view, supporting your answer with reference to the poem.

Sample Paragraph

All human beings face death. So I do not think Donne's poem 'At the round earth's imagined corners' is all that remote from people today. The difference between the modern reader and Donne is the outdated language used. Biblical references wouldn't be as familiar to today's readers. These describe the angels blowing their trumpets would not be widely known.

I think the first eight lines would appeal to the modern reader as the poet shouts 'blow', 'arise', 'go'. I don't think Donne's personal tone in the sestet, 'on this lowly ground', would be familiar today. In some ways, I can relate to Donne's fear of death – which is still the one great unknown. At times of trouble, believers often light candles in hope. Donne's personal hope was for salvation bought by the death of Christ, 'with thy blood'.

EXAMINER'S COMMENT

This is an uneven attempt at a challenging question. While the paragraph touches on some noteworthy points about the poem's archaic expressions and references which might alienate modern readers, it lacks in-depth discussion of Donne's central concern – his own relationship with God. An average mid-grade standard.

✏ Class/Homework Exercises

1. 'A feature of Donne's poetry is that his vocabulary is easy to understand, but his ideas are difficult to follow.' Discuss this statement in relation to the poem 'At the Round Earth's Imagined Corners', quoting in support of your response.

2. Donne is well known for the power of his dramatic imagery. To what extent is this true of 'At the Round Earth's Imagined Corners'? Support your answer with reference to the poem.

⊙ Points to Consider

• **Holy Sonnet imagining Judgement Day.**

• **Themes include the poet's intense relationship with God, sin and repentance.**

• **Dramatic language, memorable images, emphatic verbs, rhythm and repetition.**

• **Contrasting moods/atmospheres; effective use of assonant sounds.**

Thou Hast Made Me, and Shall Thy Work Decay?

JOHN DONNE

Thou hast made me, and shall thy work decay?
Repair me now, for now mine end doth haste,
I run to death, and death meets me as fast,
And all my pleasures are like yesterday;
I dare not move my dim eyes any way,   5
Despair behind, and death before doth cast
Such terror, and my feeble flesh doth waste
By sin in it, which it towards hell doth weigh.
Only thou art above, and when towards thee
By thy leave I can look, I rise again;   10
But our old subtle foe so tempteth me,
That not one hour myself I can sustain;
Thy grace may wing me to prevent his art,
And thou like adamant draw mine iron heart.

Repair: renew, rescue.
doth: does.

dim: blurred, unseeing.

feeble: weak.

weigh: pull down, think about.

old subtle foe: Satan, the old enemy.

adamant: a naturally occurring magnet or lodestone.
iron: hard, uncompromising.

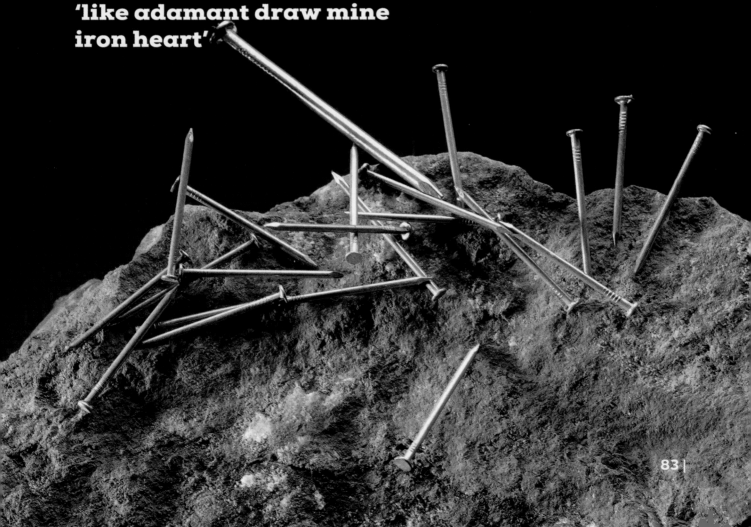

'like adamant draw mine iron heart'

👤 Personal Response

1. Donne's poem begins on a sharp demanding note. In your opinion, what does the poet mean by the question in line 1?
2. What characteristics of the Devil are implied in the phrase 'old subtle foe'?
3. In your view, is the conclusion of the poem optimistic or pessimistic? Refer closely to the text in your response.

👁 Critical Literacy

The religious poems of John Donne explore the intense spiritual struggle which preoccupied his mind and soul. Sonnets such as 'Thou Hast Made Me, and Shall Thy Work Decay?' are personal dialogues or 'conversations' which show his passionate relationship with God as he privately meditates on the reality of life and death.

Donne begins this poem in a similar way to his love poetry, in mid-action, addressing God directly. His bold question ('Thou hast made me, and shall thy work decay?') manipulatively suggests that God will be unsuccessful in his great work on behalf of sinners if he does not redeem the poet. **Donne's lifelong search for truth is channelled into this simple, dramatic confrontation**. He regards it as a priority that God should forgive him without delay, 'Repair me now', as he is facing imminent death, 'for now mine end doth haste'. Throughout this first quatrain, the poet bluntly admits his spiritual distress. Ironically, while Donne accepts his dependence on God, he uses an authoritative tone in demanding God's immediate help.

The urgency of this impatient request is evident in the personification of death as a familiar figure hurrying towards him, 'I run to death, and death meets me as fast'. **Powerfully monosyllabic language** emphasises the surging movement of this crucial encounter, which is further underlined by the mid-line repetition of 'death'. The running action of two lovers rushing to meet is evoked in this daring image. There is a sense of both intimacy and inevitability as Donne now accepts the chilling realisation that the many sensual delights he once enjoyed are gone: 'And all my pleasures are like yesterday'. Is the remorse of an indulgently sinful life flashing before the eyes of this vulnerable man who is about to die?

In the second quatrain, Donne appears to be haunted by this intense realisation: 'I dare not move my dim eyes any way'. Terrified of looking back at a past that is full of sin, he is equally petrified by the future of certain death and possible damnation. The fragility of his human condition is shown in the adjective 'dim'. He is horrified by the shocking prospect of his decaying body, rotting with sin: 'my feeble flesh doth waste'. An increasing **sense of hopelessness dominates his restless mind**, as Donne imagines his doomed

JOHN DONNE

soul being dragged into eternal punishment, 'towards hell doth weigh'. The mood throughout is fearful and guilt-ridden, focusing on a negative view of man's mortal condition: 'decay', 'dim', 'terror', 'hell'.

However, the sestet signals a change of direction, an acknowledgment that the only hope of salvation is the complete surrender of the poet's strong individual will to the will of God, **an act of submission**. Donne's humble tone is liberating. He asks permission to raise his eyes to God, 'By thy leave I can look'.

Now there is a real possibility of redemption, 'I rise again'. If the poet accepts God's power to forgive, he 'can look' again and focus his 'dim' eyes. The weight of all Donne's sinfulness – which seemed so heavy in the octet – dissolves as he takes a leap of faith towards his Creator. For a moment, the downward spiral of the poem's opening is reversed into an upward movement towards God. Nevertheless, the poet is not quite completely free – since he is so easily tempted by the Devil, the 'old subtle foe'. Donne's use of 'our' suggests his **closeness to God**, in their common struggle against Satan. In eventually coming to terms with his own weakness and constant dependence on God's grace, the poet has found a way to 'sustain' himself.

The rhyming couplet sums up Donne's continuing need of divine power against the Devil's scheming, 'to prevent his art'. God must act on his behalf, so that 'Thy Grace may wing me'. It is **God's choice whether Donne is saved or not**. The vision of his immortal soul soaring upwards is graphically conveyed in the verb 'wing'. The sonnet concludes with a typical metaphysical image drawn from science. God is compared to 'adamant', a magnetic stone which can guide ('draw') iron, a symbol of the poet's sinful heart. To his relief, Donne's newly confident faith reassures him that God has the ability to secure his soul with ease. The poet's appealing tone is clearly seen in his reserved form of address to God. This is in sharp contrast to the curt opening question. Throughout these final lines, personal pronouns underline the intimate intensity of the poet's all-consuming relationship with God.

Donne has adapted two sonnet forms for his poem. The basic structure is Petrarchan, divided into the despairing octet and a more hopeful sestet. However, he also uses the compact rhyme scheme of the Shakespearean sonnet.

✒ Writing About the Poem

'The language of Donne's poetry ranges from violence to tenderness, and from the unfamiliar to the paradoxical.' Using close reference to the text, discuss this view in relation to the sonnet 'Thou Hast Made Me, and Shall Thy Work Decay?'

Sample Paragraph

Donne's religious poem, 'Thou Hast Made Me, and Shall Thy Work Decay?' contains both forceful and gentle expressions as he insists, 'Repair me now'. An unexpected image of two lovers rushing to meet describes the terrifying end of life, 'death meets me at last'. The genuine agony of his position is clear, 'I dare not move my dim eyes any way'. His eyes are closed by sin. For me, the sestet shows a gentler voice as the poet realises that God's grace alone can save him. His tone is softly submissive, 'By thy leave I can look'. The warm, effortless language suggests the possibility of his saved soul which 'may wing' its way to heaven with the power of God. All through this poem, I was impressed by Donne's turbulent yet sensitive expressions which explored a highly dramatic exchange between himself and God.

EXAMINER'S COMMENT

Well-written paragraph which focuses firmly on the poet's style. Effective use is made of a great many accurate quotations to illustrate the variation in tone and range of language evident in the poem. There is also some good personal engagement with the text. Top-grade response.

✎ Class/Homework Exercises

1. 'Donne's religious poetry is both stimulating and challenging.' Discuss this statement in relation to 'Thou Hast Made Me, and Shall Thy Work Decay?' Refer to the poem in your response.

2. 'Many of Donne's poems are noted for their vibrancy of language, urgent tone and inventiveness of metaphor.' In your opinion, is this true of 'Thou Hast Made Me'? Give reasons for your answer, using reference to the text.

⊙ Points to Consider

- **Themes include Donne's spiritual struggle and his complete dependence on God.**

- **Varying tones: demanding, persuasive, reliant.**

- **Use of logic, debate, question-and-answer format.**

- **Dramatic atmosphere, effective sounds, memorable images.**

10 Batter My Heart, Three-Personed God

JOHN DONNE

Batter my heart, three-personed God; for, you
As yet but knock, breathe, shine, and seek to mend;
That I may rise, and stand, o'erthrow me and bend
Your force, to break, blow, burn, and make me new.
I, like an usurped town, to another due,   5
Labour to admit you, but oh, to no end,
Reason your viceroy in me, me should defend,
But is captived, and proves weak or untrue,
Yet dearly I love you, and would be loved fain,
But am betrothed unto your enemy,   10
Divorce me, untie, or break that knot again,
Take me to you, imprison me, for I
Except you enthrall me, never shall be free,
Nor ever chaste, except you ravish me.

Batter: strike, knock down. (Donne wants God to attack his heart as if it were the gates of a fortress town.)

three-personed God: Christianity teaches that God is three separate beings: God the Father, Jesus Christ the Son, and the Holy Spirit.

usurped: occupied, taken over.

viceroy: ruler on God's behalf.

fain: willingly, readily.

betrothed: engaged to be married.

break that knot again: dissolve that marriage union.

enthrall: enslave.

Nor ever chaste, except you ravish me: paradox asserts that true freedom can only be achieved by surrendering.

'Take me to you'

👤 Personal Response

1. 'Donne's poem is an unusual prayer to God.' To what extent do you agree? Consider the poet's use of language and imagery in your response.
2. 'Donne unashamedly thinks of no one but himself.' In your opinion, is this the case in 'Batter My Heart, Three-Personed God'? Give reasons, quoting closely from the poem.
3. 'This sonnet shows a troubled mind in a continuous search for certainty.' To what extent would you agree with this assessment? Refer to the text in your answer.

👁 Critical Literacy

Donne is a poet deeply divided between religious spirituality and a sensual lust for life. In 'Batter My Heart, Three-Personed God', he dares to introduce the powerful, sensuous language of secular love poetry into his treatment of a profoundly religious theme. He claims that he can only overcome his sinful nature if he is forced by God in the most violent ways imaginable.

This sonnet begins with a dramatic exclamation: 'Batter my heart, three-personed God'. The force of this powerful opening line sets a determined tone that is maintained all through the poem. **In this daring image, the poet wants God to attack his heart as if it were the gates of a fortress town.** The fearsome knocking of a battering ram echoes from the heavily stressed verb and pounding rhythm. This was a common metaphor in courtly love poetry to suggest the reluctance of a woman to yield to a lover's advances, but it is a shocking – almost bizarre – conceit when presented in this religious context. This exaggeration is used to highlight how the poet is challenging God to enter his heart, not gently, but aggressively.

The initial commanding tone of the verb 'Batter' with its explosive 'B' sound gives way to a bitter complaint against God's considerate behaviour. In line 2, the poet describes God as a careful craftsman, carrying out superficial repairs to 'mend' Donne's sinful soul. The poet makes use of a forceful paradox, asking God to rebuild him spiritually – 'o'erthrow' me' and 'make me new'. He seems to show neither respect nor humility. Instead, throughout this first quatrain, he is busily putting up a challenge to God. The underlying sense of entitlement is insidious. Donne is convinced that he deserves all God's attention. The tender approach, where the Father knocks, the Son shines and the Holy Spirit breathes, is not sufficient. A series of strong alliterative verbs ('break', 'blow', 'burn') convey the poet's intense emotional conviction. He is pinning all his hopes on divine intervention to rid him of sin.

The second quatrain is dominated by the symbol of a besieged town. Donne sees his helpless soul as 'usurped' from God, its rightful ruler. His greatest wish now is that God will reclaim what is rightfully his. But who is the real enemy – Satan or Donne himself? **The poet's tone becomes less imperative and more apologetic** as he admits his longing to find God's grace – 'Labour to admit you'. Unfortunately, his own conscience lacks willpower and strength ('Reason' is proving 'weak or untrue') and therefore his sinful soul remains at risk. Ironically, Donne uses the language of unrequited love to express his personal dilemma, caught between life's temptations and spiritual renewal.

The poet's candid admission ('Yet dearly I love you') at the start of the sestet marks a crucial turning-point. Donne exchanges the clever metaphysical comparisons for **a more direct, personal approach**. His open declaration of love for God is reminiscent of the courtly language of romantic poetry as he wistfully requests: 'and would be loved fain'. But the change of tone is short-lived and Donne immediately introduces a new metaphor. He assumes the persona of a 'betrothed' woman, engaged to be married 'unto your enemy' (Satan). The horrifying reality of facing eternal damnation leads him back to the frantic demand that God should do whatever it takes ('Divorce me, untie, or break that knot') in order to rescue his immortal soul. In the midst of this panic, the castle siege metaphor reappears as Donne insists that God 'imprison' him. The initial problem established in the octave is drawing to a solution.

The final rhyming couplet contains a fascinating double paradox. First, Donne states that unless God entices him ('enthrall me'), he will never be free. The second dramatic paradox is even more shocking as he asserts that he can only ever be holy ('chaste') if God will 'ravish' him. He acknowledges his absolute dependence on God to forcibly save him from his own human weakness. Although the word 'ravish' has an obvious violent intent, the tone is soft, almost a whisper, as though Donne deeply relishes the idea of spiritual unity with God. Although he is struggling to define a sacred, spiritual relationship, the language he chooses is the metaphor of brutal, physical love. However, Donne's agonised perseverance ensures that the readers are left in no doubt of the poem's central message: **sinners must first be broken before being made whole again in God's love**.

✎ Writing About the Poem

'Donne is a poet who is full of contradictions.' Discuss this statement in relation to the poem 'Batter My Heart, Three-Personed God'. Refer to the text in your answer.

Sample Paragraph

Donne wants God to save him from himself as if God was somehow physically present. This is the contradiction at the centre of the poem. Donne wants God to 'Batter' the poet into a state of grace. Another inconsistency is that he actually insists that a more forceful approach be taken. For me, the paradox is that the poet must be conquered in order to be made 'new'. Donne complains that his own common sense is actually behaving irrationally. Donne wants to be freed from sin so he can be imprisoned in God's forgiveness. Donne likes the idea of God taking responsibility. As usual, the focus is all about Donne – 'me, me'. This is a contradictory poem, but it has a strong argument to force God to accept the poet's view, even though he is the one who actually needs the favour, and to deliver the poet's solution. Not God's.

EXAMINER'S COMMENT

This lively response touches on interesting aspects of Donne's contradictory views of his complex relationship with God. The discussion is aptly illustrated and includes some good personal engagement. However, expression is note-like and awkward at times (with overuse of 'actually') and there are some inaccurate quotations. Mid-grade response.

✍ Class/Homework Exercises

1. In your view, is 'Batter My Heart, Three-Personed God' a good example of metaphysical poetry? Refer to both content and style in your response, using evidence from the poem to support your opinions.

2. Donne's use of sound effects is a recurring characteristic of his poetry. To what extent is this true of 'Batter My Heart, Three-Personed God'? Support your answer with reference to the poem.

⊙ Points to Consider

- **Another highly charged personal address to God.**

- **Dramatic opening, emphatic rhythms, violent/daring imagery.**

- **Varying tones of urgency, desperation, tenderness.**

- **Effective use of alliteration, repetition, paradox.**

- **Sonnet form, demanding first quatrain, apologetic second quatrain, candid sestet, paradoxical rhyming couplet.**

Sample Leaving Cert Questions on John Donne's Poetry

1. 'John Donne's inventive language and imagery often result in startling dramatic moments throughout his poems.' Discuss this statement, with reference to both the themes and language found in the poetry of Donne on your course.

2. Discuss how effectively John Donne makes use of forceful language and rich imagery to create moods that range from joy and hope to sorrow and despair in his poetry. Develop your answer with reference to the poetry of Donne on your course.

3. 'Donne's personal experiences of love – both physical and spiritual – are expressed in a highly distinctive poetic style.' To what extent do you agree with this view? Develop your answer with reference to the poetry of John Donne on your course.

How do I organise my answer?

(Sample question 1)

'John Donne's inventive language and imagery often result in startling dramatic moments throughout his poems.' Discuss this statement, with reference to both the themes and language found in the poetry of Donne on your course.

Sample Plan 1

Intro: *(Stance: agree with viewpoint in question)* Donne startles, provokes and challenges using dramatic scenes, far-fetched imagery, complex metaphors, rigorous argument and clever sound effects in intense scenes of love, parting, seduction and divine judgement.

Point 1: *(Intimate scene explored through conceit and sound effects)* 'The Sun Rising' – exuberant scene of passionate young love captured through extended image which shrinks the expanding newly discovered lands of the globe to the enclosed lovers' bedroom ('This bed thy centre is').

Point 2: *(Lovers' parting produces gripping emotions of sadness and comfort)* 'A Valediction: Forbidding Mourning' – couple's stirring farewell seen as mini-death through mournful sibilance ('sad friends do say,/The breath goes now'). Consolation in striking metaphor of compass celebrating inevitable return ('makes me end, where I begun').

Understanding the Prescribed Poetry Question

Marks are awarded using the PCLM Marking Scheme: P = 15; C = 15; L = 15; M = 5 Total = 50

- **P** (Purpose = 15 marks) refers to the set question and is the launch pad for the answer. This involves engaging with all aspects of the question. Both theme and language must be addressed, although not necessarily equally.

- **C** (Coherence = 15 marks) refers to the organisation of the developed response and the use of accurate, relevant quotation. Paragraphing is essential.

- **L** (Language = 15 marks) refers to the student's skill in controlling language throughout the answer.

- **M** (Mechanics = 5 marks) refers to spelling and grammar.

- Although no specific number of poems is required, students usually discuss at least 3 or 4 in their written responses.

- Aim for at least 800 words, to be completed within 45–50 minutes.

Point 3: *(Clever argument and rhetorical language evokes erotic seduction)* 'The Flea' – playful encounter between ardent lover and reluctant mistress uses intellectual and emotional appeals ('This flea is you and I, and this/Our marriage bed'). Melodramatic rhetorical language heightens the pressure on the woman ('Cruel and sudden, hast thou since/Purpled thy nail, in blood of innocence?')

Point 4: *(Chaotic Judgement Day created through innovative sound effects and contrasts)* 'At the Round Earth's Imagined Corners' – dramatic turmoil of divine judgement, urgent repetitive command ('arise, arise') adds to the uproar. Confident tone replaced by submissive plea for salvation expressed in legal language ('As if thou hadst sealed my pardon, with thy blood').

Conclusion: Impact of Donne's original poetic style engages readers. Fresh energetic use of language creates combative tender and sorrowful scenes of love between man and woman, and man and God.

Sample Paragraph: Point 2

The farewell scene of a departing husband and abandoned wife is presented in a fresh way through Donne's language use throughout 'A Valediction: Forbidding Mourning'. While the sorrow of the occasion is acknowledged as a kind of death by soft sibilance 'Whilst some of their friends do say,/The breath goes now', it is the inventive use of the compass metaphor to represent the couple's relationship that is so impressive. This instrument recognises both the individuality of the man and woman as well as the unity of the couple. She is 'the fixed foot' who remains steady and true, 'makes no show/To move', enabling the other foot, the poet, to complete his circuit, 'far doth roam'. The instrument then draws a complete circle, a symbol of unity and infinity, representing Donne's spiritual love, balanced, and intellectual. He concludes with a compliment to his wife, assuring her of his inevitable return, 'Thy firmness makes my circle just, And makes me end, where I begun'.

EXAMINER'S COMMENT

As part of a complete examination essay, this paragraph engages closely with both the question and Donne's poem. Good detailed explanation of the compass metaphor. Expression is clear, varied and well controlled. Excellent use of apt and accurate quotes integrated fluently into the discussion ensure the top-grade standard.

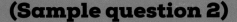

(Sample question 2)

Discuss how effectively John Donne makes use of forceful language and rich imagery to create moods that range from joy and hope to sorrow and despair in his poetry. Develop your answer with reference to the poetry of Donne on your course.

Sample Plan 2

Intro: *(Stance: agree with viewpoint in question)* Donne's poetry ranges from the dizzy heights of young love to the depths of despair at rejection. Religious sonnets range from anguish at his sinfulness to unwavering hope in God's grace to forgive. He uses powerful language, intense imagery, strong conceits, dynamic verbs and inventive syntax.

Point 1: *(Joy of young love expressed through assertive language, paradox and developed metaphor)* 'The Anniversary' – joyous mood of young couple celebrating first year together. Short defiant lines proclaim their never-changing love ('Only our love hath no decay'). Clever paradox ('Running it never runs from us away') details endurance of their feelings.

Point 2: *(Sensual poem uses robust argument and powerful imagery to highlight hope and sorrow of love)* 'The Dream' – rich simile ('As lightning, or a taper's light/Thine eyes') expresses tender emotion. Sharp mood change at woman's reluctance to submit using image of discarded torch ('light and put out'). Hope re-emerges in concluding paradox ('Thou cam'st to kindle, goest to come').

Point 3: *(Desire and frustration explored through shocking extended comparison and ingenious argument)* 'The Flea' – repetition marks peevish disappointment of rejected lover ('Mark but this flea, and mark in this'). Exaggerated self-pitying tone contrasts flea's success at touching woman to the poet's own failure ('And this, alas, is more than we would do').

Point 4: *(Terror and despair at possible damnation conveyed in intense language)* 'Thou Hast Made Me, And Shall Thy Work Decay?' – terrified by his sinful past, the poet fears to look back at his life ('I dare not move my dim eyes away'). Alliteration and assonance capture physical decay ('my feeble flesh doth waste'). Stunning simile of naturally occurring magnet portrays hope in God's grace ('thou like adamant draw mine iron heart').

NOTE
──────
In keeping with the PCLM approach, the student has to explore poems of John Donne's on the course that include:

– **effective use of forceful language and rich imagery** (assertive tones, ingenious arguments appealing to mind and heart, dramatic scenes, clever wordplay, unlikely images, extended metaphors, paradoxes, sensual exaggeration, etc.)

... that creates:

– **moods that range from joy and hope to sorrow and despair** (confidence of young lovers, feelings of expectation and disappointment, despair and hope of spiritual salvation, etc.)

Conclusion: Donne startles and coaxes in passionate poems spanning the intensity of young love and sexual experience to extreme frustration. Religious sonnets also range from deep despair at his sinful condition to an overwhelming belief in God's salvation for humanity.

Sample Paragraph: Point 3

'The Flea' explores desire and disappointment through the poet's shocking comparison of a fleabite to the lovers' act of making love. The poet's disappointment at being rejected is forcefully stated through repetition, 'Mark but this flea, and mark in this/How little that which thou deny'st me is'. Falling into despair, Donne melodramatically declares 'And this, alas, is more than we would do'. The heavily punctuated exaggeration emphasises his mood. He then turns the woman's resistance against her, using a stern tone and more emphatic alliteration, 'learn how false, fears be'. Donne casually dismisses the possible loss to her good name if she gives in to him, 'Just so much honour … Will waste, as this flea's death took life from thee'. Argumentative language recreates an age-old lovers' quarrel, leaving the poet feeling frustrated. Will this woman submit?

EXAMINER'S COMMENT

Succinct, top-grade paragraph that would make an excellent contribution to a full-length exam essay. Focuses well on the key aspects of the question (forceful language and varying moods). Clear appreciation of Donne's poetic techniques – particularly repetition, tone and argument. Effective textual support throughout. Commentary is clearly expressed and rounded off with a lively conclusion.

EXAM FOCUS

- As you may not be familiar with some of the poems referred to in the sample plans, substitute poems that you have studied closely.
- Key points about a particular poem can be developed over more than one paragraph.
- Paragraphs may also include cross-referencing and discussion of more than one poem.
- Remember that there is no single 'correct' answer to poetry questions, so always be confident in expressing your own considered response.

Leaving Cert Sample Essay

'Donne's personal experiences of love – both physical and spiritual – are expressed in a highly distinctive poetic style.' To what extent do you agree with this view? Develop your answer with reference to the poetry of John Donne on your course.

Sample Essay

INDICATIVE
MATERIAL

• **Donne's personal
experiences of love
– both physical
and spiritual**
(desire, frustration
seduction, joy,
satisfaction,
spiritual salvation,
dependence,
everlasting love,
etc.)

... expressed in:

• **a highly
distinctive poetic
style** (dramatic
rhetorical language,
intellectual
argument,
emotional appeal,
intimate tones,
vivid imagery,
paradox, unusual
references, conceits,
comparisons, etc.)

1. John Donne is an original poet. He creates intimate yet unusually poetry appealing to his lover's mind as well as feelings in 'The Anniversary' and 'Song (Sweetest Love I Do Not Go)'. His spiritual poetry is passionate, even using erotic imagery. This is seen in 'Thou Hast Made Me' and 'Batter My Heart, Three-Personed God'. In both his love poetry and his Holy Sonnets, Donne longs for union, either with a lover or God.

2. The love poem, 'The Anniversary', opens with the dramatic claim that nobody escapes 'destruction'. Donne uses emphatic repetition, 'All kings and all their favourites'. Only the lovers will have 'an everlasting day'. They are unaffected by the cruel passage of time. A stunning paradox, 'Running it never runs from us away', supports the idea of true love's immortality. Donne sets this argument in an intimate moment, the first anniversary of a young couple's love. A rhetorical question asks, 'Who is so safe as we?' He states that the couple must preserve their love as long as they can because 'Here upon earth we're kings'. He believes that happiness is shared by everyone in heaven, 'we no more than all the rest', so they should enjoy their human love while they can. The logic and self-assured tone are all elements of Donne's unique voice.

3. A couple's separation is presented in 'Song (Sweetest Love I Do Not Go)'. A personal occasion is established through the sympathetic phrase, 'Sweetest love'. Clever arguments are used to persuade both emotionally and intellectually. Donne tries to convince his sad wife that this parting is a good preparation for him for their inevitable separation at death, 'Thus by feigned deaths to die'. He reminds her that the sun returns every morning, 'yet is here today'. He promises to make even 'Speedier journeys' because, unlike the sun, he has the 'wings and spurs' of his feelings for her to hurry him along. He makes a simple request of his wife, 'think that we/ Are but turned aside to sleep', recalling a beautiful private moment in their relationship. Donne uses an affectionate conversational tone and a rigorous argument to ease this moment of separation. 'The Anniversary' ends with an optimistic image of the lovers' eternal 'reign'.

4. In 'Thou Hast Made Me', the poet issues a forceful challenge to God, 'Repair me now'. The fear of his soul's sinful state is vividly portrayed, 'I dare not move my dim eyes any way'. Powerful sound effects convey his hopelessness, 'Despair behind, and death before'. Alliteration highlights his wickedness, 'feeble flesh', which is about to be dragged down to hell by. Similarly to 'Song', the poet acknowledges his dependence on another, 'not one hour myself I can sustain'. The concluding powerful image from science again ends the poem on a hopeful note, thou like adamant draw mine iron heart'. God's forgiveness even to the most hardened sinner who repents is like a powerful magnet pulling the poet to salvation. Donne's personal spiritual struggle is powerfully conveyed through a unique variety of distinctive techniques, including tones (anger, fear and submission), evocative sound effects and scientific imagery.

5. 'Batter My Heart', Three Personed God', is another religious sonnet where Donne demands that God 'Batter' him. This is rather than requesting him to stop sinning by a gentle 'knock'. Again, he takes an unusual aggressive tone, asking God the Father to 'breathe' on him, the Holy Spirit to 'shine' on him and for Jesus Christ to 'seek to mend'. Violent verbs graphically display the aggressive force the sinful poet needs to be renewed, such as 'break', 'blow', 'burn'. A simile is presented of the sinful poet as a 'usurped town', enslaved by 'another military enemy, a reference to the devil. Military terms and images are used, such as including 'defend', 'captived' showing his hopelessness because 'Reason' has proved 'untrue'. Then Donne compares himself to a married woman, 'betrothed unto your enemy', again the devil reference. Erotic language is used to express the unexpected idea that only being a prisoner of God's will is the only way to be free, 'except you ravish me'.

6. Donne's experience of his love for God is complicated. His comparisons are still seen as shocking. To compare the relationship between himself and God in sexual terms is highly unusual. He is like an unwilling woman forced to marry against her will. Donne suggests that God must act in a similarly violent manner to rescue him from a life of sin and then eternal damnation

7. The distinct voice of Donne is found in his spiritual poems through the violence of his demanding tones, his unusual comparisons and his passionate sexual references. Readers are drawn into his very personal experiences of love, both romantic and spiritual, through his intimate conversational poetic voice, his confidence and humility, clever comparisons, the violence of his feelings and his witty arguments.

(810 words)

EXAMINER'S COMMENT

Focused response with evidence of critical thinking throughout. Points make consistent links back to the task, displaying close engagement with specific poems – both secular and religious. Good illustrations of Donne's characteristic poetic style, including his use of argument, strong tones, imagery and rhetoric. Relevant discussion is developed in structured paragraphs and apt quotations are integrated into the commentary. Expression is clear and impressive, overall, although there is some repetition and awkwardness (e.g. in paragraph 5).

GRADE: H1
P = 15/15
C = 14/15
L = 13/15
M = 5/5
Total = 47/50

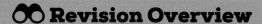 Revision Overview

'The Sun Rising'
Delightful, witty celebration of young love, dismissing external world's importance for the warm interior kingdom of the lovers' bedroom.

'Song (Go, And Catch A Falling Star)' (OL)
Distinctive love poem, cynically undermining love and fidelity. Donne argues that it is impossible to find a woman who is both faithful and honest.

'The Anniversary'
The lovers' sense of being forever young is central to this beautiful poem celebrating the first anniversary of their passionate relationship.

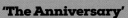

'Song (Sweetest Love, I Do Not Go)'
Emotional, dramatic poem about a couple's brief separation conveyed through tender appeal and logical argument.

'A Valediction: Forbidding Mourning'
Donne insists that genuine feelings transcend physical distance, comparing the couple's relationship to a spiritual bond between two souls.

'The Dream'
Intimate, sensual poem arguing forcefully for the physical union of the couple's relationship. Passionate and metaphorical language convey the intense feelings Donne has for his lover.

'The Flea' (OL)
Donne's famous poem uses direct language and a comic conceit to play with the idea of sex and seduction.

'At the Round Earth's Imagined Corners'
One of Donne's Holy Sonnets dealing with the subject of death. This dramatic, spiritual poem addresses his personal relationship with God, sin and repentance.

'Thou Hast Made Me, And Shall Thy Work Decay?'
Devotional sonnet examining the poet's deep religious faith. Donne seeks comfort from the only source able to give it – his Creator.

'Batter My Heart, Three-Personed God'
Another of Donne's powerful Holy Sonnets using the sensuous language of romantic poetry to explore sin and spiritual fulfilment.

Last Words

'No man is an island.'
John Donne

'Poetry is not a turning loose of emotion, but an escape from emotion; it is not the expression of personality, but an escape from personality. But, of course, only those who have personality and emotions know what it means to want to escape these things.'
T. S. Eliot

'Rave on, John Donne.'
Van Morrison

  LOVE JOY/HOPE UNFAITHFULNESS IMMORTALITY DEATH DESIRE MORTALITY SALVATION FAITH

Seamus Heaney
1939–2013

'Walk on air against your better judgement.'

Seamus Heaney was born in 1939 in Co. Derry, the eldest of nine children. He was accepted into Queen's University, Belfast in 1957 to study English Language and Literature. Heaney's poetry first came to public attention in the 1960s, when he and a number of other poets, including Michael Longley and Derek Mahon, came to prominence. They all shared the same fate of being born into a society that was deeply divided along religious grounds and was to become immersed in violence, intimidation and sectarianism. In 1966, Heaney's first poetry collection, *Death of a Naturalist*, was published. Throughout the 1970s, he was publishing prolifically and giving public readings. He also wrote several volumes of criticism. Widely regarded as the finest poet of his generation, he was awarded the Nobel Prize for Literature in 1995 'for works of lyrical beauty and ethical depth, which exalt everyday miracles and the living past'. In accepting the award, Heaney stated that his life had been 'a journey into the wideness of language, a journey where each point of arrival … turned out to be a stepping stone rather than a destination'.

Investigate Further

To find out more about Seamus Heaney, or to hear readings of his poems not already available in your eBook, you could search some useful websites, such as YouTube, BBC Poetry, poetryfoundation.org and poetryarchive.org, or access additional material on this page of your eBook.

Prescribed Poems

(OL) indicates poems that are also prescribed for the Ordinary Level course.

1 🔊 The Forge

All I know is a door into the dark.
Outside, old axles and iron hoops rusting;
Inside, the hammered anvil's short-pitched ring,
The unpredictable fantail of sparks
Or hiss when a new shoe toughens in water.   5
The anvil must be somewhere in the centre,
Horned as a unicorn, at one end square,
Set there immoveable: an altar
Where he expends himself in shape and music.
Sometimes, leather-aproned, hairs in his nose,   10
He leans out on the jamb, recalls a clatter
Of hoofs where traffic is flashing in rows;
Then grunts and goes in, with a slam and a flick
To beat real iron out, to work the bellows.

axles: bars or shafts on which wheels rotate.
anvil: iron block that the smith uses as a work surface.

unicorn: mythical animal (usually a white horse) with a spiralled horn growing from its forehead.
expends: burns up, expresses.

jamb: upright door support.

bellows: instrument for drawing air into a fire.

'The unpredictable fantail of sparks'

👤 Personal Response

1. Describe the poet's attitude to the forge. Is he fascinated or fearful, or both? Support your answer with reference to the poem.
2. Based on your study of the poem, what is your impression of the blacksmith?
3. Comment on the effectiveness of the phrase 'The unpredictable fantail of sparks'.

👁 Critical Literacy

'The Forge' comes from Seamus Heaney's second collection, *Door into the Dark*, which was published in 1969. The sonnet form has a clear division of an octave (the first eight lines) and a sestet (the final six lines). While the octave, apart from its initial reference to the narrator, focuses on the inanimate objects and occurrences inside and outside the forge, the sestet describes the blacksmith and his work.

The poem's opening line ('All I know is a door into the dark') is both modest and assured. There is also a **mystical undertone** (a sense of otherworldliness) as Heaney revisits his childhood and his fascination with a local forge. The image, with its negative and mysterious connotations, incites our curiosity and invites us to find out what answers lie beyond. The poet recalls unwanted objects strewn outside, 'old axles and iron hoops rusting'. The irregular rhythm in line 2 suggests the disorder of what has been discarded. He **contrasts** the lifeless exterior scene with the vigorous atmosphere ('the hammered anvil's short-pitched ring') inside the forge. The world outside is decrepit and old, a wasteland, whereas the noisy forge is a place of brilliant sparks where iron is beaten out and renewed.

Heaney's visual and aural images are characteristically striking. His vivid metaphor of 'The unpredictable fantail of sparks' (line 4) lets us see the glorious flurry of erratic flashing light and hear the twang of reverberating iron.

Onomatopoeic effects add to our sense of the physical activity taking place as the blacksmith works on a new horseshoe. Suddenly, the incandescent metal begins to 'hiss when a new shoe toughens in water'. The **tone is sympathetic** and attentive as the poet reimagines the smells, sounds and tactile impressions of the blacksmith's workshop.

Lines 6–9 contain the sonnet's central image of the smith's anvil: 'an altar/ Where he expends himself in shape and music'. Interestingly, the transition from the octave to the sestet is a run-on (or enjambment) based on this key metaphor. One effect of this is to enable us to experience the anvil as a **sacred or magical point of transition** between the material and immovable world of everyday life and the fluid, imaginative world of human consciousness. Heaney stresses the **mystery of the creative process**, associating it with the mythical creature of medieval fiction, 'Horned as a unicorn'. Although the simile seems somewhat strained, the comparison with a legendary beast still serves to highlight the mysterious qualities ('shape and music') of poetry.

The final lines focus on the blacksmith's physical characteristics. **Heaney leaves us with a down-to-earth image of a gruff, hardworking man**, 'leather-aproned, hairs in his nose'. Is the poet suggesting that art – and poetry in particular – is independent of education and social class? Seemingly wary of the world at large, the smith remembers an earlier era of horse-drawn carriages, when his skills were fully appreciated. Contrasting images of 'a clatter/Of hoofs' and modern traffic 'flashing in rows' reflect the changes he has lived through. In the end, he grudgingly accepts that he must return 'into the dark' and resume doing what he does best: 'To beat real iron out, to work the bellows'.

Heaney's poem can immediately be read as an elegy to the past and a lament for the lost tradition of the blacksmith. Readers can also interpret the anvil as a metaphor of an unreachable heritage, a traditional craft made redundant by modernisation. Many critics have seen the blacksmith figure as a **symbol or construction of the role of the poet**, one who opens the 'door into the dark', the creative artist who ritually 'expends himself in shape and music' and who 'grunts' and flicks words and language, forging his poems. As with so much of Heaney's work, the poem shows his ability to subtly evoke resonance by making us wonder.

⬛ Writing About the Poem

'Seamus Heaney's imaginative use of descriptive language often adds a mythic quality to his poems.' Discuss this statement with reference to 'The Forge'.

Sample Paragraph

In his nostalgic poem, 'The Forge', the disappearing tradition of the local blacksmith is brought vividly to life. Through dynamic sound effects ('ring', 'hiss') combined with the use of the compound word 'short-pitched', Heaney presents us with the portrait of a craftsman turning metal into useful farming tools. This unassuming blacksmith is given another persona, one of epic quality. He becomes a High Priest at his 'altar', the anvil. We get a sense of legendary times, suggested by the image of the anvil shape, 'Horned as a unicorn'. The poet envisions the surly craftsman in a mythical role, changing one everyday substance into something special. Like Heaney himself, the priest is involved in the mysterious creative process. The blacksmith is described in detail, 'warts and all'. He stands, 'leather-aproned, hairs in his nose', but he has the ability to control the power of fire. Reality and legend blend seamlessly.

EXAMINER'S COMMENT

This mature top-grade response focuses well on Heaney's powers of description – particularly his use of aural effects. The more challenging aspect of 'mythic qualities' is handled successfully, with clear points linking the anvil and altar. Expression is carefully controlled, using varied sentence lengths and a wide-ranging vocabulary (e.g. 'dynamic', 'persona', 'envisions'). Apt quotations are also used throughout.

✒ Class/Homework Exercises

1. 'Heaney's visual and aural imagery depict a harsh, rural life with lyrical beauty.' Discuss this statement in relation to 'The Forge'.
2. 'Many of Heaney's carefully crafted poems are populated with characters who have made a deep impression on him.' Discuss this view with reference to 'The Forge'.

◉ Points to Consider

- Lament for and preservation of a traditional craft and rural life.
- Interesting experimental use of structure and rhyme scheme of sonnet form.
- Clever contrasts – exterior/interior, past/present, reality/legend.
- Striking sound effects – onomatopoeia, assonance, sibilant 's'.
- Sensuous visual images and symbols create a powerful sense of time and place.

2 🔊 **Bogland**

for T.P. Flanagan

We have no prairies
To slice a big sun at evening –
Everywhere the eye concedes to
Encroaching horizon,

Is wooed into the cyclops' eye   5
Of a tarn. Our unfenced country
Is bog that keeps crusting
Between the sights of the sun.

They've taken the skeleton
Of the Great Irish Elk   10
Out of the peat, set it up
An astounding crate full of air.

Butter sunk under
More than a hundred years
Was recovered salty and white.   15
The ground itself is kind, black butter

Melting and opening underfoot,
Missing its last definition
By millions of years.
They'll never dig coal here,   20

Only the waterlogged trunks
Of great firs, soft as pulp.
Our pioneers keep striking
Inwards and downwards,

Every layer they strip   25
Seems camped on before.
The boxholes might be Atlantic seepage.
The wet centre is bottomless.

prairies: large open areas of grassland (in North America).

concedes: gives way to; admits defeat.
Encroaching: advancing gradually beyond acceptable limits.
wooed: courted, enticed.
cyclops' eye: in Greek mythology, a race of one-eyed giants.
tarn: small mountain lake.

Great Irish Elk: large northern deer (now extinct) found preserved in Irish bogland.

definition: transformation (into coal).

pioneers: adventurers, explorers.

seepage: the slow escape of liquid through a material.

👤 Personal Response

1. In your opinion, what is Heaney's central theme or point in this poem? Briefly explain your response.
2. How does Heaney employ the senses to allow the reader to share in his experience of the bogland? Refer closely to the poem in your answer.
3. Trace the poet's tone throughout the poem. Comment on where, how and why, in your opinion, the tone changes. Support your views with reference to the text.

👁 Critical Literacy

'Bogland' (1969) is the result of a Hallowe'en holiday Heaney spent with T.P. Flanagan (the artist to whom this poem is dedicated). Flanagan recalls that 'the bogland was burnt the colour of marmalade'. Heaney felt it was 'one of the most important poems' he had written because 'it was something like a symbol. I felt the poem was a promise of something else ... it represented a free place for me.' He thought the bogland was a 'landscape that remembered everything that happened in and to it'. Heaney recalled when they were children that they were told 'not to go near the bog because there was no bottom to it'.

The poem is written in seven spare, unrhymed stanzas and uses casual, almost colloquial language. In the opening stanza, a **comparison** is drawn

'Encroaching horizon,
Is wooed into the cyclops' eye
Of a tarn'

105

between the American prairies ('We have no prairies') and Ireland's bogs. Heaney said, 'At that time, I had … been reading about the frontier and the west as an important myth in the American consciousness, so I set up – or rather, laid down – the bog as an answering Irish myth'. The prairie in America represents the vastness of the country, **its unfenced expanse a metaphor for the freedom of its people** to pursue their dreams and express their beliefs. At first, Ireland's bog represents opposite values. It seems narrow, constricting and inward-looking: 'the eye concedes', 'Encroaching horizon', 'cyclops' eye'. In America, the pioneers moved across the country. In Ireland, the pioneers looked 'Inwards and downwards', remembering, almost wallowing in, the past. Is the poet suggesting that Ireland is defined by the layers of its difficult history? Or is each set of pioneers on an adventure, one set discovering new places, the other set rediscovering forgotten places?

Stanza two captures the **bog's fluidity** in the onomatopoeic phrase 'keeps crusting/Between the sights of the sun'. Heaney draws the changing face of the bog, its element of mystery and danger, as it does not always remain exactly the same, but subtly fluctuates. The poet's sense of awe at this place is expressed in stanza three as he recounts the discovery of the Great Irish Elk as 'An astounding crate full of air'. Here the poet is referring to another aspect of the bog – its **ability to preserve the past**.

In stanza four, the bog's capacity to hold and preserve is emphasised when 'Butter sunk under/More than a hundred years' was recovered fit for use, 'salty and white'. This place is 'kind'. Stanza four runs into stanza five in a parallel reference to the bog's fluidity. The bog never becomes hard; 'its last definition' is 'Missing', so it will never yield coal. The squidgy nature of the bog is conveyed in stanza six in the phrase 'soft as pulp'. The phrases of the poem are opening and melting into each other in imitation of the bog. Is this in stark contrast to the hardening prejudices of the two communities in Northern Ireland? **The Irish explore their past**; to them, history is important as they 'keep striking/Inwards and downwards'.

Heaney leaves us with an **open-ended conclusion** in stanza seven. He remembers that the bog 'seemed to have some kind of wind blowing through it that could carry on'. The boglands are feminine, nurturing, welcoming: 'The wet centre is bottomless'. The poet is aware of the depth and complexity of the national consciousness. Should we, like the bog, embrace all aspects of our national identity? Is this how we should carry on? Is there a final truth? Is it unreachable?

Writing About the Poem

'Through the rich musicality of his poetry, Seamus Heaney evokes the difficulty of establishing a national identity.' Discuss this statement with reference to 'Bogland'.

Sample Paragraph

A collective pronoun, 'We', opens 'Bogland'. However, the poet suggests that the Irish define themselves negatively in comparison to the vast expanse of America, 'We have no prairies'. While their pioneers move forward in their exploration of new territories, ours dig 'Inwards and downwards'. Yet, through his visual and aural description of the bogland, Heaney succeeds in creating a proud symbol of nationhood. The bog – just like our history – preserves treasures, both natural ('the Great Irish Elk') and manmade ('Butter ... recovered salty and white'). We, the Irish, have a long history. 'Every layer they strip/Seems camped on before'. The bog symbolises a nation in a perpetual state of change. Hard 'k' and 'c' sounds ('keeps crusting') capture the thin surface which breaks to reveal the soft interior of the bog, 'kind black butter'. Run-on lines echo the ever-changing nature of the bog, 'soft as pulp'. History continues forever.

EXAMINER'S COMMENT

A close sensitive analysis of the poem, engaging with the subtle connections between its musical language and the theme of identity. Very good range of informed and incisive points on symbolism, sound effects and run-on lines. Expression is varied and controlled. Excellent use of reference and quotation throughout add to the quality of the discussion in this top-grade response.

✎ Class/Homework Exercises

1. 'Heaney's sensuous imagery often evokes a haunting and dramatic sense of place.' To what extent is this true of 'Bogland'? Support your answer with reference to the poem.

2. 'Through his succinct and exact use of language, Seamus Heaney enables us to make sense of the world and ourselves.' Discuss this view with reference to 'Bogland'.

⊙ Points to Consider

- **Importance of history and identity expressed through the central symbol of bogland.**

- **Free verse, lack of rhyme and rhythm mimic the fluid nature of the bog.**

- **Contrasting tones of insecurity, awe and amazement turn to quiet reflection.**

- **Use of striking sound effects, visual imagery, personification and allusions to myth.**

- **Structure of poem imitates activity of digging – short lines drill down the page, while stacked stanzas reflect the layered nature of the bog.**

3 # The Tollund Man

The Tollund Man: a reference to the well-preserved body found in 1950 by two turfcutters in Tollund, Denmark. The man had been hanged over 2,000 years earlier. One theory suggested that his death had been part of a ritualistic fertility sacrifice. The Tollund Man's head was put on display in a museum at Aarhus.

I

Some day I will go to Aarhus
To see his peat-brown head,
The mild pods of his eye-lids,
His pointed skin cap.

In the flat country near by   5
Where they dug him out,
His last gruel of winter seeds
Caked in his stomach,

Naked except for
The cap, noose and girdle,   10
I will stand a long time.
Bridegroom to the goddess,

She tightened her torc on him
And opened her fen,
Those dark juices working   15
Him to a saint's kept body,

Trove of the turfcutters'
Honeycombed workings.
Now his stained face
Reposes at Aarhus.   20

II

I could risk blasphemy,
Consecrate the cauldron bog
Our holy ground and pray
Him to make germinate

The scattered, ambushed   25
Flesh of labourers,
Stockinged corpses
Laid out in the farmyards,

Aarhus: a city in Jutland, Denmark.

pods: dry seeds.

gruel: thin porridge.

girdle: belt.

torc: decorative metal collar.

fen: marsh or wet area.

kept: preserved.

Trove: valuable find.

Honeycombed workings: patterns made by the turfcutters on the peat.

blasphemy: irreverence.

Consecrate: declare sacred.
cauldron bog: basin-shaped bogland (some of which was associated with pagan rituals).
germinate: give new life to.

Tell-tale skin and teeth
Flecking the sleepers   30
Of four young brothers, trailed
For miles along the lines.

          III
Something of his sad freedom
As he rode the tumbril
Should come to me, driving,   35
Saying the names

Tollund, Grauballe, Nebelgard,

Watching the pointing hands
Of country people,
Not knowing their tongue.   40

Out there in Jutland
In the old man-killing parishes
I will feel lost,
Unhappy and at home.

sleepers: wooden beams underneath railway lines.
four young brothers: refers to an infamous atrocity in the 1920s when four Catholic brothers were killed by the police.

tumbril: two-wheeled cart used to carry a condemned person to execution.

Tollund, Grauballe, Nebelgard: places in Jutland.

'Something of his sad freedom'

👤 Personal Response

1. Comment on Heaney's tone in the first three stanzas of the poem.
2. Select one image from the poem that you find startling or disturbing and explain its effectiveness.
3. What is your understanding of the poem's final stanza? Refer closely to the text in your answer.

👁 Critical Literacy

Seamus Heaney was attracted to a book by P.V. Glob, *The Bog People*, which dealt with preserved Iron Age bodies of people who had been ritually killed. It offered him a particular frame of reference or set of symbols he could employ to engage with Ireland's historical conflict. The martyr image of the Tollund Man blended in the poet's mind with photographs of other atrocities, past and present, in the long rites of Irish political struggles. This elegiac poem comes from Heaney's third collection, *Wintering Out* (1972).

Part I opens quietly with the **promise of a pilgrimage**: 'Some day I will go to Aarhus'. The tone is expectant, determined. Yet there is also an element of detachment that is reinforced by the Danish place name, 'Aarhus'. Heaney's placid, almost reverential mood is matched by his economic use of language, dominated by simple monosyllables. The evocative description of the Tollund Man's 'peat-brown head' and 'The mild pods of his eye-lids' conveys a sense of gentleness and passivity.

Lines 5–11 focus on the dead man's final hours in a much more realistic way. Heaney suggests that the Tollund Man's own journey begins when 'they dug him out', destroyed and elevated at the same time. The poet's meticulous observations ('His last gruel of winter seeds/Caked in his stomach') emphasise the dead man's **innocent vulnerability**. In the aftermath of a ritualistic hanging, we see him abandoned: 'Naked except for/The cap, noose and girdle'. While the poet identifies himself closely with the victim and makes a respectful promise to 'stand a long time', the action itself is passive.

Heaney imagines the natural boglands as the body of a fertility goddess. The revelation that the sacrificial victim was 'Bridegroom to the goddess' (**line 12**) conveys a more **ominous, forceful tone** as the bleak bog itself is also equated with Ireland, female and overwhelming: 'She tightened her torc on him'. Sensuous and energetic images in **lines 13–16** suggest the physical intimacy of the couple's deadly embrace. The Tollund Man becomes 'a saint's kept body', almost a surrogate Christ, buried underground so that new life would spring up. He is left to chance, 'Trove of the turfcutters', and finally resurrected so that 'his stained face/Reposes at Aarhus'. The delicate blend of sibilance and broad vowel sounds suggest tranquillity and a final peace.

Part II suddenly becomes more emphatic and is filled with references to religion. Heaney addresses the spirit of the Tollund Man, invoking him 'to make germinate' (**line 24**) and give life back to the casualties of more recent violence in Northern Ireland. He acknowledges his own discomfort ('I could risk blasphemy') for suggesting that we should search for an alternative deity or religious symbol to unite people. But although it appears to be in contrast with the earlier violence, the poet's restrained style actually accentuates the horror of one infamous sectarian slaughter ('Of four young brothers'). The callous nature of their deaths – 'trailed/For miles along the lines' – is associated with the repulsive rituals in ancient Jutland. Heaney's **nightmarish images** ('Stockinged corpses') are powerful and create a surreal effect. However, the paradoxical 'survival' and repose of the Tollund Man should, the poet implies, give him the power to raise others.

Part III returns to the mellow beginning, but instead of anticipation, there is sorrow and a sense of isolation. Heaney hopes that the 'sad freedom' (**line 33**) of the Tollund Man 'Should come to me'. Along with religion and a sense of history and myth, evocative language is central to Heaney's poetry, and here the idea of isolation is brought sharply to the reader through the sense of being 'lost' in a foreign land. Yet ultimately the paradoxical nature of exile is realised: the poet feels at home in a state of homelessness, and welcomes the feeling of not belonging to society which he shares with the Tollund Man, who is no longer tied to religious forces. This estrangement from society is emphasised by the list of foreign names ('Tollund, Grauballe, Nebelgard'). **The poem ends on a note of pessimistic resignation** that describes both the familiar sense of isolation and hopelessness Heaney experiences: 'I will feel lost,/Unhappy and at home'.

Heaney's imaginary pilgrimage to Aarhus has led to a **kind of revelation**. By comparing modern Ulster to the 'old man-killing parishes' (line 42) of remote Jutland, the poet places the Northern Irish conflict in a timeless, mythological context. It is as though the only way Heaney can fully express the horrific scenes he has seen in Ireland is to associate them with the exhumed bodies of ancient bog corpses.

✒ Writing About the Poem

'Heaney often addresses the ugliness of human cruelty in subtle poems that are rich in imagery and language use.' Discuss this statement with reference to 'The Tollund Man'.

Sample Paragraph

Throughout 'The Tollund Man', Heaney reflects on the universal experience of human cruelty. He links the ritually murdered body of the Iron Age victim to the executions of 'four young brothers' in the Northern Ireland Troubles. A statement of quiet determination opens the poem, 'Some day I will go to Aarhus', its subtle monosyllables emphasising the poet's resolve. The vulnerability of the victim of Jutland's 'man-killing parishes' is shown in the gentle assonance of the vivid image, 'mild pods of his eye-lids'. The pathetic fate of the victims who were dragged 'miles along lines' is conveyed through the assonance of the letter 'i'. Harsh 't' sounds suggest the suffering of the young men, 'Tell-tale skin and teeth'. The barbarity of the Tollund Man's hanging is also expressed through abrupt sounds. The terrifying goddess 'tightened her torc' around her 'Bridegroom'. Through the meticulous observation of a detached observer, Heaney succeeds in engaging our sympathy for these victims.

EXAMINER'S COMMENT

This is a first-rate response that shows a very close appreciation of both the poem's subject matter and style. Points are clear, succinct and successfully supported with accurate quotations. The two central elements of the question are addressed, with some particularly incisive commentary on subtle sound effects (e.g. 'subtle monosyllables' and 'gentle assonance'). Expression is also impressive ('the meticulous observation of a detached observer').

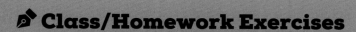

✒ Class/Homework Exercises

1. 'Heaney explores the unpalatable truth of cyclical violence and complicit acceptance through a lyrical examination of the living past.' Discuss this view, supporting your answer with reference to 'The Tollund Man'.

2. 'There is a haunting dreamlike quality to Seamus Heaney's fascination with history and mythology.' Discuss this statement, supporting your answer with reference to 'The Tollund Man'.

⊙ Points to Consider

- Examination of cyclical human violence, vulnerable victims and foreignness.

- Varying tones – resolve, reverence, detachment, uncertainty, despair, empathy.

- Use of similarity and contrast – Tollund Man/four young brothers; colloquial sound patterns; individual human experience/universal experience.

- Lyrical and musical qualities; onomatopoeia, assonance, harsh cacophonous sounds.

- Short lines and fragmented rhythm convey the disturbing reality of death.

- List of foreign place names has intriguing, unsettling effect.

4 🔊 Mossbawn: Sunlight

SEAMUS HEANEY

for Mary Heaney

There was a sunlit absence.
The helmeted pump in the yard
heated its iron,
water honeyed

in the slung bucket   5
and the sun stood
like a griddle cooling
against the wall

of each long afternoon.
So, her hands scuffled   10
over the bakeboard,
the reddening stove

sent its plaque of heat
against her where she stood
in a floury apron   15
by the window.

Now she dusts the board
with a goose's wing,
now sits, broad-lapped,
with whitened nails   20

and measling shins:
here is a space
again, the scone rising
to the tick of two clocks.

And here is love   25
like a tinsmith's scoop
sunk past its gleam
in the meal-bin.

Title: Mossbawn was Heaney's birthplace. 'Bawn' refers to the name the English planters gave to their fortified farmhouses. 'Bán' is Gaelic for 'white'. Heaney wonders if the name could be 'white moss' and has commented, 'In the syllables of my home, I see a metaphor of the split culture of Ulster.'

Dedication: the poem is dedicated to the poet's aunt, Mary Heaney, who lived with the family throughout Heaney's childhood. He shared a special relationship with her, 'a woman with a huge well of affection and a very experienced, dry-eyed sense of the world'.

griddle: circular iron plate used for cooking food.

scuffled: moved quickly, making a scraping noise.

plaque: intensity

measling: red spots on legs made by standing close to heat.

the tick of two clocks: the two time sequences in the poem, past and present.

tinsmith: person who made pots and pans from tin.

meal-bin: a container used to hold flour, etc.

'to the tick of two clocks'

👤 Personal Response

1. Describe the atmosphere in the poem 'Mossbawn: Sunlight', with particular reference to Heaney's treatment of time.
2. What image of Mary Heaney, the aunt, is drawn? Do you find the picture appealing or unappealing? Quote from the poem in support of your views.
3. Choose one image or phrase from the poem that you found particularly effective, and briefly explain why you found it so.

👁 Critical Literacy

'Sunlight' appeared in the collection *North* (1975) and was the first of two poems under the title 'Mossbawn', the name of Heaney's family home. To the poet, this farm was 'the first place', an idyllic Garden of Eden, full of sunlight and feminine grace, a contrast to the reality of the outside world. At this time, terrible atrocities were being committed in the sectarian struggle taking place in Northern Ireland.

This poem opens with a **vivid, atmospheric portrayal of the silent sunlit yard**, a beautiful, tranquil scene from Heaney's boyhood in the 1940s. The pump marked the centre of this private world, which was untroubled by the activities outside. For the impressionable Heaney growing up, the water pump was a symbol of purity and life. This guardian of domestic life is described as 'helmeted', a sentry soldier on duty, ready to protect. (The American army had bases in Northern Ireland during the Second World War.) The phrase 'water honeyed' (line 4) emphasises this slender iron idol as an image of deep and hidden goodness, the centre of another world. The poet creates a nostalgic picture of a timeless zone of domestic ritual and human warmth. These were childhood days of golden innocence and security. The repetition of 'h' (in 'helmeted', 'heated' and 'honeyed') portrays the heating process as the reader exhales breath. The sun is described in the striking simile 'like a griddle cooling/against the wall'. This homely image of the iron dish evokes a view of a serene place.

Line 10 moves readers from the place to the person. 'So' introduces us to a **warm, tender portrait of Heaney's beloved Aunt Mary at work.** She is a symbol of the old secure way of life, when a sense of community was firm and traditional rural values were held in high esteem. We are shown the unspectacular routine of work; she 'dusts the board' for baking. We see her domestic skill, her hands 'scuffled' as she kneads the dough. Visual detail paints this picture as if it were a Dutch still life from the artist Vermeer: 'floury apron', 'whitened nails'. The simplicity of this special atmosphere is evident as Heaney acknowledges: 'here is love'. The people in this scene are not glamorous. Realistic details remind us of their ordinariness: 'broad-lapped', 'measling shins'.

The **closing simile** in lines 26–8, 'like a tinsmith's scoop/sunk past its gleam/ in the meal-bin', **shows how the ordinary is transformed into the extraordinary** by the power of love. The two time zones of passing time and a timeless moment are held in the alliterative phrase 'the tick of two clocks'. We are invited to listen to the steady rhythm of the repetitive 't'. As the life-giving water lies unseen beneath the cold earth, the aunt's love is hidden, but constant, like the water in the pump. The radiant glow of love is hidden like buried light. The change of tenses at the word 'Now' brings the moment closer as the abstract becomes concrete, and the outside becomes inside. The short four-line stanzas run on, achieving their own momentum of contained energy in this still scene, which reaches its climax in the poignant final stanza.

⬛ Writing About the Poem

'Seamus Heaney often uses childhood memories to shape sensuous poetry.' Discuss this statement with reference to 'Mossbawn: Sunlight'.

Sample Paragraph

Using a tight structure of seven quatrains, Heaney re-creates his childhood experience through the details of his home life. In recalling his family's farm-yard, the 'helmeted pump' stands as if guarding this special place. It represents the hidden energies of this setting and the people. Everything Heaney writes appeals to our senses. The steady rhythm, run-on lines and assonance ('slung bucket') create a still painting of a quiet landscape. The cinematic quality zooms to an interior shot of his aunt baking in the kitchen. The poet changes the tense from past to present ('There was', 'here is') while he re-creates the living memory of Mossbawn, which resonates to the sound of the 'tick of two clocks', then and now. Love, in the person of his aunt, fills this timeless place, conveyed in the beautiful simile of the final lines, like the 'tinsmith's scoop/ sunk past its gleam/in the meal-bin'.

EXAMINER'S COMMENT

Succinct top-grade standard that focuses on the effectiveness of Heaney's sensual language. Confidently written and aptly supported by quotations.

✒ Class/Homework Exercises

1. Seamus Heaney's Nobel Prize for Literature was awarded for 'lyrical beauty ... which brings out the miracles of the ordinary day and the living past'. Discuss this statement using reference to both the content and style of 'Mossbawn: Sunlight'.
2. 'Heaney presents readers with small domestic dramas that explore recurring themes of love and longing in his poems.' Discuss this view with particular reference to 'Mossbawn: Sunlight'.

⊙ Points to Consider

- **Recurring themes of love and yearning.**
- **Slow-moving rhythm complements poignant childhood memories.**
- **Evocative tones of fondness, longing and nostalgia.**
- **Exterior scene contrasted with gentle domestic activity within.**
- **Simple language; warm, homely images.**
- **Striking use of personification, simile and evocative sound effects.**

5 A Constable Calls

SEAMUS HEANEY

His bicycle stood at the window-sill,
The rubber cowl of a mud-splasher
Skirting the front mudguard,
Its fat black handlegrips

Heating in sunlight, the 'spud'   5
Of the dynamo gleaming and cocked back,
The pedal treads hanging relieved
Of the boot of the law.

His cap was upside down
On the floor, next his chair.   10
The line of its pressure ran like a bevel
In his slightly sweating hair.

He had unstrapped
The heavy ledger, and my father
Was making tillage returns   15
In acres, roods, and perches.

Arithmetic and fear.
I sat staring at the polished holster
With its buttoned flap, the braid cord
Looped into the revolver butt.   20

'Any other root crops?
Mangolds? Marrowstems? Anything like that?'
'No.' But was there not a line
Of turnips where the seed ran out

In the potato field? I assumed   25
Small guilts and sat
Imagining the black hole in the barracks.
He stood up, shifted the baton-case

Further round on his belt,
Closed the domesday book,   30
Fitted his cap back with two hands,
And looked at me as he said goodbye.

cowl: covering shaped like a hood.

'spud': potato-like shape.

the boot of the law: heavy footwear of policemen, suggesting power and oppression.

bevel: line on policeman's forehead made by his cap.

ledger: book containing records of farm accounts.
tillage returns: amount harvested from cultivated land.

braid: threads woven into a decorative band.

Mangolds: beets grown for animal feed.
Marrowstems: long, green vegetables.

black hole: small cell in the police station.

domesday book: a survey of all the land in England and its value, ordered by William the Conqueror, the 11th-century English king; also refers to Judgement Day, when all will be brought to account.

POETRY FOCUS

A shadow bobbed in the window.
He was snapping the carrier spring
Over the ledger. His boot pushed off   35
And the bicycle ticked, ticked, ticked.

bobbed: moved up and
down.
carrier spring: spiral metal
coil on the back of a bike
used to secure a bag, etc.

'the boot of the law'

 Personal Response

1. How does the poet create an atmosphere of tension in this poem? Support your response with reference to the text.
2. What type of relationship do you think the young boy has with his father? Refer closely to the text in your response.
3. Critics disagree about the ending of the poem. Some find it 'false', others 'stunning'. How would you describe the ending? Give reasons for your response.

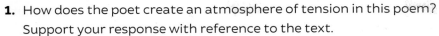 Critical Literacy

'A Constable Calls' was written in 1975 and forms the second part of the poem sequence 'Singing School'. The Heaneys were a Catholic family. The constable would have been a member of the Royal Ulster Constabulary (RUC) and probably a Protestant. This poem illustrates the underlying tensions between the two communities in Northern Ireland. Heaney's 'country of community … was a place of division'.

'A Constable Calls' is told from the **viewpoint of a young boy** caught up in the bubbling tensions in Northern Ireland. The conflict erupted into serious violence during the Troubles, usually dated from the late 1960s until the Good Friday Agreement of 1998. The poem explores fear and power from the perspective of the Nationalist community. Catholics did not trust the RUC. In the opening stanzas, crude strength, power and violence are all inherent in the cold, precise language used to describe the constable's bicycle. The 'handlegrips' suggest handcuffs, while the 'cocked back' dynamo hints at a gun ready to be fired, its trigger ready for action. It also signifies confidence and cockiness. The oppression of the local authorities is highlighted in the phrase 'the boot of the law'. Heaney personifies the bicycle, which he describes as being 'relieved' of the pressure of the weight of the constable. This poem was written during the civil rights protest marches, when Nationalists were sometimes treated very severely by the RUC. This is evoked in the assonance of the broad vowels in 'fat black' and the harsh-sounding repetition of 'ck' in the phrase 'cocked back'. Here are the observations of the child of a divided community. The character (and symbolic significance) of the constable is implicit in the description of his bicycle.

In stanzas three to five, Heaney gives us an explicit **description of the constable**. His uniform and equipment are all symbols of power, which the young boy notes in detail: 'the polished holster/With its buttoned flap, the braid cord/Looped into the revolver butt'. This is no friendly community police officer. The repetition of 'his' tells us that the possession of power belongs to him and what he represents. He is not a welcome visitor. His hat lies on the ground. He is not offered refreshment, although he is presumably thirsty from his work. Even the one human detail ('slightly sweating hair') revolts us. Is he as tense as the Catholic family in this time of sectarian conflict? The print of his great authority is stamped on him like a 'bevel', but does his power weigh heavily on him?

The policeman's function was to oblige the boy's father to give an account of his farm crop returns. Their terse exchange underlines the **tension in this troubled community**. The interrogation by the constable consists of four questions: 'Any other root crops?/Mangolds? Marrowstems? Anything like that?' This is met by the father's short, clipped, monosyllabic reply: 'No'. The encounter is summed up succinctly in the line 'Arithmetic and fear'. In the seventh stanza, the young boy becomes alarmed as he realises that his father has omitted to account for 'a line/Of turnips'. He 'assumed/Small guilts'. His perceived Catholic inferiority is graphically shown in the reference to the 'domesday book', or 'ledger', belonging to the constable. The child imagines a day of reckoning, almost like Judgement Day, when God calls every individual to account for past sins. He imagines the immediate punishment of 'the black hole in the barracks', the notorious police cell where offenders were held. This terror of being incarcerated by the law ran deep in the Catholic psyche throughout the Troubles.

In the end, the constable takes his leave (stanzas seven and eight), formally fitting 'his cap back with two hands'. We can empathise with the boy as he 'looked at me'. In the final stanza, the oppressive presence of the visitor ('A shadow') is wryly described as 'bobbed', an ironic reference to the friendly English bobby – which this particular constable was not. The verbs in this stanza continue the underlying ominous mood: 'snapping', 'pushed off'. The **poem concludes** with an intimidating reference to the sound of the departing bicycle as a slowly ticking time bomb: 'And the bicycle ticked, ticked, ticked'. Does this suggest that the tension in this divided community was always on the verge of exploding? Do you consider this an effective image or do you think the symbolism is too obvious?

✍ Writing About the Poem

'Seamus Heaney often presents insightful coming-of-age moments using autobiographical experience.' Discuss this statement in relation to 'A Constable Calls'.

Sample Paragraph

In 'A Constable Calls', Heaney recalls a tense incident from his childhood during the 1950s. A local policeman calls to interview the boy's father about the taxes due on his farm crops. The focus is placed on the constable's bicycle which 'stood at the window-sill' and then zooms to a close-up of the 'rubber cowl of a mud-splasher'. This vivid description suggests the repressive power felt by Nationalists. The metaphor, 'the boot of the law', reinforces this impression. After a tense interrogation between the officer and the boy's father ('Any other root crops?'), the boy is filled with guilt at his father's lie. Although he is not fully aware of the significance of the encounter, the youthful Heaney experiences a sense of the sectarian world around him. The menacing final line describing the spokes of the bicycle wheels as they 'ticked, ticked, ticked' predicts the terrible violence of bombs that will define Northern Ireland during the so-called Troubles of the 1970s and 80s.

EXAMINER'S COMMENT

A top-grade response, successfully describing the setting for this dramatic confrontation between the constable and Heaney's father. There is a clear explanation of the uneasy atmosphere in which the poet gains an early awareness of sectarian conflict. Supporting quotations are integrated effectively into the commentary and the expression is excellent. The impressive final sentence succinctly sums up the poem's narrative very well.

✒ Class/Homework Exercises

1. 'The question of identity looms large in Seamus Heaney's precisely controlled poetry.' Discuss this statement with reference to 'A Constable Calls'.
2. 'Heaney frequently writes evocative poems that explore the harsh reality of ordinary life.' Discuss this view, referring both to the content and style of 'A Constable Calls'.

⊙ Points to Consider

- **Key themes include conflict, repressive authority and the loss of innocence.**
- **Engaging use of first-person narrative and closely observed detail.**
- **Tension between divided community results in child's discomfort.**
- **Compelling psychological drama (threat, interrogation, lies, guilt, danger recedes).**
- **Dynamic cinematic movement (zooms, pans, slow motion, close-up).**
- **Short snappy lines juxtaposed with flowing lines and run-on quatrains.**
- **Ominous conclusion.**

6 🔊 The Skunk

Up, black, striped and damasked like the chasuble
At a funeral mass, the skunk's tail
Paraded the skunk. Night after night
I expected her like a visitor.

The refrigerator whinnied into silence.   5
My desk light softened beyond the verandah.
Small oranges loomed in the orange tree.
I began to be tense as a voyeur.

After eleven years I was composing
Love-letters again, broaching the word 'wife'   10
Like a stored cask, as if its slender vowel
Had mutated into the night earth and air

Of California. The beautiful, useless
Tang of eucalyptus spelt your absence.
The aftermath of a mouthful of wine   15
Was like inhaling you off a cold pillow.

And there she was, the intent and glamorous,
Ordinary, mysterious skunk,
Mythologized, demythologized,
Snuffing the boards five feet beyond me.   20

It all came back to me last night, stirred
By the sootfall of your things at bedtime,
Your head-down, tail-up hunt in a bottom drawer
For the black plunge-line nightdress.

damasked: patterned; rich, heavy damask fabric.
chasuble: garment worn by a priest saying Mass.

whinnied: sound a horse makes.
verandah: roofed platform along the outside of a house.

voyeur: a person who watches others when they are being intimate.

broaching: raising a subject for discussion.

mutated: changed shape or form.

eucalyptus: tree with scented leaves commonly found in California.
aftermath: consequences of an unpleasant event.

Mythologized: related to or found in myth.

sootfall: soft sound (like soot falling from a chimney).

plunge-line: low-cut.

'the skunk's tail/
Paraded the skunk'

👤 Personal Response

1. In your opinion, how effective is Heaney in creating the particular sense of place in this poem? Refer closely to the text in your answer.
2. The poet compares his wife to a skunk. Does this image work, in your view? Quote from the poem in support of your response.
3. Comment on the poem's dramatic qualities. Refer to setting, characters, action and sense of tension/climax, particularly in the first and last stanzas.

👁 Critical Literacy

'The Skunk' comes from Heaney's 1979 collection, *Field Work*. The poet called it a 'marriage poem'. While spending an academic year (1971–2) teaching in the USA, he had been reading the work of Robert Lowell, an American poet. Lowell's poem, 'Skunk Hour', describes how isolation drives a man to become a voyeur of lovers in cars. Heaney's reaction to his own loneliness is very different; he rediscovers the art of writing love letters to his wife, who is living 6,000 miles away in Ireland. This separation culminated in an intimate, humorous, erotic love poem which speaks volumes for the deep love and trust between husband and wife.

In the opening stanza, we are presented with four words describing the skunk's tail, 'Up, black, striped and damasked'. The punctuation separates the different aspects of the animal's tail for the reader's observation. An unusual simile occurs in line 1. In a **playfully irreverent tone**, Heaney likens the skunk's tail to the black and white vestments worn by a priest at a funeral. He then gives us an almost cartoon-like visual image of the animal's tail leading the skunk. The self-importance of the little animal is effectively captured in the verb 'Paraded'. All the ceremony of marching is evoked. The poet eagerly awaits his nightly visitor: 'Night after night/I expected her'. Skunks are small black-and-white striped American mammals, capable of spraying foul-smelling liquid on attackers.

In stanza two, the poet's senses are heightened. The verbs 'whinnied', 'softened' and 'loomed' vividly capture the **atmosphere of the soft, exotic California night**. The bright colours of orange and green are synonymous with the Golden State. The anticipation of stanza one now sharpens: 'I began to be tense'. He regards himself as a 'voyeur', but here there is no sense of violation. He is staring into darkness, getting ready to communicate with his wife. In stanza three, the poet, after a break of 11 years, is penning love letters again. In this separation period, he realises how much he misses her. His wife's presence, although she is absent, fills his consciousness. He is totally preoccupied with her. He uses the simile 'Like a stored cask' to show how he values her as something precious. The word 'wife' is savoured like fine wine and his affection is shown in his appreciation of 'its slender vowel', which reminds him of her feminine grace. She is present to him in the air he breathes, 'mutated into the night earth and air/Of California'.

Heaney's depth of longing is captured in the **sensuous language** of stanza four. The smell of the eucalyptus 'spelt your absence'. The word 'Tang' precisely notes the penetrating sensation of loneliness. Even a drink of wine, 'a mouthful of wine', does not dull this ache. Instead it intensifies his desire, 'like inhaling you off a cold pillow'. Now, the skunk, long awaited, appears. It is full of contradictions: 'glamorous', 'Ordinary'. We hear in stanza five the sound the little animal makes in the onomatopoeic phrase 'Snuffing the boards'. Only in stanza six is the comparison between the wife and the skunk finally drawn: 'It all came back to me last night'. Heaney imagines himself back home. His wife is rummaging in the bottom drawer for a nightdress. She adopts a slightly comic pose, 'head-down, tail-up', reminding him of the skunk as she 'hunt[s]'. The sibilance of the line 'stirred/By the sootfall of your things' suggests the tender intimacy between the married couple. The word 'sootfall' conveys the gentle rustle of clothes falling. The reader's reaction is also 'stirred' to amused surprise as the realisation dawns that the adjectives 'intent and glamorous,/Ordinary, mysterious ... Mythologized, demythologized' also apply to his wife. A **mature, trusting relationship** exists between the couple.

Longer lines suggest ease. The poet is relaxed and playful, his language conversational and sensuous. All our senses are 'stirred'. The light is romantic ('softened') and the colour black is alluring. The touch of the 'cold pillow' will now be replaced by the warm, shared bed. The sounds of California and the couple's bedroom echo: 'Snuffing', 'sootfall'. The 'aftermath of a mouthful of wine' lingers on the tongue. This is something of a rarity, a **successful love poem about marriage**, tender but not cosy, personal but not embarrassingly self-revealing.

✒ Writing About the Poem

'Seamus Heaney makes use of a wide range of striking images to explore experiences of people, places and events.' Discuss this statement in relation to 'The Skunk'.

Sample Paragraph

Heaney writes about subjects that are sometimes tinged with loneliness and often filled with love, as in 'The Skunk'. Through the innovative image of the little nocturnal animal, whose tail paraded, 'Up, black, striped and damasked', he conveys the wonder of married love. It is both mundane and mysterious. Evocative personification is used along with powerful

aural imagery, 'The refrigerator whinnied'. The poet is separated from his wife and recalls her presence, 'inhaling you off a cold pillow'. Detailed images connect her to the skunk in the yard outside. He observes the animal's posture, 'head-down, tail-up' and the sultry atmosphere is suddenly replaced by the sensuous 'sootfall of your things'. The close intimacy of the couple is highlighted in the detail of the 'black plunge-line nightdress'. By linking people, places and events, Heaney presents a moment of insight about romantic love.

✒ Class/Homework Exercises

1. 'Relationships, personal or otherwise, lie at the heart of Heaney's most accessible poems.' Discuss this view with reference to the poem, 'The Skunk'.
2. 'Throughout his lyrical poems, Seamus Heaney conjures up a sense of the universal, even when focusing on distinct personal experiences.' Discuss this statement with reference to both the content and style of 'The Skunk'.

◉ Points to Consider

- **Unusual, playful, intimate love poem.**
- **Range of tones – irreverent, reflective, wistful, emotive.**
- **Striking visual, aural, tactile imagery.**
- **Personification and onomatopoeia evoke atmosphere, people and places.**
- **Disconcerting juxtaposition of past/present, animal/person, loss/love, ordinary/mysterious.**
- **Contrasting line lengths (brief end-stopped lines, flowing run-on lines and stanzas) create urgency, tension and longing.**

7 🔊 The Harvest Bow

Title: the harvest bow, an emblem of traditional rural crafts, was made from straw and often worn in the lapel to celebrate the end of harvesting. Sometimes it was given as a love-token or kept in the farmhouse until the next year's harvest.

As you plaited the harvest bow
You implicated the mellowed silence in you
In wheat that does not rust
But brightens as it tightens twist by twist
Into a knowable corona,   5
A throwaway love-knot of straw.

implicated: intertwined; revealed indirectly.
mellowed: matured, placid.

corona: circle of light, halo.

Hands that aged round ashplants and cane sticks
And lapped the spurs on a lifetime of game cocks
Harked to their gift and worked with fine intent
Until your fingers moved somnambulant: 10
I tell and finger it like braille,
Gleaning the unsaid off the palpable,

lapped the spurs: tied the back claws of fighting birds.
game cocks: male fowl reared to take part in cock-fighting.
Harked: listened, attuned.
somnambulant: automatically, as if sleepwalking.
braille: system of reading by touching raised dots.
Gleaning: gathering, grasping, understanding.
palpable: what can be handled or understood.

And if I spy into its golden loops
I see us walk between the railway slopes
Into an evening of long grass and midges,   15
Blue smoke straight up, old beds and ploughs in hedges,
An auction notice on an outhouse wall –
You with a harvest bow in your lapel,

midges: small biting insects that usually swarm near water.

Me with the fishing rod, already homesick
For the big lift of these evenings, as your stick   20
Whacking the tips off weeds and bushes
Beats out of time, and beats, but flushes
Nothing: that original townland
Still tongue-tied in the straw tied by your hand.

flushes: rouses, reveals.

The end of art is peace   25
Could be the motto of this frail device
That I have pinned up on our deal dresser –
Like a drawn snare
Slipped lately by the spirit of the corn
Yet burnished by its passage, and still warm.   30

The end of art is peace: art brings contentment (a quotation from the English poet Coventry Patmore, 1823–1896). It was also used by W.B. Yeats.
device: object, artefact.
deal: pine wood.
snare: trap.

burnished: shining.

'A throwaway love-knot of straw'

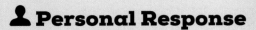

👤 Personal Response

1. Based on your reading of the poem, what impression do you get of Heaney's father? Refer to the text in your answer.
2. In your view, is the harvest bow a symbol of love? Give reasons for your answer, using reference to the poem.
3. What do you understand by the line 'The end of art is peace'? Briefly explain your answer.

👁 Critical Literacy

'The Harvest Bow' (from the 1972 collection *Field Work*) is an elegiac poem in which Heaney pays tribute to his father and the work he did with his hands, weaving a traditional harvest emblem out of stalks of wheat. Remembering his boyhood, watching his father create the corn-dolly, he already knew that the moment could not last. The recognition of his father's artistic talents leads the poet to a consideration of his own creative work.

The poem begins with a measured description of Heaney's reticent father as he twists stalks of wheat into decorative love-knots. The delicate phrasing in stanza one ('You implicated the mellowed silence in you') reflects the poet's awareness of how the **harvest bow symbolised the intricate bond between father and son**. The poet conveys a subdued but satisfied mood as another farm year draws to a close. Autumnal images ('wheat that does not rust') add to the sense of accomplishment. Heaney highlights the practised techniques involved in creating this 'throwaway love-knot of straw'. The harvest bow 'brightens as it tightens twist by twist'. Emphatic alliteration and internal rhyme enliven the image, almost becoming a metaphor for the father's expertise. The bow is likened to 'a knowable corona', a reassuring circle of light representing the year's natural cycle.

In stanza two, the intricate beauty of the straw knot prompts Heaney to recall some of the other manual skills his father once demonstrated, 'round ashplants and cane sticks'. He acknowledges the older man's 'gift' of concentration and 'fine intent' as he fashioned the harvest bow ('your fingers moved somnambulant') **without conscious effort towards artistic achievement**. Is Heaney also suggesting that poets should work that way? Carefully handling the bow 'like braille', the poet clearly values it as an expression of undeclared love: 'Gleaning the unsaid off the palpable'.

The pleasurable sentiments of Heaney's childhood memories are realised by the strength of detailed imagery in stanza three: 'I see us walk between the railway slopes'. Such **ordinary scenes are enhanced by sensuous details** of 1940s rural life: 'Blue smoke straight up, old beds and ploughs in hedges'. Many of the sounds have a plaintive, musical quality ('loops', 'slopes', 'midges', 'hedges'). The poet seems haunted by his father's ghost, and the silence that once seemed to define their relationship is now recognised as a secret code of mutual understanding.

Stanza four focuses on the relentless passing of time. The **tone is particularly elegiac** as Heaney recalls his father 'Whacking the tips off weeds' with his stick. In retrospect, he seems to interpret such pointless actions as evidence of how every individual 'Beats out of time' – but to no avail. The poet extends this notion of time's mystery by suggesting that it is through art alone ('the straw tied by your hand') that 'tongue-tied' communities can explore life's wonder.

At the start of stanza five, Heaney tries to make sense of the corn-dolly, now a treasured part of his own household 'on our deal dresser'. It mellows in its new setting and gives out heat. While 'the spirit of the corn' may have disappeared from the knot, the power of the poet's imagination can still recreate it there. So rather than being merely a nostalgic recollection of childhood, the poem takes on universal meaning in the intertwining of artistic forces. We are left with a deep sense of lost rural heritage, the unspoken joy of a shared relationship and the rich potential of the poet's art. For Heaney, **artistic achievements produce warm feelings of lasting contentment**. Whatever 'frail device' is created, be it a harvest bow or a formal elegy, *The end of art is peace*.

🖊 Writing About the Poem

'Heaney makes effective use of striking imagery to explore universal themes of love and loss.' Discuss this statement with reference to 'The Harvest Bow'.

Sample Paragraph

Heaney's poem, 'The Harvest Bow', is a powerful elegy for his father. Its imagery and sound effects describe the traditional straw bow which celebrates the end of the farming year. Remembering this 'frail device' allows Heaney to go back in time like a 'drawn snare', enabling him to 'spy into its golden loops' and re-experience treasured moments. Strong aural images, broad vowels and enjambment evoke the serene mood, 'I see us walk between the railway slopes/Into an evening of long grass and midges'. Poignant memories of childhood are universal and symbolise family love. Heaney's father 'Beats out of time' with his stick, an image that lives forever in his memory. The phrase suggests the bond shared by father and son, but also hints at the sense of loss. For Heaney, the presence of his father lives again in the poet's heart, 'still warm'.

EXAMINER'S COMMENT

This is a sustained top-grade response that shows close engagement with the poem. All the elements of the question (imagery, love and loss, universal significance) are addressed. Relevant quotations – referring to a range of imagery patterns – are used to support discussion points. Expression is well controlled and the critical vocabulary is very impressive.

🖋 Class/Homework Exercises

1. 'Seamus Heaney frequently uses detailed observation and a lyrical style to explore close family relationships.' Discuss this view with reference to 'The Harvest Bow'.
2. 'Heaney's carefully judged language enables readers to relate to recurring themes that are often grounded in the past.' Discuss this statement with reference to both the subject matter and style of 'The Harvest Bow'.

⊙ Points to Consider

- Elegy directly addresses the poet's father.
- Warm, emotional tone, consoling perfection of the past.
- Similarity drawn between intricate artistry of the bow maker and poet.
- Contrasting aspects of his father – tough, practical, silent, tender, skilled.
- Multiple word meanings, e.g. 'implicate' = 'show', 'entrap', 'include'.
- Clever aural word-play imitates the complexity of the harvest bow.
- Concluding reassuring motto – art confronts every destructive life experience and creates order.

8 The Underground

There we were in the vaulted tunnel running,
You in your going-away coat speeding ahead
And me, me then like a fleet god gaining
Upon you before you turned to a reed

Or some new white flower japped with crimson   5
As the coat flapped wild and button after button
Sprang off and fell in a trail
Between the Underground and the Albert Hall.

Honeymooning, mooning around, late for the Proms,
Our echoes die in that corridor and now   10
I come as Hansel came on the moonlit stones
Retracing the path back, lifting the buttons

To end up in a draughty lamplit station
After the trains have gone, the wet track
Bared and tensed as I am, all attention   15
For your step following and damned if I look back.

vaulted: domed, arched.

going-away coat: new coat worn by the bride leaving on honeymoon.
fleet: fast; momentary.
reed: slender plant; part of a musical instrument.

japped: tinged, layered.

the Albert Hall: famous London landmark and concert venue.

the Proms: short for Promenade Concerts, a summer season of classical music.
Hansel: fairytale character who, along with his sister Gretel, retraced his way home using a trail of white pebbles.

'Our echoes die in that corridor'

Note: in Greek mythology, Eurydice, the beloved wife of Orpheus, was killed by a venomous snake. Orpheus travelled to the Underworld (Hades) to retrieve her. It was granted that Eurydice could return to the world of the living, but on condition that Orpheus should walk in front of her and not look back until he had reached the upper world. In his anxiety, he broke his promise, and Eurydice vanished again – but this time forever.

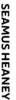

SEAMUS HEANEY

 Personal Response

1. Comment on the atmosphere created in the first two stanzas. Refer to the text in your answer.
2. From your reading of this poem, what do you learn about the relationship between the poet and his wife? Refer to the text in your answer.
3. Write a short personal response to 'The Underground', highlighting the impact it made on you.

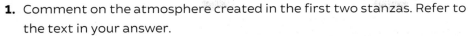 Critical Literacy

'The Underground' is the first poem in *Station Island* (1984). It recounts a memory from Heaney's honeymoon when he and his wife (like a modern Orpheus and Eurydice) were rushing through a London Underground Tube station on their way to a BBC Promenade Concert in the Albert Hall. In Dennis O'Driscoll's book *Stepping Stones*, Heaney said, 'In this version of the story, Eurydice and much else gets saved by the sheer cussedness of the poet up ahead just keeping going.'

The poem's title is filled with a sense of threat. Underground journeys are shadowed with a certain menace. Not only is there a mythical association with crossing into the land of the dead, but there is also the actuality of accidents and terrorist outrages. The first stanza of Heaney's personal narrative uses everyday colloquial speech ('There we were in the vaulted tunnel running') to introduce his **dramatic account**. The oppressively 'vaulted' setting and urgent verbs ('speeding', 'gaining') increase this sense of disquiet. For the poet, it is a psychic and mythic underground where he imagines his own heroic quest ('like a fleet god'). What he seems to dread most is the possibility of change and that, like a latter-day Orpheus, he might somehow lose his soulmate.

Cinematic images and run-on lines propel the second stanza forward. This **fast-paced rhythm is in keeping with the restless diction** – 'the coat flapped wild'. The poet's wife is wearing her going-away wedding outfit and in the course of her sprint, the buttons start popping off. Internal rhyme adds to the tension; 'japped' and 'flapped' play into each other, giving the impression that whatever is occurring is happening with great intensity.

The poem changes at the beginning of the third stanza and this is evident in the language, which is much more playful, reflecting Heaney's assessment of the occasion in hindsight. He now recognises the youthful insecurity of the time: 'Honeymooning, mooning around'. The reference to the fictional Hansel and Gretel hints at the immaturity of their relationship as newlyweds and emphasises the couple's initial fretfulness. But recalling how he carefully gathered up the buttons, like Hansel returning from the wilderness, **Heaney appears to have now come to terms with his uneasy past**: 'Our echoes die in that corridor'.

This new-found confidence underscores the poet's recollections in the fourth stanza. The action and speed have now ceased. After the uncertainty of the 'draughty lamplit station', he has learned to trust his wife and his own destiny. Unlike Orpheus, the tragic Greek hero, Heaney has emerged from his personal descent into Hades, 'Bared and tense'. Although **he can never forget the desolation of being threatened with loss**, the poet has been well served by the experience, having realised that it will always be him – and not his wife – who will be damned if he dares to look back.

The ending of the poem is characteristically compelling. Commenting on it in *Stepping Stones*, Heaney has said, 'But in the end, the "damned if I look back" line takes us well beyond the honeymoon.' Although some critics feel that the final outlook is more regretful, it is difficult to miss the sheer determination that is present in the poem's last line. The **poet's stubborn tone leaves us with overwhelming evidence of his enduring devotion to love**, an emotional commitment which seems to be even more precious with the passing of time.

✒ Writing About the Poem

'Heaney's poetry operates successfully across several levels, dramatically observing and quietly reflecting.' Discuss this statement with reference to 'The Underground'.

Sample Paragraph

EXAMINER'S COMMENT

An intelligent top-grade response that addresses both elements of this challenging question. Some focused commentary on dramatic aspects ('frantic dash', 'reality and nightmare', 'cinematic detail'). Apt quotations are successfully integrated into the discussion. Assured vocabulary ('interweaves', 'alternative') is also impressive.

'The Underground' is another of Heaney's autobiographical poems in which he gives a dramatic account of a frantic dash by his wife and himself through London's Underground train station. What is interesting is how he interweaves past and present into reality and nightmare throughout the poem. Urgent verbs ('speeding', 'gaining') and run-on lines further suggest the headlong rush. Heaney's observations lead to deep reflection. The poet introduces the Orpheus and Eurydice tale of tragic loss in the Underworld. Suddenly, the personal has become universal. Another cinematic detail – the falling buttons – is associated with the 'moonlit stones' from the fairytale of Hansel and Gretel. Heaney, like Hansel, goes back, 'retracing the path', to find a way forward. The poem's final phrase, 'damned if I look back', also works on two levels. Heaney is determined to put real effort into the couple's relationship. The alternative is loss of love – a kind of damnation that he fears.

✒ Class/Homework Exercises

1. 'Heaney frequently invokes a vivid range of memories and mythological echoes to reveal intense feelings in his poetry.' Discuss this view with reference to 'The Underground'.

2. 'Heaney's love poems celebrate his subjects warmly, yet realistically, through the use of precise visual imagery and aural detail.' Discuss this statement with reference to both the subject matter and style of 'The Underground'.

◉ Points to Consider

- Nostalgic love poem of a specific event infused with Greek myth and fairy story.

- Personal narrative using colloquial speech and engaging imagery.

- Dramatic atmosphere, pacy rhythm, dynamic verbs, run-on lines.

- Aural music of internal rhyme and assonance.

- Fear of loss contrasted with the poet's determined commitment to his wife.

Postscript

And some time make the time to drive out west
Into County Clare, along the Flaggy Shore,
In September or October, when the wind
And the light are working off each other
So that the ocean on one side is wild   5
With foam and glitter, and inland among stones
The surface of a slate-grey lake is lit
By the earthed lightning of a flock of swans,
Their feathers roughed and ruffling, white on white,
Their fully grown headstrong-looking heads   10
Tucked or cresting or busy underwater.
Useless to think you'll park and capture it
More thoroughly. You are neither here nor there,
A hurry through which known and strange things pass
As big soft buffetings come at the car sideways   15
And catch the heart off guard and blow it open.

the Flaggy Shore: stretch of coastal limestone slabs in the Burren, Co. Clare.

working off: playing against.

cresting: stretching, posing.

buffetings: vibrations, shudderings.

👤 Personal Response

1. Choose one image from the poem that you find particularly effective. Briefly explain your choice.
2. What is your understanding of the poem's final line?
3. In your opinion, is the advice given by Heaney in 'Postscript' relevant to our modern world? Give reasons to support your response.

👁 Critical Literacy

This beautiful pastoral lyric comes at the end of Seamus Heaney's 1996 collection, *The Spirit Level*. The title suggests an afterthought, something that was missed out earlier. As so often in his poetry, Heaney succeeds in conveying the extraordinary by way of an everyday experience – in this case, the vivid memory of a journey westwards. The poem resonates with readers, particularly those who have also shared moments when life caught them by surprise.

Line 1 is relaxed and conversational. The poet invites others (or promises himself, perhaps) to 'make the time to drive out west'. The phrase 'out west' has connotations both of adventurous opportunity and dismal failure. By placing 'And' at the start of the poem, Heaney indicates a link with something earlier, some unfinished business. **Keen to ensure that the journey will be worthwhile**, he recommends a definite destination ('the Flaggy Shore') and time ('September or October').

'along th Flaggy Shore'

The untamed beauty of the Co. Clare coastline is described in some detail: 'when the wind/And the light are working off each other' (lines 3–4). The phrase 'working off' is especially striking in conveying the **tension and balance between two of nature's greatest complementary forces: wind and light**. Together, they create an effect that neither could produce singly.

Close awareness of place is a familiar feature of the poet's writing, but in this instance he includes another dimension – the notion of in-betweeness. The road Heaney describes runs between the ocean and an inland lake. Carefully chosen images **contrast** the unruly beauty of the open sea's 'foam and glitter' with the still 'slate-grey lake' (line 7). In both descriptions, the sounds of the words echo their sense precisely.

The introduction of the swans in line 8 brings unexpected drama. Heaney captures their seemingly effortless movement between air and water. The poet's **vigorous skill with language** can be seen in his appreciation of the swans' transforming presence, which he highlights in the extraordinary image of 'earthed lightning'. His expertly crafted sketches are both tactile ('feathers roughed and ruffling') and visual ('white on white'). Tossed by the wind, their neck feathers resemble ruffled collars. To Heaney, these exquisite birds signify an otherworldly force that is rarely earthed or restrained. In response, he is momentarily absorbed by the swans' purposeful gestures and powerful flight.

In line 12, the poet cautiously accepts that such elemental beauty can never be fully grasped: 'Useless to think you'll park and capture it'. Because we are 'neither here nor there', we can only occasionally glimpse 'known and strange things'. Despite this, the poem concludes on a redemptive note, acknowledging those special times when we edge close to the miraculous. These **experiences transcend our mundane lives** and we are shaken by revelation, just as unexpected gusts of winds ('soft buffetings') can rock a car.

Heaney's journey has been both **physical and mystical**. It is brought to a climax in line 16, where it ends in the articulation of an important truth. He has found meaning between the tangible and intangible. The startling possibility of discovering the ephemeral quality of spiritual awareness is unnerving enough to 'catch the heart off guard and blow it open'. The seemingly contradictory elements of comfort and danger add to the intensity of this final image. Heaney has spoken about the illumination he felt during his visit to the Flaggy Shore as a 'glorious exultation of air and sea and swans'. For him, the experience was obviously inspirational, and the poem that it produced might well provide a similar opportunity for readers to experience life beyond the ordinary material world.

✒ Writing About the Poem

'Heaney's work often addresses the wonder of poetic inspiration through the use of carefully chosen images.' Discuss this statement in relation to 'Postscript'.

Sample Paragraph

'Postscript' starts with a casual invitation, 'And some time make the time', building to a crescendo and concluding with a highly charged insight. The poem evokes the creative process of poetry, the ability of language to transport a person to a magical place ('when the wind/And the light are working off each other'). The unexpected satisfaction of creativity is caught in the interaction of wind, light, ocean, lake and swans. He focuses on nuances of colour ('white on white') and texture ('roughed and ruffling') to capture the enchanting moment. The swans are also carefully noted – their arrogance ('headstrong-looking') and their paddling feet ('busy underwater'). Quietly, the poet cautions readers to appreciate this moment, 'Useless to think you'll park and capture it'. The final explosive line is filled with the emotion of being truly alive. The wind, like the poem itself, triggers uncontrollable emotion. Both come like 'big soft buffetings' to 'catch the heart off guard and blow it open'.

EXAMINER'S COMMENT

An insightful response to the question. Informed discussion points focused throughout on the theme of the creative process and Heaney's use of language. Good choice of accurate quotations integrated effectively into the commentary. Expression is impressive also: varied sentence length, wide-ranging vocabulary ('crescendo', 'nuances', 'triggers uncontrollable emotion') and good control of syntax. A top-grade standard.

✒ Class/Homework Exercises

1. 'Seamus Heaney's poems are capable of capturing moments of insight in a strikingly memorable fashion.' Discuss this statement with reference to 'Postscript'.
2. 'Heaney evokes the beauty and mystery of Ireland's natural landscape through the precision of his language.' Discuss this view with reference to both the subject matter and style of 'Postscript'.

◎ Points to Consider

- Conversational description of a car drive 'out west' into Co. Clare.
- The poem pays tribute to the sheer power of perception.
- Resonance of memory, contrasting joy at visual experience with sadness at realisation of its transience.
- Vivid visual imagery and subtle sound effects used to convey the scene.
- Cautious, reflective tone contrasts with exhilarating description.

10 A Call

'Hold on,' she said, 'I'll just run out and get him.
The weather here's so good he took the chance
To do a bit of weeding.'
              So I saw him
Down on his hands and knees beside the leek rig,   5
Touching, inspecting, separating one
Stalk from the other, gently pulling up
Everything not tapered, frail and leafless,
Pleased to feel each little weed-root break,
But rueful also ...   10
                Then found myself listening to
The amplified grave ticking of hall clocks
Where the phone lay unattended in a calm
Of mirror glass and sunstruck pendulums ...

And found myself then thinking: if it were nowadays,   15
This is how Death would summon Everyman.

Next thing he spoke and I nearly said I loved him.

tapered: slender; reducing in thickness towards the end.
frail: weak.

rueful: expressing regret.

amplified: increased the strength of the sound.

pendulums: weights that hang from a fixed point and swing freely, used to regulate the mechanism of a clock.

Everyman: character in fifteenth-century morality plays.

'Pleased to feel each little weed-root break'

👤 Personal Response

1. How does Heaney dramatise this event? Refer to setting, mood, dialogue, action and climax in your response.
2. Describe the mood of 'A Call'. Does it change during the course of the poem? Support your answer with suitable quotations.
3. One literary critic said that the 'celebration of people and relationships in Heaney's poetry is characterised by honesty and tenderness'. To what extent do you agree or disagree with this view? Refer to the text in your response.

👁 Critical Literacy

'A Call' comes from Heaney's collection *The Spirit Level* (1996) and deals with two of the poet's recurring themes: the father–son relationship and the passing of time. The setting is a routine domestic scene of a mother talking, a father weeding, a son calling. *The Spirit Level* refers to balance, getting the level right, measuring. It also suggests poetry, which is on another plane, free-floating above the confines of the earth. Heaney spoke about this in his Nobel Prize speech, saying 'I am permitting myself the luxury of walking on air'.

This personal narrative opens with a conversational directness, as Heaney is told to 'Hold on'. Heaney has phoned his parents' home and his mother is responding to her son's request to speak with his father. When she puts the receiver down (these were the days of the land line), the poet has time to imagine the old man at work in his garden: 'The weather here's so good, he took the chance/To do a bit of weeding'. The rhythm of colloquial dialogue is realistically caught by the use of everyday expressions and a **simple scene of domesticity is established**. In line 4, the poet becomes the engrossed spectator on the fringes of the scene: 'So I saw him'. The detail of 'Down on his hands and knees beside the leek rig' invites the reader to observe for themselves.

Fragmented description shows the care and skill of the gardener's activity, 'Touching, inspecting, separating', as the father tends his vegetable patch. All farming tradition is associated with decay and growth, and the weakest is usually discarded, 'gently pulling up/Everything not tapered'. The onomatopoeia of the word 'break', with its sharp 'k' sound, suggests the snap of the root as it is pulled from the soil. The father takes pleasure ('Pleased to feel') in his work ('each little weed-root break') but he is, perhaps, regretful too ('rueful') that a form of life is ending, snapped from the nurturing earth.

In line 11, the **visual imagery is replaced by aural effects**. The mood in the deserted hallway indicates a significant change in the tone of the poem. Sounds are 'amplified' due to the subdued atmosphere of the location and Heaney's long wait to hear his father's voice. Time is passing, not just for the weeds but also for the man, measured by the 'grave ticking of hall clocks'. Here the poem begins to move between earthbound reality and airiness. The image of ticking clocks in a sea ('calm') of 'mirror glass and sunstruck pendulums' is almost surreal. Broad vowel sounds create an air of serenity and otherworldliness. The word 'amplified' vividly conveys the echo of the clocks and we can imagine their loud ticking as the sound increases in intensity. The inclusion of the word 'grave' is an obvious reminder that death is edging closer – and not just for the poet's father.

In **line 15**, Heaney moves from observation to meditation, walking on air, 'And found myself then thinking'. Death is depicted as a personal communication, like a phone call from a loved one. The poet is pushing at the boundaries of what is real. His father, like the weeds, will be uprooted, spirited away to some afterlife. Here Heaney is 'seeing things'; he is mediating between states of awareness. **A keen sense of mortality informs the poem**. The **last line** stands apart, as Heaney is jolted out of his daydreaming: 'Next thing he spoke'. Family love is an important theme throughout Heaney's poetry. In this case, he considers the deep-rooted closeness of the father–son relationship and we witness the frustrating attempts at communication between them, 'and I nearly said I loved him'. Was it an awareness of his father's mortality which prompted this reaction from the poet? The careful phrasing, relaxed and casual, reflects the powerful love between these silent men and the heart-breaking tension of the impossibility of articulating their feelings. In the poem's poignant conclusion ('Next thing he spoke and I nearly said I loved him'), father and son are both united and separated at the same time.

The title of this poem is intriguing. Apart from referring to a telephone call, it also signals the final summons that 'Everyman' will receive from Death. While the dominant tone of 'A Call' celebrates the poet's father and his regard for nature, there is an underlying elegiac quality that reveals Heaney's deep awareness of mortality and loss.

✒ Writing About the Poem

'Seamus Heaney's poetry engages the reader through his use of striking imagery and thought-provoking themes.' Discuss this statement with reference to 'A Call'.

Sample Paragraph

'A Call', engages readers from the closely observed domestic scene to the dreamlike imagery depicting tender emotion, 'I nearly said I loved him'. We hear Heaney's mother's natural speaking voice, 'Hold on', while she rushes to get his father. We also imagine the father working quietly in

his garden through a carefully punctuated list of verbs, 'Touching, inspecting, separating'. Heaney also depicts a surreal scene of passing time through the broad vowels of the 'sunstruck pendulums'. His dark humour continues through the image of Death using the telephone to call human beings to the next world. The tender scene gives way to reflections on transience. As often in Heaney's poems, he celebrates life while accepting the reality of death. Through his multi-layered images, he teaches his readers about the significance of ordinary experiences.

✏ Class/Homework Exercises

1. 'Seamus Heaney's reflective poetry often reveals moments of sensitivity that can enrich our experience of life.' Discuss this statement with reference to 'A Call'.
2. 'Heaney's lyrical poems go beyond description to disclose rich insights into universal themes.' Discuss this view with reference to both the subject matter and style of 'A Call'.

◉ Points to Consider

- **Autobiographical poem expands into profound meditation.**
- **Colloquial, direct speech is engaging.**
- **Effective use of carefully observed visual detail.**
- **Assonance, internal rhyme and alliteration heighten the musicality of the poem.**
- **Personification adds an ominous note.**
- **Unusual line breaks highlight the poem's focus on transience.**
- **Final line poignantly evokes both the communication and the lack of communication between father and son.**

11 Tate's Avenue

Title: Tate's Avenue is located in South Belfast, a popular student area. Heaney's girlfriend (later his wife) lived there in the late 1960s.

Not the brown and fawn car rug, that first one
Spread on sand by the sea but breathing land-breaths,
Its vestal folds unfolded, its comfort zone
Edged with a fringe of sepia-coloured wool tails.

vestal: innocent, untouched (Heaney is comparing the crumpled rug to the modest dresses of vestal virgins in ancient Rome).
sepia-coloured: faded brownish colour; old looking.

Not the one scraggy with crusts and eggshells   5
And olive stones and cheese and salami rinds
Laid out by the torrents of the Guadalquivir
Where we got drunk before the corrida.

Guadalquivir: river in Andalusia, Spain.
corrida: bullfight.

Instead, again, it's locked-park Sunday Belfast,
A walled back yard, the dust-bins high and silent   10
As a page is turned, a finger twirls warm hair
And nothing gives on the rug or the ground beneath it.

locked-park: Belfast's public parks were closed on Sundays in the 1960s.

I lay at my length and felt the lumpy earth,
Keen-sensed more than ever through discomfort,
But never shifted off the plaid square once.   15
When we moved I had your measure and you had mine.

plaid: checked, tartan.

'As a page is turned, a finger twirls warm hair'

👤 Personal Response

1. Comment on the poet's use of sound effects in the first two stanzas.
2. 'I had your measure and you had mine.' Briefly explain what you think Heaney means by this statement.
3. Write your own personal response to the poem.

👁 Critical Literacy

'Tate's Avenue' (from the 2006 collection *District and Circle*) is another celebration of Heaney's love for Marie Devlin. They married in 1965 and lived just off Tate's Avenue in South Belfast during the late 1960s. Here, the poet reviews their relationship by linking three separate occasions involving a collection of car rugs spread on the ground by the couple over the years.

Stanza one invites us to eavesdrop on a seemingly mundane scene of everyday domesticity. It appears that the poet and his wife have been reminiscing – presumably about their love life over the years. Although the negative opening tone is emphatic ('Not the brown and fawn car rug'), we are left guessing about the exact nature of the couple's discussion. A few tantalising details are given about 'that first' rug, connecting it with an early seaside visit. Heaney can still recall the tension of a time when the couple **were caught between their own desire and strong social restrictions**. He describes the rug in terms of its texture and colours: 'Its vestal folds unfolded' (suggesting their youthful sexuality) contrasting with the 'sepia-coloured wool tails' (symbolising caution and old-fashioned inhibitions). As usual, Heaney's tone is edged with irony as he recalls the 'comfort zone' between himself and Marie.

The repetition of 'Not' at the start of stanza two clearly indicates that the second rug is also rejected, even though it can be traced back to a more exotic Spanish holiday location. Sharp onomatopoeic effects ('scraggy with crusts and eggshells') and the list of Mediterranean foods ('olive stones and cheese and salami rinds') convey **a sense of freedom and indulgence**. Although the couple's hedonistic life is communicated in obviously excessive terms ('Laid out by the torrents of the Guadalquivir'), Heaney's tone is somewhat dismissive. Is he suggesting that their relationship was mostly sensual back then?

'Instead' – the first word in stanza three – signals a turning point in the poet's thinking. Back in his familiar home surroundings, he recalls the rug that mattered most and should answer whatever doubts he had about the past. He has measured the development of their relationship in stages associated with special moments he and Marie shared. The line 'it's locked-park Sunday Belfast' conjures up memories of their early married life in the Tate's Avenue district. The sectarian 1960s was marked by dour

Protestant domination, a time when weekend pleasures were frowned upon and even the public parks were closed. Despite such routine repression and the unromantic setting ('A walled back yard, the dust-bins high and silent'), **the atmosphere is sexually charged**.

Heaney is aware of the scene's **underlying drama**; the seconds tick by 'As a page is turned, a finger twirls warm hair'. The unfaltering nature of the couple's intimacy is evident in the resounding declaration: 'nothing gives on the rug or the ground beneath it'.

This notion of confidence in their relationship is carried through into stanza four and accentuated by the alliterative 'I lay at my length and felt the lumpy earth'. The resolute rhythm is strengthened by the robust adjectival phrase 'Keen-sensed' and the insistent statement: 'But never shifted off the plaid square once'. Heaney builds to a discreet and understated climax in the finely balanced last line: 'When we moved I had your measure and you had mine'. While there are erotic undertones throughout, the poet presents us with restrained realism in place of excessive sensuality. 'Tate's Avenue' is a **beautiful, unembarrassed poem of romantic and sexual love within a committed relationship**. Characteristically, when Heaney touches on personal relationships, he produces the most tender and passionate emotions.

✒ Writing About the Poem

'Seamus Heaney's poetry frequently explores intense relationships in a style that is fresh and innovative.' Discuss this statement with reference to 'Tate's Avenue'.

Sample Paragraph

'Tate's Avenue' is one of Heaney's most romantic poems. The poet traces the progress of his relationship with his wife through recalling three rugs that mark stages in their lives together. The breathless nature of early courtship is revealed in the colour ('sepia-coloured', reminiscent of an old photo) and texture ('vestal folds unfolded') of the first rug. Yet the strong physical attraction is revealed through sibilance and personification, 'Spread on sand by the sea but breathing land-breaths'. An emphatic 'Not' adds to the drama of the poem as the first two rugs are rejected. The adverb 'Instead' signals the decision to choose a 'plaid square' to truly sum up their feelings. The poem concludes in a wonderful sense of unity between the lovers, 'I had your measure and you had mine'. Overall, restrained, sensuous tension is presented in this lively study of intimacy.

EXAMINER'S COMMENT

An excellent top-grade response that shows a very good understanding of this unusual love poem. Detailed examination of language use (dramatic settings, contrasting atmospheres, energetic imagery and aural effects) is supported by apt and accurate quotations. Expression is also skilfully controlled and the paragraph is well rounded off in the concise final sentence.

✒ Class/Homework Exercises

1. 'Heaney's poetry realistically depicts people and places through carefully chosen language and imagery.' Discuss this view with reference to 'Tate's Avenue'.
2. 'Seamus Heaney's poems are often filled with vivid sensuousness and evocative description.' Discuss this statement with reference to 'Tate's Avenue'.

⊙ Points to Consider

- Tender, compelling poem celebrates love in a committed relationship.

- Precise, vibrant details illustrate the various scenes.

- The headlong rush of young love is conveyed in the enjambment of the second quatrain.

- In contrast, the more measured pace of mature love is found in the final stanza.

- Compound words, onomatopoeia, alliteration and assonance create a rich aural texture.

- Compact four-quatrain structure adds to the understated quality of the poem.

12 The Pitchfork

SEAMUS HEANEY

Of all implements, the pitchfork was the one
That came near to an imagined perfection:
When he tightened his raised hand and aimed with it,
It felt like a javelin, accurate and light.

So whether he played the warrior or the athlete   5
Or worked in earnest in the chaff and sweat,
He loved its grain of tapering, dark-flecked ash
Grown satiny from its own natural polish.

Riveted steel, turned timber, burnish, grain,
Smoothness, straightness, roundness, length and sheen.   10
Sweat-cured, sharpened, balanced, tested, fitted.
The springiness, the clip and dart of it.

And then when he thought of probes that reached the farthest,
He would see the shaft of a pitchfork sailing past
Evenly, imperturbably through space,   15
Its prongs starlit and absolutely soundless –

But has learned at last to follow that simple lead
Past its own aim, out to an other side
Where perfection – or nearness to it – is imagined
Not in the aiming but the opening hand.   20

javelin: long spear thrown in a competitive sport, also used as a weapon.

chaff: husks of grain separated from the seed.
grain: wheat.
tapering: reducing in thickness towards one end.

Riveted: fastened.
burnish: the shine on a polished surface.

clip: clasp; smack (colloquial).
dart: follow-on movement; small pointed missile thrown as a weapon.
probes: unmanned, exploratory spacecraft; a small measuring or testing device.
imperturbably: calmly, smoothly; unable to be upset.
prongs: two or more projecting points on a fork.

'When he tightened his raised hand and aimed with it'

👤 Personal Response

1. What is the tone of this poem? Does it change or not? Refer closely to the text in your response.
2. Select one image (or one line) that you find particularly interesting. Briefly explain your choice.
3. What do you think about the ending of this poem? Do you consider it visionary or far-fetched? Give reasons for your answer.

👁 Critical Literacy

'The Pitchfork' was published in Heaney's 1991 collection, *Seeing Things*. These poems turn to the earlier concerns of the poet. Craft and natural skill, the innate ability to make art out of work, is seen in many of his poems, such as 'The Forge'. Heaney is going back, making 'a journey back into the heartland of the ordinary'. The poet is now both observer and visionary.

In stanza one, Heaney describes a pitchfork, an ordinary farming 'implement'. Through **looking at an ordinary object with intense concentration**, the result is a fresh 'seeing', where the ordinary and mundane become marvellous, 'imagined perfection'. For Heaney, the creative impulse was held in the hand, in the skill of the labourer ('tightened his raised hand and aimed with it'). This skill is similar to the skill of the poet. They both practise and refine their particular ability. The pitchfork is now transformed into a piece of sporting equipment, 'a javelin'. The heaviness of physical work falls away as it becomes 'accurate and light' due to the practised capability of the worker. This is similar to the lightness of being and the **freeing of the poet's spirit** that Heaney allows himself to experience in this collection of poetry.

The worker is described as sometimes playing 'the warrior or the athlete' (stanza two). **Both professions command respect** and both occupations require courage and skill. But the worker's work is also described realistically, 'worked in earnest in the chaff and sweat'. This is heavy manual labour, and Heaney does not shirk from its unpleasant side. However, the worker is not ground down by it because he 'loved' the beauty of the pitchfork. Here we see both the poet and the worker dazzled, as the intent observation of the humble pitchfork unleashes its beauty, its slender 'dark-flecked ash'. The shine of the handle is conveyed in the word 'satiny'. Such tactile language allows the reader to feel the smooth, polished wooden handle. Now three pairs of eyes (the worker's, the poet's and our own) observe the pitchfork.

Close scrutiny of the pitchfork in stanza three continues with a virtuoso display of description, as **each detail is lovingly depicted**, almost like a slow sequence of close-ups in a film. The meeting of the handle and fork is caught in the phrase 'Riveted steel'. The beauty of the wood is evoked in the alliteration of 'turned timber'. The marvellous qualities of the wood are itemised with growing wonder: its shine ('burnish'), its pattern ('grain'). It is as if the worker and the poet are twirling the pitchfork round as they exclaim over its 'Smoothness, straightness, roundness, length and sheen'. This is more like the description one would give to a work of art or a thoroughbred animal than to a farm implement. The skill that went into the making of the pitchfork is now explored in a list of verbs beginning with the compound word 'Sweat-cured'. This **graphically shows the sheer physical exertion that went into making this instrument**, as it was 'sharpened, balanced, tested, fitted'. The tactile quality of the pitchfork is praised: 'The springiness, the clip and dart of it'. The worker, just like the athlete or warrior, tests his equipment.

In stanza four, the labourer imagines space 'probes' searching the galaxy, 'reached the farthest'. **The long line stretches out in imitation of space**, which pushes out to infinity. The pitchfork now becomes transformed into a spaceship, 'sailing past/Evenly, imperturbably through space'. This ordinary pitchfork now shines like the metal casing of a spaceship, 'starlit', and moves, like the spacecraft, through the vastness of outer space, 'absolutely soundless'.

Stanza five shows the poet becoming a mediator between different states, actual and imagined, ordinary and fantastical. He stands on a threshold, philosophising about the nature of his observation as a familiar thing grows stranger. Together (poet, worker and reader), all follow the line of the pitchfork to 'an other side', a place where 'perfection' is 'imagined'. Perfection does not exist in our world. But it is not the 'tightened' hand, which was 'aiming' at the beginning of the poem, which will achieve this ideal state, but the 'opening hand' of the last stanza. Is the poet suggesting we must be open and ready to receive in order to achieve 'perfection'? Heaney states: '**look at the familiar things you know. Look at them with ... a quality of concentration ... you will be rewarded with insights and visions**.'

✒ Writing About the Poem

'In celebrating traditional rural crafts in his poetry, Heaney reveals his own skills as a master craftsman of the written word.' Discuss this view with reference to 'The Pitchfork'.

POETRY FOCUS

Sample Paragraph

'The Pitchfork' is based on a treasured memory of Heaney's father who spent his life working on the family farm in Co. Derry. The poem begins with a dynamic image as Heaney remembers his father in an idealised way, holding the fork 'like a javelin'. In his innocent eyes, his father was god-like – 'imagined perfection'. Hard 't' sounds suggest the father's strength in handling the pitchfork with confidence. The sense of deep respect for the traditional work of the farm as well as for his father is found in the tone of admiration when Heaney imagines the older man playing 'the warrior or the athlete'. The poet moves from describing the everyday activity of gathering in the hay to a visionary level as the fork hangs in the air, 'starlit and absolutely soundless'. He transforms the implement into a mysterious spacecraft. Through his own precise language skills, Heaney celebrates the working life of the father he idealised.

EXAMINER'S COMMENT

Clear, top-grade response tackling all elements of the question and showing a good understanding of the poem. Impressive awareness of Heaney's expertise with language (particularly imagery, tone and sound effects). Focused quotations are used effectively to support key points and the expression is varied and well controlled.

✒ Class/Homework Exercises

1. 'Seamus Heaney's poetry addresses thought-provoking themes in language that is both realistic and mystical.' Discuss this view with reference to 'The Pitchfork'.
2. 'In Heaney's most compelling poems, ordinary objects are lovingly and exactly described.' Discuss this statement with particular reference to 'The Pitchfork'.

⊙ Points to Consider

- Exploration of commitment, craft and creativity.
- Focus on physical details in the first four stanzas.
- Impact of cinematic imagery and energetic rhythm.
- Sudden change of pace and mood in the last stanza.
- Compelling ending reinforces poet's devotion to generosity and acceptance.

| 148

13 🔊 Lightenings viii

Lightenings: insights, transcendent experiences.

SEAMUS HEANEY

The annals say: when the monks of Clonmacnoise
Were all at prayers inside the oratory
A ship appeared above them in the air.

The anchor dragged along behind so deep
It hooked itself into the altar rails   5
And then, as the big hull rocked to a standstill,

A crewman shinned and grappled down the rope
And struggled to release it. But in vain.
'This man can't bear our life here and will drown,'

The abbot said, 'unless we help him.' So   10
They did, the freed ship sailed, and the man climbed back
Out of the marvellous as he had known it.

annals: monastic records.
Clonmacnoise: established in the sixth century, the monastery at Clonmacnoise was renowned as a centre of scholarship and spirituality.
oratory: place of prayer, small chapel.

shinned: climbed down, clambered.

abbot: head of the monastery.

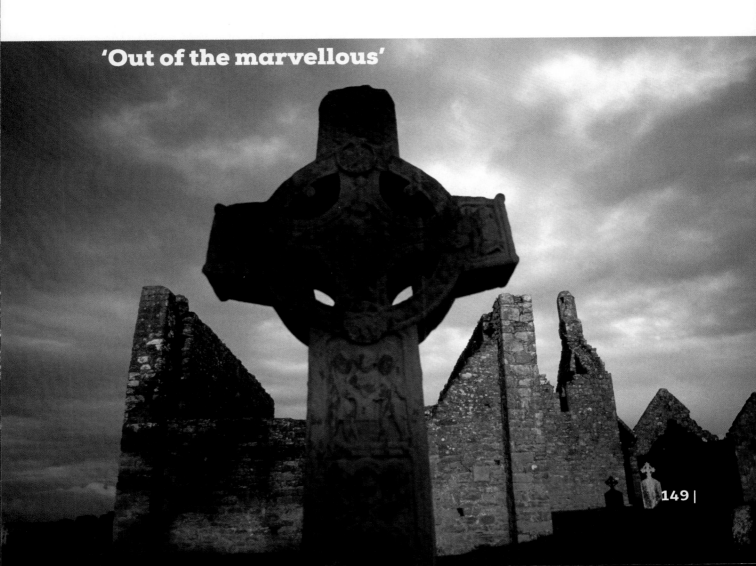

'Out of the marvellous'

👤 Personal Response

1. How is the surreal atmosphere conveyed in this poem? Quote in support of your response.
2. Choose one striking image from the poem and comment on its effectiveness.
3. In your view, what does the air-ship symbolise? Refer to the text in your answer.

👁 Critical Literacy

Written in four tercets (three-line stanzas), 'Lightenings viii' (from Seamus Heaney's 1991 collection, *Seeing Things*), tells a legendary story of a miraculous air-ship which once appeared to the monks at Clonmacnoise, Co. Offaly. Heaney has said: 'I was devoted to this poem because the crewman who appears is situated where every poet should be situated: between the ground of everyday experience and the airier realm of an imagined world.'

Heaney's matter-of-fact approach at the start of stanza one leads readers to expect a straightforward retelling of an incident recorded in the 'annals' of the monastery. The story's apparently scholarly source seems highly reliable. While they were at prayers, the monks looked up: 'A ship appeared above them in the air'. We assume that the oratory is open to the sky. The simplicity of the colloquial language, restrained tone and run-through lines all ease us into a **dreamlike world** where anything can happen. But as with all good narratives, the magic ship's sudden appearance raises many questions: Why is it there? Where has it come from? Is this strange story all a dream?

Then out of the air-ship came a massive anchor, which 'dragged along behind so deep' (stanza two) before lodging itself in the altar rails. The poet makes **effective choices in syntax (word order) and punctuation**, e.g. placing 'so deep' at the end of the line helps to emphasise the meaning. The moment when the ship shudders to a halt is skilfully caught in a carefully wrought image: 'as the big hull rocked to a standstill'.

A crewman clambered down the rope to try to release the anchor, but he is unsuccessful. Heaney chooses his words carefully: 'shinned', 'grappled', 'struggled' (stanza three) are all powerful verbs, helping to create a clear picture of the sailor's physical effort. The phrase 'But in vain' is separated from the rest of the line to emphasise the man's hopelessness. The contrasting worlds of magic and reality seem incompatible. Ironically, the story's turning point is the abbot's instant recognition that the **human, earthly atmosphere will be fatal to the visitor**: 'This man can't bear our life here and will drown'.

But a solution is at hand: 'unless we help him' (stanza four). The unconditional generosity of the monks comes naturally to them: 'So/They did'. The word 'So' creates a pause and uncertainty before the prompt, brief opening of the next line: 'They did'. When the anchor is eventually disentangled and 'the freed ship sailed', **the crewman will surely tell his travel companions about the strange beings he encountered** after he 'climbed back out of the marvellous as he had known it'. This last line is somewhat surprising and leaves the reader wondering – marvelling, even.

Heaney's poem certainly raises interesting questions, blurring the lines between reality and illusion, and challenging our ideas about human consciousness. **The story itself can be widely interpreted**. Is the ship a symbol of inspiration while the monks represent commitment and dedication? Presumably, as chroniclers of the annals (preserving texts on paper for posterity), they were not aware of the miracle of their own labours – crossing the barrier from the oral tradition to written records – which was to astonish the world in the forthcoming centuries and help spread human knowledge.

'Lightenings viii' is a beautiful poem that highlights the fact that **the ordinary and the miraculous are categories defined only by human perception**. For many readers, the boat serves as an abstract mirror image, reversing our usual way of seeing things. In Heaney's rich text, we discover that from the outsider's perspective, the truly marvellous consists not of the visionary or mystical experience, but of the seemingly ordinary experience.

✒ Writing About the Poem

'Heaney's evocative language often makes room for everyday miracles and otherworldly wisdom.' Discuss this statement with reference to 'Lightenings viii'.

Sample Paragraph

Heaney's poem 'Lightenings viii' is an account of a surreal experience when the Clonmacnoise monks imagined a ship above them in the sky. Heaney's tone is dreamlike – particularly the narrative style. The long lines and broad vowel sounds suggest an unhurried atmosphere where anything can happen – 'as the big hull rocked to a standstill'. The monks believe that the mysterious sailors have come out 'of the marvellous' – but the stranded sailors see the monks in the same way. Indeed, their rescue is arranged by the abbot. The poet seems to be saying that everything in life can be viewed as a wonder. The abbot chooses to save the desperate crewman – 'This man can't bear our life here and will drown'. For me, this is the poet's central lesson – we should help others when we can. If we do, then our lives will be filled with everyday miracles.

✒ Class/Homework Exercises

1. 'Heaney's poetic world is one of wonder and mystery that is matched by the energy of his language.' Discuss this view with reference to 'Lightenings viii'.
2. 'Many of Seamus Heaney's poems communicate intense observations through thought-provoking images and symbolism.' Discuss this statement with reference to both the subject matter and style of 'Lightenings viii'.

⊙ Points to Consider

- Characteristic narrative style and use of colloquial language.

- Dramatic qualities – characters, setting, tension, dialogue, resolution.

- The poem is concerned with visionary experiences, yet rooted in the physical world.

- Effective use of vivid imagery, assonance, powerful verbs.

- Contrasting worlds – mundane monks and magical sailors.

Sample Leaving Cert Questions on Heaney's Poetry

1. **Discuss how Heaney uses detailed observation and a reflective tone to address aspects of identity and belonging in his poetry. Develop your response with reference to themes and language evident in the poems by Seamus Heaney on your course.**
2. **'Heaney frequently reveals a deep sense of love and loss through the effective use of evocative language in his poetry.' Develop your response with reference to the poems by Seamus Heaney on your course.**
3. **'Heaney creates memorable characters often in dramatic settings, to explore experiences of great emotional intensity.' Develop your response with reference to the poems by Seamus Heaney on your course.**

How do I organise my answer?

(Sample question 2)

'Heaney frequently reveals a deep sense of love and loss through the effective use of evocative language in his poetry.' Develop your response with reference to the poems by Seamus Heaney on your course.

Sample Plan 1

Intro: *(Stance: agree with viewpoint in the question)* Heaney's poetry discloses aspects of love and loss in relationships with people, places and culture. Using vivid imagery, mythical reference, colloquial speech, personification and comparisons, the poet invites readers to share these intense experiences.

Point 1: *(Love of home and family – visual and aural imagery)* 'Mossbawn: Sunlight' recreates the rural idyll of Heaney's childhood home through effective similes ('the sun stood/like a griddle cooling'). Detailed visual and aural effects ('floury apron', 'scuffled') paint a picture of Heaney's beloved Aunt Mary at work in the kitchen.

Point 2: *(Loss of love – mythical allusion/dynamic verbs)* 'The Underground' uses the myth of Orpheus and Eurydice to describe the breathless dash of two lovers to a concert in London, widening the appeal from the personal to the universal. Dramatic verbs convey the headlong rush of each lover ('speeding', 'gaining').

Understanding the Prescribed Poetry Question

Marks are awarded using the PCLM Marking Scheme:
P = 15; C = 15; L = 15; M = 5
Total = 50

- **P** (Purpose = 15 marks) refers to the set question and is the launch pad for the answer. This involves engaging with all aspects of the question. Both theme and language must be addressed, although not necessarily equally.
- **C** (Coherence = 15 marks) refers to the organisation of the developed response and the use of accurate, relevant quotation. Paragraphing is essential.
- **L** (Language = 15 marks) refers to the student's skill in controlling language throughout the answer.
- **M** (Mechanics = 5 marks) refers to spelling and grammar.
- Although no specific number of poems is required, students usually discuss at least 3 or 4 in their written responses.
- Aim for at least 800 words, to be completed within 45–50 minutes.

NOTE

In keeping with the PCLM approach, the student has to take a stance by agreeing, disagreeing or partially agreeing that Heaney's:

- **deep sense of love and loss** (love of family, friends, places and people; lost culture, lost love, lost memories, change, etc.)

... is revealed through:

- **effective use of evocative language** (vivid visual/ aural imagery, personification, mythical allusions, striking comparisons, dark humour, cinematic detail, colloquial speech, varying tones/ atmospheres, innovative poetic structures, etc.)

Point 3: *(Love/passing time – colloquial speech/personification)* 'A Call' details the personal narrative of a phone call home. Colloquial language ('Hold on') sets the mood. Rich vowels recreate the inescapable passage of time ('amplified grave ticking of hall clocks'). Effective personification evokes the universal experience of death ('Death would summon Everyman').

Point 4: *(Vanished memory/change – unusual comparisons, poetic structure)* 'Bogland' is the container of lost memories and culture ('Great Irish Elk', 'Butter sunk'). Aural imagery captures the nature of the ever-changing bog ('Melting and opening'). Poetic structure mirrors act of digging peat.

Conclusion: Heaney offers vivid, evocative descriptions of cherished memories of intense love and loss. The poet's skilful use of language reveals these experiences with exactness.

Sample Paragraph: Point 4

For Heaney, 'Bogland' is the holder of lost memories and culture. Heaney sees Ireland's peat bogs as both concealing and revealing the past. These bogs record the transitions in natural history – 'the Great Irish Elk', 'waterlogged trunks'. Long forgotten Celtic traditions are revealed, 'Butter sunk under … recovered salty and white'. Soft 'm' and 's' sounds suggest the moving, oozing nature of the bog, 'Melting', 'Missing'. Lost history is preserved in the bog, waiting to be discovered, 'Every layer they strip/Seems camped on before'. Heaney's clever poetic structure is used to mirror the neat piles of turf on the bogland through a series of short lines and stacked stanzas, a nostalgic memory of a lost age. The endless search for the past is conveyed in a tone of aching longing, 'The wet centre is bottomless'.

EXAMINER'S COMMENT

An insightful response that directly responds to the question and shows excellent understanding of the poem. Heaney's skilful use of sound and structure to express feelings of loss is very well illustrated. Expression throughout is impressive and quotations are carefully integrated into the answer. An assured top-grade standard.

(Sample question 3)

'Heaney creates memorable characters often in dramatic settings, to explore experiences of great emotional intensity.' Develop your response with reference to the poems by Seamus Heaney on your course.

NOTE

In keeping with the PCLM approach, the student has to explore poems of Heaney's on the course that include:

– **memorable characters often in dramatic settings** (real people from the poet's past, striking natural landscape, cultural/political tensions in Northern Ireland, etc.)

… to explore:

– **experiences of great emotional intensity** (feelings of love, fear, wonder, etc. heightened by sensuous imagery, vivid details, striking comparisons, energetic sound effects, engaging conversational language, evocative tones, mythical allusions, etc.)

Sample Plan 2

Intro: *(Stance: agree with viewpoint in the question)* Heaney's autobiographical poems create unforgettable characters in powerful settings. Intense memories of meaningful encounters with people and experiences expressed through visual and aural imagery, contrast, cinematic detail, dark humour and dramatic dialogue.

Point 1: *(Dramatic encounter with RUC policeman – imagery, dialogue)* 'A Constable Calls' recreates an uneasy meeting between the poet's father and an RUC policeman at a time of tense relations between Ulster's two cultures ('the boot of the law'). Terse dialogue ('Any other root crops?') and ominous repetition ('the bicycle ticked, ticked, ticked') capture the oppressive atmosphere.

Point 2: *(Absent wife/exotic location – sensuous imagery/edgy humour)* 'The Skunk' is a playful love poem to his wife using an irreverent image of the pompous little animal ('damasked like the chasuble/At a funeral mass'). Sensuous language conjures up the exotic setting ('Tang of eucalyptus') and desperate longing ('aftermath of a mouthful of wine/Was like inhaling you off a cold pillow').

Point 3: *(Dead father – metaphor, dynamic verbs)* 'The Harvest Bow' brings to life Heaney's reticent father ('tongue-tied') carefully creating the harvest bow ('tightens twist by twist'). Onomatopoeic verbs convey restless energy ('Beats out'). Natural setting reflecting the deep love between father and son nostalgically captured, the memory 'still warm' ('I see us walk').

Point 4: *(Personal relationship – striking contrasts, cinematic detail)* 'Tate's Avenue' describes the evolving relationship between Heaney and his wife through the image of a car rug. Young hedonistic love in an exotic location is shown in the cinematic close-up of a picnic. Mature love ('nothing gives') is sharply contrasted through dour description of the confines ('walled back yard') of a Sunday in Belfast.

Conclusion: Heaney presents memorable characters in dramatic locations and uses a range of language techniques to investigate experiences of intense emotional depth.

Sample Paragraph: Point 3

In 'The Harvest Bow', Heaney creates a precise description of his father, a reserved Irish farmer ('tongue-tied'). The reserved man's artistic skill in crafting 'A throwaway love-knot of straw' is eloquently conveyed through alliteration ('tightened twist by twist'). The intricate harvest bow symbolises the natural bond between father and son. It awakens precious memories of the poet who spies 'into its golden loops'. He remembers their walk in the quiet countryside in the stillness of an Irish evening 'of long grass and midges'. Sensuous sibilant sounds suggest the bittersweet sense of past times and the love they once experienced. Heaney's father may be gone but his memory lives 'still warm' in the 'frail device' of the harvest bow 'pinned up' on the poet's kitchen dresser.

EXAMINER'S COMMENT

A successful top-grade paragraph that focuses on both parts of the question (characters in dramatic settings and intense emotion). The response shows a real appreciation of Heaney's poetic techniques, particularly his use of descriptive details and sound effects. Apt quotes are used effectively to support discussion points and there is assured expression throughout.

EXAM FOCUS

- As you may not be familiar with some of the poems referred to in the sample plans, substitute poems that you have studied closely.
- Key points about a particular poem can be developed over more than one paragraph.
- Paragraphs may also include cross-referencing and discussion of more than one poem.
- Remember that there is no single 'correct' answer to poetry questions, so always be confident in expressing your own considered response.

Leaving Cert Sample Essay

Discuss how Heaney uses detailed observation and a reflective tone to address aspects of identity and belonging in his poetry. Develop your response with reference to the themes and language evident in the poems by Seamus Heaney on your course.

Sample Essay

1. Seamus Heaney, growing up in Co. Derry, inherited a divided identity. He occupied the in-between space of Irish identity resulting from centuries of conflict with England and sectarian disagreement between Protestant and Catholic. 'The Forge' and 'The Pitchfork' are rooted in his rural Irish upbringing. Alienation and conflict are themes explored in 'The Tollund

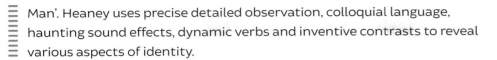
Man'. Heaney uses precise detailed observation, colloquial language, haunting sound effects, dynamic verbs and inventive contrasts to reveal various aspects of identity.

2. In 'The Forge', Heaney reflects on a disappearing way of life. This scene from his childhood is lovingly recreated from closely observed details. The untidy pile of discarded objects, 'old axles and iron hoops rusting', recalls an earlier time when people depended on horse transport. We get a sense of a very different and simpler way of living among Ireland's farming community. Onomatopoeic verbs, 'short-pitched ring', 'hiss', bring the forge to life and reveal the skill of the blacksmith to 'beat real iron out'. Flashes of light erupt in a forceful image, 'The unpredictable fantail of sparks'. Heaney's aural effects and vivid images emphasise the poet's deep-rooted belonging in this Irish rural society.

3. Heaney also explores his own identity as a poet in this poem. The blacksmith's anvil sits proudly at the centre of the forge, 'Horned as a unicorn'. It seems to possess magical powers that can transform things. The poet, like the blacksmith, makes patterns with words. Each man 'expends himself in shape and music' in a creative act. Heaney is claiming his place in the literary tradition of poetry. The poet is 'immoveable' and like the anvil, he is at home here.

4. 'The Tollund Man' compares ancient and modern conflict. Heaney imagines that 'Some day I will go to Aarhus', the museum in Denmark, to see the remains of the executed Iron Age man. He establishes the man's individuality, using a vivid metaphor to show the victim's gentle innocence, 'The mild pods of his eye-lids'. He enables readers to experience the man's fear as he 'rode the tumbril'. The poet considers the names of the places he might pass on his car journey to Aarhus, 'Tollund, Grauballe', the very same places the Tollund Man passed on his final journey. Both men share a history of experiencing violence in Jutland and Northern Ireland, and 'feel lost' in 'man-killing parishes'.

5. The harsh alliterative phrase, 'tightened her torc on him', highlights the cruelty of the ritual killing, sacrificed to a pagan goddess. Focusing on this victim of the goddess allows Heaney to reflect on the victims of a more recent conflict in Northern Ireland. The reality of sectarian division is conveyed through another jarring alliterative phrase, 'Tell-tale skin and teeth' of four murdered 'young brothers'. The poet compares the Tollund Man's sacrifice for his people to the murdered brothers sacrificed back home. They are hoping their lives might mean something and in the end benefit their local community and country. The experience of the Tollund Man has helped Heaney clarify his own identity. They have both experienced violent pasts. He now feels as 'Unhappy and at home' in the murderous bogs of Jutland as he does in his native Ulster back home.

INDICATIVE MATERIAL

- **Heaney's detailed observation and reflective tone** (descriptive details, vivid sensuous images, aural effects, inventive contrasts, personal narratives, variety of tones – introspective, insightful, elegiac, nostalgic, romantic, inspirational, etc.)

... addresses:

- **aspects of identity and belonging** (sense of the past, Irish cultural identity and nationalism, landscape and placenames, autobiographical focus on real people at home and abroad, etc.)

6. Heaney's vivid memory of his father working the land inspires his poem 'The Pitchfork'. He observes his father working 'in earnest in the chaff and sweat'. The ordinary becomes transformed into the extraordinary, his pitchfork 'imagined perfection'. Once again, Heaney is not only claiming his place in the rural Irish tradition, but his individuality as poet. In this poem, both father and son practise their skill so that their everyday work becomes 'accurate and light'. A close-up image allows us to observe the pitchfork's 'Riveted steel, turned timber, burnish, grain'.

7. Heaney's language also appeals to our sense of touch as he describes the feel of the pitchfork in his father's hand, 'The springiness, the clip and dart of it'. Soft alliteration describes the labourer's dream of 'Its prongs starlit and absolutely soundless'. As he remembers his father quietly working in the field, Heaney reflects on how everyday activities can become mysterious and timeless through the power of the imagination.

8. Identity and belonging are explored by Heaney through reflective reconstructions of rural Irish life, through his detailed observations of people, places and agricultural implements. His identity as poet causes him to understand his place as a native of a divided society. Heaney believed in the power of poetry to know who you are and where you belong.

(745 words)

EXAMINER'S COMMENT

A solid critical response, showing good engagement with Heaney's poetry. Sustained focus on the use of detailed observation and reflection to address aspects of identity. Impressive commentary on stylistic features (sound effects, imagery and tone) in paragraphs 2, 4 and 7. The discussion is supported by accurate quotation ranging over several poems. Points are generally well-developed – although there is some repetition in paragraph 5. Overall, expression is clear (e.g. 'deep-rooted belonging in this Irish rural society', 'The ordinary becomes transformed into the extraordinary') adding to the essay's top-grade standard.

GRADE: H1
P = 15/15
C = 14/15
L = 13/15
M = 5/5
Total = 47/50

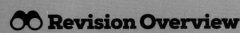 # Revision Overview

'The Forge'
Sonnet celebrating traditional rural crafts and exploring the mysterious creative process of achieving poetic identity.

'Bogland'
Ireland's boglands function as a metaphor for the poet's search to find his national identity.

'The Tollund Man'
In responding to the violence in Northern Ireland during the 1970s, Heaney draws parallels with earlier victims in Jutland.

'Mossbawn: Sunlight'
Reflective recollection of the poet's childhood and the loving relationship he had with his Aunt Mary.

'A Constable Calls'
Coming-of-age experience illustrating the divisions between Northern Irish Catholics and the Protestant community.

'The Skunk'
In this celebration of enduring love, the poet uses an affectionately teasing tone to express how he feels about his wife.

'The Harvest Bow'
A tender exploration of the father/son relationship and the unspoken understanding between them.

'The Underground'
Beautiful love poem that draws upon myth to revisit a hectic scene from the poet's honeymoon.

'Postscript'
The poet's description of experiencing transcendent beauty in the natural Irish landscape evokes powerful feelings.

'A Call'
Elegiac reflection on the passing of time and the poet's complex relationship with his father.

'Tate's Avenue'
Memories of particular places and moods are central to this poem which explores the theme of love in all of its richness.

'The Pitchfork'
Vivid recollection of rural life and the way everyday objects can become more than themselves through the power of the imagination.

'Lightenings viii'
In this curious and thought-provoking poem, Heaney makes room for everyday miracles and otherworldly wisdom.

Last Words

'A poet for whom sound is crucial, who relishes the way words and consonants knock around.'
Tim Nolan

'Heaney has achieved a hard-won clarity of vision.'
Heather Clark

'The best moments are those when your mind seems to implode and words and images rush of their own accord into the vortex.'
Seamus Heaney

 NATURE LOVE IDENTITY CREATIVITY CONFLICT PLACES HISTORY/ MEMORY RELATIONSHIPS WONDER

Gerard Manley Hopkins

1844–1889

'Every poet must be original.'

Gerard Manley Hopkins, a priest and poet, was born in Stratford, outside London, in 1844. In 1863 he began studying classics at Balliol College, Oxford, where he wrote a great deal of poetry. Hopkins converted to Catholicism and was later ordained a Jesuit priest in 1877. It was while studying for the priesthood that he wrote some of his best-known religious and nature poems, including 'The Windhover' and 'Pied Beauty'. His compressed style of writing, especially his experimental use of language, sound effects and inventive rhythms, combined to produce distinctive and startling poetry. In 1884 Hopkins was appointed Professor of Greek at University College, Dublin. He disliked living in Ireland, where he experienced failing health and severe depression. In 1885 he wrote a number of the so-called 'terrible sonnets', including 'No Worst, There is None', which have desolation at their core. Hopkins died of typhoid fever in June 1889 without ever publishing any of his major poems. He is buried in Glasnevin Cemetery.

Investigate Further

To find out more about Gerard Manley Hopkins, or to hear readings of his poems, you could search some useful websites, such as YouTube, BBC Poetry, poetryfoundation.org and poetryarchive.org, or access additional material on this page of your eBook.

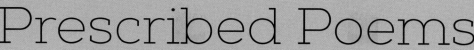

Prescribed Poems

GERARD MANLEY HOPKINS

(OL) indicates poems that are also prescribed for the Ordinary Level course.

1 God's Grandeur

The world is charged with the grandeur of God.
   It will flame out, like shining from shook foil;
   It gathers to a greatness, like the ooze of oil
Crushed. Why do men then now not reck his rod?
Generations have trod, have trod, have trod;   5
   And all is seared with trade; bleared, smeared with toil;
   And wears man's smudge and shares man's smell: the soil
Is bare now, nor can foot feel, being shod.

And for all this, nature is never spent;
   There lives the dearest freshness deep down things;   10
And though the last lights off the black West went
   Oh, morning, at the brown brink eastward, springs –
Because the Holy Ghost over the bent
   World broods with warm breast and with ah! bright wings.

charged: powered; made responsible.
foil: shimmering gold or silver.

Crushed: compressed from olives or linseed.
reck his rod: pay heed to God's power.

seared: scorched; ruined.
bleared: blurred.
toil: industrialisation.

shod: covered; protected.

spent: exhausted.

last lights: the setting sun.

Note: Hopkins's philosophy emphasised the uniqueness of every natural thing, which he called inscape. He believed that there was a special connection between the world of nature and an individual's consciousness. Hopkins viewed the world as an integrated network created by God. The sensation of inscape (which the poet termed 'instress') is the appreciation that everything has its own unique identity. The concept is similar to that of epiphanies in James Joyce's writing.

'nature is never spent'

👤 Personal Response

1. Describe Hopkins's tone in the first four lines of this poem. Refer closely to the text in your answer.
2. How are human beings portrayed in the poem? Support your points with reference.
3. Select two unusual images the poet uses. Comment on the effectiveness of each.

👁 Critical Literacy

Hopkins wrote many Italian (or Petrarchan) sonnets (consisting of an octave and a sestet). The form suited the stages in the argumentative direction of his themes. Like many other Christian poets, he 'found' God in nature. His poetry is also notable for its use of sprung rhythm (an irregular movement or pace which echoed ordinary conversation). 'God's Grandeur' is typical of Hopkins in both its subject matter and style. The condensed language, elaborate wordplay and unusual syntax – sometimes like a tongue-twister – can be challenging.

The poem's opening quatrain (four-line section) is characteristically dynamic. The **metaphor ('charged') compares God's greatness to electric power**, brilliant but hazardous. The visual effect of 'flame out' and 'shook foil' develops this representation of God's constant presence in the world. The image of oozing oil signifies a natural richness. The reference to electricity makes a subtle reappearance in line 4, where the 'rod' of an angry Creator is likened to a lightning bolt. The tone is one of energised celebration, but there is also a growing frustration: 'Why do men then now not reck his rod?' Hopkins seems mystified at human indifference to God's greatness.

The second quatrain is much more critical. We can sense the poet's own weariness with the numberless generations who have abandoned their spiritual salvation for the flawed material benefits of 'trade' and 'toil'. Hopkins's laboured repetition of 'have trod' is purposely heavy-handed. The internal rhymes of the negative verbs ('seared', 'bleared' and 'smeared') in line 6 convey his deep sense of disgust at a world blighted by industry and urbanisation. **Humankind's neglect of the natural environment is closely linked to the drift away from God**. Hopkins symbolises this spiritual alienation through the image of the 'shod' foot out of touch with nature and its Creator.

However, in response to his depression, the mood changes in the sestet (the final six lines of the sonnet). Hopkins's tone softens considerably, aided by the gentle, sibilant effect in line 10: 'There lives the dearest freshness deep down things'. As in many of his religious poems, he takes comfort in conventional Christian belief. For him, 'nature is never spent'. The world is

filled with 'freshness' that confirms God's presence. This **power of renewal** is exemplified in the way morning never fails to follow the 'last lights' of dark night.

The reassuring image in the last line is of God guarding the world and promising rebirth and salvation. The source of this constant regeneration is 'the Holy Ghost' (God's grace) who 'broods' over a dependent world with the patient devotion of a bird protecting its young. In expressing his faith and surrendering himself to divine will, the poet can truly appreciate the grandeur of God. The final exclamations ('Oh, morning' and 'ah! bright wings') echo Hopkins's **sense of euphoria**.

✒ Writing About the Poem

'Hopkins's original voice explores God's presence in this weary world.' Discuss this statement, with particular reference to the poem 'God's Grandeur'.

Sample Paragraph

EXAMINER'S COMMENT

A solid discussion on Hopkins's twin themes of God's power and man's indifference. There is a keen awareness of Hopkins's innovative use of language: 'A dynamic alliterative metaphor dramatically opens the poem'. Varied expressive language and accurate use of quotation also contribute to this top grade.

Hopkins uses the sonnet form to examine man's lack of awareness of the beauty of God's world. A dynamic alliterative metaphor dramatically opens the poem, 'The world is charged with the grandeur of God'. His power and brilliance are conveyed through references to electricity, 'It will flame out, like shining from shook foil'. Yet man remains unconcerned at God's lightning bolt and does 'not reck his rod'. The tone in the second quatrain suggests the drudgery of man's mechanical world. Industrialisation has 'smeared' God's glorious creation. The repetition of 'have trod' coupled with the verbs ('seared' and 'bleared') show the horrendous effects of urbanisation on both man and landscape. Hopkins suggests that man is no longer in touch with his natural environment. A gentler tone emerges in the sestet. Hopkins realises the power of nature to regenerate itself, 'nature is never spent'. I was impressed with Hopkins's religious belief expressed in the lovely natural image of the bird protecting its young, 'the Holy Ghost over the bent/World broods with warm breast'.

✒ Class/Homework Exercises

1. Comment on Hopkins's use of sound in this poem. Refer closely to the text in your answer.
2. Hopkins is a poet of intense emotion, ecstasy and distress. Discuss this view, tracing how the poet expresses intense emotions throughout 'God's Grandeur'.

⊙ Points to Consider

- Combination of conflicting emotions, ecstasy and distress.
- Natural world enlivened by God's presence.
- Assonance and alliteration emphasise despondency, humankind's neglect of natural environment associated with drift away from God.
- Belief in nature's ability to regenerate.
- Sonnet concludes with a benevolent image of Holy Ghost as benevolent mother bird.
- Tone becomes more reassuring in the sestet.

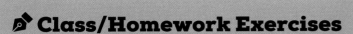

2 Spring

Nothing is so beautiful as Spring –
   When weeds, in wheels, shoot long and lovely and lush;
   Thrush's eggs look little low heavens, and thrush
Through the echoing timber does so rinse and wring
The ear, it strikes like lightnings to hear him sing;   5
   The glassy peartree leaves and blooms, they brush
   The descending blue; that blue is all in a rush
With richness; the racing lambs too have fair their fling.

What is all this juice and all this joy?
   A strain of the earth's sweet being in the beginning   10
In Eden garden. – Have, get, before it cloy,
   Before it cloud, Christ, lord, and sour with sinning,
Innocent mind and Mayday in girl and boy,
   Most, O maid's child, thy choice and worthy the winning.

in wheels: radiating out like spokes; rampant; pivoting movement.
lush: growing thickly, luxuriantly.
Thrush's eggs: songbird's eggs, which are light blue.
rinse: wash out with fresh water.
wring: to twist or squeeze; drain off excess water.

have fair their fling: the lambs are enjoying their freedom.

strain: a trace; streak; a segment of melody.

cloud: darken; depress.

Mayday: innocence of the young.
Most: the best choice.
maid's child: Jesus, son of Mary.

'Nothing is so beautiful as Spring'

👤 Personal Response

1. Describe Hopkins's tone in the first eight lines of the poem. Refer to the text in your response.

2. What is the mood in the second section of the poem? What reasons would you give for this change in the sestet? Use reference or quotation to support your point of view.

3. Write your own personal response to this poem, commenting on both the subject matter and style.

👁 Critical Literacy

'Spring' was written in May 1877. Hopkins had a special devotion to Mary, Queen of Heaven, and May is the month that is devoted to her. The poem was written after a holiday spent walking and writing poetry in Wales. Hopkins's emphatic language captures the exuberance of nature bursting into life.

The simple opening sentence in the first section, 'Nothing is so beautiful as Spring', is a deliberately exaggerated statement (hyperbole) used to emphasise a feeling. This Petrarchan sonnet's octet starts with an **ecstatic account of the blooming of nature in spring**. As we examine the poet's use of language, we can understand why it should be heard rather than read. Here in the second line – 'When weeds, in wheels, shoot long and lovely and lush' – the alliteration of 'w' and 'l', the assonance of 'ee' and the slow, broad vowels 'o' and 'u' add to this description of abundant growth. We can easily imagine the wild flowers growing before our eyes, as if caught by a slow-motion camera, uncurling and straightening to reach the heavens.

The **energy of the new plants** is contained in the verb 'shoot'. Just as the plants are shooting from the fertile earth, so one word seems to sprout out of another in the poem, e.g. 'thrush' springing from 'lush'. Now we are looking down, carefully examining a delicately beautiful sight among the long grasses: 'Thrush's eggs look little low heavens'. Note the speckled appearance of the eggs, similar to the dappling of blue and white in the sky. The oval shape is like the dome of the heavens.

The poet's **breathless excitement** at the sight of Heaven on earth is caught by the omission of the word 'like'. We hear the song of the bird as the assonance of 'rinse' and 'wring' fills our ears with strikingly rich sounds. It has a powerful effect, like a bolt of lightning. The focus shifts to the gleam on the leaves of the pear tree, as its 'glassy' appearance is observed. Hopkins looked closely at objects to try to capture their essence (inscape).

Hopkins **pushes language** to its boundaries as nouns become verbs ('leaves' and 'blooms'). The sky seems to bend down to reach the growing trees: 'they brush/The descending blue'. The blueness of the sky is captured in the alliteration of 'all in a rush/With richness'. Meanwhile, newborn lambs are frolicking happily, 'fair their fling'. This octet is a joyous exploration of a kaleidoscope of the colours, sounds and movement of spring. The poet's imagination soars as he strains language to convey the immediacy of the moment.

In the sestet, **the mood becomes reflective** as the poet considers the significance of nature: 'What is all this juice and all this joy?' As he meditates, he decides it is 'A strain of the earth's sweet being', a fleeting glimpse of a perfect world 'In Eden garden', before it was sullied with sin. Hopkins **had a deep love of God**, especially as the Creator. His tone becomes insistent as he urges God to grasp the world in order to preserve it in its perfect state. The hard 'c' sound of 'cloy' and 'cloud' shows how the beauty will become stained and imperfect if Christ does not act swiftly. Hopkins desires virtue and purity: 'innocence', 'Mayday in girl and boy'. He refers to Christ as Mary's child ('O maid's child') as he attempts to persuade God that this world is worth the effort ('worthy the winning').

The regular rhyme scheme adds to the music of the poem as well as emphasising key words: 'joy', 'cloy', 'boy', 'beginning', 'Sinning', 'winning'. The poet was influenced by reading the medieval theologian Duns Scotus, who said that the material world was an incarnation of God. Thus Hopkins felt justified in his preoccupation with the material world, as it had a sacramental value.

🖊 Writing About the Poem

'Hopkins uses poetry to speak of the glory of God.' Write a paragraph in response to this statement, using reference or quotation from 'Spring' to support your views.

Sample Paragraph

Hopkins had felt uneasy loving the natural world in case it distracted him from loving God. But after reading the theologian Duns Scotus, who maintained that the material world was a representation of God, Hopkins felt if he loved nature, he was loving its creator. So in giving us the glorious octet of this poem 'Spring', with the weeds 'long and lovely and lush', the thrush's eggs like 'little low heavens', Hopkins is worshipping God.

In the sestet he becomes more reflective. He links the poem to the glory of God as he meditates on the meaning of all this 'juice' and 'joy'. He asks God to preserve the world in its sinless state. We also see his devotion to the Mother of God, Our Lady in this poem. The references to 'O maid's child' and 'Mayday' confirm this. May is the month associated with the worship of Mary, Queen of Heaven.

EXAMINER'S COMMENT

This confident answer has noted one of the key influences on Hopkins (Duns Scotus) in his decision to glorify God in his poetry. Personal engagement with the poem is evident in the lively language, e.g. 'in giving us the glorious octet of this poem'. Expression throughout is clear: 'He asks God to preserve the world in its sinless state.' The effective use of accurate quotation is central to this successful top-grade response.

✒ Class/Homework Exercises

1. Hopkins uses language in an energetic, intense and religious way. Do you agree? Refer to the poem 'Spring' in your answer.
2. Hopkins is fascinated by the uniqueness of things. How does he convey the wonder of the individuality of an object through his use of language in this poem?

⊙ Points to Consider

- **Euphoric declaration of beauty of nature.**
- **Jubilant tone, rush of energy, one word sprouts from another.**
- **Rich visual detail and stunning sound effects.**
- **Religious impulse, reflection on innocence, God's beauty in nature and man.**
- **Sonnet form – descriptive octet and reflective sestet.**

3 As Kingfishers Catch Fire, Dragonflies Draw Flame

As kingfishers catch fire, dragonflies draw flame;
  As tumbled over rim in roundy wells
  Stones ring; like each tucked string tells, each hung bell's
Bow swung finds tongue to fling out broad its name;
Each mortal thing does one thing and the same: 5
  Deals out that being indoors each one dwells;
  Selves – goes itself; myself it speaks and spells,
Crying *What I do is me: for that I came.*

I say more: the just man justices;
  Keeps grace: that keeps all his goings graces;   10
Acts in God's eye what in God's eye he is –
  Christ. For Christ plays in ten thousand places,
Lovely in limbs, and lovely in eyes not his
  To the Father through the features of men's faces.

kingfishers: brilliantly coloured birds that hunt small fish.
dragonflies: brightly coloured insects with transparent wings.
tucked: plucked.
Bow: rim of bell that makes a sound when struck.

Selves: (used as a verb) defining or expressing its distinctiveness.

justices: (as a verb) acting justly.
Keeps grace: obeys God's will.

'dragonflies draw flame'

👤 Personal Response

1. Comment on the nature images in the poem's opening line.
2. Select two interesting sound effects from the poem and briefly explain the effectiveness of each.
3. 'Celebration is the central theme in this poem.' Write your response to this statement, supporting your answer with reference to the text.

👁 Critical Literacy

This sonnet is often cited as an example of Hopkins's theory of inscape, the uniqueness of every created thing as a reflection of God's glory. The poet believed that human beings had the uniqueness to recognise the divine presence in everything around us. The poem is written in an irregular ('sprung') rhythm that gives it a more concentrated quality.

The poem begins with two strikingly vivid images as Hopkins describes some of nature's most dazzling creatures. In **line 1**, he observes their vivid colour and dynamic movement (note the sharp alliteration and fast-paced rhythm) in the brilliant sunlight. The poet associates both the kingfisher and the dragonflies with fire. Aural images dominate **lines 2–4**. He takes **great delight in the uniqueness of existence** by listing a variety of everyday sounds: the tinkling noise of pebbles ('Stones ring') tossed down wells, the plucking of a stringed instrument and the loud ringing of a bell are all defined through their own distinctive sounds.

Hopkins is certain that the same quality applies to humans – 'Each mortal thing'. **We all express our unique inner selves**. Every individual does the same by presenting their inner essence (that dwells 'indoors'). The poet invents his own verb to convey how each of us 'Selves' (or expresses) our individual identity. The didactic tone of **lines 7–8** clearly reflects his depth of feeling, summed up by his emphatic illustration about our god-given purpose on earth: 'What I do is me: for that I came'.

Hopkins's enthusiasm ('I say more') intensifies at the start of the **sestet**. His central argument is that **people should fulfil their destiny by being themselves**. Again, he invents a new verb to illustrate his point: 'the just man justices' (good people behave in a godly way). Acting 'in God's eye' and availing of God's grace is our purpose on earth. The poet focuses on his belief that human beings are made in God's image and have the capacity to become like the omnipresent Christ.

Hopkins's **final lines** are filled with the devout Christian faith that **God will redeem everyone who 'Keeps grace'**. The poet repeatedly reminds us of the 'Lovely' personal relationship between God and mankind. It is Christ's presence within every human being that makes 'the features of men's faces' lovely in God's sight. Typically, Hopkins is fully convinced of the reality of Christ and the existence of the spirit world. He sees his own role as a 'kingfisher' catching fire – reeling in souls with his mystical poems of hope and spirituality.

Some critics have commented that the poem is too instructive and that Hopkins was overly concerned with getting across his message at the expense of method. The poet himself did not consider it a success. Yet there is no denying the poetic language of feeling and excitement in every line of the poem.

☐ Writing About the Poem

What aspects of this poem are typical of Hopkins's distinctive poetic style? Refer closely to the text in your answer.

Sample Paragraph

Hopkins the priest is the key speaker in 'As Kingfishers Catch Fire'. To me, the poem is not as typical as 'God's Grandeur' or 'Spring'. However, his writing is full of energy and unusual language. It starts with lively images drawn from nature – 'As kingfishers catch fire, dragonflies draw flame'. There is an immediacy about his images that demands attention. The alliteration of 'f' and 'd' sounds suggest blinding flashes of colour, darting flames and dramatic movements – exactly what fish and insects do in their natural habitats. Hopkins uses personification to show the vitality of the natural world – 'Stones ring'. He makes up new words of his own, such as 'justices'. Again, this is typical of his vibrant style. Hopkins reduces sentences to childlike phrases to show his joy in being aware of the mystery of creation – 'For Christ plays in ten thousand places'. Even here, the alliteration adds energy to the language. This is typical of so much of his poetry.

EXAMINER'S COMMENT

This is a reflective top-grade response that shows a good understanding of the poem. Points address Hopkins's distinctive writing style. There is a good focus on visual imagery, sound effects and personification. Supportive quotations are also integrated into the commentary throughout.

Class/Homework Exercises

1. Hopkins admitted that his poetry had an 'oddness' about it. Comment on his management of language in this poem. Refer closely to the text in your answer.

2. Hopkins uses the Petrarchan sonnet form of an octet (eight lines) and sestet (six lines) in this poem. How does the poet's treatment of his theme of wonder change in these two sections? Support your answer with close reference to the text.

Points to Consider

- **Distinctive quality of everything in the natural world.**
- **Invents verb, 'selves', to suggest unique quality of nature and man.**
- **Aural imagery, onomatopoeia, use of everyday sounds, sprung rhythm.**
- **Emphasises the importance of acceptance of God's will.**

4 The Windhover

Windhover: a kestrel or small falcon; resembles a cross in flight.

To Christ our Lord

I caught this morning morning's minion, kingdom
  of daylight's dauphin, dapple-dawn-drawn Falcon, in his riding
  Of the rolling level underneath him steady air, and striding
High there, how he rung upon the rein of a wimpling wing
In his ecstasy! then off, off forth on swing,   5
  As a skate's heel sweeps smooth on a bow-bend: the hurl
   and gliding
  Rebuffed the big wind. My heart in hiding
Stirred for a bird, – the achieve of, the mastery of the thing!

Brute beauty and valour and act, oh air, pride, plume here
  Buckle! AND the fire that breaks from thee then, a billion   10
Times told lovelier, more dangerous, O my chevalier!

  No wonder of it: sheer plod makes plough down sillion
Shine, and blue-bleak embers, ah my dear,
  Fall, gall themselves, and gash gold-vermilion.

minion: favourite; darling.
dauphin: prince, heir to French throne.
dapple-dawn-drawn: the bird is outlined in patches of colour by the dawn light, an example of Hopkins's use of compression.
rung upon the rein: circling movement of a horse at the end of a long rein held by a trainer; the sound of the bird pealing like a bell as it wheels in the sky.
wimpling: pleated.
bow-bend: a wide arc.
Rebuffed: pushed back; mastered.
My heart in hiding: the poet is afraid, unlike the bird.

Buckle: pull together; clasp; fall apart.
chevalier: medieval knight; Hopkins regards God as a knight who will defend him.
sheer plod: back-breaking drudgery of hard work, similar to Hopkins's work as a priest.
sillion: track, furrow.
ah my dear: intimate address to God.
Fall, gall ... gash: a reference to the crucifixion of Christ as he fell on the way to Cavalry, was offered vinegar and gashed by a spear on the cross.
gold-vermilion: gold and red, the colours of Christ the Saviour and also of the Eucharist, the body and blood of Christ, which offers redemption.

'how he rung upon the rein of a wimpling wing'

👤 Personal Response

1. In your opinion, has the poet been as daring in his use of language as the bird has been in its flight? Support your view by referring closely to the poem.
2. The sonnet moves from description to reflection. What does the poet meditate on in the sestet? Refer to the poem in your answer.
3. Write your own personal response to the poem, referring closely to the text in your answer.

👁 Critical Literacy

'The Windhover' was Hopkins's favourite poem, 'the best thing I ever wrote'. It is dedicated to Christ – Hopkins wrote it in 1877, when he was thirty-three years old, the same age as Christ when he died. The poet celebrates the uniqueness of the bird and his own deep relationship with God the Creator.

The name of the bird comes from its custom of hovering in the air, facing the wind, as it scans the ground for its prey. The opening lines of the octet are **joyful and celebratory** as Hopkins rejoices in the sight of the bird, 'daylight's dauphin'. The verb 'caught' suggests not just that the poet caught sight of the bird, but also that he 'caught' the essence of the bird on the page with words. This is an example of Hopkins's compression of language where he edges two meanings into one word or phrase. Hopkins shaped language by omitting articles, conjunctions and verbs to express the energy of the bird, 'off forth on swing'. **Movement fascinated the poet**. The bird is sketched by the phrase 'dapple-dawn-drawn'. A vivid image of the flecks of colour on his wings (as the dawn light catches him) is graphically drawn here.

The **momentary freshness** is conveyed by 'this morning', with the bird in flight beautifully captured by the simile 'As a skate's heel sweeps smooth on a bow-bend'. The 's' sound mimics the swish of the skater as a large arc is traced on the ice. This curve is similar to the strong but graceful bend of a bow stretched to loose its arrow, with all its connotations of beauty of line and deadly strength.

In the octet, there is typical **energetic language**: 'how he rung upon the rein of a wimpling wing/In his ecstasy!' This carries us along in its breathless description. The word 'wimpling' refers to the beautiful, seemingly pleated pattern of the arrangement of the outstretched wings of the bird. The capital 'F' used for 'Falcon' hints at its symbolism for Christ. This very personal poem uses 'I' in the octet and 'my' in the sestet. Hopkins lavishes praise on the bird: 'dauphin' (young prince, heir) and 'minion' (darling). Run-on lines add to the poet's excitement. He acknowledges that the bird has what he himself does not possess: power, self-belief and grace ('My heart in hiding'). The lively rhyme, such as 'riding'/'striding', never becomes repetitive because of the varying line breaks. The octet concludes with Hopkins's admiration of 'the thing', which broadens the focus from the particular to the general. All of creation is magnificent.

This leads to the sestet, where **God the Creator becomes central to the poem**. The essence (inscape) of the bird is highlighted: 'air, pride, plume here'. The bird is strong, brave, predatory, graceful and beautiful. The word 'Buckle' is paradoxical, as it contains two contradictory meanings: clasp together and fall apart. The bird is holding the line when it rides the rolling wind and falls apart as it swoops down on its prey. Capital letters for the conjunction 'AND' signal a moment of insight: 'the fire that breaks from thee'. The pronoun refers to God, whose magnificence is shown by 'fire'. The Holy Spirit is often depicted as a bird descending with tongues of flame. A soft tone of intimacy emerges: 'O my chevalier!' It is as if Hopkins wants God to act as the honourable knight of old, to take up his cause and fight on his behalf against his enemy. God will be Hopkins's defender against evil.

The sestet concludes with **two exceptional images**, both breaking apart to release their hidden brilliance. The ploughed furrow and the 'bluebleak embers' of coal both reveal their beauty in destruction: 'sillion/Shine', 'gash gold-vermilion'. Christ endured Calvary and crucifixion, 'Fall, gall … gash', and through his sacrifice, the 'Fall', achieved redemption for us. So too the priest embracing the drudgery of his service embraces his destiny by submitting to the will of God. In doing so, he reflects the greatness of God. Earthly glory is crushed to release heavenly glory. The phrase 'ah my dear' makes known the dominant force of Hopkins's life: to love God. The colours of gold and red are those of Christ the Saviour as well as the colours associated with the Eucharist, the body and blood of Christ. When Christians receive the sacrament of Holy Communion, they are redeemed. So, as the poem begins, 'dapple-dawn-drawn Falcon', it ends with 'gold-vermilion' in a triumph of glorious colour.

✒ Writing About the Poem

'Hopkins's intense reflections on Christ in his poetry are always conveyed with visual energy.' Discuss this statement, with particular reference to 'The Windhover'.

Sample Paragraph

In 'The Windhover', Hopkins uses the image of the falcon as a symbol of Christ. Using strong images, the poet describes the bird's magnificent beauty, 'dapple-dawn-drawn', and its strength, 'rebuffed the big wind'. In the sestet, Hopkins calls God 'O my chevalier'. This gives a vivid picture of a highly moral individual. The verb 'Buckle' reminds me of the knight putting on his armour and stumbling in battle. Hopkins felt it was right to focus on nature as evidence of the power and beauty of God. In glorifying Him through the dramatic emblem of the windhover, he is glorifying divine creation, and therefore God Himself. The flash of red and gold, with which this visually powerful poem ends, 'gash gold-vermilion', reminds me that the priest carrying out his ordinary duties is also revealing the beauty of God's creation. I think Hopkins's reflections on Christ add a real spiritual quality to his poetry.

EXAMINER'S COMMENT

Close reading of the poem is evident in this top-grade personal response: 'The verb "Buckle" reminds me of the knight putting on his armour'. Quotations are very well used here to highlight Hopkins's commitment to his Christian faith, 'The flash of red and gold, with which this visually powerful poem ends, "gash gold-vermilion", reminds me that the priest carrying out his ordinary duties is also revealing the beauty of God's creation.' Well-controlled language use throughout.

✒ Class/Homework Exercises

1. Would you agree that 'The Windhover' illustrates much that is both spiritual and Christian in Hopkins's poetry? Give reasons for your response.
2. Hopkins creates a powerful sense of drama throughout 'The Windhover'. Discuss this view, using reference to the poem.

⊙ Points to Consider

- **Deeply personal poem, engaging opening.**
- **Relationship with God accentuated by poet's ability to see the divine in nature.**
- **Medieval chivalric imagery.**
- **Bird's movement depicted by alliteration and assonance.**
- **Optimistic ending, illustrated by 'blue-black' becoming 'gold-vermilion'.**

Pied Beauty

Pied: varied.

GERARD MANLEY HOPKINS

Glory be to God for dappled things –
   For skies of couple-colour as a brinded cow;
   For rose-moles all in stipple upon trout that swim;
Fresh-firecoal chestnut-falls; finches' wings;
   Landscape plotted and pieced – fold, fallow, and plough;   5
   And all trades, their gear and tackle and trim.

All things counter, original, spare, strange;
   Whatever is fickle, freckled (who knows how?)
   With swift, slow; sweet, sour; adazzle, dim;
He fathers-forth whose beauty is past change: 10
               Praise him.

dappled: speckled, spotted.

brinded: streaked.

rose-moles: red-pink spots.
stipple: dotted.
Fresh-firecoal chestnut falls: open chestnuts bright as burning coals.
pieced: enclosed.
fold: sheep enclosure.
fallow: unused.
trades: farmwork.
gear: equipment.
tackle: implements.
trim: fittings.
counter: contrasting.
spare: special.
fickle: changeable.
He: God.
fathers-forth: creates.

'skies of couple-colour'

👤 Personal Response

1. In your view, what is the central theme in this poem? Refer to the text in your answer.
2. Discuss the poet's use of sound effects in the poem. Support your answer with quotations.
3. Choose two striking images from the poem and comment on the effectiveness of each.

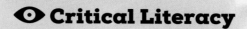 Critical Literacy

'Pied Beauty' is one of Hopkins's 'curtal' (or curtailed) sonnets, in which he condenses the traditional sonnet form. It was written in the so-called sprung rhythm that he developed, based on the irregular rhythms of traditional Welsh verse. The poem's energetic language – particularly its sound effects – reflects Hopkins's view of the rich, abundant diversity evident within God's creation.

The simplicity of the prayer-like opening line ('Glory be to God') is reminiscent of biblical language and sets the poem's devotional tone. From the start, Hopkins displays a **childlike wonder** for all the 'dappled things' around him, illustrating his central belief with a series of vivid examples from the natural world.

Included in his panoramic sweep of nature's vibrant delights are the dominant blues and whites of the sky, which he compares to the streaked ('brinded') patterns of cowhide. The world is teeming with contrasting colours and textures, captured in **detailed images**, such as 'rose-moles all in stipple upon trout' and 'Fresh-firecoal chestnut-falls'.

For the exhilarated poet, everything in nature is linked. It is ironic, of course, that what all things share is their god-given individuality. In line 4, he associates broken chestnuts with burning coals in a fire, black on the outside and glowing underneath. In turn, the wings of finches have similar colours. Condensed imagery and compound words add even greater energy to the description.

Hopkins turns his attention to human nature in lines 5–6. The farmland features he describes reflect hard work and efficiency: 'Landscape plotted and pieced – fold, fallow, and plough'. The range of man's impact on the natural world is also worth celebrating, and this is reinforced by the **orderly syntax and insistent rhythm**. Human activity in tune with nature also glorifies God.

Hopkins's **final four lines** focus on the **unexpected beauty of creation** and further reveal the poet's passionate Christianity. As though overcome by the scale and variety of God's works – 'who knows how?' – the poet meditates on a range of contrasting adjectives ('swift, slow; sweet, sour; adazzle, dim'), all of which indicate the wonderful diversity of creation. As always, the alliteration gives an increased dynamism to this image of abundance and variety in nature.

The poem ends as it began – with a shortened version of the two mottoes of St Ignatius of Loyola, founder of the Jesuits: *Ad majorem Dei gloriam* (to the greater glory of God) and *Laus Deo semper* (praise be to God always). For Hopkins, **God is beyond change**. The Creator ('He fathers-forth') and all the 'dappled' opposites that enrich our ever-changing world inspire us all to 'Praise him'.

🖋 Writing About the Poem

'Hopkins's appreciation of the energy present in the world is vividly expressed in his unique poetry.' Discuss this statement, with particular reference to 'Pied Beauty'.

Sample Paragraph

'Pied Beauty' is more like a prayer than an ordinary poem. It begins with 'Glory be to God' and continues to the final words 'Praise him'. In between, Hopkins lists examples of the variety of the natural environment, the 'landscape plotted and pieced'. The pace of the poem is rapid, as though he is in a rush to explain his astonishment: 'Fresh-firecoal chestnut-falls'. There is an overwhelming sense of God's mystery and greatness. This is partly due to the compound phrases, such as 'couple-colour' and 'rose-moles' which make us more aware of the varied appearances of natural things. The energetic rhythm builds to a climax in the last line. This is almost breathless – just one simple phrase that sums up Hopkins's awareness of God's creation: 'Praise him'.

EXAMINER'S COMMENT

A short, focused response that ranges over a number of interesting features of Hopkins's style, particularly his description of nature's energy: 'The pace of the poem is rapid, as though he is in a rush to explain his astonishment'. The rapidity of Hopkins's verse is effectively explored, particularly in the reference to the lead-up to the climax in the poem's final line. A successful top-grade answer.

🖋 Class/Homework Exercises

1. In your opinion, what is Hopkins's attitude towards God in this poem? Refer to his use of imagery and pay particular attention to the concluding four lines.
2. Compare and contrast the views expressed in 'Pied Beauty' with any other 'religious' poem by Hopkins from your course. Support your answer with reference to both poems.

⊙ Points to Consider

- Condensed version (ten and a half lines) of traditional sonnet form (fourteen lines).
- Anthem of praise to God for nature's variety.
- Catalogue of vibrant examples of 'dappled beauty'. Effective use of compound words.
- Alliteration conveys how man's activities are in harmony with God's design.

6

Felix Randal

Felix Randal: the parishioner's name was Felix Spenser. 'Felix' in Latin means 'happy'. Randal can also mean a lowly, humble thing or trodden on.

Felix Randal the farrier, O he is dead then? my duty all ended,
Who have watched his mould of man, big-boned and
   hardy-handsome
Pining, pining, till time when reason rambled in it, and some
Fatal four disorders, fleshed there, all contended?

Sickness broke him. Impatient he cursed at first, but mended   5
Being anointed and all; though a heavenlier heart began some
Months earlier, since I had our sweet reprieve and ransom
Tendered to him. Ah well, God rest him all road ever he offended!

This seeing the sick endears them to us, us too it endears.
My tongue had taught thee comfort, touch had quenched thy
   tears   10
Thy tears that touched my heart, child, Felix, poor Felix Randal;

How far from then forethought of, all thy more boisterous years,
When thou at the random grim forge, powerful amidst peers,
Didst fettle for the great grey drayhorse his bright and battering
   sandal!

farrier: blacksmith.
O he is dead then?: reaction of priest at Felix's death.
hardy-handsome: compound word describing the fine physical appearance of the blacksmith.

disorders: diseases.
contended: competitively fought over Felix.

anointed: sacraments administered to the sick by a priest.
reprieve and ransom: the sacraments of confession and communion through which Christians are redeemed from sin.
Tendered: offered.
all road ever: in whatever way (local dialect).

random: casual; irregular.
fettle: prepare.
drayhorse: big horse used to pull heavy carts.
sandal: type of horseshoe.

'at the random grim forge'

👤 Personal Response

1. 'Hopkins is a poet who celebrates ordinary life and simple religious faith in his poem, "Felix Randal".' Discuss this statement with reference to the poem, illustrating your answer with quotations.
2. How does the octet differ from the sestet in this Petrarchan sonnet? Refer to theme and style in your response. Use quotations in support of your views.
3. Choose two aural images that you found interesting and briefly explain their effectiveness.

👁 Critical Literacy

'Felix Randal' was written in Liverpool in 1880. The poem contrasts with others such as 'Spring'. Hopkins had been placed as a curate to the city slums of Liverpool, 'a most unhappy and miserable spot', in his opinion. He didn't communicate successfully with his parishioners and he didn't write much poetry, except this one poem about the blacksmith who died of tuberculosis, aged thirty-one.

The opening of the octet identifies the man with his name and occupation, 'Felix Randal the farrier'. Then the poet shocks us with the priest's reaction: 'O he is dead then? my duty all ended'. On first reading, this sounds both dismissive and cold. However, when we consider that the death was expected and that the priest had seen all this many times, we realise that the line rings with authenticity. For Hopkins, 'duty' was a sacred office. **The farrier is recalled in his physical prime**, using the alliteration of 'm', 'b' and 'h' in the phrase 'mould of man, big-boned and hardy-handsome'. The repetition of 'Pining, pining' marks his decline in health. His illness is graphically conveyed as his mental health deteriorated ('reason rambled') and the diseases attacked his body ('Fatal four disorders, fleshed there, all contended'). **The illnesses took possession of the body** and waged a horrific battle to win supremacy, eventually killing Felix.

The word 'broke' is suitable in this context, as in the world of horses it refers to being trained. Is Felix trained ('broke') through suffering? His realistic reaction to the news – 'he cursed' – changes when he receives the sacraments ('being anointed'). Felix was broken but is now restored by 'our sweet reprieve and ransom', the healing sacraments. **The tone changes** with the personal pronoun. The priest–patient relationship is acknowledged: we, both priest and layperson, are saved by God. A note of resigned acceptance, almost an anti-climax, is evident in the line 'Ah well, God rest him all road ever he offended!' The use of the Lancashire dialect ('all road') by the priest shows a developing relationship between the two men.

The detached priest's voice resurfaces in the sestet: 'seeing the sick'. This section of the sonnet focuses on the **reality of sickness** and its effects. Both Felix and the priest received something from the experience. We respond to the sick with sympathy ('the sick endears them to us'), but we also appreciate ourselves and our own health more ('us too it endears') as we face another's mortality. The priest comforted the dying man with words ('My tongue') and the last sacraments, anointing by 'touch' and becoming a father figure to 'child' Felix. Is there a suggestion that one must become like an innocent child to enter the kingdom of Heaven? The tercet (three-line segment) is intimate: 'thee', 'thy', 'Thy tears', 'my heart'. The last tercet explodes in a **dramatic flashback** to the energy of the young blacksmith in his prime, when there was little thought of death: 'How far from then forethought'. Onomatopoeia and alliteration convey the lifeforce (inscapes) of the young Felix, 'boisterous' and 'powerful amidst peers'.

Sprung rhythm adds to the force of the poem as the six main stresses are interspersed with an irregular number of unstressed syllables. Felix did a man's job at the 'grim forge' when he made the 'bright and battering sandal' for the powerful carthorse, powerfully conveyed in the assonance of 'great grey drayhorse'. The poem ends not with Felix in heavenly glory, but in his former earthly glory: 'thou ... Didst fettle'. God has fashioned Felix through his suffering just as Felix had fashioned the horseshoe. Both required force and effort to bend them to the shape in which they can function properly. The poem is a celebration of God's creation of the man.

✒ Writing About the Poem

'Hopkins is a poet who celebrates unique identities and individual experiences, exploring their meaning and worth.' Discuss this statement in relation to one or more of the poems on your course, quoting in support of your points.

Sample Paragraph

In 'Felix Randal', Hopkins captures the unique essence of a strong man struck down by illness. He was 'big-boned and hardy-handsome', and the alliteration emphasises his physique. His understandable reaction to his own misfortune is evident in 'he cursed at first', the assonance echoing the deep voice. The repeated 'f' of 'Fatal four disorders' conveys the impossible odds stacked against Felix. Hopkins has given us the unique identity of the man. He also gives us the dismissive voice of the priest: 'O he is dead then? my duty all ended'. Here is a man who has seen too much suffering. His use of the expression 'all road' shows how he has tried to enter the world of his parishioners, but he quickly reverts back to his professional capacity. He has a strong belief that the sacraments will help: 'sweet reprieve and ransom'. The poem leaves us feeling that the priest has received as much from the sick man as the sick man has received from the priest: 'Thy tears that touched my heart'.

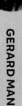

EXAMINER'S COMMENT

This paragraph has dealt comprehensively with the various elements of the question. The close attention to the poet's use of language, assonance and alliteration, enhances the answer. Real personal engagement is evident in the discussion of the priest's transition from tiredness to his regained 'professional capacity'. A successful answer that merits the top grade.

✎ Class/Homework Exercises

1. Hopkins deals with suffering in his poetry. Has this any relevance to the modern reader? Use reference to 'Felix Randal' in your answer.
2. Hopkins gives a vivid portrait of the farrier. Discuss how his changing tone conveys his view of Felix Randal. Support your answer with close reference to the text.

⊙ Points to Consider

- Inscape (essence captured) of blacksmith in this Petrarchan sonnet.
- Focus on man's insignificance; glory only achieved through Christian faith.
- Sprung rhythm (many unstressed syllables) add to poem's energy.
- Simple everyday speech and colloquialisms root poem firmly in north of England.
- Final image is positive; 'b' sound accentuates energy.

7 Inversnaid

Title: Inversnaid is a remote area located near Loch Lomond in the Scottish Highlands.

This darksome burn, horseback brown,
His rollrock highroad roaring down,
In coop and in comb the fleece of his foam
Flutes and low to the lake falls home.

A windpuff-bonnet of fawn-froth   5
Turns and twindles over the broth
Of a pool so pitchblack, fell-frowning,
It rounds and rounds Despair to drowning.

Degged with dew, dappled with dew
Are the groins of the braes that the brook treads through,   10
Wiry heathpacks, flitches of fern,
And the beadbonny ash that sits over the burn.

What would the world be, once bereft
Of wet and of wildness? Let them be left,
O let them be left, wildness and wet;   15
Long live the weeds and the wilderness yet.

burn: stream.

coop: hollow.
comb: moving freely.

Flutes: grooves; whistles.

twindles: spins.

fell: fiercely.

Degged: sprinkled about.

groins of the braes: sides of hills.
heathpacks: heather outcrops.
flitches: ragged tufts.
beadbonny: mountain ash tree with bright berries.

bereft: deprived.

'the fleece of his foam'

👤 Personal Response

1. From your reading of the first stanza, explain how the poet conveys the stream's energy.
2. Sound effects play a key part in the second and third stanzas. Choose two aural images that convey Hopkins's excited reaction to the mountain stream. Comment on the effectiveness of each.
3. Write your own personal response to the poem, referring closely to the text in your answer.

👁 Critical Literacy

'Inversnaid' was written in 1881 after Hopkins visited the remote hillsides around Loch Lomond. He disliked being in cities and much preferred the sights and sounds of the wilderness. The poem is unusual for Hopkins in that there is no direct mention of God as the source of all this natural beauty.

The opening lines of stanza one are dramatic. Hopkins compares the brown, rippling stream ('This darksome burn') to a wild horse's back. The forceful alliteration – 'rollrock highroad roaring' – emphasises the power of this small stream as it rushes downhill, its course directed by confining rocks. A sense of immediacy and energy is echoed in the **onomatopoeic effects**, including end rhyme ('brown', 'down'), repetition and internal rhyme ('comb', 'foam'). This is characteristic of Hopkins, as is his use of descriptive details, likening the foamy 'fleece' of the water to the fluted surface ('Flutes') of a Greek or Roman column.

Stanza two begins with another effective metaphor. The poet compares the yellow-brown froth to a windblown bonnet (hat) as the water swirls into a dark pool on the riverbed. The **atmosphere is light and airy**. Run-on lines reflect the lively pace of the noisy stream. However, the tone suddenly darkens with the disturbing image of the 'pitchblack' whirlpool which Hopkins sees as capable of drowning all in 'Despair'. The sluggish rhythm in lines 7–8 reinforces this menacing mood.

Nature seems much more benign in stanza three. The language is softer sounding – 'Degged with dew, dappled with dew' – as Hopkins describes the **steady movement of the water** through 'the groins of the braes'. Enclosed by the sharp banks, the stream sprinkles nearby branches of mountain ash, aflame with their vivid scarlet berries. As always, Hopkins delights in the unspoiled landscape: 'Wiry heathpacks, flitches of fern,/And the beadbonny ash'. Throughout the poem, he has also used traditional Scottish expressions ('burn', 'braes') to reflect the vigorous sounds of the Highlands.

The language in stanza four is rhetorical. Hopkins wonders what the world would be like without its wild qualities. The tone is personal and plaintive: 'O let them be left, wildness and wet'. While repetition and the use of the exclamation add a sense of urgency, his plea is simple: let nature remain as it is. The final appeal – 'Long live the weeds and the wilderness yet' – is reminiscent of his poem 'Spring'. Once again, there is no doubting Hopkins's **enthusiasm for the natural beauty of remote places** and the sentiments he expresses are clearly heartfelt. Although written in 1881, the poem has obvious relevance for today's generation.

🖋 Writing About the Poem

'Hopkins's deep appreciation of nature is a central feature of his striking poetry.' Discuss this statement, with particular reference to 'Inversnaid'.

Sample Paragraph

The immediate thing that emerges about Hopkins is his extraordinary closeness to nature. He seems to have a heightened awareness of the sights and sounds of the remote mountain 'burn' in 'Inversnaid'. He details the colours of the water. It is 'darksome', 'horseback brown'. Hopkins is always excited by his natural environment. To him, the river is alive. It is 'roaring down'. In the last section of the poem, Hopkins openly states his fears for nature. He begs us to preserve the 'wildness and wet'. For him, all of nature deserves respect. He ends the poem with his own slogan, 'Long live the weeds and the wilderness'. He repeats the words 'wet' and 'wildness' a number of times in the final lines, leaving us in no doubt about how much the natural landscape meant to him.

EXAMINER'S COMMENT

Hopkins's awareness of the unruly aspects of nature is effectively explored: 'He details the colours of the water. It is "darksome".' There is a convincing sense of close engagement with the poem: 'Hopkins is always excited by his natural environment.' Accurate textual references and impressive, fluent expression ensure the top grade.

🖋 Class/Homework Exercises

1. In your opinion, does the poem 'Inversnaid' have relevance to our modern world? Support the points you make with reference to the text.
2. How does Hopkins reveal his intense love of nature in this poem? Refer to his subject matter and writing style in your response.

⊙ Points to Consider

- Celebration of nature's unruly beauty; unusually no reference to God.
- Colloquial Scots–English language locates poem in Scottish Highlands.
- Steady movement of water conveyed through onomatopoeic effects.
- Plea on behalf of unspoilt natural scenes.

8 I Wake and Feel the Fell of Dark, Not Day

I wake and feel the fell of dark, not day.
What hours, O what black hours we have spent
This night! what sights you, heart, saw; ways you went!
And more must, in yet longer light's delay.
   With witness I speak this. But where I say   5
Hours I mean years, mean life. And my lament
Is cries countless, cries like dead letters sent
To dearest him that lives alas! away.

   I am gall. I am heartburn. God's most deep decree
Bitter would have me taste: my taste was me;   10
Bones built in me, flesh filled, blood brimmed the curse.
   Selfyeast of spirit a dull dough sours. I see
The lost are like this, and their scourge to be
As I am mine, their sweating selves; but worse.

fell: threat; blow; knocked down; past tense of fall (fall of Adam and Eve cast into darkness); also refers to the mountain.

dead letters sent/To dearest him: communication which is of no use, didn't elicit a response.

gall: bitterness; anger; acidity; vinegar.
deep decree: command that cannot easily be understood.
Bones built in me, flesh filled, blood brimmed the curse: the passive tense of the verb might suggest how God created Man, yet Man has sinned.
Selfyeast of spirit a dull dough sours: yeast makes bread rise; Hopkins feels he cannot become good or wholesome.
The lost: those condemned to serve eternity in Hell with no hope of redemption, unlike the poet.

'I wake and feel the fell of dark, not day'

👤 Personal Response

1. How is the oppressive atmosphere conveyed in this sonnet? Support your response with reference to the poem.
2. How does the poem conclude, on a note of hope or despair? Illustrate your answer by referring closely to the text.
3. Comment on the use of alliteration to convey Hopkins's sense of dejection. Mention at least three examples.

👁 Critical Literacy

'I Wake and Feel the Fell of Dark, Not Day' was written in Dublin, where Hopkins was teaching at UCD and was burdened by a massive workload of examination papers. After a long silence, he wrote the 'terrible sonnets'. Hopkins said of these, 'If ever anything was written in blood, these were.' This sonnet was discovered among his papers after his death.

The last three sonnets on the course are called the 'terrible sonnets'. Here Hopkins reaches the **darkest depths of despair**. The sonnet opens in darkness and the only mention of light in the whole poem is 'light's delay' in line 4, as it is postponed. He wakes to the oppressive blow of the dark ('the fell of dark'), not to the brightness of daylight. The heaviness of depression is being described, the oppressive darkness which Adam woke to after his expulsion from the Garden of Eden. Hopkins and his soul have shared these 'black hours' and they will experience 'more'. It is not just hours they have spent in darkness, but 'years', 'life'.

The formal, almost biblical phrase 'With witness I speak this' emphasises that what he has said is true. The hard 'c' sounds in 'cries countless' and the repetition of 'cries' keenly describe the **fruitless attempts at communication** ('dead letters'). There is no response: he 'lives alas! away'. We can imagine the poet in the deep dark of the night attempting to gain solace from his prayers to God ('dearest him'), but they go unanswered.

Hopkins feels this deep depression intensely. **Note the repetition of 'I'**: 'I wake', 'I speak', 'I am gall', 'I am heartburn', 'I see', 'I am'. He is in physical pain, bitter and burning. The language might well refer to Christ's crucifixion, when he was offered a sponge soaked in vinegar to drink, and pierced through his side. However, the poet recognises that it is God's unfathomable decision that this is the way it should be: 'God's most deep decree'. **The poet is reviled by himself** in line 10: 'my taste was me'. He describes how he was fashioned: 'Bones built in me, flesh filled, blood brimmed'. The alliteration shows the careful construction of the body by the Creator, but Hopkins is full of 'the curse'.

Could this sense of revulsion be related to original sin emanating from the fall of Adam and Eve? The deadening 'd' sound of 'dull dough' shows that there is no hope of rising. The body is tainted, soured. It does not have the capacity to 'Selfyeast', to resurrect or renew. Is it being suggested that Hopkins needs divine intervention? Is there an overtone of the bread of communion, the wholesome Body of Christ? The scope of the poem broadens out at the end as the poet gains an **insight into the plight of others**. All those condemned to Hell are like this and in fact are worse off: 'but worse'. The horrific atmosphere of Hell is conveyed in the phrase 'sweating selves'. For those 'lost', it is permanent. For Hopkins, perhaps it is just 'longer light's delay'. Some day **he will be redeemed**.

✒ Writing About the Poem

'Hopkins's poetry displays a deeply personal and passionate response to the human condition.' Discuss with reference to 'I Wake and Feel the Fell of Dark, Not Day', illustrating your answer with relevant quotations.

Sample Paragraph

Many people can identify with Hopkins suffering from depression. This is evident in 'I Wake and Feel the Fell of Dark, Not Day'. To me he is describing waking over and over again at night. The long vowel sounds in 'O what black hours' give an idea of the man tossing and turning, trying to sleep. Hopkins's personal relationship with God was the focus of his life. His passionate pleas to God, 'To dearest him', are useless, 'dead letters'. So he is devastated. He despises himself: 'the curse', 'dull dough'. The poem is filled with self-disgust. The only slight glimmer for the poet is that those condemned to Hell are in a worse situation 'and their scourge to be ... their sweating selves; but worse'. Hopkins writes passionately about being human and the feeling of unworthiness.

EXAMINER'S COMMENT

This is a mature response to the assertion that Hopkins reacts deeply and passionately to the human condition: 'The poem is filled with self-disgust.' There is also in-depth exploration of the poem's sound effects: 'The long vowel sounds in "O what black hours" give an idea of the man tossing and turning'. Vocabulary and expression are impressive, adding to a successful, high-grade paragraph.

🖋 Class/Homework Exercises

1. 'Hopkins charts an extraordinary mental journey in "I Wake and Feel the Fell of Dark, Not Day".' Write a short personal response to this statement, quoting in support of your opinions.

2. Hopkins graphically explores his deep feeling of despair through light and dark imagery in 'I Wake and Feel the Fell of Dark, Not Day'. Pick one image of brightness and one of darkness which you considered effective and explain your choice.

⊙ Points to Consider

- Feeling of abandonment by God; spiritual suffering.

- Depressive's experience of waking into night vividly conveyed by imagery.

- Long vowel sounds and dragging repetition emphasise the prevailing darkness.

- Sense of self-disgust balanced by the poet's concluding empathy.

9 No Worst, There is None

GERARD MANLEY HOPKINS

No worst, there is none. Pitched past pitch of grief,
More pangs will, schooled at forepangs, wilder wring.
Comforter, where, where is your comforting?
Mary, mother of us, where is your relief?
My cries heave, herds-long; huddle in a main, a chief   5
Woe, world-sorrow; on an age-old anvil wince and sing –
Then lull, then leave off. Fury had shrieked 'No ling-
ering! Let me be fell: force I must be brief.'

   O the mind, mind has mountains; cliffs of fall
Frightful, sheer, no-man-fathomed. Hold them cheap   10
May who ne'er hung there. Nor does long our small
Durance deal with that steep or deep. Here! creep,
Wretch, under a comfort serves in a whirlwind: all
Life death does end and each day dies with sleep.

Pitched past pitch: pushed beyond.
pangs: sudden pains.
schooled at forepangs: prepared by earlier sorrows.
Comforter: the Holy Spirit.

main: crowd.

fell: harsh; cruel.
force: perforce; therefore.

Durance: endurance; determination.
whirlwind: turmoil.

'frightful, sheer, no-man-fathomed'

👤 Personal Response

1. Comment on how Hopkins creates a sense of suffering and pessimism in the first four lines of the poem.
2. Discuss the effectiveness of the mountain images in lines 9–12.
3. In your opinion, is this a completely negative poem? Support your response by referring closely to the text.

👁 Critical Literacy

This Petrarchan sonnet was written in Hopkins's final years, at a time when he suffered increasingly from ill health and depression. It was one of a short series of sonnets of desolation, now known as the 'terrible sonnets' or 'dark sonnets'. In 'No Worst, There is None', we see a man experiencing deep psychological suffering and struggling with his religious faith. The poem reveals a raw honesty from someone close to despair.

The opening is curt and dramatic, revealing the intensity of Hopkins's suffering: 'No worst, there is none'. He is unable to imagine any greater agony. The emphatic use of monosyllables in line 1 reflects his **angry frustration**. Having reached what seems the threshold of torment, 'Pitched past pitch of grief', the poet dreads what lies ahead and the horrifying possibility that his pain ('schooled at forepangs') is likely to increase. The explosive force of the verb 'Pitched', combined with the harsh onomatopoeic and alliterative effects, heighten the sense of uncontrollable anguish. Both 'pitch' and 'pangs' are repeated, suggesting darkness and violent movement.

The rhythm changes in line 3. The three syllables of 'Comforter' slow the pace considerably. This is also a much softer word (in contrast to the harshness of the earlier sounds) and is echoed at the end of the line by 'comforting'. Hopkins's desolate plea to the Holy Spirit and the Virgin Mary emphasises **his hopelessness**: 'where, where is your comforting?' The tone, reminiscent of Christ's words on the Cross ('My God, why hast thou forsaken me?'), is both desperate and accusatory.

The poet likens his hollow cries for help to a herd of cattle in line 5. The metaphor highlights his lack of self-worth – his hopeless prayers 'heave' and 'huddle in a main'. He feels that his own suffering is part of a **wider universal 'world-sorrow'**. There is an indication here that Hopkins recognises that experiencing a crisis of faith can affect any Christian from time to time. This possibility is supported by the memorable image of the anvil being struck in line 6. He realises that the Christian experience involves suffering the guilt of sin and doubt to achieve spiritual happiness: 'on an age-old anvil wince and sing'.

But for the poet, any relief ('lull') from suffering is short-lived. His unavoidable feelings of shame and the pain of remorse are hauntingly personified: 'Fury had shrieked'. Once again, the severe sounds and the stretching of the phrase 'No lingering!' over two lines reinforce the relentlessness of Hopkins's troubled conscience.

This tormented tone is replaced by a more reflective one in the opening lines of the **sestet**, where Hopkins moves from the physical world of his 'cries' into the metaphorical landscape of towering mountains, with their dark, unknown depths. This **dramatic wasteland**, with its 'no-man-fathomed' cliffs, is terrifyingly portrayed. The poet reminds us that the terror of depression and separation from God cannot be appreciated by those 'who ne'er hung there'. The terror of being stranded on the 'steep or deep' rock face cannot be endured for long.

In the **last two lines**, Hopkins resigns himself to the **grim consolation** that all the depression and pain of this world will end with death, just as everyday troubles are eased by sleep. The final, chilling image of the wretched individual taking refuge from the exhausting whirlwind is less than optimistic. There is no relief from the terrible desolation and Hopkins's distracted prayers have yet to be answered.

✒ Writing About the Poem

'Hopkins's deep despair is evident in the 'terrible sonnets'. Discuss this statement, with particular reference to 'No Worst, There is None'.

Sample Paragraph

At the start of 'No Worst, There is None', the tone is totally despondent. The first sentence is short and snappy, emphasising that Hopkins has reached rock bottom. Hopkins was a manic depressive and obsessed with religion. In many ways he was caught between his role as a priest and his human desires. Rhetorical questions emphasise his dependence on his religious faith – 'Comforter, where, where is your comforting?' This gives a heartfelt tone. Hopkins uses effective images which always make us feel sympathy for him, for example 'My cries heave, herds-long'. His tone is sorrowful and this is emphasised by comparisons. The prayers he offers to Heaven are just useless words: 'My cries heave, herds-long'.

EXAMINER'S COMMENT

This response includes a number of relevant examples of the varying tones throughout. Accurate quotations are effectively used in support and there is some good engagement with the poem. The expression was slightly awkward in places: 'This gives a heartfelt tone', and there is overuse of the verb 'emphasises'. Overall, a solid high-grade standard.

The end of the poem is even more negative. Hopkins obviously had issues with his own faith in God. He uses a tone of despair as he compares himself to a stranded wanderer finding shelter from a 'whirlwind'. His only comfort is sleep and eventually death, which will silence his inner pain.

✍ Class/Homework Exercises

1. The poet feels utterly abandoned by God in this poem. Trace the development of thought in 'No Worst, There is None' and discuss how Hopkins uses vivid description to explore his negative feelings. Support your answer with close reference to the text.

2. Write your own personal response to 'No Worst, There is None'. Refer closely to the text in your answer.

⊙ Points to Consider

- **Most despairing and bleakest of 'terrible sonnets'.**

- **Alarming metaphors and powerful sound effects reveal inner suffering.**

- **Ups and downs of man's spiritual journey suggested by mountain imagery.**

- **Slightly optimistic end, death brings end to suffering for man.**

10 Thou Art Indeed Just, Lord, if I Contend

GERARD MANLEY HOPKINS

*Justus quidem tu es, Domine, si disputem tecum: verumtamen
justa loquar ad te: Quare via imporium prosperatur? &c.*

Thou art indeed just, Lord, if I contend
With thee; but, sir, so what I plead is just.
Why do sinners' ways prosper? And why must
 Disappointment all I endeavour end?
  Wert thou my enemy, O thou my friend,   5
 How wouldst thou worse, I wonder, than thou dost
Defeat, thwart me? Oh, the sots and thralls of lust
Do in spare hours more thrive than I that spend,
Sir, life upon thy cause. See, banks and brakes
Now leaved how thick! laced they are again   10
With fretty chervil, look, and fresh wind shakes
Them; birds build – but not I build; no, but strain,
Time's eunuch, and not breed one work that wakes.
Mine, O thou lord of life, send my roots rain.

Latin quotation: Indeed you are just, O Lord, if I dispute with you; yet I would plead my case before you. Why do the wicked prosper? The first lines of the poem are a version of a Latin quotation that is taken from the Bible.
contend: dispute; argue; challenge.

sots: drunkards.
thralls: slaves.

brakes: thickets; groves of trees.

fretty: fretted; interlaced; the herb chervil has lacy leaves.
chervil: garden herb; the 'rejoicing leaf'.

eunuch: a castrated male, incapable of reproducing.

'laced they are again/
With fretty chervil, look'

👤 Personal Response

1. List the questions put to God. What tone is evident in each – anger, rebelliousness, reverence, trust, despair, etc.?
2. Is there a real sense of pain in the poem? At what point is it most deeply felt? Refer to the text in your response.
3. Is the image of God in the poem stern or not? Do you think that Hopkins had a good or bad relationship with God? Illustrate your answer with reference to this poem.

👁 Critical Literacy

'Thou Art Indeed Just, Lord, if I Contend' was written in 1889 at a time of great unhappiness for Hopkins in Dublin. He had written in a letter that 'all my undertakings miscarry'. This poem is a pessimistic yet powerful plea for help from God. It was written just three months before he died.

This sonnet opens with the **formal language of the courtroom** as the poet, in clipped tones, poses three questions in the octet. With growing frustration, he asks God to explain why sinners seem to prosper. Why is he, the poet, continually disappointed? If God was his enemy instead of his friend, how could he be any worse off? God, he allows, is just, but he contends that his own cause is also just. The language is that of a coherent, measured argument: 'sir', 'I plead'.

However, in lines 3–4, 'and why must/Disappointment all I endeavour end?', the inversion of the natural order makes the reader concentrate on the notable point that 'Disappointment' is the 'end' result of all the work the poet has done. But **the tone remains rational**, as Hopkins points out to 'sir' that the worst doing their worst 'more thrive' than he does. But his frustration at his plight makes the line of the octet spill over into the sestet, as the poet complains that he has spent his life doing God's will ('life upon thy cause').

The sestet has the ring of the real voice breaking through as Hopkins urgently requests God to 'See', 'look'. Here is **nature busily thriving**, producing, building, breeding, growing. The movement and pace of continuing growth and regrowth is caught in the line 'Now leaved how thick! laced they are again'. The **alliteration** of 'banks and brakes', 'birds build' vividly portrays the abundance of nature, as does the **assonance** of 'fretty' and 'fresh'. **Flowing run-on lines** describe the surge of growing nature. Hopkins is the exception in this fertile scene. The negatives 'not', 'no', the punctuation of semi-colon and comma and the inversion of the phrase 'but not I build; no, but strain' depict the **fruitless efforts of the poet to create**. The dramatic, sterile image of 'Time's eunuch', the castrated male, contrasts the poet's unhappy state of unsuccessful effort with the ease of fruitful

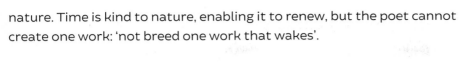

nature. Time is kind to nature, enabling it to renew, but the poet cannot create one work: 'not breed one work that wakes'.

The last line of the poem pleads for help and rescue. An image of a drought-stricken plant looking for life-giving water is used to describe the poet's plight of unsuccessful poetic creativity. **He looks to the 'lord of life'** for release. Hopkins had written in one of his final letters, 'If I could produce work ... but it kills me to be time's eunuch and never to beget'. It is intriguing that someone of such great faith can argue ('contend') so vehemently with God. Hopkins stretches the disciplined structure of the sonnet form to echo his frustration as he strains to create.

⌨ Writing About the Poem

'Hopkins's poetry deals with the theme that God's will is a mystery to us.' Discuss this statement, illustrating your response with relevant quotation from 'Thou Art Indeed Just, Lord, if I Contend'.

Sample Paragraph

In the sonnet, 'Thou Art Indeed Just, Lord', Hopkins asks God several questions: 'Why do sinners' ways prosper? And why must/ Disappointment all I endeavour end?' The poet is frustrated that God's will is such a mystery and that so much suffering is allowed to happen in the world. This mood of puzzlement continues in the sestet as he urgently points out how nature is thriving ('fretty chervil', 'birds build'). But he, in contrast, is far from happy. He concludes with the striking image of himself as 'Time's eunuch', a castrated slave unable to reproduce. Hopkins makes one final plea to God to nourish his infertile 'roots' with 'rain'. The alliteration associates him closely with the fertile world of nature, 'banks and brakes'. In the end, he accepts that God is the 'lord of life', his divine plan a mystery to us, but we can still trust in his love and forgiveness.

EXAMINER'S COMMENT

Close reading of the text is evident in this insightful paragraph – particularly in the developed discussion on the theme of doubting God's will. Effective use is made of Hopkins's imagery and alliteration. Expression is assured and there is supportive quotation throughout. An impressive top-grade standard.

✒ Class/Homework Exercises

1. Hopkins's innovative poetic style makes his work accessible to the modern reader. How true is this of 'Thou Art Indeed Just, Lord, if I Contend'? Use reference to the poem in your answer.
2. Hopkins complains and questions throughout this poem. What conclusion does he reach in the end? Did you find this ending satisfactory or not? Give reasons for your opinion.

⊙ Points to Consider

- **Deeply personal and direct address to God.**
- **Hurt and frustration as poet wrestles with his religious faith.**
- **Struggle to control anger and frustration.**
- **Effective use of alliteration and vivid imagery.**
- **Contrast between abundance of nature and man's infertility.**
- **Concluding prayer to enable creativity to blossom.**

Sample Leaving Cert Questions on Hopkin's Poetry

1. **Discuss how Hopkins's unique approach to language conveys a sense of his intense spiritual awareness. Develop your response with reference to the poems by Gerard Manley Hopkins on your course.**

2. **'Gerard Manley Hopkins celebrates the wonder and beauty of nature through the effective use of evocative visual and aural imagery.' Discuss this view, developing your answer with reference to the poems by Hopkins on your course.**

3. **'Hopkins's distinctive poetic style highlights his struggle with what he believes to be important truths.' Discuss this statement, developing your response with reference to the themes and language evident in the poems by Gerard Manley Hopkins on your course.**

How do I organise my answer?

(Sample question 1)

Discuss how Hopkins's unique approach to language conveys a sense of his intense spiritual awareness. Develop your response with reference to the poems by Gerard Manley Hopkins on your course.

Sample Plan 1

Intro: *(Stance: agree with viewpoint in the question)* Hopkins's poems highlight his personal religious vision. His innovative poetry uses rich imagery and stunning sound effects. While celebrating God's creation, he also acknowledges man's suffering and weakness.

Point 1: *(Celebration of uniqueness – vivid imagery, alliteration)* 'The Windhover' celebrates the distinctive bird as a symbol of Christ the Saviour. Rich alliteration describes its special appearance ('wimpling wing').

Point 2: *(Prayerful praise – striking sound effects)* 'Pied Beauty', another powerful hymn of praise to God ('Glory be to God') for the dazzling variety of nature ('dappled things'). Emphatic language shows man and nature in harmony ('Landscape plotted and pieced – fold, fallow, and plough'). Simple confident conclusion ('Praise him').

Understanding the Prescribed Poetry Question

Marks are awarded using the PCLM Marking Scheme:
P = 15; C = 15; L = 15; M = 5
Total = 50

- **P** (Purpose = 15 marks) refers to the set question and is the launch pad for the answer. This involves engaging with all aspects of the question. Both theme and language must be addressed, although not necessarily equally.

- **C** (Coherence = 15 marks) refers to the organisation of the developed response and the use of accurate, relevant quotation. Paragraphing is essential.

- **L** (Language = 15 marks) refers to the student's skill in controlling language throughout the answer.

- **M** (Mechanics = 5 marks) refers to spelling and grammar.

- Although no specific number of poems is required, students usually discuss at least 3 or 4 in their written responses.

- Aim for at least 800 words, to be completed within 45–50 minutes.

Point 3: *(Despair/optimism – startling opening)* In contrast 'No Worst, There is None' shows the negative impact of suffering in this imperfect world. Poem concludes with a glimmer of hope that each day's suffering is eased by sleep ('each day dies with sleep'). Troubles do end.

Point 4: *(Delight in/concern for wilderness – colloquialism, onomatopoeia, run-on lines)* 'Inversnaid' located in the wilds of the Scottish Highlands. An earnest plea is made for man to stop destroying the natural beauty of wild places ('Let them be left').

Conclusion: Hopkins creates dynamic poetry celebrating nature as God's wonderful creation. He acknowledges the sin, suffering and destruction of this world but believes a merciful God will save it. Stunning visual imagery and sound effects involve the reader in Hopkins's intense vision.

Sample Paragraph: Point 1

Hopkins celebrates an extraordinary bird in 'The Windhover'. It soars on the wind in a cross shape, a dramatic symbol of Christianity. The poem's sub-title, 'To Christ our Lord', shows Hopkins's own deep religious faith. The bird reflects God's glory. Its appearance is highlighted through the alliterative description of its outstretched 'wimpling wing'. Hopkins believed Christ was crucified to save the world. The verb 'Buckle' has two opposite meanings – fall apart and pull together. It describes the mysterious movement of the bird as it breaks from its gliding motion to swoop down on its prey. This verb also refers to God descending to earth to save mankind with tongues of flame, 'the fire that breaks from thee'. To the poet, the bird is a magnificent symbol of Christ who will be his defender ('chevalier') against the evil of this world. The poem concludes in a riot of Christ's colours, 'gold-vermilion'.

EXAMINER'S COMMENT

A focused and analytical paragraph. Effective use of selected text references supports discussion points about the poet's central theme of spiritual awareness and his distinctive language use. Quotes are skilfully interwoven into the main commentary. Confident, varied expression throughout adds to the top-grade quality.

(Sample question 2)

'Gerard Manley Hopkins celebrates the wonder and beauty of nature through the effective use of evocative visual and aural imagery.' Discuss this view, developing your answer with reference to the poems by Hopkins on your course.

Sample Plan 2

Intro: *(Stance: agree with viewpoint in the question)* Hopkins creates inspired visions of nature's abundant variety. He also contrasts nature's ability to renew itself with humanity's destructive actions.

Point 1: *(Appreciation of natural world – elaborate wordplay)* 'God's Grandeur' reveals poet's wonder at nature's power to grow again in contrast to his dismay at human destruction ('wears man's smudge'). Yet God's reassuring presence in nature guards like the bird protecting its young ('broods with warm breast').

Point 2: *(Admiration of nature's/humans' beauty/diversity – striking imagery)* 'As Kingfishers Catch Fire, Dragonflies Draw Flame' captures two of nature's most brilliant creatures, the kingfisher and dragonfly in powerful images ('catch fire', 'draw flame'). Aural effects echo a variety of sounds ('ring', 'tells', 'fling').

Point 3: *(Exuberant reflection on the natural world – aural music, inscape)* 'Spring' uses imaginative sound effects to express joy – alliteration ('long and lovely and lush'), assonance ('weeds', 'wheels'), onomatopoeia ('wring'). Close observation results in inscape, capturing the essence of an object, such as the shine on leaves ('glassy').

Point 4: *(Contrast fertile nature/sterile man – legal language, unusual syntax)* 'Thou Art Indeed Just, Lord, if I Contend' directs accusatory questions at God ('Why do sinners' ways prosper?') Sharp contrast in imagery between nature's fertility and humanity's sterility.

Conclusion: Hopkins explores the wonder of nature through exuberant description and stunning aural effects. This leads him to consider humans' destruction of nature as well as our inability to constantly create.

Sample Paragraph: Point 4

'Thou Art Indeed Just' opens with Hopkins asking God challenging questions, 'Why do sinners' ways prosper?' The awkward order of words highlights the poet's frustration at his own useless efforts, 'why must/Disappointment all I endeavour end?' Meanwhile, nature is thriving. This is suggested in run-on lines and vivid visual imagery, 'laced they are again/With fretty chervil'. Hopkins describes the wild beauty of the natural scene around him. The wind shakes the 'banks and brakes' but they still remain intact. It is here that 'birds build' – unlike the poet who is unable to build anything. The sterile image, 'Time's eunuch', describes his hopeless attempts to produce work. At the end of the poem, Hopkins's reflections on the wonder of nature widen out to include the many different emotions experienced by human beings when we observe nature's beauty and mystery.

EXAM FOCUS

- As you may not be familiar with some of the poems referred to in the sample plans, substitute poems that you have studied closely.
- Key points about a particular poem can be developed over more than one paragraph.
- Paragraphs may also include cross-referencing and discussion of more than one poem.
- Remember that there is no single 'correct' answer to poetry questions, so always be confident in expressing your own considered response.

Leaving Cert Sample Essay

'Hopkins's distinctive poetic style highlights his struggle with what he believes to be important truths.' Discuss this statement, developing your response with reference to the themes and language evident in the poems by Gerard Manley Hopkins on your course.

Sample Essay

INDICATIVE MATERIAL

- **Hopkins's distinctive style** (experimental language – sound, imagery, symbolism, repetition, sprung rhythm, dramatic effects, range of tones and poetic forms, etc.)

... highlights:

- **his struggle** (conflicting feelings, intense sense of delight and dejection, self-doubt, etc.)

... with:

- **important truths** (deeply-held beliefs – God as Creator, celebration of nature, as source of salvation, etc.)

1. Hopkins is known for his unusual writing style. His use of language is odd and unexpected. He often omits words and includes vivid visual images and dramatic sound effects. Two key themes in his poetry are the beauty of nature and his deep belief in God. Hopkins engages readers in his personal struggle with religious faith in several of his poems.

2. In 'Spring', Hopkins expresses great delight in the mystery and beauty of the season. He believed that loving nature was almost like loving God, its creator. This is seen in the dynamic description of common weeds, 'long and lovely and lush'. He draws attention to the intense blue of the sky, a 'rush with richness'. Hopkins links all this 'juice' and 'joy'. It's all evidence of God's work. As a Jesuit priest, he believes this is a glimpse of the earth like it was before Adam and Eve were expelled from the Garden of Eden. This idea of innocent purity is further highlighted by references to Mary, the mother of God, 'O maid's child' and 'Mayday'. May is a special month. It is traditionally associated with the worship of Mary, to whom Hopkins had a special devotion.

3. Hopkins uses language in various ways to express spiritual beliefs through sensuous imagery. He is fascinated by the sounds of nature. The high-pitched piercing cry of the thrush is described using slender vowel assonance, 'rinse and wring'. The deep blue sky sweeps down to meet the tree branches overhead – which is suggested in the sibilance of 'brush'. Throughout the poem, he uses language to capture the excitement of the moment. In some cases, Hopkins uses nouns as verbs, for example, 'leaves' and 'blooms'. Run-on lines re-create the growth and activity happening at springtime. In pushing language beyond the usual limits, Hopkins successfully captures the spirit of the magical spring season, created by God.

4. 'Felix Randal' was written during a very unhappy period of the poet's life when he cared for sick people in a slum area of Liverpool. Man replaces nature here as the main subject of the poem. The young blacksmith is first described in his prime at the height of his powers. This is done through alliteration and compound adjectives, 'big-boned' and 'hardy-handsome'. Felix used metal for horses' shoes by beating out iron. But his health has now failed and he has suffered terrible sickness, 'Fatal four disorders, fleshed there, all contended'. The unusual order of words is typical of Hopkins. In a way, he is trying to draw attention to how life can be cruel and that nobody can ever fully understand why there is suffering in the world.

5. However, the poet's deep faith consoles him. He sees Felix as a man who has to become a 'child' to enter heaven. Hopkins's earlier attitude seemed detached, 'O he is dead then?'– but this is now replaced by deep compassion for another human being. He uses the local dialect, 'all road ever he offended'. He hopes that God will forgive Felix for whatever sins he has committed and will welcome him into heaven. Hopkins ends the poem by celebrating the gift of life while it lasts. He remembers when Felix Randal was in full health and had little 'forethought' of his death, standing at the forge when he worked hard, making a 'bright and battering sandal' or horseshoe for a great drayhorse.

6. 'I Wake and Feel the Fell of Dark, Not Day' is one of the so-called 'terrible sonnets' written during the poet's unhappy time working in Dublin. He draws attention to the personal pain of sleepless nights by using emphatic alliteration, 'I wake and feel the fell of dark, not day'. The unsuccessful prayers for relief from this torment are suggested by the harsh phrase, 'cries countless'. Hopkins uses first person pronouns to stress his pain, 'I am gall. I am heartburn'. While he acknowledges God's love, he complains that he is trapped in an endless cycle. All he can taste is his own 'bitter' self and he seems to be cursed. The only glimmer of hope is his realisation that he has a possibility of salvation unlike those souls cast down to the fires of Hell, their suffering vividly described as 'sweating selves'.

GRADE: H1
P = 15/15
C = 13/15
L = 12/15
M = 5/5
Total = 45/50

7. Hopkins writes passionately about the beauty of nature which to him is the physical symbol of God's glory. But he also writes about the darker aspects of life, sickness, suffering and feelings of abandonment. Whether celebrating God's presence in beauty or struggling with pessimism, Hopkins's innovative use of language allows readers to engage with his deeply-held conviction that God, not man, is the creator of the universe.

(770 words)

👓 Revision Overview

'God's Grandeur'
In this dramatic sonnet, Hopkins explores how God's reassuring presence is infused in the world of nature.

'Spring'
A beautifully crafted reflection on the beauty, innocence and spiritual significance of nature.

'As Kingfishers Catch Fire, Dragonflies Draw Flame'
Central themes include nature's beauty, variety and uniqueness. Hopkins relates mankind's ultimate spiritual purpose to the natural world.

'The Windhover'
The sense of religious wonder is a key feature of this striking sonnet in which Hopkins presents the beauty of nature as a compelling metaphor for Christ's beauty.

'Pied Beauty'
Another hymn to creation. Hopkins praises the variety and beauty of the world, glorifying the infinite power of God and the hope that can be found in faith.

'Felix Randal'
Italian sonnet tracing the relationship between a spiritual healer and the sufferer. Both complement each other in the act of attaining eternal salvation.

'Inversnaid'
Hopkins wonders what would become of the world without unspoiled remote landscapes and he urges people to retain such beautiful places.

'I Wake and Feel the Fell of Dark, Not Day'
In this 'dark sonnet', Hopkins explores the theme of exile from God, the personal doubt that many believers feel at times.

'No Worst, There is None'
Another of the 'terrible sonnets'. As a Christian, Hopkins is intensely aware of the spiritual torment of feeling alienated from God.

'Thou Art Indeed Just, Lord, if I Contend'
Another powerful examination of the mystery of faith. Hopkins questions the existence of evil in the world but concludes by placing his own trust in God.

💬 Last Words

'What you look hard at seems to look hard at you.'
G. M. Hopkins

'Hopkins is more concerned with putting across his perceptions than with fulfilling customary expectations of grammar.'
Robert Bernard Martin

'Design, pattern, or what I am in the habit of calling inscape is what I above all aim at in poetry.'
G. M. Hopkins

NATURE

MEANING OF LIFE

SUFFERING

RELIGION/ SPIRITUALITY

TRANSIENCE

Paula Meehan
1955–

'When I go into poetry, I go into a kind of dream time.'

Paula Meehan was born in 1955 and spent her early years in Dublin's north inner city. While at secondary school, she wrote lyrics for local bands and began publishing her poems in a young people's magazine. After studying at Trinity College, she travelled round Europe and America before returning to Ireland, where she taught creative writing in universities, prisons and in the wider community. During the mid–1980s, Meehan's first poetry collections, *Return and No Blame* and *Reading the Sky*, were published. However, her work gained broader attention with *The Man who was Marked by Winter* in 1991 and since then her numerous collections have won consistent praise.

Meehan is innovative in experimenting with form, and her poems are haunting in their evocation of Irish places and speech patterns. Many draw their energy from the poet's vivid reminiscences of childhood, family and community. Her poetry also offers a powerful critique of Ireland's recent social history.

Paula Meehan's uncompromising engagement with the politics of gender and class, and her love of the natural world, make her one of Ireland's most distinctive and influential voices.

Investigate Further

To find out more about Paula Meehan, or to hear readings of her poems not already available in your eBook, you could search some useful websites, such as YouTube, BBC Poetry, poetryfoundation.org and poetryarchive.org, or access additional material on this page of your eBook.

Prescribed Poems

(OL) indicates poems that are also prescribed for the Ordinary Level course.

POETRY FOCUS

1 🔊 **Buying Winkles**

Title: winkles are edible snail-like shellfish. Also called periwinkles or whelks.

My mother would spare me sixpence and say,
'Hurry up now and don't be talking to strange
men on the way.' I'd dash from the ghosts
on the stairs where the bulb had blown
out into Gardiner Street, all relief.   5
A bonus if the moon was in the strip of sky
between the tall houses, or stars out,
but even in rain I was happy — the winkles
would be wet and glisten blue like little
night skies themselves. I'd hold the tanner tight   *— Childhood innocence*   10
and jump every crack in the pavement,
I'd wave up to women at sills or those
lingering in doorways and weave a glad path through
men heading out for the night.

difference between the role of men & women

She'd be sitting outside the Rosebowl Bar   *— sense of place*   15
on an orange-crate, a pram loaded
with pails of winkles before her.
When the bar doors swung open they'd leak
the smell of men together with drink   *— role of men*
and I saw light in golden mirrors.   20
I envied each soul in the hot interior.

I'd ask her again to show me the right way
to do *it*. She'd take a pin from her shawl —
'Open the eyelid. So. Stick it in
till you feel a grip, then slither him out.   25
Gently, mind.' The sweetest extra winkle
that brought the sea to me.
'Tell yer Ma I picked them fresh this morning.'

Dublin accent

I'd bear the newspaper twists
bulging fat with winkles
proudly home, like torches.   30

sixpence: coin worth six old pence, discontinued since 1980. Worth about fifty cent in today's money.

Gardiner Street: long Georgian street in Dublin's north inner city.

tanner: slang for sixpence.

sills: window ledges.

orange-crate: wooden box sometimes used as a seat.
pails: small buckets.

eyelid: tiny 'cap' which covers the winkle.

newspaper twists: small rolls of paper used to wrap fish.

'the tall houses'

PAULA MEEHAN

 Personal Response

1. How does the poet create a sense of childhood innocence in the opening stanza? Comment on the effect of the tone, rhythm and verbs, using suitable reference to the text.
2. In your opinion, why did the child envy the people who were in the Rosebowl Bar? Briefly explain your response.
3. Do you think Meehan's account of 1960s Dublin life is realistic or is it a sentimental poem that glorifies the old days? Give reasons for your answer, using reference to the text.

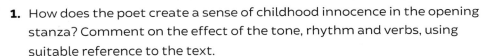 Critical Literacy

Memory and continuity are recurring themes in Paula Meehan's work. Her third collection, *The Man who was Marked by Winter* (1991), recalls significant moments from her childhood, several of which combine a wonderful energy with a warm tone. 'Buying Winkles' is not only a vibrant snapshot of Dublin's social history in the early 1960s, it also evokes the mystery and charm of the act of writing poetry.

The poem's opening lines present a tender image of Paula Meehan's early days in Dublin's inner city. She recalls the eager anticipation and excitement of being sent to buy winkles for her mother, who would 'spare her sixpence'. The **close child–mother bond** is highlighted by the verb 'spare', suggesting that she has been specially chosen and trusted with an important task.

This small domestic drama is immediately brought to life with the mother's words of warning: 'don't be talking to strange/men on the way'. The poet recalls her younger self, leaving behind imaginary 'ghosts' on the dark tenement stairs where she lived to 'dash' along the neighbouring streets on her important errand. Everything delights her on this **magical journey**: 'even in rain I was happy' (line 8).

Closely observed details recreate a vivid picture of **the young girl's zest for life** and its many mysteries. Sibilant 's' sounds used to describe the wet winkles that 'glisten blue like little/night skies' add a tactile quality to the image. Energetic run-on lines emphasise the child's intense feeling of freedom: 'I'd hold the tanner tight/and jump every crack in the pavement'.

A dynamic picture of working-class communal living during the 1960s emerges in this scene, yet history is not entirely romanticised. Despite all the friendliness and good humour, society is shaped by both **poverty and gender roles**. To a great extent, women are depicted as being marginalised in this crushingly patriarchal environment. Some are restricted to the shadows, 'at sills', while prostitutes wait patiently, 'lingering in doorways'. Meanwhile, the men are free, 'heading out for the night'.

209 |

In line 15, the poet introduces a larger-than-life figure from her past. The winkle-seller is found in her usual location 'outside the Rosebowl Bar'. Using a discarded orange-crate as a makeshift seat, she exhibits her merchandise on an old pram. Equally fascinating is the forbidden male world behind the bar doors where the child would occasionally get an alluring glimpse of 'light in golden mirrors'. Naturally, this only increases her **keen sense of wonder**: 'I envied each soul in the hot interior'.

The evocative description of the winkle-seller's **playful language** is heard as she uses a pin to coax the whelks out of their spiral shells. It conveys the local colour and dialect of the times: 'Stick it in/till you feel a grip, then slither him out./Gently, mind' (lines 24–26). The onomatopoeic verb 'slither' indicates the slow movement and sound of the juicy winkles being de-shelled. Again, there is a suggestion of how the moment was significant in opening up new worlds for Meehan beyond the confines of Dublin, 'the sweetest extra winkle that brought the sea to me'. We are left with the reassurance of the winkle-seller's colloquial voice: 'Tell yer Ma I picked them fresh this morning'.

The poem ends with an engaging picture of the young girl taking the shellfish back home. The concluding lines are short, reflecting the self-assurance she feels after her street adventure: 'I'd bear the newspaper twists/bulging fat with winkles/proudly home, like torches'. The simile is particularly effective in illustrating her innocent **sense of triumph** as she relishes the edgy freedom of the city streets at night. It also suggests that such simple experiences as buying winkles were already lighting the way to her creative future.

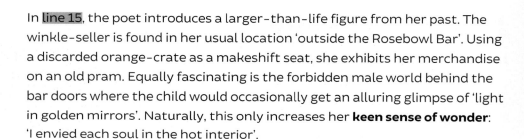

✒ Writing About the Poem

'Paula Meehan's poetry often has a powerful dramatic quality which engages readers.' Discuss this view, with reference to 'Buying Winkles'.

Sample Paragraph

'Buying Winkles' is about a time when the poet was young and felt a little bit scared of the adult world. The poem has a number of stand-out characters who appear powerful and intimidating. The poet's mother warns her to avoid 'strange men'. The girl is also slightly afraid of the local women 'lingering in doorways'. The old lady selling winkles really fascinates her. She sits outside the pub and shows her how to scoop out the shellfish with a clothes pin. She speaks like a true Dub, adding an extra touch of realism. The bar itself is a mystery to the girl who can only dream about what is going on inside what seems like a palace with 'golden mirrors'. The back streets are an exciting setting and I could imagine the night-time atmosphere creating a lot of drama. The central character is the young narrator herself and she is very engaging – particularly at the end when she can't wait to get 'proudly home' with her precious winkles wrapped up in newspapers.

EXAMINER'S COMMENT

A focused top-grade response that makes good use of accurate quotations integrated well into the commentary. The two elements of the question ('dramatic quality' and 'engages readers') are addressed throughout. Discussion points range across the entire poem, showing close understanding of the text. Expression is also clear, varied and controlled.

✒ Class/Homework Exercises

1. 'Paula Meehan often makes effective use of vivid descriptive details to celebrate ordinary people and everyday Irish life.' Discuss this statement with reference to 'Buying Winkles'.

2. 'Meehan's poetry can be highly emotional, but always manages to avoid sentimentality.' To what extent is this true of 'Buying Winkles'? Develop the points you make with suitable reference to the poem.

⊙ Points to Consider

- **Enduring impact of family and community, childhood innocence, and the joys of life are central to the poem.**

- **Other themes include memory, exclusion, creativity and social history.**

- **Authentic sense of atmosphere, time and place.**

- **Appealing dramatic elements including characters, storyline and dialogue.**

- **Contrasting tones: nostalgic, reflective, insightful and celebratory.**

2 🔊 **The Pattern**

Title: a repeated decorative design; set of instructions; an example for others to follow.

Little has come down to me of hers,
a sewing machine, a wedding band,
a clutch of photos, the sting of her hand
across my face in one of our wars

when we had grown bitter and apart.   5
Some say that's the fate of the eldest daughter,
I wish now she'd lasted till after
I'd grown up. We might have made a new start

as women without tags like *mother*, *wife*,
sister, *daughter*, taken our chances from there.   10
At forty-two she headed for god knows where,
I've never gone back to visit her grave.

*

First she'd scrub the floor with Sunlight soap,
an armreach at a time. When her knees grew sore
she'd break for a cup of tea, then start again   15
at the door with lavender polish. The smell
would percolate back through the flat to us,
her brood banished to the bedroom.

And as she buffed the wax to a high shine
did she catch her own face coming clear?   20
Did she net a glimmer of her true self?
Did her mirror tell her what mine tells me?

I have her shrug and go on
knowing history has brought her to her knees.
She'd call us in and let us skate around   25
in our socks. We'd grow solemn as planets
in an intricate orbit about her.

*

She's bending over crimson cloth,
the younger kids are long in bed.
Late summer, cold enough for a fire,   30
she works by fading light
to remake an old dress for me.
It's first day back at school tomorrow,

*

clutch: handful.

tags: labels, definitions.

Sunlight soap: all-purpose household soap.

percolate: filter gradually.

brood: young family.

buffed: polished.

net a glimmer: catch a trace.

intricate orbit: elaborate circle.

'Pure lambswool. Plenty of wear in it yet.
You know I wore this when I went out with your Da.   35
I was supposed to be down in a friend's house,
your Granda caught us at the corner.
He dragged me in by the hair — it was long as yours then —
in front of the whole street.
He called your Da every name under the sun,   40
cornerboy, lout; I needn't tell you
what he called me. He shoved my whole head
under the kitchen tap, took a scrubbing brush
and carbolic soap and in ice-cold water he scrubbed
every spick of lipstick and mascara off my face.   45
Christ but he was a right tyrant, your Granda,
'It'll be over my dead body anyone harms a hair of your head.'

                                *

She must have stayed up half the night
to finish the dress. I found it airing at the fire,
three new copybooks on the table and a bright   50
bronze nib, St Christopher strung on a silver wire,

as if I were embarking on a perilous journey
to uncharted realms. I wore that dress
with little grace. To me it spelt poverty,
the stigma of the second hand. I grew enough to pass   55

it on by Christmas to the next in line. I was sizing
up the world beyond our flat patch by patch
daily after school, and fitting each surprising
city street to city square to diamond. I'd watch

the Liffey for hours pulsing to the sea   60
and the coming and going of ships,
certain that one day it would carry me
to Zanzibar, Bombay, the land of the Ethiops.

                                *

There's a photo of her taken in the Phoenix Park
alone on a bench surrounded by roses   65
as if she had been born to formal gardens.
She stares out as if unaware
that any human hand held the camera, wrapped
entirely in her own shadow, the world beyond her
already a dream, already lost. She's   70
eight months pregnant. Her last child.

                                *

lambswool: fine soft wool.

cornerboy: idler.
lout: thug.

carbolic soap: harsh disinfectant soap.

St Christopher: holy medal of the patron saint of travellers.

embarking: setting out.
perilous: dangerous.
uncharted realms: unknown lands.

stigma: shame, disgrace.

pulsing: beating, throbbing.

Zanzibar: island off East Africa.
Bombay: Indian city.
Land of the Ethiops: East African country.

Phoenix Park: public parkland in Dublin.

Her steel needles sparked and clacked,
the only other sound a settling coal
or her sporadic mutter
at a hard part in the pattern.   75
She favoured sensible shades:
Moss Green, Mustard, Beige.

I dreamt a robe of a colour
so pure it became a word.

Sometimes I'd have to kneel   80
an hour before her by the fire,
a skein around my outstretched hands,
while she rolled wool into balls.
If I swam like a kite too high
amongst the shadows on the ceiling   85
or flew like a fish in the pools
of pulsing light, she'd reel me firmly
home, she'd land me at her knees.

Tongues of flame in her dark eyes,
She'd say, 'One of these days I must   90
teach you to follow a pattern.'

clacked: clicked.

sporadic: occasional, random.

skein: loosely coiled length of wool.

kite: light air-borne toy.

reel: roll or wind back.

'a hard part in the pattern'

👤 Personal Response

1. In your opinion, what is the poet's dominant mood in the first three stanzas? Is it confused, bitter, nostalgic, reflective, affirming? Support your answer with reference to the text.

2. Pick two examples of onomatopoeia (words or phrases whose sound echo the meaning) from the poem which you found particularly effective. Briefly explain your choices.

3. Write a short personal response to the poem, outlining the impact it made on you.

👁 Critical Literacy

Throughout much of her poetry, Paula Meehan explores the complex reality of her own working-class origins and family relationships. Her 1991 collection, *The Man who was Marked by Winter*, includes candid, deeply personal poems which provide beautiful haunting images of her past. Meehan has spoken of 'going back and taking things from the negative in your life and trying to transform them into ... something much more powerful and clear'. 'The Pattern' is an autobiographical series of snapshots portraying a poignant and conflicted mother–daughter relationship.

The poet has only inherited a few modest items from her mother, 'a sewing machine, a wedding band,/a clutch of photos'. Suddenly she thrusts the reader into the furious immediacy of her childhood. The bitter conflict between mother and 'eldest daughter' is vividly conveyed through flowing run-on lines and a sharp onomatopoeic 'sting' of her mother's hand across the poet's face. Wistfully, Meehan reflects on what might have been, had they known each other as adults, unhampered by the restrictive familial labels of '*mother, wife/sister, daughter*' (line 9). The poet records her mother's early death and comments – with droll humour – 'she headed for god knows where'. Their **fractured relationship** is evident in the frank admission, 'I've never gone back to visit her grave'.

Meehan's upbringing in Dublin's inner city is recreated through **dramatic sensory recollections**. Her mother is engaged in routine housework. Soft sibilance recalls the gentle 'Sunlight soap' she used to 'scrub the floor' (line 13). The heady smell of 'lavender polish' filters through the small flat where the 'brood' of children have been confined to the bedroom until the work is complete. Rhetorical questions probe whether the mother has ever recognised her 'true self', her unique identity as a person, in the reflective surfaces. The poet now wonders what her subservient mother might have seen in her reflection. Meehan is keenly aware that Irish society 'brought her to her knees'. Yet she recovers and acknowledges that her childhood was supportive and nurturing. Her pragmatic mother just kept going, allowing the children to skate on the newly polished floor, shining it further with their stockinged feet. Like satellites, they repeatedly circled her as if orbiting their centre of the universe.

The poet presents another significant episode from the past in line 34. Her mother is busy altering old clothes for her daughter. The **practical maternal voice is heard**, 'Plenty of wear in it yet', while she remakes the crimson dress she wore 'when I went out with your Da'. Suddenly the viciousness of male power in working-class communities erupts. Her mother recollects 'Granda' dragging her home 'by the hair' because she was 'caught' meeting her boyfriend. Harsh 'carbolic soap' with 'ice-cold water' is used to scrub every trace of make-up from her face. Meehan also remembers her mother's angry reaction, swearing to protect her from such male violence, 'It'll be over my dead body anyone harms a hair of your head'. But was this always the case?

However, in line 48, there is further **recognition of her mother's caring nature**, 'She must have stayed up half the night/to finish the dress'. Another list itemises the careful preparation for her daughter's return to school, 'three new copybooks', a 'bright/bronze nib' and a 'St Christopher' medal. The poet believes her mother imagined her going off on 'a perilous journey' of discovery. Despite this, all the loving care is met with petulance from the child who wore the second-hand dress with 'little grace'. Meehan is reminded of the acute shame and 'stigma' of her family's poverty. Run-through lines echo the growing independence of this young girl who looked outwards at a 'world beyond'. She discovers a 'surprising/city street' which fits into a 'city square' and then transforms into a 'diamond' or parallelogram. Is she mirroring her mother's creativity by patterning? Is she making her own unique design?

Hemmed in by disadvantage and gender repression, the poet **desires to escape the oppressive atmosphere of her home**. This is conveyed in the vivid image of the 'pulsing' dynamic flow of the River Liffey with its ever-changing scenes of incoming and departing ships. She tries to transcend her repressive circumstances by dreaming of far-off exotic places, the Moorish island of Zanzibar, bustling Bombay and the dramatic landscapes of Ethiopia.

Line 65 brings the reader back to the present, beside the poet while she looks at a photo of her heavily pregnant mother sitting in the Phoenix Park, 'surrounded by roses'. There is a striking contrast between the beauty of the formal gardens and a woman worn out with poverty and constant child-bearing, 'already lost'. Meehan now sees her mother as a victim, someone who never really discovered herself, but sits 'wrapped/entirely in her own shadow'. She only exists in her prescribed place in society, **obscured from her individual identity** as a person in her own right.

Vibrant visual and aural imagery in line 72 recreate another episode depicting the mother's creativity, 'Her steel needles sparked and clacked'. But now her voice has dimmed to a 'sporadic mutter' while she tries to negotiate a 'hard part in the pattern'. Once again her daughter dismisses her mother's efforts by ridiculing her colour choices as 'sensible shades'. Two emphatic lines stand alone, however. Her daughter dares to dream of 'a robe of a colour/so pure it became a word'. Unlike her mother, the poet chooses language rather than wool to fashion her dream.

In the final lines, Meehan expresses her feelings about **the effect of her mother's influence**. The daughter is engaged in the mind-numbing activity of holding knitting wool on 'outstretched hands' while her mother rolls the wool into balls. The daunting challenge of longing to escape is captured in the clever swapping of expected verbs, 'swam like a kite', 'flew like a fish'. Meehan's tone is ambiguous as she describes the 'Tongues of flame in her dark eyes'. Beneath the menace and mystery in this powerful image, there is a sense of a manic puppeteer, reeling back the line of the kite to bring her daughter to her proper place within the community, 'at her knees'. Is she repeating the grandfather's tyrannical behaviour, enforcing submission? Is she demanding that her daughter submit to her expected role in Irish patriarchal society?

Interestingly, the poet bears witness to the richness and dignity of her working-class background while refusing to idealise it. We are left to wonder about the extent to which the poet has broken free of 'The Pattern', her mother's legacy. What did she inherit in the end? Was the 'clutch of photos' a loving hug or a devastating embrace? While family tensions have run through the entire poem, Meehan still feels an **intense connection** to her mother, leaving readers to consider the complexity of their troubled relationship.

✒ Writing About the Poem

'Paula Meehan's poetry is starkly conflicted between her desire to recover the past and her need to move beyond it.' Discuss this view, with reference to 'The Pattern'.

Sample Paragraph

'The Pattern' presents a clear contrast between Meehan's desire to recreate working-class Dublin life in the 1960s while desperately wanting to escape its limitations. Rich imagery recreates this past, 'lavender polish' and 'The smell would percolate', while the children waited for the cleaning of the floor to finish. Meehan appreciates her mother's hopes for her daughter to do well. This is evident in the list of things she buys her

for going back to school. Yet in contrast to such concern, violence is used to enforce discipline, the harsh 'sting' of a hand on the young girl's face or the dragging home by the hair. The pattern of society's rules had to be adhered to. Meehan rejects this conformity by dreaming of a 'pulsing' Liffey bringing her to exotic places. Unlike her 'sensible' mother, the poet imagines a 'robe of a colour so pure it became a word'. She acknowledges her past, but refuses to be 'wrapped' like her mother 'entirely in her own shadow' with no identity except for her oppressed place in the family.

EXAMINER'S COMMENT

Assured top-grade response that included several focused discussion points based on the poet's successful use of contrast. Good sense of engagement with the text and effective use of apt reference. Accurate quotations well integrated into critical commentary. Clarity and control of varied expression throughout.

✒ Class/Homework Exercises

1. 'Paula Meehan's poetry presents dramatic and complex perspectives on her Irish working-class background.' Discuss this statement with reference to 'The Pattern'.
2. 'Meehan's reflective poetry candidly explores her Irish identity through stunning aural and visual effects.' To what extent is this true of 'The Pattern'? Develop your answer with suitable textual evidence.

◉ Points to Consider

- **Conflict between warm acknowledgement of Irish working-class past and a more critical adult view of its negative impact.**

- **Other key themes include memory, creativity and identity.**

- **Authentic evocation of character, atmosphere, time and place.**

- **Contrasting tones: nostalgic, reflective, critical, insightful and cynical.**

- **Engaging poetic techniques: visual and aural imagery, contrasts, direct speech.**

3 The Statue of the Virgin at Granard Speaks

PAULA MEEHAN

It can be bitter here at times like this,
November wind sweeping across the border.
Its seeds of ice would cut you to the quick.
The whole town tucked up safe and dreaming,
even wild things gone to earth, and I   5
stuck up here in this grotto, without as much as
star or planet to ease my vigil.

grotto: ornamental religious shrine built into rock.
vigil: night watch.

The howling won't let up. Trees
cavort in agony as if they would be free
and take off — ghost voyagers   10
on the wind that carries intimations
of garrison towns, walled cities, ghetto lanes
where men hunt each other and invoke
the various names of God as blessing
on their death tactics, their night manoeuvres.   15
Closer to home the wind sails over
dying lakes. I hear fish drowning.
I taste the stagnant water mingled
with turf smoke from outlying farms.

cavort: twist, shake.
voyagers: travellers, messages.
intimations: suggestions, memories.
garrison towns: places where troops were stationed.
ghetto lanes: backstreet slums.
invoke: pray to.
manoeuvres: movements, plots.

mingled: mixed.

They call me Mary — Blessed, Holy, Virgin.   20
They fit me to a myth of a man crucified:
the scourging and the falling, and the falling again,
the thorny crown, the hammer blow of iron
into wrist and ankle, the sacred bleeding heart.
They name me Mother of all this grief   25
though mated to no mortal man.
They kneel before me and their prayers
fly up like sparks from a bonfire
that blaze a moment, then wink out.

myth of a man crucified: story of Jesus Christ.
scourging: flogging, torture.

thorny crown: Jesus was mocked and a crown of thorns was placed on his head.
sacred bleeding heart: also known as the Sacred Heart. Catholic symbol of Christ's sacrifice and love for humanity.

It can be lovely here at times. Springtime,   30
early summer. Girls in Communion frocks
pale rivals to the riot in the hedgerows
of cow parsley and haw blossom, the perfume
from every rushy acre that's left for hay
when the light swings longer with the sun's push north.   35

Communion frocks: white dresses symbolising purity worn at the Holy Communion ceremony.
cow parsley: fern-like leaves with delicate white flowers.

Or the grace of a midsummer wedding
when the earth herself calls out for coupling
and I would break loose of my stony robes,
pure blue, pure white, as if they had robbed
a child's sky for their colour. My being   40
cries out to be incarnate, incarnate,
maculate and tousled in a honeyed bed.

Even an autumn burial can work its own pageantry.
The hedges heavy with the burden of fruiting
crab, sloe, berry, hip; clouds scud east   45
pear scented, windfalls secret in long
orchard grasses, and some old soul is lowered
to his kin. Death is just another harvest
scripted to the season's play.

But on this All Souls' Night there is   50
no respite from the keening of the wind.
I would not be amazed if every corpse came risen
from the graveyard to join in exaltation with the gale,
a cacophony of bone imploring sky for judgement
and release from being the conscience of the town. 55

On a night like this I remember the child
who came with fifteen summers to her name,
and she lay down alone at my feet
without midwife or doctor or friend to hold her hand
and she pushed her secret out into the night,   60
far from the town tucked up in little scandals,
bargains struck, words broken, prayers, promises,
and though she cried out to me *in extremis*
I did not move,
I didn't lift a finger to help her,   65
I didn't intercede with heaven,
nor whisper the charmed word in God's ear.

On a night like this I number the days to the solstice
and the turn back to the light.
                              O sun,   70
centre of our foolish dance,
burning heart of stone,
molten mother of us all,
hear me and have pity.

coupling: physical union, intimacy.

incarnate: alive, embodied.

maculate: flawed, human.

pageantry: spectacle, ceremony.

scud: rush, sail.

keening: wailing, grieving.

exaltation: intense praise.

cacophony: loud outburst.

secret: baby.

in extremis: on the point of death.

intercede: plead.

solstice: year's shortest day.

molten: liquified.

👤 Personal Response

1. Describe the tone of voice in the opening stanza, using close reference to the text.
2. Select one image or phrase from the poem that you find particularly startling or disturbing. Briefly explain your choice.
3. Write a short personal response to the poem, highlighting the overall impact it made on you.

◉ Critical Literacy

On 31 January 1984, a fifteen-year-old girl died after giving birth at the hillside grotto on the outskirts of Granard, Co. Longford. Ann Lovett was found by passers-by. Her baby boy also died. Ann had kept the pregnancy hidden from her family, teachers and friends. Meehan is well known as an activist who raises poetry into public consciousness. In this dramatic monologue, she remembers the heartbreak associated with one young woman's tragedy. Set on All Souls' Night, the iconic statue comes alive as the poet assumes the voice of the Blessed Virgin in the grotto recalling the past year. 'The Statue of the Virgin at Granard Speaks' was published in 1991.

The colloquial 'voice' Meehan gives to the iconic statue is out of character with the Blessed Virgin's usual timid image. Mary complains about the 'bitter' cold and northerly winds carrying 'seeds of ice' from which nothing good will grow. She envies 'the whole town tucked up safe' while she is 'stuck up here in this grotto'. Nothing eases her 'vigil'. Her **resentful tone** is evident throughout the opening stanza. There is an emphasis on rejection and alienation. Harsh winter weather is an obvious symbol of cruel times. The isolation of the statue highlights the experience of the young girl who died here and her loneliness in death.

Graphic details of the desolate landscape in stanza two provide a disquieting context for the anguish of the terrible event. Even the trees 'cavort in agony'. Meehan creates **a surreal scene of chaos and suffering**. The windswept branches become 'ghost voyagers', reminders of death elsewhere in Ireland: 'garrison towns, walled cities, ghetto lanes'. Through the statue's 'voice', Meehan expresses contempt for the way murders have sometimes been carried out in the name of religion. She references other dark periods in Irish history – particularly the sectarian conflict in the North where men use 'God as blessing/on their death tactics'. Meanwhile, all around the grotto, the natural world offers further evidence of lifeless images: 'dying lakes', 'stagnant water'.

Stanza three is filled with seething resentment: 'They call me Mary – Blessed, Holy, Virgin'. The insistent repetition creates a religious rhythm. All Mary can do is witness. She 'voices' her disappointment at the way her public image has been reduced to a stone statue, a symbolic presence, unable to act. She is primarily associated with her **passive maternal role,** confined to the background in the story of Christ's suffering and death on the cross: 'They fit me to a myth of a man crucified'. She is uneasy with the focus on violence: 'the scourging and the falling'. The Virgin feels distanced from her role as an icon unable to help those who 'kneel before me'. She has no illusions about her own lack of influence, 'their prayers/fly up like sparks'.

Following the graphic description of the crucifixion, an unexpected change of tone occurs in stanza four. Echoing the first line, the poem becomes **more positive and nostalgic**: 'It can be lovely here at times'. The statue goes on to describe the budding greenery surrounding the graveyard. The loveliness of nature is even greater than human beauty: 'Girls in Communion frocks/pale rivals to the riot in the hedgerows'. A series of dynamic images across several run-on lines describe the energy and beauty of springtime: 'the perfume/ from every rushy acre'.

The seasonal references continue in stanza five with a particularly vivid description of midsummer, 'when the earth herself calls out for coupling'. For the first time, the statue exchanges her anger with passionate desire. She **yearns for natural physical intimacy**, to 'break loose of my stony robes'. The statue longs to break free, 'to be incarnate, incarnate'. Repetition emphasises her yearning to feel truly alive. In place of Mary's traditional 'immaculate' image, she cries out to be 'maculate and tousled in a honeyed bed'.

Although summer excites the statue the most, she acknowledges the rich pageantry of autumn in stanza six, describing the hedges 'heavy with the burden of fruiting'. But she also **appreciates the realities of life**. In stark contrast to the cheerful images of bright grottos, communion frocks and midsummer weddings, there are images of darkness and pain. Mary is acutely aware of the appropriateness of autumn burial, observing that 'Death is just another harvest/scripted to the season's play'. Dying is part of the cycle of nature too.

Stanza seven takes the reader back to the icy present. It is All Souls' Night and the relentless 'keening' gale returns, bringing more reminders of death. The statue imagines corpses rising from their graves 'to join in exaltation'. The **wild supernatural scene** and disturbing image of the ghosts celebrating death becomes increasingly intense: 'a cacophony of bone'. The dead souls demand 'judgement' and 'release from being the conscience of the town'. It is time for the living to take responsibility for the horrific events that happened here.

The tone in stanza eight alternates between pity and remorse as the statue recalls a young girl ('with fifteen summers to her name') who secretly came to give birth at the grotto. The similarity between the girl's sad history and the story of the Virgin Mary is striking. Both would risk being marginalised by their community, 'the town tucked up in little scandals'. The sense of frustration and guilt is heightened, 'and though she cried out to me *in extremis*/I did not move'. As the forceful voice reaches **a dramatic climax**, short lines intensify the emotional impact: 'I didn't lift a finger to help her,/I didn't intercede with heaven'. The poem's irony is that the Virgin herself is ineffectual. Though the lines are ambiguous as to whether she cannot or will not help the girl, her powerlessness is beyond doubt.

In the final stanza, the statue's monologue becomes a **prayerful lament**. Looking ahead to the winter solstice and turning to pre-Christian pagan values, the speaker appeals directly to nature, addressing the 'molten mother' sun. She describes human existence as 'our foolish dance' and begs for mercy: 'hear me and have pity'. Poignantly, the Virgin herself is now praying for forgiveness. There is little sign, however, of any prospect of a more humanitarian world. Indeed, all that is certain is that the natural cycle of life and death will continue.

From the outset, the statue's disembodied and haunting narration has implicated a sense of **communal involvement** based on the repressiveness of Irish society. In voicing such a central Christian icon as the Blessed Virgin, Meehan obviously points to the complicity of organised religion in Ann Lovett's tragedy. In the meantime, the victim herself remains voiceless. While the poet's views are clearly expressed, it is up to individual readers to make up their own minds about the many issues explored in this unsettling, powerful poem.

'It can be bitter here at times'

✒ Writing About the Poem

'Paula Meehan's deep sense of outrage is often evident in her poetry.' Discuss this view, with reference to 'The Statue of the Virgin at Granard Speaks'.

Sample Paragraph

In 'The Statue of the Virgin', Meehan uses the voice of Our Lady to protest about a schoolgirl who died in childbirth back in 1984. The poet is channelling her own angry feelings through the talking statue. It's clear that religion has not helped the tragic victim. The statue is furious about being left abandoned in the freezing grotto – while the townspeople are 'tucked up safe'. Meehan's frantic tone is really directed at the locals who still go through the motions of praying even though it did the teenager no good whatsoever. Irish people are 'tucked up' in prayers. The phrase is repeated for emphasis. The poet's anger is at its most intense when the statue admits, 'I didn't lift a finger to help her'. Nobody else did either despite our so-called Christian community. Meehan concludes by portraying Our Lady helplessly imploring the sun for mercy – 'hear me and have pity'. Unfortunately, there is no hope at the end of this poem.

EXAMINER'S COMMENT

This clearly focused personal response shows good engagement with both the question and the poem. The focus on the poet's sense of outrage is illustrated effectively and sustained throughout. Valuable use is made of references to tone, repetition and symbolism. Expression is varied and well controlled. Overall, an impressive top-grade standard.

✒ Class/Homework Exercises

1. 'Paula Meehan often makes use of contrasting images of nature that make a powerful impact.' To what extent is this true of 'The Statue of the Virgin at Granard Speaks'? Develop your answer with suitable textual support.
2. 'Meehan's poetry has subversive and feminist qualities that engage readers.' Discuss this view in relation to 'The Statue of the Virgin at Granard Speaks'.

⊙ Points to Consider

- Meehan challenges various aspects of Irish society.
- Themes include religion, nature, inhumanity and the role of women.
- Effective use of dramatic monologue, imagery and irony.
- Varying tones: critical, indignant, compassionate, elegiac and reflective.

PAULA MEEHAN

4 🔊 Cora, Auntie

Title: Cora is the name of Meehan's aunt; the Irish form means honest and fair.

Staring Death down
with a bottle of morphine in one hand,
a bottle of Jameson in the other:

morphine: pain-relieving drug.
Jameson: Irish whiskey.

laughing at Death —
love unconditional keeping her just this side   5
of the threshold

unconditional: total.

threshold: divide.

as her body withered
and her eyes grew darker and stranger
as her hair grew back after chemo

chemo: chemotherapy, used to treat cancer.

thick and curly as when she was a girl;   10
always a girl in her glance
teasing Death — humour a lance

lance: weapon.

she tilted at Death.
Scourge of Croydon tram drivers and High Street dossers
on her motorised invalid scooter   15

tilted: leaned, attacked.
Scourge: tormentor.
Croydon: suburban area in London.
dossers: homeless people.

that last year:
bearing the pain,
not crucifixion but glory

crucifixion: agony, execution.

in her voice.
Old skin, bag of bones,   20
Grinning back at the rictus of Death:

rictus: fixed grimace.

always a girl in her name —
Cora, maiden from the Greek Κόρη,
promising blossom, summer, the scent of thyme.

Κόρη: Cora is derived from the Greek word, Κόρη (pronounced *kopp*), the goddess Persephone.
thyme: scented herb.

*

Sequin: she is standing on the kitchen table.   25
She is nearly twenty one.
It is nineteen sixty one.

Sequin: small, shiny disc sewn on clothing for decoration.

They are sewing red sequins, the women,
to the hem of her white satin dress
as she moves slowly round and round.   30

Sequins red as berries,
red as the lips of maidens
red as blood on the snow

in Child's old ballads,   35
as red as this pen
on this white paper

Child's old ballads:
traditional British folk songs
collected by Frances James
Child.

I've snatched from the chaos
to cast these lines
at my own kitchen table —

Cora, Marie, Jacinta, my aunties,   40
Helena, my mother, Mary, my grandmother —
the light of those stars

only reaching me now.
I orbit the table I can barely see over.
I am under it singing.   45

orbit: travel round.

She was weeks from taking the boat to England.
Dust on the mantlepiece,
dust on the cards she left behind:

a black cat swinging in a silver horseshoe,
a giant key to the door,   50
emblems of luck, of access.

emblems: symbols.
access: opportunity.

All that year I hunted sequins:
roaming the house I found them
in cracks and crannies,

crannies: small spaces.

in the pillowcase,   55
under the stairs,
in a hole in the lino,

lino: linoleum, floor
covering.

in a split in the sofa,
in a tear in the armchair
in the home of the shy mouse.   60

split: rip, slit.

With odd beads and single earrings,
a broken charm bracelet, a glittering pin,
I gathered them into a tin box

charm bracelet: a chain
with small jewelled
ornaments.

which I open now in her memory —
the coinage, the sudden glamour   65
of an emigrant soul.

coinage: currency,
invention.
emigrant: person who
settles in a foreign country,
exile.

| 226

'sewing red sequins'

👤 Personal Response

1. What impression do you get of Aunt Cora in the opening 16 lines? Comment on the effect of the imagery, tone, verbs and run-on lines, using suitable reference to the text.
2. In your opinion, was Cora an object of admiration or ridicule? Briefly explain your response.
3. In your view, what is the dominant mood in this poem? Happy? Sad? Nostalgic? Celebratory? Briefly explain your response, using reference to the text.

👁 Critical Literacy

Paula Meehan's collection *Painting Rain* (2009) includes poems linking landscape, community and selfhood. She dedicates several to family members. The elegy 'Cora, Auntie' encourages readers not to regard the negativity of death as an end but as a journey towards meaning. The poem also works as a way of re-establishing a lost connection between the past and present. Meehan sees her aunt's red sequins not just as an evocation of memory, but also in terms of feminine interconnection.

The poem's opening lines present a picture of **a vivacious woman**, the poet's aunt, Cora, defiantly 'Staring Death down'. The powerful presence of the encroaching end of life is captured in the personification, capitalisation and repetition of the word 'Death'. Despite this, the aunt careers merrily on her 'motorised invalid scooter', clutching a bottle of painkillers in one hand and a bottle of whiskey in the other. Vivid verbs ('laughing', 'teasing') catch the essence of this dynamic character. Yet the poet also acknowledges the realistic details of the ravages of cancer and mortality, 'body withered', 'hair grew back after chemo'. However, it is the **aunt's determined spirit** which predominates, described in the humorous metaphor of a chivalrous knight challenging death with a 'teasing' glance. In her final year, she spins around her adopted home in London, tormenting everyone.

Cora's courage in the face of life's trials is recorded in line 17. She is not broken by suffering, 'crucifixion', but endures, 'bearing the pain'. Meehan's admiration for this display of human spirit is evident in the phrase, 'glory/ in her voice'. Life conspires against the aunt. This is highlighted in the chilling images of the destructive effects of time, 'Old skin, bag of bones'.

Nevertheless, she still dares to grin at the ugly grimace ('rictus') of death. The ominous present then slips into a more optimistic past as the aunt is imagined in all her girlish glory, 'Cora, maiden from the Greek Κόρη' (line 23). Persephone was addressed as Κόρη, the goddess of vegetation and a true nature child. The youthful **Cora also symbolised this abundance of life**, vividly evoked in gentle sibilance and vivid imagery, 'promising blossom, summer, the scent of thyme'.

In line 25, the italicised word '*Sequin*' and its colon suggest that the rest of the poem is an exploration of this tangible aid to memory which links all the women in the poem. Cora is brought to life, 'standing on the kitchen table', slowly twirling around as red sequins are attached to the hem of her white satin dress. Meehan nostalgically recalls the collaborative activity of the women's craft. As a child, she can only sense the complexity of the 'red sequins'. It will be years before she will be able to articulate their significance. However, three similes emphasise their image as folk-tale emblems. The sequins are as 'red as berries', 'the lips of maidens' and 'as blood on the snow'. The vibrant colours also form **a strong connection between women, past and present**, who create order in contrast to 'the chaos' of life. Meehan's fluid poetry flows through time, rather like her free-spirited aunt. The '*Sequin*', fleeting yet twinkling, maintains the female line.

The poet **recalls her female ancestors** like a litany of sacred names, 'Cora, Marie, Jacinta, my aunties,/Helena, my mother, Mary, my grandmother'. She encases these ghost shadows in constellation imagery, 'the light of those stars' (line 42). Their wisdom transcends time and space to become a liberating source of knowledge to her. Once more the poem drifts back into the past, showing the young poet circling her aunt. Line 46 recalls harsh times of enforced emigration from Ireland, 'She was weeks from taking the boat to England'. Home was left behind, gathering 'dust', a sharp reminder of human mortality. Cards wishing the aunt a happy twenty-first birthday, 'a giant key to the door', and good luck, 'a black cat swinging on a silver horseshoe', are all left behind. Cora has crossed the threshold into her new life as an exile in England and won't return.

Line 52 recalls the summer after her aunt had emigrated. In an **act of recollection**, the poet searched the house for the discarded red sequins. Like memories they surfaced in the most unlikely places, 'in cracks and crannies'. The alliterative hard 'c' suggests Meehan's effort in her search for memories. A list of hiding places for the sequins also reminds readers of the harsh effects of time on objects and people, 'a split', 'a tear'. The poet is now aware that she is repeating this action in opening the 'tin box' and by composing an elegy for her beloved aunt. Once again, she discovers the 'glamour' of the alluring Cora who has given her the wealth, 'coinage', of her example on **how to live life with humour and determination**. The emigrant aunt made the transition from her home in Ireland and forged a new life for herself in her adopted London. She has now crossed the threshold between life and death.

🏠 Writing About the Poem

'Paula Meehan's poetry often confronts darkness in dynamic language which reveals, questions and heals.' Discuss this view, with reference to 'Cora, Auntie'.

Sample Paragraph

In 'Cora, Auntie', Meehan recalls her glamorous, independent aunt who refused to give up even when faced with serious illness. The use of verbs 'laughing' and 'teasing' illustrate Cora's upbeat spirit. But the grim reality of old age is acknowledged through powerful images, 'withered body', 'old bag of bones'. Overall, it is the defiant Cora who is most remembered, 'grinning back at the rictus of Death'. Meehan has a close bond with her aunt. This is shown in the link she sees between the sewing of the 'red sequins' for Cora's dress and the poet's creation of her poem in red ink 'on white paper'. Meehan begins to appreciate the lessons of these women from the past who are now distant as 'those stars'. Her precious memories are her wealth or 'coinage', to deal with loss. Her aunt has taught her that the way to approach life is with courage and humour.

> **EXAMINER'S COMMENT**
>
> *Focused, confident response to both the task and the poem. Some insightful engagement with the text, backed by supportive commentary – particularly on the effectiveness of imagery and verbs. Points are expressed clearly and quotations are well integrated into the discussion – although there are slight misquotes. Otherwise, a solid high-grade standard.*

✒️ Class/Homework Exercises

1. 'Paula Meehan makes effective use of language to praise ordinary people and their approach to everyday life.' Discuss this statement with reference to 'Cora, Auntie'.
2. 'Meehan's poetry can be highly dramatic, but always manages to avoid exaggeration.' To what extent is this true of 'Cora, Auntie'? Support the points you make with suitable reference to the poem.

⊙ Points to Consider

- The poem's loose structure and time frame reflects the free-spirited aunt.
- Vivid visual imagery provides stark contrast between the ravages of life and the spirited personality of Meehan's aunt.
- Graphic recreation of atmosphere, time and place through the use of specific details.
- Contrasting tones: wistful, reflective, intuitive, triumphant and elegiac.
- Greek mythological reference widens the poem's impact.

5 🔊 The Exact Moment I Became a Poet

for Kay Foran

was in 1963 when Miss Shannon
rapping the duster on the easel's peg
half obscured by a cloud of chalk

said *Attend to your books, girls,*
or mark my words, you'll end up   5
in the sewing factory.

It wasn't just that some of the girls'
mothers worked in the sewing factory
or even that my own aunt did,

and many neighbours, but   10
that those words 'end up' robbed
the labour of its dignity.

Not that I knew it then,
not in those words — labour, dignity.
That's all back construction,   15

making sense; allowing also
the teacher was right
and no one knows it like I do myself.

But: I *saw* them: mothers, aunts and neighbours
trussed like chickens   20
on a conveyor belt,

getting sewn up the way my granny
sewed the sage and onion stuffing
in the birds.

Words could pluck you,
leave you naked,
your lovely shiny feathers all gone.

easel's peg: blackboards supported on wooden frames used in classrooms.

trussed: bound, tied.
conveyor belt: mechanical system for moving goods.

'I *saw* them'

👤 Personal Response

1. What is your impression of the teacher in the poem? Does she mean well in advising her young pupils? Or is she misleading them?
2. In your opinion, what key point is the poet making in the concluding stanza? Refer to the text in your response.
3. Do you think this is an optimistic or pessimistic poem, overall? Briefly explain your response.

👁 Critical Literacy

In 2000, Paula Meehan published her sixth poetry collection, *Dharmakaya*. The word comes from *The Tibetan Book of the Dead* and can be loosely translated as 'Truth-body'. Several of the poems touch on childhood memories, urban poverty, coming of age and self-awareness. 'The Exact Moment I Became a Poet' focuses on familiar themes of social class and oppressive gender relations in Irish society.

The title leads directly into the first stanza where Meehan recalls a significant moment from her childhood when she was eight years old. She sets the scene in an inner-city Dublin national school and recalls Miss Shannon standing at the blackboard. Through 'a cloud of chalk', the poet remembers hearing the teacher's stern advice: '*Attend to your books, girls*'. The use of italics emphasises the **ominous tone**: '*or mark my words, you'll end up/in the sewing factory*'.

For the young pupil, these words represent the beginning of class consciousness and an early sign of a possible future life as a writer. The schoolroom becomes the location where **middle-class values and prejudice are handed down**. Meehan is astounded by what she hears and the expression 'end up' makes an instant impact. The poet's tone wavers between antagonism towards the teacher and natural empathy for the many working women she knew – her aunt, neighbours, friends' mothers. She immediately senses that both the women and their work are being degraded. She describes their labour as being 'robbed' of its dignity in stanza four, reflecting how resentful she feels about the idea that some types of employment are undervalued.

The poet is caught between what she initially sensed as a child about attitudes to different jobs and careers ('Not that I knew it then') and what she eventually came to understand ('back construction') as an adult. She is uncomfortable with the idea that certain occupations are given a social position and that work in a sewing factory was considered inferior in the **class hierarchy**.

Experience has taught Meehan that the 'the teacher was right' about the prejudiced world where academic achievement could directly determine a young person's social position. She is also acutely aware of how education has affected her own life, 'no one knows it like I do myself'. An obvious irony, of course, is that **she herself chose 'books'** and literature as a means of escape from the downgraded world of factories and domesticity.

At the same time, Meehan expresses her solidarity with women who are powerless to change the way Irish society views them. She '*saw*' her local community for what it was and related closely to individual women. Once again, italics highlight how she resists the teacher's middle-class values because she feels they **demean and dehumanise working women** as 'trussed like chickens/on a conveyor belt'. The simile suggests controlled mechanical lives of dreary confinement. This comparison is extended into the two final stanzas as the poet recalls how her granny 'sewed the sage and onion stuffing/in the birds'.

The poem ends with a **rich image about the power of language** to deprive people of their individual identity, 'Words could pluck you,/ leave you naked,/your lovely shiny feathers all gone'. Meehan argues that definitions can undervalue individuals, sometimes diminishing them. This is reinforced by the plucked chicken image, adding to the sense of violation and powerlessness. Opposition and resistance are recurring themes in Meehan's poetry. In this case, she challenges class discrimination, restoring dignity to lives that have been overlooked.

While readers may not always agree with the poet about her views on class and gender, there is no denying that poetry has become her way of coming to terms with the past. The memory of an extraordinary school lesson back in 1963 marks a **crucial turning point** that illustrates the origins of a young girl's personal development. Throughout her adult life, Meehan's identity as a poet has never been separated from her self-awareness as a working-class woman.

✒ Writing About the Poem

'The effective use of powerful and compassionate language is a recurring feature of Paula Meehan's poetry.' Discuss this view, with reference to 'The Exact Moment I Became a Poet'.

Sample Paragraph

'The exact moment I became a poet' is typical of Paula Meehan. All through, she defends women in jobs who are looked down on. As a young girl, she objects to a teacher saying the factory is somewhere where failures 'end up'. The teacher has a position of privilage. She is in authority and this is what Meehan challanges, showing compassion towards ordinary girls. She uses very forceful language, saying the privilaged middle class 'robbed the labour of dignity'. Meehan confronts people treating factory-girls as non-human, using a powerful image – 'trussed up like chickens on a conveyor belt'. This idea is repeated when she says nothing has changed since her granny's time. Meehan's tone is challanging all through. The ending image is very forceful – 'words pluck you, leave you naked' and shows sympathy for how women can be unfairly treated by society.

EXAMINER'S COMMENT

There are several good discussion points here that address the question and focus on language use throughout the poem. Reference to tone, repetition and imagery show reasonably close engagement with the text. Expression is repetitive, however, with some mechanical flaws (e.g. 'privilage', 'challanging') and slight misquotations. A solid middle-grade response.

✐ Class/Homework Exercises

1. 'Paula Meehan's most compelling poems often explore painful memories of childhood.' To what extent is this true of 'The Exact Moment I Became a Poet'? Support the points you make with reference to the text.

2. In your view, how relevant is 'The Exact Moment I Became a Poet' to Ireland today? Develop your answer with reference to the poem.

⊙ Points to Consider

- Meehan takes up the struggle for self-definition on behalf of women.

- Themes include work, social class divisions, prejudice and resistance.

- Variety of tones: indignant, empathetic, reflective, impassioned and critical.

- Effective use of direct speech, developed metaphor, imagery and repetition.

6 My Father Perceived as a Vision of St Francis

POETRY FOCUS

for Brendan Kennelly

It was the piebald horse in next door's garden
frightened me out of a dream
with her dawn whinny. I was back
in the boxroom of the house,
my brother's room now,   5
full of ties and sweaters and secrets.
Bottles chinked on the doorstep,
the first bus pulled up to the stop.
The rest of the house slept

except for my father. I heard   10
him rake the ash from the grate,
plug in the kettle, hum a snatch of a tune.
Then he unlocked the back door
and stepped out into the garden.

Autumn was nearly done, the first frost   15
whitened the slates of the estate.
He was older than I had reckoned,
his hair completely silver,
and for the first time I saw the stoop
of his shoulder, saw that   20
his leg was stiff. What's he at?
So early and still stars in the west?

They came then: birds
of every size, shape, colour; they came
from the hedges and shrubs,   25
from eaves and garden sheds,
from the industrial estate, outlying fields,
from Dubber Cross they came
and the ditches of the North Road.

The garden was a pandemonium   30
when my father threw up his hands
and tossed the crumbs to the air. The sun

Title: Paula Meehan's father recognised as an image of the Italian friar who lived in poverty, and is the patron saint of animals and the environment.

Dedication: Meehan studied with the distinguished Irish poet Brendan Kennelly, who was one of her teachers at Trinity College.

piebald: dappled, white and black.

whinny: high-pitched sound made by a horse.
boxroom: small bedroom.

chinked: jingled, tinkled.

rake the ash: clear the dust.
grate: metal grid.
snatch: fragment, short piece.

slates: roof tiles.

reckoned: imagined.

stoop: bend, droop.

stiff: rigid, unable to bend.

eaves: lower edges of a roof.

industrial estate: factory area.
outlying: distant.
Dubber Cross: location in North Dublin.
ditches: drains.

pandemonium: uproar, confusion.

| 234

cleared O'Reilly's chimney
and he was suddenly radiant,
a perfect vision of St Francis,
made whole, made young again,
in a Finglas garden.

35

cleared: rose above.

radiant: glowing, transformed.
vision: image, apparition.

whole: complete, unspoiled.

Finglas: Dublin suburb.

PAULA MEEHAN

'a pandemonium'

👤 Personal Response

1. In your view, what was Meehan's attitude towards her father? Does she pity, ridicule or admire the elderly man? Briefly explain your response with reference to the poem.
2. What is your impression of the Dublin suburb of Finglas portrayed in the poem? Support your answer with reference to the text.
3. Meehan's poem is a powerful statement about time and ageing. In your opinion, what is the poet's central theme or message?

👁 Critical Literacy

Paula Meehan creates a loving song of praise and triumph in her observational poem, 'My Father Perceived as a Vision of St Francis', from her 1994 collection *Pillow Talk*. She recounts a story of an overnight stay she made as an adult in the family home in Finglas. Intrigued by her father's early morning rising and activity, she witnessed a man who was transformed.

A striking opening recalls the poet's frightened reaction to a piebald horse in a neighbouring garden. The gentle phrase, 'dawn whinny,' evokes the animal's soft neighing sound. A series of alliterative 'b' sounds ('back', 'boxroom', 'brother's') reinforce the confined sense of her claustrophobic bedroom. Another onomatopoeic sound, 'chinked', announces the early morning arrival of the milkman, delivering bottles of milk. Everyday life is slowly resuming its normal activity. Sibilance

235 |

is used to suggest the quiet household, 'The rest of the house slept' (line 9). One person is already downstairs, however. Meehan describes her father's routine activities. He is busy preparing for the day ahead – clearing the grate, boiling the kettle. The noise of the plug in the electric socket is accompanied by his singing 'a snatch of a tune'. This colloquial phrase roots the family in their Dublin **working-class environment**.

Everything changes when her father crosses the threshold from the mundane domestic interior to the dream-like exterior, and 'stepped out into the garden'. The world of nature is described in line 15. Personification conjures up the changing seasons, 'Autumn was nearly done'. Alliteration suggests the onset of cold, withering winter, 'first frost/whitened'. Suddenly the poet realises that her father has aged more than she had thought. His 'completely silver' hair mirrors the early white frost on the dark roof slates of the housing estate. **The poet's compassionate eye notices the wear and tear of time**. A run-on line suggests the 'stoop/of his shoulder'. Rhetorical questions reflect the poet's fascination as she observes her father closely, 'What's he at?/So early and still stars in the west?'

Line 23 marks a **dramatic development**. A rush of birds replaces the orderly early morning movement. Suddenly, this riotous abundance of nature is on full display. The birds were of 'every size, shape, colour'. They flew in from 'hedges and shrubs', 'garden sheds', 'outlying fields'. The noise in the garden is described as 'pandemonium'. Meehan watches her father greet the dawn with what appears to be his daily ritual of feeding the birds. Raising his arms, 'he tossed the crumbs to the air'.

The old man's gesture is transformative. Amid the commotion of wings moving and the sun rising above a neighbour's chimney, the poet's perception of her father is altered. He had become 'radiant', **ecstatic in his happiness**. In his daughter's estimation, he had replicated the caring action of St Francis of Assisi, the patron saint of animals and the environment. No longer was her father stiff and stooped but vibrant ('young again') in his simple suburban garden. Like the saint, he was 'whole' and at one with nature's creatures.

The poem is firmly anchored in **autobiographical experience**. While Meehan celebrates a local community, she has a heightened awareness of changing times and human mortality. Her sympathetic, intuitive tone recollects and transforms her father. In the vision of the poem's title, he is by no means a stereotypical patriarchal figure, but an iconic nurturing man. For the poet, this simple ritual of her father feeding the birds is a moment of revelation when she unexpectedly sees him in an entirely different light, associating him closely with the sanctity and goodness of the gentle St Francis. The focus on vivid images, small details and the poem's free-flowing form are all in keeping with this eye-opening epiphany.

🖋 Writing About the Poem

'Paula Meehan's specific use of language creates a place where private memory and ecology meet.' Discuss this view, with reference to 'My Father Perceived as a Vision of St Francis'.

Sample Paragraph

In 'My Father Perceived as a Vision of St Francis', Meehan uses everyday Dublin speech to create a loving portrait of her father. His recreation as a 'perfect vision of St Francis' is the point where an intimate family memory, mythic story and love for the environment all meet. Onomatopoeia recreates the sleepy housing estate where an ordinary man prepares for a new day, plugging in the kettle for tea. He hums a 'snatch of a tune', the colloquial expression placing her father in his Finglas community. But one simple action of his transforms him into a symbol of the saint of wildlife and nature, 'my father threw up his hands and tossed the crumbs'. St Francis is often depicted in paintings holding a bird in his hand. Meehan's father has also shown empathy with the creatures of the wild. He is now transfigured, no longer old but 'young again'. He has crossed into a spiritual existence, sharing with Francis an autumnal holy day, 'in a Finglas garden'.

> **EXAMINER'S COMMENT**
>
> *Clear and sustained top-grade response that focuses on the three elements of this challenging question (memory, myth and ecology). The commentary succeeds in tracing the progress of thought in the poem and is rounded off with an impressive overview. Quotations are integrated into the discussion and used effectively to support points.*

✒ Class/Homework Exercises

1. 'Paula Meehan places lyrical moments of transcendence into everyday life.' Discuss this statement with reference to 'My Father Perceived as a Vision of St Francis'.
2. 'Meehan's most heart-rending poems highlight the twin themes of love and loss.' To what extent is this true of 'My Father Perceived as a Vision of St Francis'? Support the points you make with suitable reference to the poem.

⊙ Points to Consider

- **Moving tribute expressing enthusiastic praise for the poet's father.**
- **Intriguing parallels between Meehan's father and the Italian saint.**
- **Keen evocation of a particular person, place and time.**
- **Range of tones: wistful, nostalgic, compassionate, illuminating and respectful.**

7 🔊 Hearth Lesson

Title: A hearth is the front area of a fireplace, often associated with home and family.

Either phrase will bring it back —
money to burn, burning a hole in your pocket.

burn: waste.
burning a hole: eager to spend cash.

I am crouched by the fire
in the flat in Seán MacDermott Street
while Zeus and Hera battle it out: 5

Zeus and Hera: In Greek mythology, Zeus was king of the gods and had a tempestuous relationship with his wife Hera, goddess of women.
thunderbolt: violent outburst.
fancyman: lover, boyfriend.

for his every thunderbolt
she had the killing glance;
she'll see his fancyman
and raise him the Cosmo Snooker Hall;
he'll see her 'the only way you get any   10
attention around here is if you neigh';
he'll raise her airs and graces
or the mental state of her siblings,
every last one of them.

neigh: high-pitched cry horses make.
airs and graces: pretentiousness, showing off.
siblings: sisters and brothers.

I'm net, umpire, and court; most balls   15
are lobbed over my head.
Even then I can judge it's better
than brooding and silence and the particular hell of the unsaid,
of 'tell your mother…' 'ask your father…'.

umpire: adjudicator, referee.
lobbed: hurled.
brooding: sulking.

Even then I can tell it was money,   20
the lack of it day after day,
at the root of the bitter words
but nothing prepared us one teatime
when he handed up his wages.

She straightened each rumpled pound note, then   25
a weariness come suddenly over her,
she threw the lot in the fire.

rumpled: crumpled, creased.
pound note: banknote used in Ireland until 2002.

The flames were blue and pink and green,
A marvellous sight, an alchemical scene.

alchemical: magical, transformative, cathartic.

'It's not enough,' she stated simply.   30
And we all knew it wasn't.

The flames sheered from cinder to chimney breast
like trapped exotic birds;
the shadows jumped floor to ceiling, and she'd
had the last, the astonishing, word.   35

sheered from cinder to chimney breast: spread upwards.
exotic: strange and colourful.

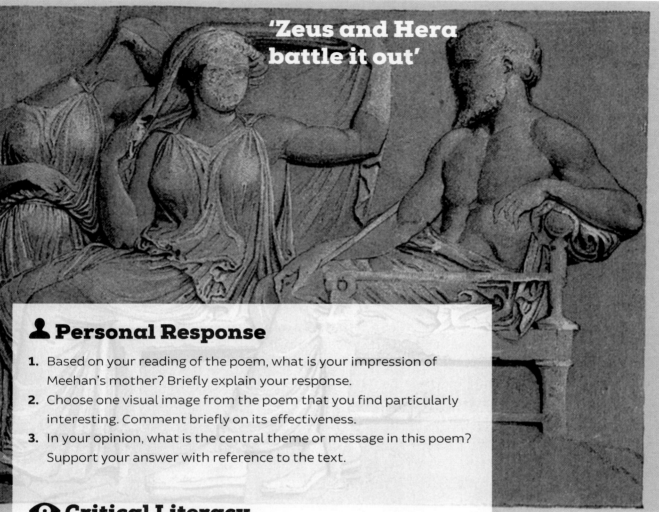

'Zeus and Hera battle it out'

👤 Personal Response

1. Based on your reading of the poem, what is your impression of Meehan's mother? Briefly explain your response.
2. Choose one visual image from the poem that you find particularly interesting. Comment briefly on its effectiveness.
3. In your opinion, what is the central theme or message in this poem? Support your answer with reference to the text.

👁 Critical Literacy

Paula Meehan has written many biographical poems mourning the loss of family and remembrances of childhood. Some of these, including 'Hearth Lesson', are found in her 2010 collection *Painting Rain*, and reflect on the politics of the family as a place of unrest. The poet has spoken about her interest in such confessional poetry: 'I wrote what one of my friends calls "the shallow grave poems", excavations of material in my own family life, material that has always disturbed and frightened me'.

The colloquial expressions Meehan quotes in the poem's opening lines trigger stressful childhood memories of family conflict: '*money to burn, burning a hole in your pocket*'. Economic issues were central to the disagreements between her parents. Indeed, the poet is still haunted by the **sarcastic phrases** she remembers from the harsh quarrels between her mother and father. The use of italics emphasises the derisive nature of their rows. Meehan's image of herself as a young child 'crouched by the fire' and already crushed by the tension surrounding her adds poignancy to the unhappy domestic scene.

The adult poet finds inspiration in classical references, using Greek mythology to evoke the confrontational mood and her own enduring feelings of hurt. Reflecting on the turbulent relationship between her parents, she imagines this ordinary inner-city Dublin couple into Zeus and Hera. Meehan can now express the **exaggerated perception** she first had when she witnessed her mother and father 'battle it out'. The sadness of their seemingly epic encounters remains, even though the poet has developed a clearer understanding of their lives.

In stanza three, their stormy **marriage is compared to a mock-heroic poker match** between Zeus and his goddess wife. Using an extended metaphor, the poet recollects several dramatic scenes from their vicious exchanges: 'for his every thunderbolt/she had the killing glance'. Card game terminology illustrates how the couple traded spiteful insults. In response to his accusations of unfaithfulness ('she'll see his fancyman'), her mother complains about him wasting time and money on gambling ('raise him the Cosmo Snooker Hall').

Meehan recognises the cynical frustration of a wife who feels unloved because her husband spends so much time betting on horses: 'the only way you get any/attention around here is if you neigh'. As the recriminations continue, the father resorts to sneering. He accuses the poet's mother of putting on 'airs and graces'. Tempers flare and he ends up questioning the sanity of her entire family, 'every last one of them'. **Short lines and brisk rhythms** emphasise the sharp tone of their vindictive dialogue.

Throughout all of this, Meehan is able to cross time and space to re-establish this lost connection with her early home life. We get a poignant sense of the trauma of a child who was powerless to ease the tension. The **tennis metaphor** in stanza four develops the idea that the strained mood was played out like another point-scoring game around her: 'I'm net, umpire and court'. In particular, she remembers experiencing the awkward 'brooding and silence'. Even worse was the 'hell' of being used as a means of communication between her parents, 'tell your mother …', 'ask your father …'.

The tone becomes more analytical in stanza five as Meehan acknowledges that poverty was always a factor in the 'bitter' disagreements between her parents: 'Even then I can tell it was money,/the lack of it day after day'. The poet is then reminded of **a defining moment** 'one teatime' when her father 'handed up his wages'. Nothing prepared the family for her mother's extraordinary reaction. Slowly and deliberately, 'she threw the lot in the fire'.

Looking back on this **dramatic event**, the poet remembers the vivid colours of the flames, 'blue and pink and green'. She recalls her mother's weary words, 'It's not enough' – something which she and her siblings instinctively understood at the time, 'we all knew it wasn't'. Indeed, the mother's stark statement captures the hopelessness of someone whose unhappiness is not simply caused by lack of money, but who is disillusioned by a life of quiet desperation.

In the final stanza, Meehan focuses on how inspired she is by her mother's unexpected act of defiance. **Vivid descriptive details** of the burning banknotes create a startling situation that is charged with energy; it is almost surreal. The force of the flames is 'like trapped exotic birds', an evocative simile that reflects the poet's intense awareness of her mother's troubled life. In the end, she is left in awe of a woman who has triumphed by having 'the last, the astonishing, word'.

The concluding lines seem to range over various emotional responses from excitement to empathy and ultimately, admiration. The poet clearly celebrates her mother's courage in challenging a patriarchal world that forces many women to rely on their husbands. Yet there is also a broader appreciation of her parents as two unhappy people who are both victims of their times. Throughout the poem, Meehan's mother has been presented as angry, spirited, unpredictable and enigmatic. However, she has taught her daughter to resist oppression and be true to herself. Is this the crucial lesson Meehan has learned?

✒ Writing About the Poem

'Meehan's attitude to family relationships is often conflicted and unresolved.' To what extent is this the case in 'Hearth Lesson'? Support your answer with reference to the text.

Sample Paragraph

Paula Meehan was born in 1955 and grew up in the inner city before moving to Finglas, a suburb just north of Dublin. Many of her poems deal with family and especially her mother who died in her forties. Meehan had an uneasy relationship with her, but in 'Hearth Lesson', she shows it was complicated. She remembers the rows between her parents – usually over money – the 'lack of it'. Meehan 'crouched by the fire'. Once, her mother was so depressed she threw the weekly pay-packet into the flames. I got the impression she was a woman with nothing to lose. The poet is astonished by such a rebellious thing. She is in shock, but it was 'a marvellous sight'. Basically, Meehan is conflicted. She sees both parents under pressure, but she

EXAMINER'S COMMENT

Good personal response that engages reasonably well with the question. Time spent on unnecessary biographical details at the start could have been used to examine the poem in greater depth. More discussion about the poet's own relationship with her parents – as the 'umpire' caught up in their rows – would have improved the basic middle-grade standard.

understands her mother's desperation. Through her own 'astonishing' writing, Meehan will avoid following in her mother's footsteps.

✍ Class/Homework Exercises

1. 'Meehan's carefully chosen language is ideally suited to the disturbing subject matter she often addresses in her poetry.' Discuss this view, with particular reference to 'Hearth Lesson'.

2. 'Readers engage with Paula Meehan's poems because she writes about everyday human experiences that have a universal relevance.' To what extent is this true of 'Hearth Lesson'? Support your answer with reference to the text.

⊙ Points to Consider

- Family life, Irish society and gender roles in the 1960s are all central themes.

- Good use of extended metaphors: mythology, poker and tennis.

- Variety of tones: nostalgic, realistic, reflective, regretful and admiring.

- Effective use of dramatic language, dialogue and vivid imagery.

- Interesting, thought-provoking ending.

8 🔊 Prayer for the Children of Longing

PAULA MEEHAN

A poem commissioned by the community of Dublin's north inner city for the lighting of the Christmas tree in Buckingham Street, to remember their children who died from drug use.

Great tree from the far northern forest
Still rich with the sap of the forest
Here at the heart of winter
Here at the heart of the city

Grant us the clarity of ice   5
The comfort of snow
The cool memory of trees
Grant us the forest's silence
The snow's breathless quiet

For one moment to freeze   10
The scream, the siren, the knock on the door
The needle in its track
The knife in the back

In that silence let us hear
The song of the children of longing   15
In that silence let us catch
The breath of the children of longing

The echo of their voices through the city streets
The streets that defeated them
That brought them to their knees   20
The streets that couldn't shelter them
That spellbound them in alleyways
The streets that blew their minds
That led them astray, out of reach of our saving
The streets that gave them visions and dreams   25
That promised them, everything
That delivered nothing

The streets that broke their backs
The streets that we brought them home to

Great tree: large Christmas tree erected annually at Buckingham Street by the community to remember the children's tragic deaths.
sap: liquid energy and strength.

clarity: transparency, intelligibility.

siren: warning alarm on police car or ambulance.

longing: craving, wishing for something, often something unattainable.

spellbound: fascinated, mesmerised.
alleyways: narrow laneways.
astray: off course.

visions: ideas, hallucinations, revelations.

Let their names be the wind through the branches   30
Let their names be the song of the river
Let their names be the holiest prayers

Under the starlight, under the moonlight
In the light of this tree

Here at the heart of winter   35
Here at the heart of the city

'In the light of this tree'

👤 Personal Response

1. Meehan refers to two different locations in the opening nine lines of the poem. Comment on how she establishes these contrasting settings through her choice of poetic techniques (directly addressing the tree, natural imagery, repetition, etc.).

2. Why, in your opinion, is the tone of the poem bitter and accusatory in lines 18–29? Briefly explain your response.

3. Do you regard Meehan's depiction of the tragedy of the young people's deaths from drug use as sentimental or realistic? Give reasons for your answer, using reference to the text.

PAULA MEEHAN

◉ Critical Literacy

The community of Dublin's north inner city commissioned Paula Meehan to write a poem commemorating young people who had died as a result of a heroin epidemic in the city during the 1980s. Meehan's warm response, published in her collection *Painting Rain* (2009), explores the threads which link trauma, memory, natural imagery and recovery in the form of a spiritual request. The poem also demonstrates Meehan's commitment to her local community and her role as a spokesperson for its residents.

This **tender elegy of love and loss** begins with a direct address to the Christmas tree erected annually by the Buckingham Street community in memory of their children who died from drug abuse. The tree still contains the life-giving 'sap' of the 'far northern forest' where it grew, in contrast to those who have lost their lives so tragically. Meehan's repetition of 'heart' not only refers to the new location of the festive tree in the middle of the city but also to the enduring love within the community. On behalf of the distraught residents of the inner city, she asks for the gifts of the forest – particularly 'the clarity of ice' (line 5), so that families can fully come to terms with the past.

Meehan also asks for the healing of nature, the 'comfort of snow' which blankets everything, beautiful and ugly, in pristine white. She wants its 'breathless quiet' to clear a place where relatives can come together to grieve and understand the terrible events of what happened to all the children they mourn. The verb 'freeze' (line 10) serves as a pivotal point, taking the poem back in time to those raw, cruel memories.

The poet details the **horror of the drug scene** on the city streets in the sibilant spine-chilling 'scream' and the high-pitched sound of the approaching 'siren'. Meehan's unsettling phrase 'the knock on the door' is a poignant reminder of the announcement of yet another heart-rending death when the authorities break the tragic news to anxious parents. In lines 12 and 13, the grim reality of drug use is further conveyed in equally disturbing language ('The needle in its track', 'The knife in the back') adding a devastating impact.

It is in this sacred location, presided over by the Christmas tree, that the poet wants everyone to remember 'the song of the children'. **Their inarticulate cry of 'longing' was ignored** by the busy modern world. Meehan's belief is that these young people were victims of unemployment and poverty, regarded by society as waste material. This lack of a future, of the possibility of love and building a family 'defeated them'. So they disappeared into the oblivion of drugs, 'spellbound in alleyways', excluded from 'streets that couldn't shelter them' (line 21). The angry tone and striking visual imagery reflect the poet's sense of a whole generation of children who have been failed.

245 |

From Meehan's point of view, the children were led astray, disconnected from their past and families, 'out of reach of our saving'. She acknowledges the wasted potential of these vulnerable young people, who were exploited by drug dealers and a ruthless world which 'gave them visions and dreams' – only to dash them. In turn, the children wandered in the maze of an impersonal society which 'delivered nothing'. The alliterative phrase 'broke their backs' emphasises the pressure which resulted in the fracturing and crushing of the young. However, in line 29, the phrase 'we brought them home' marks a pivotal change as Meehan's bitter, accusatory voice is replaced by a much more sympathetic tone.

The soothing mantra of the final lines references the natural rhythms of the universe, those of 'the wind' and the 'river'. Meehan has used repetition throughout the poem to convey the **sense of a public choral prayer**. The spiritual quality of the conclusion is even more explicit, 'Let their names be the holiest prayers'. The poet restores dignity to a broken community, living through the anguish of burying their children. Her powerful voice breaks the silence 'Under the starlight, under the moonlight'. The repetition of 'Here' demonstrates how a special place has been set aside at Christmas to remember, honour and console.

The poem ends as it began, 'at the heart'. With **characteristic compassion,** Meehan has succeeded in changing our perception of the dead children by bringing them home to their families, their community and the natural world. The soft aural effects and flowing lines, without any punctuation, mirror the ceaseless blowing of the wind and the endless movement of the river.

🖋 Writing About the Poem

'Paula Meehan's deep sense of anger is often evident in her most compelling poems.' Discuss this view, with reference to 'Prayer for the Children of Longing'.

Sample Paragraph

Paula Meehan's outrage can be felt in 'Prayer for the Children of Longing' when she describes the waste of young lives by modern society. Yet it is the poet's empathetic approach which I remember. This is seen in the image of the 'Great tree' which will bring 'comfort' to heal the grieving families. Run-on lines convey powerful emotion, 'let us hear/The song of the children of longing'. The poem is based on the rhythms of a prayer, 'Grant us', 'Let us'. I felt that it summed up the tragedy of drug addiction, 'The scream, the siren'. What was interesting to me was that it transformed this violent reality by linking it to the healing beauty of nature, 'the song of the river'. This symbolised that there is more support for young addicts these days. No longer are they social outcasts. Instead, Meehan restores their self-worth by the final request, 'Let their names be the holiest prayers'. I found calmness, not anger, in the conclusion, where there was a strong feeling of communal love.

✒ Class/Homework Exercises

1. 'Paula Meehan's dynamic, positive poetry depicts the cruelty and deprivation of her working-class background.' Discuss this statement with reference to 'Prayer for the Children of Longing'.

2. 'Meehan's poetry uses effective poetic techniques, such as repetition, sound effects and descriptive detail to convey her themes.' To what extent is this true of 'Prayer for the Children of Longing'? Support the points you make with suitable reference to the poem.

⊙ Points to Consider

- **Key themes of loss, alienation, waste, longing and belonging.**

- **Exact visual and aural details contrast the squalid inner city with the cool beauty of nature.**

- **Simple direct language appropriate to the subject matter adds authenticity.**

- **Use of long incantatory lines, prayer-like rhythms and deep spiritual yearning.**

- **Variety of tones: pleading, objective, scathing, reflective and consolatory.**

- **Repetition and lack of punctuation intensify the poem's momentum.**

 🔊 Death of a Field

The field itself is lost the morning it becomes a site
When the Notice goes up: Fingal County Council — 44 units

The memory of the field is lost with the loss of its herbs

Though the woodpigeons in the willow
And the finches in what's left of the hawthorn hedge   5
And the wagtail in the elder
Sing on their hungry summer song

The magpies sound like flying castanets

And the memory of the field disappears with its flora:
Who can know the yearning of yarrow   10
Or the plight of the scarlet pimpernel
Whose true colour is orange?

The end of the field is the end of the hidey holes
Where first smokes, first tokes, first gropes
Were had to the scentless mayweed   15

The end of the field as we know it is the start of the estate
The site to be planted with houses each two or three bedroom
Nest of sorrow and chemical, cargo of joy

The end of dandelion is the start of Flash
The end of dock is the start of Pledge   20
The end of teazel is the start of Ariel
The end of primrose is the start of Brillo
The end of thistle is the start of Bounce
The end of sloe is the start of Oxyaction
The end of herb robert is the start of Brasso   25
The end of eyebright is the start of Persil

Who amongst us is able to number the end of grasses
To number the losses of each seeding head?

site: land set aside for building.
Notice: official sign, poster.

herbs: plants used for flavouring food or for medicine.

woodpigeons: common garden birds.
willow: willow tree.
finches: small birds.
wagtail: colourful bird.
elder: flowering tree.

castanets: clackers, percussion instruments.

flora: vegetation, plant life.

yarrow: white flowering plant.
plight: predicament.
scarlet pimpernel: plant with brightly coloured flowers.

tokes: cannabis smoking.

mayweed: common summer-flowering wildflower.

cargo: load.

Flash: cleaning product (the first of several listed).
dock: perennial weed.
teazel: tall flowering plant.

sloe: blackthorn.
Oxyaction: popular chemical cleanser.
herb robert: flowering plant with pink flowers.
eyebright: wildflower with small white flowers.

PAULA MEEHAN

I'll walk out once
Barefoot under the moon to know the field   30
Through the soles of my feet to hear
The myriad leaf lives green and singing   **myriad:** countless.
The million million cycles of being in wing

That — before the field become map memory
In some archive on some architect's screen   35   **archive:** database.
I might possess it or it possess me
Through its night dew, its moon white caul   **caul:** cover.
Its slick and shine and its profligacy   **profligacy:** extravagance.
In every wingbeat in every beat of time   **wingbeat:** motion of a bird's
                                                      wings in flight.

'the end of grasses'

👤 Personal Response

1. Select one image or line from the poem that you find particularly interesting. Briefly explain your choice.
2. Comment on Meehan's use of repetition throughout the poem. In your view, is it effective or over-done? Give a reason for your answer.
3. Describe the poet's tone throughout lines 29–39. In your opinion, is it angry, reflective, nostalgic or sentimental? Briefly explain your response.

◉ Critical Literacy

This is another of Paula Meehan's signature public poems taken from her 2009 collection *Painting Rain*. It addresses change and loss – particularly nature's losses. 'Death of a Field' is a response to the rampant planning and housing development that characterised much of 'Celtic Tiger' Ireland during the nineties and noughties. Set in a suburban construction site, the poem becomes an elegy for traditional communities during those so-called boom years.

In keeping with the impassioned title, Meehan's opening line reflects her own deep feeling of sorrow. The field is personified and its loss will affect the poet directly. She draws attention to the functional business-like language used on the local planning authority's written 'Notice'. What was once a 'field' is already 'lost' and redefined as a 'site'. A single isolated line emphasises the **irreversible transformation of landscape**: 'The memory of the field is lost with the loss of its herbs'

The poet recognises birds as familiar presences. For the moment, their sounds and rituals are unchanged. The woodpigeons, finches and wagtail all depend for survival on this natural environment where they sing 'their hungry summer song'. Sibilance and soft aural effects ('willow', 'elder') add to the tender elegiac tone. Nature's vibrancy is also acknowledged: 'The magpies sound like flying castanets' (line 8). This vivid simile – referring to exotic Spanish music – highlights Meehan's awareness of the dynamism and excitement of the natural world.

In listing the flora and fauna that will disappear with the housing project, Meehan details the process of both the field's and the humans' loss of memory of this open space. **Rhetorical language** ('Who can know the yearning of yarrow/Or the plight of the scarlet pimpernel') personifies the endangered vegetation. The choice of agonising terms ('yearning' and 'plight') are clearly aimed at appealing to the reader's sympathies.

With inevitable progress and development, the field loses identity. People also lose contact with their personal memories of growing up in the locality. **Nostalgia is tinged with humour** in lines 13 and 14 when the poet reflects on playing childhood games here in 'hidey holes' and later coming-of-age experiences, 'first smokes, first tokes, first gropes'. She also notes the way language changes over time as open space soon becomes an 'estate'.

Oddly, the word 'estate' has connotations with Ireland's grand country houses belonging to the landed gentry during colonial times. However, the end of this field is the start of the modern-day residential estate. Along **with all the new homes come consumer goods** – something else which the poet dislikes. Meehan's thoughts return to what will happen when the earth-moving machines arrive to displace the wild herbs growing here. Her bitterly ironic tone is particularly evident in line 18, 'Nest of sorrow and chemical, cargo of joy'.

As the field gives way to concrete, wild plants will disappear – including dandelion, dock, thistle and eyebright. Meehan organises lines 19–26 into a prayer-like mantra through anaphora (repetition at the beginning of successive phrases). She makes **effective use of emphatic contrast**: 'The end of primrose is the start of Brillo', placing the delicate flower beside the rough-sounding scouring pad. A list of nature's losses is compared to leading household brand names, such as Flash, Pledge, Ariel and Persil. This format allows the poet to highlight aspects of the modern world that she deplores. The rhythmic chanting leads to another apocalyptic rhetorical demand: 'Who amongst us is able to number the end of grasses' (line 27).

For Meehan, nature is mysterious and unknowable. Yet she is determined to create a lasting personal connection with the landscape. She imagines communing with it ('Barefoot under the moon') one last time before it is developed. Her intention is to 'know the field/Through the soles of my feet'. She wants to experience its 'myriad leaf lives', even though this would be like trying to understand creation itself, an experience she describes as the 'million million cycles of being in wing' (line 33). Meehan's **vibrant evocative imagery** creates a haunting sense of the untamed growth and timeless beauty of the natural world.

It could, of course, be argued that the poet is taking an unrealistic approach to an **age-old conflict of interests**. While it's vital to protect natural spaces, housing is a basic human need. In dramatising the battle between nature and urban development, the writing style – particularly the use of repetition – is somewhat laboured and some readers may find the didactic tone heavy-handed at times.

However, the poem's conclusion focuses on Meehan's intimate appreciation of landscape and her acceptance that the field is destined to end up as a 'map memory' in an architect's data bank. This makes her even more determined that readers share her fears about future environmental destruction. The poet's **voice becomes more urgent** as she expresses her heartfelt desire to be at one with nature so that 'I might possess it or it possess me'. In a poignantly beautiful image, she compares the dew-covered field to the 'moon white caul' of a vulnerable new-born child.

By challenging the recklessness of unrestrained capitalism, Meehan wishes to let nature work its magic on her so that she becomes the voice promoting the rich 'profligacy' of nature and the 'slick and shine' of what will soon be absent. Her enthusiasm is evident in the romanticised tone and fast-moving rhythm of the final lines. Having envisaged the transformation of a natural space that she values, Meehan leaves readers with a **thought-provoking elegy** about the destruction of a small ecosystem, a kind of death that signifies a much greater global threat.

⬛ Writing About the Poem

'Paula Meehan frequently uses contrast as an effective literary technique to convey key themes in her poetry.' Discuss this statement, with particular reference to 'Death of a Field'.

Sample Paragraph

'Death of a Field' uses contrast to show up the negative effects of house construction. The first example is when the 'field' is described as a 'site'. Meehan repeats two contrasting words, 'end' and 'start', to show up how the change of land use affects nature – 'The end of herb robert is the start of Brasso'. This is part of a whole list of examples where herbs are compared to detergents, like Brillo and Bounce. She is basically disgusted by the loss of herbs. Even the quiet and harsh sounds are contrasted. This made me think of the link between the field's destruction and the estate's construction. Contrast adds emphasis to the main point that people must pay an extra price for new houses in the loss of the green environment.

EXAMINER'S COMMENT

Some good personal commentary here that engages with the question. Reference to several examples of effective contrast are well supported with accurate quotations. These are integrated into the discussion and show reasonably close engagement with the text. While expression is functional, points are clear. A solid middle-grade response.

✒ Class/Homework Exercises

1. In your opinion, is 'Death of a Field' still relevant to Ireland today? Develop your answer with suitable textual support.
2. 'Many of Meehan's most heartfelt poems are elegies that lament Irish places and culture.' Discuss this view, with particular reference to 'Death of a Field'.

◉ Points to Consider

- Poet addresses the impact of urban development and consumerism on the natural world.

- Contrasting tones: angry, heartfelt, nostalgic, ironic, didactic and anguished.

- Effective use of contrast, personification, onomatopoeia and vivid imagery.

- Rhetorical style: repetition, questions, anaphora, speech rhythms, emotive language, etc.

10 🔊 Them Ducks Died for Ireland

PAULA MEEHAN

Title: humorous colloquial comment on sacrifice of ducks for Irish freedom.

'6 of our waterfowl were killed or shot, 7 of the garden seats broken and about 300 shrubs destroyed.'
Park Superintendent in his report on the damage to
St Stephen's Green, during the Easter Rising, 1916

Time slides slowly down the sash window
puddling in light on oaken boards. The Green
is a great lung, exhaling like breath on the pane
the seasons' turn, sunset and moonset, the ebb and flow

of stars. And once made mirror to smoke and fire,   5
a Republic's destiny in a Countess' stride,
the bloodprice both summons and antidote to pride.
When we've licked the wounds of history, wounds of war,

we'll salute the stretcher bearer, the nurse in white,
the ones who pick up the pieces, who endure,   10
who live at the edge, and die there and are known

by this archival footnote read by fading light;
fragile as a breathmark on the windowpane or the gesture
of commemorating heroes in bronze and stone.

Dedication: *'The Times History of the War'* recorded that St Stephen's Green 'was well stocked with waterfowl, and the keeper, who remained inside all the time, reported that his charges were well looked after and fed by him, and were very little perturbed by the bullets flying over their heads'. The park-keeper's name was James Kearney – every day, twice a day he would enter the Green to feed the ducks, and every day the opposing sides would cease firing to allow him to do so.

sash window: window with two frames of paned glass placed one above the other.
puddling: forming a small pool.
oaken: made of oak.
The Green: St Stephen's Green.
exhaling: breathing out.
pane: window glass.
ebb and flow: coming and going.
made mirror: reflected, symbolised.
Republic's destiny: Ireland's freedom.
Countess' stride: Countess Markievicz's determination. She fought in St Stephen's Green.
bloodprice: the sacrifice paid for freedom.
summons: call.
antidote: response.
edge: boundary, limit.

archival footnote: additional information in historical document.
fragile: delicate, vulnerable.
gesture: action, signal.
commemorating: honouring.

'a great lung, exhaling like breath'

👤 Personal Response

1. How effective is Meehan's use of personification and imagery in the first seven lines of the poem? Refer closely to the text in your answer.
2. Describe the dominant tone throughout this poem. Is it reflective, bitter, respectful, disappointed, ironic? Briefly explain your response.
3. In the sestet (last six lines), Meehan focuses on the untold stories of individuals who do not feature prominently in Irish history. In your view, what is her attitude to these people?

👁 Critical Literacy

Painting Rain (2009) contains a sequence of sonnets, the 'Six Sycamores'. These were based on the six sycamore trees planted by the original Anglo-Irish leaseholders of the buildings around St Stephen's Green. 'Them Ducks Died for Ireland' is set in the aftermath of the 1916 Easter Rising. Meehan has said: 'I wrote the poem out of a fragment I found in the Architectural Archive, the report of the park superintendent in the clean-up of the Revolution'. The poet has also commented: 'We are now looking back to that initiatory event, the Rising, in a different way, retrieving the stories that were written out of history in the post-revolutionary era. I think this is such a healthy thing to do, to change perspective.'

The sonnet opens with a sibilant personification of Time, which 'slides slowly' down the windows of the magnificent Georgian mansions encircling St Stephen's Green and ends in a pool of light on their polished hardwood floors, 'oaken boards'. Meehan imagines 'The Green' as 'a great lung', a simple but powerful metaphor reflecting the vitality of the changing seasons. All of nature's mystery and beauty is recorded here: 'sunset and moonset', 'the ebb and flow' of the stars. Long run-on lines add to **the stately, harmonious rhythm** in the first quatrain (four-line section).

A very different image is mirrored in the windows in line 5, 'smoke and fire'. **Revolution, destruction and violence once took hold of the Green** during the struggle to achieve Irish liberty. For Meehan, the Rising was the 'summons and antidote to pride'. Irish freedom fighters fought for the ideal of a politically independent and socially classless society. The Citizen Army had dug defensive trenches in the Green but were fired upon by the British who occupied the upper floors of the nearby Shelbourne Hotel (the 'antidote').

After an innocent civilian was killed, they withdrew to the College of Surgeons. The remarkable Countess Markievicz, 'a Countess' stride', **who was herself a member of the Anglo-Irish Ascendancy**, was one of the senior military leaders involved at the time, calling for the cessation of shooting to allow the ducks to be fed every day.

The poet imagines how people attempted to recover from the trauma of battle. Like stricken animals, they 'licked the wounds of history, wounds of war'. **Repetition and alliteration emphasise the suffering** of armed struggle. All the participants had paid the 'bloodprice' (line 7), the Irish and British forces, Dublin's citizens and even the natural inhabitants of the Green, the waterfowl.

The sestet (final six lines) moves beyond the immediate confines of the park as **Meehan personally acknowledges those dealing with the aftermath of conflict**, 'the stretcher bearer, the nurse in white' – those left cleaning up the mess and destruction, who 'pick up the pieces'. They must 'endure' and carry on living 'at the edge', the periphery of history. Their stories are not recorded in the official narrative of important events. They are only discovered by a chance reading of a government document 'by fading light'.

The poem concludes as it began, noting the reflections in the windows. **These unknown characters' beautiful 'fragile' stories disappear** like 'breath on the pane', having been relegated to the footnotes of history books. This is in stark contrast to the 'gesture', the courage and sacrifice of the 'heroes' who are formally memorialised in public statues of 'bronze and stone'.

Meehan expresses her **desire to give voice to unrecorded lives** which remain buried within historical narratives. She has rescued the unknown stories of history from oblivion. In the end, readers are left to reflect on how culture copes with revolutionary change. Were the ideals of the 1916 Rising accomplished? Was an inclusive classless society formed where all are given equal respect?

✒ Writing About the Poem

'Paula Meehan's poetry presents a range of views of Ireland's past.' Discuss this statement, with particular reference to 'Them Ducks Died for Ireland'.

Sample Paragraph

'Them Ducks Died for Ireland' recreates the beauty of St Stephen's Green through personification. 'The Green is a great lung' exhaling breath patterns of the peaceful progress of nature, 'sunset and moonset' onto the Georgian windows surrounding the park. Suddenly the peaceful atmosphere is replaced by the 'smoke and fire' of the Rising. Ireland has had a history of conflict. Meehan also makes the point that the stories of the unknown participants of these momentous events are of equal importance to the more famous 'heroes' commemorated in 'bronze and stone'. The park attendant who fed the birds is recognised in this sonnet. Just as 'The Green' made patterns of nature's beauty on the window panes of great mansions, Meehan breathes the stories of history's unknown men and women, 'the stretcher bearer' and the 'nurse in white'. In this reflective poem, she shows that Ireland's past varied from peaceful to violent and heroic.

✒ Class/Homework Exercises

1. 'Paula Meehan's carefully crafted poems offer an insightful vision of Irish history.' Discuss this statement with reference to 'Them Ducks Died for Ireland'.

2. 'Meehan's most memorable poetry can be both compassionate and critical.' To what extent is this true of 'Them Ducks Died for Ireland'? Support the points you make with suitable reference to the text.

◉ Points to Consider

• Various perspectives on places and events – the wonder of nature, the destruction of war, the revision of historical narrative.

• Provocative use of contrast, imaginative use of personification.

• Effective sonnet form – contrasting descriptive quatrains of peace and war followed by sober reflective sestet.

• Interesting rhyme/half rhyme scheme – abba, cddc, efg, efg – adds to poem's musicality.

• Long run-on lines in which spoken rhythms carry meaning across line endings, mirroring breath patterns referenced in poem.

Sample Leaving Cert Questions on Meehan's Poetry

1. 'Some of Meehan's most compelling poems are rooted in community and a sense of place.' To what extent do you agree or disagree with this view? Support your answer with reference to the poetry of Paula Meehan on your course.

2. 'Paula Meehan uses evocative language to create poems that include both personal reflection and public commentary.' Discuss this view, supporting your answer with reference to both the themes and language found in the poetry of Meehan on your course.

3. 'Meehan's distinctive poetic vision often gives voice and dignity to individuals who are marginalised or excluded.' To what extent do you agree or disagree with this statement? Develop your answer with reference to the poetry of Paula Meehan on your course.

How do I organise my answer?

(Sample question 1)

'Some of Meehan's most compelling poems are rooted in community and a sense of place.' To what extent do you agree or disagree with this view? Support your answer with reference to the poetry of Paula Meehan on your course.

Sample Plan 1

Intro: *(Stance: partially agree with viewpoint in question)* Meehan creates captivating poetry clearly established in her Dublin working-class community and environment, but she also encourages readers to look out at the wider world.

Point 1: *(Exact details paint a bleak urban landscape, but also hint at world beyond)* 'Buying Winkles' recalls a drab cityscape transformed by a child's imagination; the moon is a 'bonus', the rain makes the winkles 'glisten blue like little/night skies themselves'. But the outside world is suggested – 'The sweetest extra winkle/that brought the sea to me' – and the child's growing curiosity beyond the limits of the city.

Point 2: *(Colloquialism, vivid visual and aural detail locate the poem in community and place, gesture transforms and transcends)* 'My Father Perceived as a Vision of St Francis' includes details describing an ordinary man in his local environment. A simple transcendent gesture evokes the wider world of the saint.

Understanding the Prescribed Poetry Question

Marks are awarded using the PCLM Marking Scheme: P = 15; C = 15; L = 15; M = 5 Total = 50

- **P** (Purpose = 15 marks) refers to the set question and is the launch pad for the answer. This involves engaging with all aspects of the question. Both theme and language must be addressed, although not necessarily equally.

- **C** (Coherence = 15 marks) refers to the organisation of the developed response and the use of accurate, relevant quotation. Paragraphing is essential.

- **L** (Language = 15 marks) refers to the student's skill in controlling language throughout the answer.

- **M** (Mechanics = 5 marks) refers to spelling and grammar.

- Although no specific number of poems is required, students usually discuss at least 3 or 4 in their written responses.

- Aim for at least 800 words, to be completed within 45–50 minutes.

NOTE

In keeping with the PCLM approach, the student has to take a stance by agreeing, disagreeing or partially agreeing that Meehan's

– **compelling poems** (intimate personal memories, exact detail, resonant voice full of spiritual energy, intense vision capable of transcending family trauma and celebrating life, engaging colloquial language, vivid imagery, forceful repetition, etc.)

… are:

– **rooted in community and a sense of place** (close awareness of inner-city childhood, perception of Irishness and cultural history, enduring communal identity, place names, collective sense of overcoming hardships, folklore, oral tradition, etc.)

EXAMINER'S COMMENT

As part of a full essay, this high-grade paragraph demonstrates close engagement with the poem in addressing the question. Good use of reference and accurate quotation – all skilfully worked into the succinct critical comments. Expression is clear, overall, but could have been a little more varied ('environment' is overused).

Point 3: *(Colloquial language and details create a local environment, mythological references widen to a universal perspective)* 'Hearth Lesson' uses colloquial expressions to describe a bitter family quarrel. Mythological comparisons in the parody card game between Zeus and Hera illustrate universal the age-old struggle between men and women.

Point 4: *(Using rhetoric and private memory, the reader is forced to consider uncontrolled housing development)* 'Death of a Field' uses rhetorical questions, emotive contrasts between plants and products and a litany of repetitive phrases to reflect on the beauty of nature under threat of rampant materialism.

Conclusion: Meehan is a poet of the streets and people of working-class Dublin. She fearlessly confronts the city's tragedies and deprivations through forceful poetry. But she also points the reader to a bigger stage featuring ecology, freedom, transcendence and a universal perspective.

Sample Paragraph: Point 2

In 'My Father Perceived as a Vision of St Francis', Meehan remembers her father as 'a perfect vision'. The scene is an early morning suburb, 'a Finglas garden'. Effective onomatopoeia, 'dawn whinny', 'Bottles chinked' establish the ordinary environment. The colloquial phrase, 'hum a snatch of a tune' places her father in his working-class environment. Suddenly, a transformative gesture of her father who 'tossed the crumbs' for the birds changes the entire scene. The times in Italy when St Francis preached to the birds 'of every size, shape, colour' is recreated. Her father has transcended the boundaries of age and environment. He is 'made young again' by repeating the saint's simple act of kindness. This compelling poem broadens its outlook from the local environment to the wider world by showing how a simple act of love to our fellow creatures can free an ordinary man from the struggle to survive and become 'suddenly radiant'.

(Sample question 2)

'Paula Meehan uses evocative language to create poems that include both personal reflection and public commentary.' Discuss this view, supporting your answer with reference to both the themes and language found in the poetry of Meehan on your course.

Sample Plan 2

Intro: *(Stance: agree with viewpoint in question)* Meehan's poetry flows from her deep love of people and places. Energetic recollections of childhood, family and environment lead to a robust assessment of Ireland's recent social history. Powerful poems encourage readers to examine attitudes to gender, class, history, ecology, etc.

Point 1: *(Personal horror at event, public criticism)* 'The Statue of the Virgin at Granard Speaks' – dramatic monologue of Mary herself who is ironically ineffective in young girl's hour of need, 'I didn't lift a finger to help her'. Further irony of repressive smug Irish society 'tucked up safe and dreaming'.

Point 2: *(Memories of threatened field, public critique of uncontrolled development)* 'Death of a Field' – nostalgic recollection of teenage years, 'where first smokes, first tokes, first gropes'. Simile conjures memory of dynamic wildlife, 'magpies sound like flying castanets'. Startling list of contrasts emphasises the destruction of the precious ecosystem, 'The end of primrose is the start of Brillo'.

Point 3: *(Personal discovery, public reflection on official historical narrative)* 'Them Ducks Died for Ireland' – reflective sonnet emerges from poet's discovery of footnote in Architectural Archive. Georgian windows reflect changing seasons and scenes of the park. Repetition and alliteration detail the 'bloodprice' of the armed struggle paid not only by the combatants but also by the ordinary people, 'wounds of history, wounds of war'.

Point 4: *(Poet's own experience, public commentary on class division)* 'The Exact Moment I Became a Poet' – personal recollection of incident at school ignites poet's indignation at class prejudice, effective use of teacher's direct speech, 'end up'. Anger at degradation of working women she knew, powerfully captured in extended image of poultry, 'trussed like chickens'.

> **NOTE**
>
> In keeping with the PCLM approach, the student has to explore poems of Meehan's on the course that include:
> - **evocative language** (powerful imagery, colloquial speech, personification, repetition, contrast, irony, evocative tones of compassion, regret, reflection, etc.)
>
> ... to create poems that show:
> - **both personal reflection and public commentary** (warm recollected scenes from Irish working-class community, changing perspectives, intense criticism of patriarchal, materialistic society and the havoc it wreaks on fragile communities and natural environments, etc.)

Conclusion: Meehan's poetry shows empathy for her own people and environment. She is a fearless speaker who searches and defends her childhood and her home. Her evocative poems attack the hypocrisy, uncertainty, materialism and changing identities of a modern world.

Sample Paragraph: Point 4

EXAMINER'S COMMENT

Addresses the question directly and engages well with the text. Further emphasis on the evocative elements (moving atmospheres and tones) would have provided more development. Effective use made of apt reference and relevant quotation. Expression is generally clear and impressive (e.g. 'incensed', 'definitions undervalue and diminish'). Solid high-grade standard.

'The Exact Moment I Became a Poet' comes from a personal recollection from Meehan's childhood. At eight years of age, she heard her teacher warn the students that if they don't 'Attend' to their lessons they will 'end up' in the sewing factory, as if discarded on a rubbish heap. Meehan is incensed at the term, 'end up'. She feels that the working women she knew are being 'robbed' of their dignity because they are working to support their families. A vibrant simile illustrates the prejudice against these ordinary women, 'trussed like chickens on a conveyor belt'. The poet extends the image by declaring that class definitions undervalue and diminish a person, 'Words could pluck you … your lovely shiny feathers all gone'. Meehan's compassionate poem publicly expresses her indignation at the insult levelled at her own community in her recollection of this childhood memory.

Leaving Cert Sample Essay

'Meehan's distinctive poetic vision often gives voice and dignity to individuals who are marginalised or excluded.' To what extent do you agree or disagree with this view? Support your answer with reference to the poetry of Paula Meehan on your course.

EXAM FOCUS

- As you may not be familiar with some of the poems referred to in the sample plans, substitute poems that you have studied closely.
- Key points about a particular poem can be developed over more than one paragraph.
- Paragraphs may also include cross-referencing and discussion of more than one poem.
- Remember that there is no single 'correct' answer to poetry questions, so always be confident in expressing your own considered response.

Sample Essay

1. Paula Meehan creates poetry which often results in conversations across time where she re-imagines the past. Using innovative poetic forms, vivid visual detail and colloquial language, Meehan acknowledges the importance of working women, celebrates the vivacity of her emigrant aunt, upholds the dignity of the tragic victims of drug abuse and reinstates the memory of ordinary people who lived on the edge of history.

2. 'Prayer for the Children of Longing' is dedicated to the young people in North Dublin's inner city who died from drug abuse. Meehan's inventive use of incantatory lines without punctuation, propels the poem forward through repetitive phrasing, 'Here at', 'Grant us'. She does not avoid the grim reality of the announcement of a child's death, 'The scream, the siren, the knock on the door'. Incisively, she criticises the pressure of a modern world on an impoverished community through startling personification, 'The streets ... That promised them everything/That delivered them nothing'.

3. Yet her empathetic voice allows these neglected children to be heard at last, 'In that silence let us hear'. Meehan restores their dignity so that their names seem like a litany of 'the holiest prayers'. Her soothing voice consoles their grieving families at the foot of the Christmas tree. For the first time, these children are reclaimed from the statistics in a government report listing the victims of drug abuse. They live again 'Under the starlight, under the moonlight'. Meehan has offered a lifeline to the grieving community by naming a shared loss.

4. 'Cora, Auntie' is another elegy whose run-on lines record the vigour of Meehan's emigrant aunt, 'scourge of Croydon train drivers'. She 'tilted at death' like a chivalrous medieval knight using 'humour' as her 'lance'. Once again, Meehan truthfully visualises the sadness of life, 'her body withered', 'a split', 'a tear'. But by focusing on the rich colours and delicate communal craftwork of the women, 'sewing red sequins', the poet presents her aunt as an impressive extrovert. She stands 'on the kitchen table' in her 'white satin dress' with its sewn border of 'sequins red as berries'.

5. Sensual sibilant details, 'promising blossom, summer, the scent of thyme' convey the aunt's positive energy. Meehan's maternal family line is honoured and the lesson of how to live life, with good humour, is recalled through the symbol of a small frivolous object – the glittering sequin. The poet has 'gathered them 'into a tin box' which she now opens 'in memory' of Cora. This is not just a tribute to Meehan's aunt, but to the countless Irish migrants who had to make new lives for themselves and face untold challenges away from their own families.

6. Another elegy, 'The Pattern', allows Meehan to re-live her personal traumatic childhood memories – particularly the uneasy relationship between herself and her mother. Sharp onomatopoeic details convey the reality, 'the sting of her hand across my face in one of our wars'. As before, the poet candidly acknowledges the harsh life of North Dublin's working-class community during the 1950s. Her mother's voice is heard recalling the rough patriarchal world of the time, 'your Granda caught us at the corner./He dragged me in by the hair'. Meehan is horrified that her mother never truly discovered who she was, 'already lost'. Like so many women, she had been restricted by a male-dominated society and endless child-bearing.

INDICATIVE MATERIAL

- **Meehan's distinctive poetic vision** (probing, recording, empathising, reflecting, transforming, drawing lessons) through visual and aural imagery, contrast, direct speech, mythological reference, personification, innovative poetic structure, etc.

  ... gives voice and dignity to:

- **the marginalised** (by widening the perspective on ordinary lives not included in official historical narrative, e.g. the importance of matriarchal family influence, the courage and resilience of the reluctant emigrant, the exploited victims of drug abuse, etc.).

7. But what is even more shocking is Meehan's revelation that her mother wanted to teach her free-spirited daughter 'to follow a pattern' of conformity just as she had. She will 'reel' her daughter 'home'. The poet refuses to accept such restrictions, however, and will make her own choices in life. Overall, the use of direct speech, onomatopoeia and vivid imagery highlights the oppression of Irish women in unforgiving living conditions during earlier times.

8. The sestet in Meehan's sonnet, 'Them Ducks Died for Ireland', also commemorates the marginalised, those who are not mentioned in the history books. The poet discovers by 'fading light' the Park Superintendent's report of the damage sustained in Stephen's Green during the 1916 Rising. Meehan is inspired to honour those on the periphery of these huge national events, such as 'the stretcher-bearer, the nurse in white'. They are the unnamed people who were left to clear up the destruction of the violent military events of 'smoke and fire'. Using a delicate simile, Meehan emphasises how easily their stories can be lost, 'fragile as a breathmark on the windowpane'. Their small acts of bravery are so quickly erased. At least Meehan's poem will 'salute' these marginalised people and help restore their proper place in the historical records.

9. Paula Meehan is keen to defend the uniqueness and relevance of her Dublin working-class roots. She restores shadows of the past in the elegiac stories about her mother and her aunt. She recovers marginal voices that are usually hidden from history. Meehan's sense of solidarity and compassion is evident in so many of her poems, offering dignity to society's outcasts.

(820 words)

EXAMINER'S COMMENT

A well-sustained and clearly supported response that shows some close engagement with Meehan's poetry. Both elements of the question (poetic vision and acknowledgement of the marginalised) are generally addressed throughout, although a little more on the 'distinctive' element would have been welcome. Good examples of the poet's style illustrated – particularly in paragraphs 5 and 8. The note-like commentary in paragraph 7 could have been more developed, but in referencing all four poems, there is effective use of quotations integrated into the discussion. Overall, a well-written top-grade essay.

GRADE: H1
P = 15/15
C = 13/15
L = 13/15
M = 5/5
Total = 46/50

👀 Revision Overview

'Buying Winkles' (OL)
In this nostalgic poem, the poet creates a vivid sense of an urban working-class community and reflects on a magical journey of discovery.

'The Pattern'
Recalling various scenes in a Dublin flat, Meehan considers a difficult mother-daughter relationship. Many of her poems are informed by the voices of women in her family.

'The Statue of the Virgin at Granard Speaks'
Poignant and dramatic poem in which the self-critical 'voice' of the statue also accuses an entire society that lets young women go to waste.

'Cora, Auntie'
Investigating the lives of her family allows the poet freedom to explore her culture and become reconciled with the past. Here she pays tribute to her aunt's courage and resilience.

'The Exact Moment I Became a Poet'
In this autobiographical poem, Meehan takes up the struggle for self-definition on behalf of women. Challenging class division and prejudice is central to much of her poetry.

'My Father Perceived as a Vision of St Francis'
Set in the poet's family home in Finglas, this moving tribute expresses deep feelings of empathy while conveying an underlying sense of transience and mortality.

'Hearth Lesson' (OL)
Another confessional poem from Meehan's disquieting childhood offers a compelling poetic vision of innocence and newfound determination.

'Prayer for the Children of Longing' (OL)
Empathy and solidarity are recurring features of Meehan's poetry. This prayerful poem for victims of drug abuse explores themes of loss, exploitation and community.

'Death of a Field'
Nature is close to Meehan's heart and many of her poems are environmentalist. This plaintive poem addresses some of the adverse effects of urban development.

'Them Ducks Died for Ireland'
In considering the significance of the Easter Rising, Meehan focuses on what has been officially recorded by history – and what has been left out of history.

💬 Last Words

'I love her verbal energy and the profound compassion that I find in her work. She is a dynamic public advocate for Irish poetry.'
Maureen Kennelly

'Even in the darkness of grief and loss, Paula Meehan celebrates life with a visceral, flaying attention.'
Maura Dooley

'The great thing about poetry is that it's the human voice, the one human voice breaking the silence.'
Paula Meehan

 HISTORY/ MEMORY   **IDENTITY**   **IRELAND**   **RELATIONSHIPS**   **CREATIVITY**   **LOSS**   **RELIGION/ SPIRITUALITY**   **LOVE**   **NATURE**   **CONFLICT**

Eiléan Ní Chuilleanáin

1942–

'I chose poetry because it was different.'

Eiléan Ní Chuilleanáin is regarded by many as one of the most important contemporary Irish women poets. Her subject matter ranges from social commentary and considerations of religious issues to quiet, introspective poems about human nature. Ní Chuilleanáin is noted for being mysterious and complex; her poems usually have subtle messages that unfold only through multiple readings. She is well read in history, and a strong sense of connection between past and present characterises her work, in which she often draws interesting parallels between historical events and modern situations. Many of her poems highlight the contrast between fluidity and stillness, life and death, and the undeniable passing of time and humanity's attempts to stop change. She herself has frequently referred to the importance of secrecy in her poetry. Most critics agree that Ní Chuilleanáin's poems resist easy explanations and variously show her interest in explorations of transition, the sacred, women's experience and history.

Investigate Further

To find out more about Eiléan Ní Chuilleanáin, or to hear readings of her poems not already available in your eBook, you could search some useful websites such as YouTube, BBC Poetry, poetryfoundation.org and poetryarchive.org, or access additional material on this page of your eBook.

Prescribed Poems

(OL) indicates poems that are also prescribed for the Ordinary Level course.

1 🔊 Lucina Schynning in Silence of the Nicht

Moon shining in silence of the night
The heaven being all full of stars
I was reading my book in a ruin
By a sour candle, without roast meat or music
Strong drink or a shield from the air   5
Blowing in the crazed window, and I felt
Moonlight on my head, clear after three days' rain.

I washed in cold water; it was orange, channelled down bogs
Dipped between cresses.
The bats flew through my room where I slept safely.   10
Sheep stared at me when I woke.

Behind me the waves of darkness lay, the plague
Of mice, plague of beetles
Crawling out of the spines of books,
Plague shadowing pale faces with clay   15
The disease of the moon gone astray.

In the desert I relaxed, amazed
As the mosaic beasts on the chapel floor
When Cromwell had departed and they saw
The sky growing through the hole in the roof.   20

Sheepdogs embraced me; the grasshopper
Returned with lark and bee.
I looked down between hedges of high thorn and saw
The hare, absorbed, sitting still
In the middle of the track; I heard   25
Again the chirp of the stream running.

'shining in silence of the night'

Title: Lucina is another name for Diana, the moon goddess. In Roman mythology, Lucina was the goddess of childbirth. Ní Chuilleanáin's title comes from the opening line of 'The Antichrist', a satirical poem by the Scottish poet William Dunbar (c. 1460–1517).

cresses: small strongly flavoured leaves.

plague: curse, diseased group.

spines: inner parts, backs.

astray: off course.

mosaic: mixed, assorted.

Cromwell: Oliver Cromwell (1599–1658), controversial English military and political leader who led an army of invasion in 1649–50, which conquered most of Ireland. Cromwell is still regarded largely as a figure of hatred in the Irish Republic, his name being associated with massacre, religious persecution and mass dispossession of the Catholic community.

chirp: lively sound, twitter.

👤 Personal Response

1. How would you describe the atmosphere in the poem's opening stanza? Refer to the text in your answer.
2. Choose one image taken from the natural world that you found particularly interesting. Comment briefly on its effectiveness.
3. Based on your reading of this poem, do you think Ní Chuilleanáin presents a realistic view of Irish history? Give reasons for your response.

👁 Critical Literacy

Eiléan Ní Chuilleanáin takes her title from a Middle Scots poem by William Dunbar. 'Lucina Schynning in Silence of the Nicht' is set in a ruin somewhere in Ireland, after Oliver Cromwell had devastated the country in 1649. However, Ní Chuilleanáin's beautiful and haunting poem is much more than a meditation on an historical event. The poet achieves immediacy by means of a dramatic monologue that recreates the whisperings of desolation in the aftermath of Cromwell's march through Ireland.

As in so many of her poems, Ní Chuilleanáin invites readers into a **strangely compelling setting**. The poet personifies the moon, creating an uneasy atmosphere. Silence enhances the dramatic effect: 'The heaven being all full of stars.' This eerie scene is described in a series of random details. The language – with its archaic Scottish dialect – is note-like and seemingly timeless. There is a notable absence of punctuation and a stilted rhythm as the unknown speaker's voice is introduced: 'I was reading my book in a ruin' (**line 3**). The series of fragmentary images – 'a sour candle', 'the crazed window' – are immediately unsettling, drawing us back to a darker age in Ireland's troubled history.

Characteristically, Ní Chuilleanáin leaves readers to unravel the poem's veiled meanings and the identity of the dispossessed narrator is never made known. Instead, this forlorn figure 'without roast meat or music' is associated with material and cultural deprivation – **a likely symbol of an oppressed Ireland**? Does the absence of 'Strong drink or a shield' add to the notion of a defeated people? Despite the obvious indications of almost incomprehensible suffering, some respite can still be found: 'I felt/Moonlight on my head, clear after three days' rain' (**line 7**). This simple image of nature – illuminating and refreshing – suggests comforting signs of recovery.

Ní Chuilleanáin's startling drama moves into the wild Irish landscape: 'I washed in cold water; it was orange.' The sense of native Irish resistance against foreign invasion is clearly evident in the reference to Dutch-born Protestant William of Orange, who defeated the army of Catholic James II at the Battle of the Boyne in 1690. But the poet focuses on the speaker's experience of displacement, illustrating the **alienation which existed within nationalist Ireland**. The narrator, surrounded by animal life and the open sky, becomes an extension of animate and inanimate nature: 'The bats flew through my room … Sheep stared at me' (**line 10**).

In an increasingly surreal atmosphere, the mood becomes much more disturbed. The poet's apocalyptic dream-vision highlights the 'waves of darkness' in an uninterrupted nightmarish sequence of repulsive images: 'plague/Of mice, plague of beetles/Crawling'. The **emphatic repetition of 'plague' resonates with images of widespread misery, disease and famine**. Nor does the poet ignore the distorted history of Ireland that has resulted from prejudice, propaganda and vested interest 'Crawling out of the spines of books' (line 14). What stands out, however, is Ní Chuilleanáin's ability to suggest distressing glimpses of our island's dark past, poignantly depicted in her heart-rending language describing innocent death: 'Plague shadowing pale faces with clay/The disease of the moon gone astray.'

There is a distinctive change of mood in lines 17–20 as the speaker reflects on the aching aftermath in the period after 'Cromwell had departed'. References to Christian retreat and renewal indicate the **consolation provided by religious faith**: 'In the desert I relaxed, amazed/As the mosaic beasts on the chapel floor'. This sense of wonder through the possibility of spiritual fulfilment is developed in the metaphorical image of 'The sky growing through the hole in the roof'. As always, landscape and nature are features of Ní Chuilleanáin's poem, allowing readers access to her subtle thinking.

In sharp contrast to the earlier trauma, the final tone is remarkably composed and harmonious. The language – which has been somewhat archaic throughout much of the poem – is noticeably biblical: 'Sheepdogs embraced me; the grasshopper/Returned with lark and bee.' **There is an unmistakable sense of survival and newfound confidence** in line 23: 'I looked down between hedges of high thorn.' Ní Chuilleanáin's recognition of 'The hare, absorbed, sitting still' (a cross-reference to her poem 'On Lacking the Killer Instinct') reinforces the feeling of quiet resignation. Is she alluding to the maturity and relative peace of the present Irish state? At any rate, the poem ends on a hopeful note of vigorous resilience, with one of nature's liveliest sounds, 'the chirp of the stream running'.

Throughout this elusive poem, Ní Chuilleanáin has explored fascinating aspects of Irish history – a story that has been often lost in the 'silence of the night'. So much of Ireland's past is marked by exploitation and resistance. The poem has deep undercurrents of countless conflicts springing from both without and within. The moon has long been associated with love, beauty, loneliness, lunacy and death. Some critics have suggested that Ní Chuilleanáin's poem uses the moon to symbolise the struggle of women through the centuries. As usual, readers are free to judge for themselves. However, there is little doubt that 'Lucina Schynning in Silence of the Nicht' presents us with **an intense, self-enclosed world** – but one where the tensions and aspirations of Ireland's complex story are imaginatively encapsulated.

⬚ Writing About the Poem

'Eiléan Ní Chuilleanáin's poems offer rich rewards to the perceptive reader.' Discuss this view, with particular reference to 'Lucina Schynning in Silence of the Nicht'.

Sample Paragraph

While I first found Ní Chuilleanáin's poetry quite difficult, I really enjoyed reading 'Lucina Schynning'. The strange title and eerie atmosphere under the moonlight makes us imagine the 'world' of the poem. I found it very dramatic. The narrative voice seemed very traumatised and was convincing as it represented Ireland's troubled history – 'Behind me, waves of darkness'. What I really liked about the poet was that she suggested, rather than explained. The description of Irish people starving was very moving – especially because of the word 'plague'. Ní Chuilleanáin's images of suffering were balanced by the positive ending. The poem asked many questions about how people today look at the past. The poet used many simple nature images such as the hare 'sitting still' and the 'chirp of the stream' to show a present-day Ireland where there is peace – unlike the war-torn past of the history books. Overall, I did enjoy 'Lucina Schynning' as it reminded me that there is still meaning in the beauty of nature.

EXAMINER'S COMMENT

This sensitive reaction to Ní Chuilleanáin's poem reflected on both the subject matter and style of the text using accurate quotations to support the discussion points. The poem's narrative was disclosed by drawing together its significant details. Very impressive vocabulary throughout. A solid high-grade response.

✍ Class/Homework Exercises

1. 'Ní Chuilleanáin's distinctive poetry is filled with subtle messages.' Discuss this statement, with particular reference to 'Lucina Schynning in Silence of the Nicht'.
2. 'Eiléan Ní Chuilleanáin's "Lucina Schynning in Silence of the Nicht" is a highly atmospheric poem that has an elusive dreamlike quality.' To what extent do you agree or disagree with this statement? Support your answer with reference to the poem.

⊙ Points to Consider

- **Evocative mid-17th-century Irish setting.**

- **Dramatic monologue form recreates Irish alienation after Cromwell's invasion.**

- **Themes include suffering, loss, human resilience and the celebration of nature.**

- **Effective use of startling imagery, repetition, sibilance and alliteration.**

2 🔊 **The Second Voyage**

Odysseus rested on his oar and saw
The ruffled foreheads of the waves
Crocodiling and mincing past: he rammed
The oar between their jaws and looked down
In the simmering sea where scribbles of weed defined   5
Uncertain depth, and the slim fishes progressed
In fatal formation, and thought

                       If there was a single
Streak of decency in these waves now, they'd be ridged
Pocked and dented with the battering they've had,   10
And we could name them as Adam named the beasts,
Saluting a new one with dismay, or a notorious one
With admiration; they'd notice us passing
And rejoice at our shipwreck, but these
Have less character than sheep and need more patience.   15

I know what I'll do he said;
I'll park my ship in the crook of a long pier
(And I'll take you with me he said to the oar)
I'll face the rising ground and walk away
From tidal waters, up riverbeds   20
Where herons parcel out the miles of stream,
Over gaps in the hills, through warm
Silent valleys, and when I meet a farmer
Bold enough to look me in the eye
With 'where are you off to with that long   25
Winnowing fan over your shoulder?'
There I will stand still
And I'll plant you for a gatepost or a hitching-post
And leave you as a tidemark. I can go back
And organise my house then.   30

                    But the profound
Unfenced valleys of the ocean still held him;
He had only the oar to make them keep their distance;
The sea was still frying under the ship's side.
He considered the water-lilies, and thought about fountains   35
Spraying as wide as willows in empty squares,

Odysseus: Greek mythic king and warrior. He is also the literary hero of Homer's epic tale, *The Odyssey*, which tells of Odysseus's 10-year struggle to return home from the Trojan War.
ruffled: wrinkled, tangled.
Crocodiling: gliding.
mincing: moving daintily.

Pocked: disfigured.

notorious: infamous.

herons: long-necked wading birds.
parcel: mark, measure.

Winnowing: probing.

EILÉAN NÍ CHUILLEANÁIN

The sugarstick of water clattering into the kettle,
The flat lakes bisecting the rushes. He remembered spiders and frogs
Housekeeping at the roadside in brown trickles floored with mud,
Horsetroughs, the black canal, pale swans at dark: 40
His face grew damp with tears that tasted
Like his own sweat or the insults of the sea.

bisecting: cutting through.

'the simmering sea'

👤 Personal Response

1. From your reading of the first stanza (lines 1–15), describe Odysseus's relationship with the sea. Refer to the text in your response.
2. Select two interesting images from the poem and comment on the effectiveness of each.
3. Write your own personal response to 'The Second Voyage', supporting the points you make with reference to the text.

⦿ Critical Literacy

The relationship between past and present is one of Eiléan Ní Chuilleanáin's recurring themes. In addressing the present within the context of history, she often explores contrasts, such as life and death, motion and stillness, and the inevitable tension between time passing and people's desire to resist change. 'The Second Voyage' refers to the Greek hero Odysseus, whose first epic journey was a relentless battle with the treacherous ocean. But growing frustrated by the endless struggle against nature, he decides that his next voyage will be on land and therefore less demanding.

From the outset, Odysseus is presented as a slightly bemused and ridiculous figure. There is a cartoon-like quality to the exaggerated ocean setting as Ní Chuilleanáin immediately portrays this legendary hero resting on his oar and watching the 'ruffled foreheads of the waves/Crocodiling and mincing past' (line 3). The poet expands this metaphor, describing the waves as great beasts to be challenged: 'he rammed/The oar between their jaws.' **Ní Chuilleanáin's derisive humour mocks the great wanderer's inflated sense of his own masculinity.** But there is no denying that Odysseus is still excited by the 'Uncertain depth' beneath him. For him, anything is possible at sea, where he is truly in his element. The personification is childlike, suggesting his peevish annoyance at being unable to conquer the ocean waves, which don't possess 'a single/Streak of decency' (line 9).

Ní Chuilleanáin's tone is playfully critical. As always, the poet's skill lies in her vigorous images, such as the 'slim fishes' beneath 'scribbles of weeds'. Odysseus's powerful physicality is contrasted with the seemingly pretty waves, which somehow resist the 'battering they've had'. Lording over this surreal scene and filled with disappointment, the egotistical Greek warrior thinks about the Garden of Eden. He is soon envying Adam, who was given God-given control over all living things and had 'named the beasts' of the earth. Completely unaware of the irony of his excessive pride, Odysseus is overwhelmed by self-pity and resorts to ridiculing these foolish waves, which fail to 'rejoice at our shipwreck' (line 14).

Ní Chuilleanáin develops the whimsical drama by letting us hear Odysseus's petulant voice as he prepares to seek recognition onshore. Armed with renewed confidence and his trusty oar – ('I'll take you with me he said to the oar') – he sets out to 'face the rising ground' and seek affirmation far away 'From tidal waters'. But despite the purposeful rhythm and self-assured tone, there is a strong underlying sense that he is deluding himself. The landscape might be serenely beautiful, but it is confined. Unlike the boundless sea, birds define it: 'herons parcel out the miles of stream' (line 21). Yet the brave warrior is eager to boast of his exploits in the outside world and hopes to tell his story to the first farmer he meets who is 'Bold enough to look me in the eye'. **Odysseus even tries to convince himself that**

it is time to put down roots, to plant his oar as 'a gatepost or a hitching-post'. Then he will be ready to return home and 'organise my house'. However, the laboured rhythm and imposing multi-syllabic language convey his half-heartedness about settling down.

Indeed, there are already signs that Odysseus will never surrender the freedom and adventure of dangerous ocean voyages. The powerful oar, which once signified dynamism and exhilaration, is now seen as a decorative symbol of stillness, a 'Winnowing fan'. Unable to deny his true destiny any longer, **he accepts that he cannot ignore his urge to control the sea**: the 'Unfenced valleys of the ocean still held him' (**line 32**). But his ironic situation remains; while the freedom he yearns for is unattainable on land, he is still unable to conquer the seemingly infinite sea.

The poem's final section is sympathetic to Odysseus's dilemma. Ní Chuilleanáin replaces the pompous first-person pronouns with her own measured narrative account: 'He considered the water-lilies, and thought about fountains' (**line 35**). The poet makes extensive use of **contrasting water images to highlight land and sea**. Unlike the water 'frying under the ship's side', settled life appears controlled, but unattractive ('Horsetroughs, the black canal'). His uneasy memories of home ('water clattering', 'pale swans at dark') are ominous. For Odysseus, his second excursion into landlocked civilisation offers so little fulfilment that 'His face grew damp with tears'. The hero is forever drawn to that first epic voyage and the wonderful experience of ocean living, with which he is inextricably bound: 'Like his own sweat or the insults of the sea.'

The fluctuating water images – another familiar feature of Eiléan Ní Chuilleanáin's writing – reflect the complex narrative threads throughout the poem. Transitions of various kinds are central to her work. The poet has also been very involved in translating texts, and believes that because of the limits imposed by the translator, the process can never be completely true to the original language. Some literary critics see 'The Second Voyage' as an **extended metaphor exploring how language and culture resist translation**, but like so many of Ní Chuilleanáin's enigmatic poems, the ultimate interpretation is left to individual readers themselves.

⬤ Writing About the Poem

'Ní Chuilleanáin's poetry makes effective use of contrasts to illuminate her themes.' Discuss this view, with particular reference to 'The Second Voyage'.

Sample Paragraph

Contrasting themes, such as life and death, permanence and transience, and motion and stillness are all prominent in Ní Chuilleanáin's 'The Second Voyage'. The description of Odysseus who 'rammed' his oar against the waves shows a macho character whose extrovert behaviour could not be more unlike the silent sea which he will never tame. Momentarily, the irritated hero makes up his mind to undertake a new 'voyage' by seeking glory on land. But the reality of settled life disappoints him. Revealing images of fixed landmarks – 'a gatepost', 'tidemark' – all convey the sense of disinterest. Odysseus is immediately aware of the contrasting dynamic qualities of the sea's 'Unfenced valleys'. I found it interesting that the man-made images were all water-based – 'fountains', 'the black canal' – and all lacking the danger of the open sea which Odysseus longs for. Once again, Ní Chuilleanáin succeeds in presenting Odysseus's love-hate obsession with the mysterious ocean.

EXAMINER'S COMMENT

The introductory overview established a very good basis for exploring interesting contrasts within the poem. There is some well-focused personal engagement with the text: 'I found it interesting that the man-made images were all water-based.' Suitable quotations provide valuable support. Diction and expression – in the final sentence, for example – are also excellent. This confident response merits the top grade.

✒ Class/Homework Exercises

1. 'Eiléan Ní Chuilleanáin presents readers with unsettling scenes, both real and otherworldly.' Discuss this statement, with particular reference to 'The Second Voyage'. Refer to the text in your answer.
2. 'In "The Second Voyage", Ní Chuilleanáin addresses the idea of transition and the difficulties associated with change.' Discuss this view, supporting your answer with reference to the poem.

⊙ Points to Consider

- Imaginative use of mythic tale of Greek hero.

- Sardonic humour evident in vivid personification of the sea.

- Unsettling scenes, both real and otherworldly.

- Contrasting themes (transience, masculinity, freedom, etc.).

- Vibrant water imagery is a powerful motif.

- Alliteration and sibilance create dynamic sound effects.

- Direct dialogue adds immediacy.

3 🔊 Deaths and Engines

EILÉAN NÍ CHUILLEANÁIN

We came down above the houses
In a stiff curve, and
At the edge of Paris airport
Saw an empty tunnel
– The back half of a plane, black   5
On the snow, nobody near it,
Tubular, burnt-out and frozen.

Tubular: cylindrical, tube-shaped.

When we faced again
The snow-white runways in the dark
No sound came over   10
The loudspeakers, except the sighs
Of the lonely pilot.

The cold of metal wings is contagious:

contagious: catching.

Soon you will need wings of your own,
Cornered in the angle where   15
Time and life like a knife and fork
Cross, and the lifeline in your palm
Breaks, and the curve of an aeroplane's track
Meets the straight skyline.

The images of relief: 20
Hospital pyjamas, screens round a bed
A man with a bloody face
Sitting up in bed, conversing cheerfully

conversing: chatting.

Through cut lips:
These will fail you some time.   25

You will find yourself alone
Accelerating down a blind

Accelerating: speeding.

Alley, too late to stop
And know how light your death is;

You will be scattered like wreckage,   30
The pieces every one a different shape

lodge: settle.

Will spin and lodge in the hearts
Of all who love you.

'snow-white runways'

👤 Personal Response

1. Describe the atmosphere at the airport in lines 1–12. Refer to the text in your response.
2. Based on your reading of lines 13–25, choose one image that you found particularly memorable and comment on its effectiveness.
3. Write your personal response to 'Deaths and Engines', referring closely to the poem in your answer.

👁 Critical Literacy

'Deaths and Engines' contextualises Eiléan Ní Chuilleanáin's experience of death – and particularly her father's death – within the setting of another 'burnt-out' ruin: the abandoned wreckage of an aircraft engine. Characteristically, the poet's metaphorical sense is so complete that at times it dominates the poem, constantly inviting readers to tease out meaningful connections within the language.

As with so many of her poems, Ní Chuilleanáin begins mid-narrative – as dreams often do – with an aeroplane coming in to land in Paris. The sense of danger as the plane descends in 'a stiff curve' is typical of the edgy imagery found in stanza one. **The memory immediately suggests a moment of insight – of coming down to earth**: 'We came down above the houses/In a stiff curve.' Details are stark – particularly the absorbing description of the 'empty tunnel' and the peculiar sight of the 'back half of a plane' that has been 'burnt-out and frozen' against the wintry landscape. The contrast of the deserted 'black' wreckage 'On the snow' accentuates the visual effect, adding drama to the memory.

Stanza two emphasises the surreal nature of the hushed 'snow-white runways in the dark'. The poet continues to construct a dreamlike sense of uneasy silence and chilling alienation. The only sounds coming over the loudspeakers are the unsettling 'sighs/Of the lonely pilot'. There is an underlying suggestion of a weary individual – perhaps facing death. This is given a wider relevance by the unnerving opening of stanza three: 'The cold of metal wings is contagious.' For the poet, this insightful moment marks a changing perspective: 'Soon you will need wings of your own.' The 'you' might refer to Ní Chuilleanáin's dying father or the poet herself or possibly the reader. From this point onwards, the metaphor of the wrecked aircraft is central to the fragmentary memories of her father's illness and death. **The poet interweaves two narratives**: the trajectory of the plane as it 'Meets the straight skyline' and the mark of her father's natural life span ('the lifeline in your palm'). Ní Chuilleanáin uses the memorable image of the crossed knife and fork to suggest the inescapable destiny that confronts the dying.

The poet's familiar preoccupations of tension and mystery are even more obvious in stanza four. Disjointed scenes of 'Hospital pyjamas, screens round a bed' are introduced as 'images of relief' – at least temporarily. **But the prevailing mood is of inevitable death** – 'These will fail you some time'. The poet expresses the final reality of every human being in stanza five: 'You will find yourself alone.' Ní Chuilleanáin conveys the nightmarish realisation of irreversible death through recognisable images of losing control: 'Accelerating down a blind/Alley, too late to stop.' Run-on lines and a persistent rhythm add to the sense of powerlessness. Once again, there are echoes of the 'empty tunnel' and the 'burnt-out' plane. Nevertheless, in imagining her father's final moments, the poet can relate to his experience of dying as a release, so that they both understood 'how light your death is'.

The resigned tone of stanza six reflects Ní Chuilleanáin's deeper understanding of mortality. In celebrating her father's life within a context of enduring love, the poet is able to simultaneously dismantle and preserve the relationship she has had with her father. She returns to the image of the wrecked aeroplane, accepting that in death, 'You will be scattered like wreckage'. However, far from feeling sadness for her father's loss, **Ní Chuilleanáin takes comfort in knowing that he will live 'in the hearts/Of all who love you'**. The sentiment is subdued and poignant, and all the more powerful since it comes from a poet who rarely expresses her feelings directly.

To a great extent, the poem is about families and how they process their personal tragedies. As always, Ní Chuilleanáin's oblique approach is open to many interpretations. But she seems to be suggesting that it takes the sudden shock of death to acknowledge the closeness of relationships in our lives. Typically, in dealing with such emotional subjects as separation, grief and the death of a loved one, **the poet never lapses into sentimentality**. 'Deaths and Engines' was written during the escalation of violence in Northern Ireland, and some critics have understood the poem as a commentary on the human cost of conflict. In the end, readers are left to make up their own minds.

✒ Writing About the Poem

'Ní Chuilleanáin's poems of separation and estrangement transcend the limits of personal experience.' Discuss this view, with particular reference to 'Deaths and Engines'.

Sample Paragraph

One of the most interesting aspects of Ní Chuilleanáin's poetry is her focus on the natural life cycle. Even though she deals with her father's death in 'Deaths and Engines', I found the poem to be more uplifting than depressing. In comparing his death to the wrecked plane, 'burnt-out and frozen', she realises that the wreckage 'Will spin and lodge in the hearts/Of all who love you'. The poem also shows Ní Chuilleanáin stressing the experience of death for every human being: 'You will find yourself alone'. Her message is simple – every individual must face death unaccompanied. In 'Fireman's Lift', for example, she also came to terms with a family death – her mother – by comparing her passing to the Assumption of the Virgin Mary. I believe that such poems transcend the individual and emphasise the naturalness of separation and loss.

EXAMINER'S COMMENT

This is a well-focused response to the question and shows a close understanding of the poem, particularly in the cross-reference to 'Fireman's Lift'. Accurate quotations are used effectively to support key points. Expression is fluent, varied and clear, with some good personal engagement, such as in the final sentence. A very assured performance securing the highest grade.

✒ Class/Homework Exercises

1. 'What defines Eiléan Ní Chuilleanáin's poetry is its imaginative power and precision of language.' Discuss this statement, with particular reference to 'Deaths and Engines'.

2. 'In "Deaths and Engines", Ní Chuilleanáin explores aspects of suffering and death by effectively using the metaphor of an aeroplane coming in to land.' Discuss this view, with reference to the poem.

⊙ Points to Consider

- **Key themes – memory, family bonds and coming to terms with death.**

- **An underlying sense of tension pervades the poem.**

- **Effective use of metaphor, contrast and repetition throughout.**

- **Positive conclusion: love can transcend death.**

4 🔊 Street

EILÉAN NÍ CHUILLEANÁIN

He fell in love with the butcher's daughter
When he saw her passing by in her white trousers
Dangling a knife on a ring at her belt.
He stared at the dark shining drops on the paving-stones.

One day he followed her   5
Down the slanting lane at the back of the shambles.
A door stood half-open
And the stairs were brushed and clean,
Her shoes paired on the bottom step,
Each tread marked with the red crescent   10
Her bare heels left, fading to faintest at the top.

Dangling: hanging freely, displaying.

shambles: untidy market scene; place of slaughter.

tread: undersole of a shoe; top surface of a step in a staircase.
crescent: half-moon; sickle shape.
fading: dwindling, perishing.
faintest: weakest, exhausted.

'And the stairs were brushed and clean'

👤 Personal Response

1. Why do you think Ní Chuilleanáin chose to name her poem 'Street' and yet gives the street no name? Give reasons for your response.
2. Which image did you find most intriguing in the poem? Refer closely to the text in your answer.
3. Were you satisfied by the poem's conclusion? Briefly explain your response.

⊙ Critical Literacy

'Street' is a short lyric poem from Ní Chuilleanáin's collection *The Magdalene Sermon* (1989). Mary Magdalene was the first person to witness the Resurrection of Christ and these poems reflect on women's religious experiences. The poems also depict edges, borders and crossings between different kinds of worlds as though passing through thresholds and intersections from one realm of experience to another, just as Christ rose from the dead. Characteristically, the poet reveals and conceals women and their strange responsibilities in a graceful, luminous voice.

Ní Chuilleanáin believed in the importance of the ordinary and the domestic as new metaphors for human experience. In the first section of the poem, she quietly tells a somewhat unusual tale, giving readers a memorable glimpse into another reality. It is the story of a man falling in love with a woman, 'the butcher's daughter'. Flowing run-on lines depict the rising emotions of the man as he catches sight of her 'in her white trousers'. This colour is often associated with purity and innocence, but it is also the traditional colour butchers wear in their work. **A close-up shot captures a disturbing detail**. 'Dangling' describes the careless movement of the knife as it sways from the 'ring at her belt'. The verb is carefully positioned at the beginning of the line, as it tantalises and entices like a piece of shining jewellery; yet this knife has a deadly purpose. The man is captivated: 'He stared at the dark shining drops on the paving-stones.' Has this knife recently been used? Has blood just been spilled? Is he, as if in a fairy tale, suddenly enthralled by the glittering yet lethal trade of the slaughterer?

In the second section, the narrative continues, becoming increasingly menacing: 'One day he followed her.' The assonant 'ow' sound disquietly enhances his journey. Ní Chuilleanáin specialises in the 'poetic of descriptive places'. The man's journey takes him 'Down the slanting lane at the back of the shambles'. **Varying line lengths add to the growing tension**. The adjective 'slanting' suggests a sinister backstreet where everything is oblique, tilted, half-concealed. The 'shambles' is a rough market where meat is carved and animals are slaughtered. To the outside world, it is a place of violence and mayhem. Is Ní Chuilleanáin making a hidden reference to the slaughter of Christ on the cross? 'A door stood half-open'. Does the door admit or shut out? Is this a symbol of the threshold between life and death which Christ breached? As always, the poet invites the reader to make sense of the clues. A secret is being half-revealed, a mystery is being highlighted. Where does the door lead?

Eiléan Ní Chuilleanáin often peoples her poems with women who studiously attend to their chores. (Mary Magdalene attended to Jesus, washing his feet with her tears and drying them with her hair.) Here 'the stairs were brushed and clean'. Are they awaiting a visit or is this the attention to hygiene which is normal in the butchering trade? This poet's population of silent figures disclose little information. The 'butcher's daughter' had left 'shoes paired on the bottom step'. Yet even this tangible detail reveals only mystery. The full narrative is missing. Is there a suggestion that the man and woman will soon be a pair as well? An inviting flight of stairs leads to all sorts of possibilities. **Ní Chuilleanáin has created a typically ambivalent scenario** filled with underlying danger and excitement. This dreamlike encounter is imbued with an unforgettable atmosphere of edgy anticipation as profound silence echoes.

The poem concludes with a defined image. The girl's 'bare heels' have left traces which become more indistinct as they ascend the stairs. This is emphasised by the alliterative phrase 'fading to faintest'. These are 'marked with the red crescent', like a secret sign beckoning through the enjambed lines. **The mystery resonates**. What really is marked with the bow shapes? The stairs? Her shoes? The heels? Readers are kept wondering. What does the future hold for this couple? Detailed close-ups have been presented, yet there are tantalising gaps in the narrative as we are left like the man who was enticed by the 'Dangling' knife, lured into this ominous atmosphere. As in so many of her elusive dramas, disrupting patterns of communication allows the poet to draw attention to the problem of communication itself. Is this the rounded insight to be glimpsed in the poem?

✒ Writing About the Poem

'Poems of waiting, dramatic and incident-rich, are told quietly by Ní Chuilleanáin.' Discuss this statement in relation to the poem 'Street'.

Sample Paragraph

I felt that the poem 'Street' invited me into its surreal yet tangible world rather like the man is lured by the 'butcher's daughter'. I was caught as if in a dream where details are clearly recognisable, 'the red crescent/her bare heels left', yet their meaning is uncertain. Will the encounter take place between the man and the woman? The reader has been brought like the man on a 'slanting' journey. The full view of the lane was obscured from him, the full story is hidden by the obliqueness of the poem. Yet the atmosphere is unforgettable, the waiting is ominous. The poem disappears at its conclusion as the 'red crescent' marks flow 'fading to faintest'. Suspense and tension reverberate. The reader is led like the man, by sinister signs, a 'door', 'stairs' and footprints as if following a trail in a fairy tale. Yet the poet does not release the dramatic tensions at the poem's conclusion, leaving it in the reader's consciousness.

EXAMINER'S COMMENT

This response shows a remarkably close reading of the poem, using suitable reference and quotation to address the task in the question throughout. Discussion is coherent and the analysis incisive, especially the point about the dreamlike atmosphere. Expression is also impressive – fluent, varied and well controlled: 'the full story is hidden by the obliqueness of the poem.' Deserves the top grade.

✍ Class/Homework Exercises

1. 'Ní Chuilleanáin's poetry is oblique, yet concrete.' Discuss this statement in relation to 'Street'.
2. 'Ní Chuilleanáin creates an unnerving nightmarish atmosphere in her poem, "Street".' To what extent do you agree with this view? Support your answer with reference to the text.

⊙ Points to Consider

- **Highly dramatic poem filled with suspense and intrigue.**

- **Close-up details create interest.**

- **Run-through lines add a sense of urgency.**

- **Sense of mystery resonates at the end.**

5 🔊 Fireman's Lift

EILÉAN NÍ CHUILLEANÁIN

Fireman's Lift: The term refers to a technique commonly used by emergency service workers to carry someone to safety by placing the carried person across the shoulders of the carrier.

I was standing beside you looking up
Through the big tree of the cupola
Where the church splits wide open to admit
Celestial choirs, the fall-out of brightness.

cupola: dome-shaped roof.

Celestial: heavenly, divine.

The Virgin was spiralling to heaven,   5
Hauled up in stages. Past mist and shining,
Teams of angelic arms were heaving,
Supporting, crowding her, and we stepped

spiralling: whirling, twisting.

Back, as the painter longed to
While his arm swept in the large strokes.   10
We saw the work entire, and how the light

Melted and faded bodies so that
Loose feet and elbows and staring eyes
Floated in the wide stone petticoat
Clear and free as weeds.   15

This is what love sees, that angle:
The crick in the branch loaded with fruit,
A jaw defining itself, a shoulder yoked,

crick: arch, strain.
yoked: forced, strained.

The back making itself a roof
The legs a bridge, the hands   20
A crane and a cradle.

Their heads bowed over to reflect on her
Fair face and hair so like their own
As she passed through their hands. We saw them
Lifting her, the pillars of their arms   25

(Her face a capital leaning into an arch)
As the muscles clung and shifted
For a final purchase together
Under her weight as she came to the edge of the cloud.

capital: upper section of a column supporting a ceiling or arch.

Parma 1963 – Dublin 1994

The Assumption of the Virgin: Roman Catholic Church teaching states that the Virgin Mary, having completed the course of her earthly life, was assumed (or elevated) body and soul into heavenly glory. Antonio Allegri da Correggio (1489–1534), usually known as Correggio, was the foremost painter of the Parma school of the Italian Renaissance. One of his best-known works, The *Assumption of the Virgin*, is a fresco which decorates the dome of the Duomo (Cathedral) of Parma, in northern Italy.

'spiralling to heaven'

👤 Personal Response

1. Based on your reading of the poem, comment on the appropriateness of the title, 'Fireman's Lift'.
2. Choose one visual image from the poem which you consider particularly effective. Briefly explain your choice.
3. Write your own short personal response to the poem.

👁 Critical Literacy

This extraordinary poem describes the scene depicted in the painter Correggio's masterpiece, *Assumption of the Virgin*. In 1963 Eiléan Ní Chuilleanáin and her mother had visited Parma Cathedral. Following her mother's death in 1994, the poet used the visit as the setting for 'Fireman's Lift', describing it as a 'cheering-up poem, when my mother was dying because I absolutely knew that she would want me to write a poem about her dying …'

The poem begins with Ní Chuilleanáin's vivid memory of the moment when she and her mother were looking up at Correggio's celebrated ceiling mural. In the opening stanza, she invites readers into the Italian setting: 'I was standing beside you looking up/Through the big tree of the cupola.' There is **an immediate dreamlike sense of intimacy and closeness between mother and daughter**, as though they were both aware that something significant was happening. From the outset, the focus is on the majestic painting's mystery and symbolism, reaching heavenwards to imagined 'Celestial choirs'.

Stanza two emphasises the struggle of the angels to lift Mary into the heavens, and the awkwardness and wonder of being pushed in such a similar manner to birth. We are encouraged to become part of the dynamic scene within the reality of this great spectacle. The dynamic verbs 'spiralling' and 'heaving' suggest **the physical effort involved in raising the Virgin from her earthly life**. Line breaks and frequent commas are used to create a sluggish pace. Ní Chuilleanáin is drawn to the collective energy which becomes a fireman's lift of 'Teams of angelic arms', and the effort to raise Mary 'Past mist and shining' is relentless.

Ní Chuilleanáin then considers the overwhelming effect of Correggio's 'work entire', designed to give the illusion of real and simulated architecture within the painted fresco. This awe-inspiring achievement is reflected in the pulsating run-through rhythms and hushed tones of stanzas three and four. **Dramatic images of the angelic figures and saints assisting Mary's Assumption give expression to the artist's powerful vision**: 'Melted and faded bodies' are intermingled with 'elbows and staring eyes'. Within the dome/petticoat image, Ní Chuilleanáin describes Correggio's Virgin passing into another glorious life. All the time, this vortex of bodies and faces around her are fully engaged in assisting Mary to reach the waiting Christ. **Stanza five** defines an important turning point for the poet, who can now make sense of her mother's death through a fresh understanding of Correggio's perspective: 'This is what love sees, that angle.' **The assured tone marks a coming to terms with deep personal loss**. Ní Chuilleanáin's renewed appreciation of the painting enables her to accept the burden of letting the dead go. Her resignation is evident in the poignant image of a 'branch loaded with fruit', an obvious symbol of the natural cycle.

Stanzas six and seven return to **Correggio's mesmerising skill in his interaction of art and architecture** within the cathedral dome. This intricate collusion is seen in sharper focus, providing a context for Ní Chuilleanáin to reassert her changing relationship with her mother. The restless limbs of the painted angels are in perfect harmony with the great Duomo ceiling: 'The back making itself a roof/The legs a bridge.' This intriguingly harmonious composition merging paint and plaster adds to the urgency of ensuring that the dying soul achieves its ultimate ascension to heaven.

The final stanzas observe the figures attending on Mary, 'heads bowed over to reflect on her/Fair face'. Their tenderness is evident in both sound and tone. The poet has said that, on one level, 'Fireman's Lift' is about the nurses who looked after her mother when she was dying. Typically, the poet broadens our understanding of suffering, showing people caring and concerned. The concluding lines, however, acknowledge **the strength of spirit which Ní Chuilleanáin singles out as the hallmark of her mother's life and death**. This is reflected in the purposeful expression on the Virgin's face: 'As the muscles clung and shifted/For a final purchase.' Tactile 'u' sounds ('usc', 'ung', 'urch', etc.) and the drawn-out rhythms emphasise that body goes with soul in the movement across this threshold: 'to the edge of the cloud.'

Death and rebirth are recurring themes in Ní Chuilleanáin's work. But in honouring her mother's life and associating her passing with the Assumption of the Virgin, the poet has brought together Italian art, religion and a deep sense of sorrow. Essentially, however, **'Fireman's Lift' is a moving expression of the poet's enduring love** for her mother. It is not unusual for readers of Ní Chuilleanáin's poetry to encounter beautiful images which leave them searching. Nevertheless, this poem has a universal significance. It is infused with an astounding sense of love, loss and triumph as the ascending figure disappears into the clouds. Poised on the edge of this unknowable boundary, the rest is mystery.

🖋 Writing About the Poem

'For Eiléan Ní Chuilleanáin, boundaries and transitions are central concerns.' Discuss this view with particular reference to 'Fireman's Lift'.

Sample Paragraph

I found 'Fireman's Lift' both puzzling and interesting. Ní Chuilleanáin managed to link her mother's death with the painting *Assumption of the Virgin*. In describing her memory of a visit to Parma Cathedral, the poet seemed to enter the reality of the mural and see her own relationship with her mother in a new way – almost like one of the angels who tries to raise Mary to heaven, 'Teams of angelic arms were heaving'. The transition is shown in terms of brute strength – the Virgin is 'Hauled up in stages'. But the poet also reflects the transition between this life and the next in the optical illusions painted on the dome. Everything appears to be integrated – for example, the hands of angels act as a 'crane and a cradle' supporting Mary. She leans on the 'pillars of their arms'. The poet sees no difference between her own prayers for her mother's soul and the work of the saints who raise the Virgin. To me, Ní Chuilleanáin is absorbed in the art work. I found this typical of her poetry in that she wanders beyond borders.

EXAMINER'S COMMENT

An incisive response which addresses this challenging question directly. There is good personal interaction: 'To me, Ní Chuilleanáin is absorbed in the art work', and effective use of supportive references. Clearly made points explore the poet's emphasis on the blurred lines within the Correggio painting, and between it and Ní Chuilleanáin's own involvement. Such in-depth analysis merits the top grade.

✒ Class/Homework Exercises

1. 'Eiléan Ní Chuilleanáin's poems explore the persistence of memory in a highly distinctive style.' Discuss this statement with particular reference to 'Fireman's Lift'.
2. '"Fireman's Lift" is typical of Ní Chuilleanáin's poems in that it is layered with hidden meaning.' To what extent do you agree with this view? Support your answer with reference to the text.

⊙ Points to Consider

- **Characteristic narrative opening recalling a significant memory.**

- **Effective use of run-on lines, symbolism, dramatic images of art and architecture.**

- **Vivid details and powerful verbs suggest physical effort.**

- **Key themes – death, rebirth, family relationships and enduring love.**

6   🔊 All for You

EILÉAN NÍ CHUILLEANÁIN

Once beyond the gate of the strange stableyard, we dismount.
The donkey walks on, straight in at a wide door
And sticks his head in a manger.

The great staircase of the hall slouches back,
Sprawling between warm wings. It is for you.   5
As the steps wind and warp
Among the vaults, their thick ribs part; the doors
Of guardroom, chapel, storeroom
Swing wide and the breath of ovens
Flows out, the rage of brushwood,   10
The roots torn and butchered.

It is for you, the dry fragrance of tea-chests
The tins shining in ranks, the ten-pound jars
Rich with shrivelled fruit. Where better to lie down
And sleep, along the labelled shelves,   15
With the key still in your pocket?

wind: curve, meander.
warp: bend, buckle.
vaults: large rooms often used for storage; chambers beneath a church.
ribs: curved structures that support a vault.
brushwood: undergrowth, small twigs and branches.

👤 Personal Response

1. Would you agree that there is a dramatic trance-like atmosphere in this poem? Support your answer with reference to the text.
2. Choose one particularly vivid image from the poem and briefly explain its effectiveness.
3. Write your own individual response to the poem, referring closely to the text in your answer.

👁 Critical Literacy

'All for You' comes from Eiléan Ní Chuilleanáin's *The Brazen Serpent* (1994). The book's title refers to the biblical story of Moses and the Israelites in the desert. God had become angry with his people, as they had spoken against their leader, Moses, and He let fierce snakes crawl among them and bite them. Moses prayed for the people and God instructed Moses to make a bronze serpent and place it upon a pole in public view. Anyone who was bitten could then look on the brazen snake and they would be cured. This

'steps wind and warp/ Among the vaults'

foreshadows the raising onto the cross of Jesus Christ, who died to save sinners. Therefore, God made this sacrifice 'All for You'. Ní Chuilleanáin's collection of poems brings the possibility of hope, of getting through bad times, of being redeemed.

Ní Chuilleanáin **collapses time and distinctions betweeen places** in 'All for You'. Line by line, the reader is drawn into deeper water until the bottom can no longer be touched, a recurring feature of this poet's complex work. The first three lines describe a scene that resonates with detail from the Bible story of the birth of Jesus: 'the strange stableyard', 'The donkey', the 'manger'. Why is the stableyard 'strange'? In the biblical account, Joseph and Mary had to leave their home town and travel to Bethlehem to be listed for a tax census. As is often the case with Ní Chuilleanáin's dramatic presentations, the reader must piece together a bare minimum of narrative sense. However, there is a sense of inevitability about the journey being described.

In lines 4–11, a noticeably different time and space is realised. What follows is **a series of evocative images and metaphors relating to a transitional experience**. Personification brings a staircase vividly to life as it 'slouches back', lolling and slumping – 'Sprawling' almost like a reclining animal as it sits between the 'warm wings' of the hall. Is it ominous or welcoming? It is waiting, as the bronze serpent awaited the Israelites, like a gift 'for you'. Ní Chuilleanáin does not determine the identity of 'you', instead leaving it open to speculation so that 'you' could have a universal application and refer to anyone. Is this gift for all? The poet's descriptive talent engages the reader as the grand staircase is depicted with great clarity, yet its full significance is never defined. Alliteration ('wind and warp') conveys the stairs' sinuous movement, curling like an uncoiling animal through the 'thick ribs' of the intimidating vaults.

The architectural metaphor is a strong element in Ní Chuilleanáin's poetry, which is full of mysterious crannies and alcoves. Could this imposing building be a convent waiting to welcome a young woman as its doors open, revealing the imposing interior of 'guardroom, chapel' and 'storeroom'? The poet's three aunts were nuns and she has commented, 'One is constantly made aware of the fact that the past does not go away, that it is walking around the place causing trouble at every moment.' Is this reference therefore autobiographical or does it encompass a wider significance? Could the staircase lead to salvation and heaven?

A rush of heat from the nearby ovens is suddenly palpable – again conveyed through the poet's effective working of personification: 'the breath of ovens/Flows out.' Ní Chuilleanáin uses a violent image to describe the fierce temperature: 'the rage of brushwood.' This is continued in the savagery with which the kindling has been collected: 'roots torn out and butchered.' Is there an echo of the biblical tale of the burning bush from the **Book of Exodus**, where God directed Moses to the Promised Land? This story teaches that we should be able to obey God whenever he calls us. Is the poet also referencing the story of Christ, 'butchered' on the cross for the sins of the world? The forceful rhythm of these dramatic lines creates an intensity, a climax of dread, almost like an ecstatic spiritual experience.

There is a marked **change of tone** in the last five lines. All the tension eases within the ordered space of the building's provisions store. Readers are now immersed in the moment, smelling the 'dry fragrance of tea-chests', observing 'tins shining in ranks, the ten-pound jars'. Repetition of the rich 'r' sound suggests the store's abundance of goods. Yet there is also an unease secreted in this image of confined order. The fruit is 'shrivelled', the fragrance is 'dry'. Is there a life withering, unable to reproduce? Is this another central dimension of religious life? The poem concludes with a rhetorical question intimating that there is nowhere better to take rest, just as Joseph and Mary did long ago in that 'strange stable yard', than here 'along the labelled shelves'. The body's surrender and submission to God's will enables it to act.

Another biblical reference is suggested in the final detail of the 'key still in your pocket'. In Isaiah 33:6, faith is the key to salvation: 'He will be the sure foundation of your times, a rich store of salvation and wisdom and knowledge; the fear of the Lord is the key to this treasure.' Ní Chuilleanáin's poem focuses on the experience of Christian faith as imagined through the imposing challenge and triumph of religious vocations. The 'key' image is typically contradictory – symbolising both confinement and freedom. Is the poet presenting the central paradox of Christian belief? Can the soul's redemption only be achieved through submission to God's will? Characteristically, Ní Chuilleanáin's multi-layered narrative has been subtly woven, offering a glimpse, perhaps, of salvation and hope.

✒ Writing About the Poem

'Eiléan Ní Chuilleanáin's poetry is an unshaped fire demanding to be organised into a sequence of words and images.' Discuss this statement in relation to 'All for You'.

Sample Paragraph

'All for You' is an unsettling poem which springs from the idea of a gift. Like an 'unshaped fire', the poem's religious theme 'Flows out' like the heat from the ovens. I thought the image of the staircase which 'slouches back' was very effective. The image symbolised the ladder of life which Christians must climb to reach salvation. I got the sense of being in a strange building with old-fashioned rooms. The storeroom imagery reflected the enclosed religious world, with 'the dry fragrance' of 'shrivelled fruit'. The sense of order was also present: 'The tins shining in ranks.' The repetition of 'It is for you' suggests a generous God wishing to give a precious gift and what gift could be more important than hope? All the poet's ideas are expressed in patterns of visionary language which can be seen as a powerful 'unshaped fire'.

EXAMINER'S COMMENT

A clear personal response to a challenging question. Key discussion points are very well developed and effectively illustrated. This shows a good understanding of this complex poem – and particularly the poet's use of dense symbols and overlapping images. Expression throughout is confident, fluent and well controlled. An excellent response that deserves the highest grade.

Class/Homework Exercises

1. 'Ní Chuilleanáin's language is subtle and acute enough to undertake its most difficult subject: how we perceive and understand the world.' Discuss this statement in relation to the prescribed work of the poet on your course.

2. '"All for You" illustrates Ní Chuilleanáin's deep interest in the mysteries of Christianity.' To what extent do you agree with this view? Support your answer with reference to the poem.

Points to Consider

- The poem explores various aspects of choosing the Christian life.

- Personification and architectural imagery create a sense of mystery.

- Effective use of biblical and religious references.

- Descriptive details and provocative images add drama.

EILÉAN NÍ CHUILLEANÁIN

7 🔊 **Following**

Following: coming after in time or sequence; people about to be mentioned or listed; those who admire or support somebody.

So she follows the trail of her father's coat through the fair
Shouldering past beasts packed solid as books,
And the dealing men nearly as slow to give way –
A block of a belly, a back like a mountain,
A shifting elbow like a plumber's bend –   5
When she catches a glimpse of a shirt-cuff, a handkerchief,
Then the hard brim of his hat, skimming along,

beasts: animals at an Irish mart.
dealing men: dealers, men who bargain as they buy and sell animals at an Irish fair.
plumber's bend: length of 18 inches from the bend of the elbow to the tip of the middle finger.
brim: edge.

Until she is tracing light footsteps
Across the shivering bog by starlight,
The dead corpse risen from the wakehouse   10
Gliding before her in a white habit.
The ground is forested with gesturing trunks,
Hands of women dragging needles,
Half-choked heads in the water of cuttings,
Mouths that roar like the noise of the fair day.   15

wakehouse: house, particularly in Ireland, where a dead person is laid out; people come to console the grieving relatives and to pay their respects to the deceased.

cuttings: small pieces of plants.

She comes to where he is seated
With whiskey poured out in two glasses
In a library where the light is clean,
His clothes all finely laundered,
Ironed facings and linings.   20
The smooth foxed leaf has been hidden
In a forest of fine shufflings,
The square of white linen
That held three drops
Of her heart's blood is shelved   25
Between the gatherings
That go to make a book –
The crushed flowers among the pages crack
The spine open, push the bindings apart.

facings: strengthening linings; collar, cuffs and trimmings on a uniform coat.
linings: layers of material used to cover and protect.
foxed: soiled; marked with fox-like reddish spots and stains, often found on old books and documents.
leaf: single sheet of paper.
shufflings: walking slowly and awkwardly.

spine: vertical back of book to which pages are attached.
bindings: material which holds pages together.

👤 Personal Response

1. Based on your reading of the poem, show how Ní Chuilleanáin conjures up the atmosphere of an Irish fair day. Refer closely to the text in your response.
2. In your opinion, how many settings are there in this poem? Which one did you prefer? Give reasons for your choice, quoting to support your answer.
3. Choose one vivid image from the third stanza of the poem and briefly explain its effectiveness.

'And the dealing men nearly as slow to give way'

👁 Critical Literacy

Eiléan Ní Chuilleanáin often assumes a storytelling role in her poems as she relates memories from the past. She readjusts the perspective of readers by taking us into the lives of ordinary people who literally and physically made history. In her collection *The Brazen Serpent*, Ní Chuilleanáin highlights family and women as makers of history. She hints at the untold through her use of characters, silences and secrets. These confidential witnesses, like the poet herself, reconstruct subtle revelations of family unease and discontentment. Female imagery expresses what is silenced. The poet frequently explores religious themes as well as death and rebirth. Quietly and precisely, she offers us the comfort that the past does not go away.

In the opening section, the poet begins her story in her usual oblique, non-confessional style, yet deeply engages the reader despite her seeming detachment. A vividly realised journey by a girl through the hurly-burly of an Irish fair day catapults the reader into the story. She is trying to follow her father through the dense crowds: 'the trail of her father's coat through the fair.' Long run-on lines and broad vowels convey the difficulty of negotiating the route as she attempts to push past 'beasts packed as solid as books'. This unusual simile illustrates the tightly packed rows of animals. Nor could she easily make her way through the dealers, men caught up in the very serious business of buying and selling, making a deal. Their thick-set bodies, bulky like their animals, are described through a tumbling list of similes and metaphors to highlight their immobile weight: 'A block of a belly, a back like a mountain.' A 'shifting elbow' is like the measure used in plumbing. All these images reinforce the **tough, masculine world of the fair**. Ní Chuilleanáin has pushed the reader, through her unwavering gaze, into the poem's self-enclosed world.

Suddenly, in line 6, the girl catches a glimpse of her father. This is shown by a list of his clothing: 'a shirt-cuff, a handkerchief,/Then the hard brim of his hat.' His progress is swift and effortless. He moves as swiftly as the punctuation (a series of fast-moving commas) accelerates the motion of the line. Sharp contrast in the verbs used to describe the progress of the girl and her father **highlight their different rates of success in moving through the fair**. The girl is struggling, 'Shouldering past', while the father moves with ease, 'skimming along'. Is Ní Chuilleanáin suggesting that a woman finds it difficult to negotiate a man's world? The poet has hypnotically caught the excitement as well as the danger of the fair day.

Distance and time blur in the second section. Ní Chuilleanáin shifts the scene and time frame from the noise and physical bulk of the fair to the '**shivering bog**'. Personification and slender vowels effectively convey the cold 'starlight' scene she is revisiting, 'tracing light footsteps', mapping faint prints. **A surreal, nightmarish world is presented**, as 'The dead corpse risen from the wakehouse' appears 'before her in a white habit'. Whose corpse is this? The effortless sense of 'Gliding' suggests the agile movement of the father. Momentarily, the packed animals of the fair have given way to the ground 'forested with gesturing trunks'. Now the heavy trees are highlighting her way, she will ultimately follow her father into death. Thin waving rushes are evocatively described as 'Hands of women dragging needles'. Their slow cumbersome movement is presented in visionary terms. Is this a reference to the story from the Bible when the Pharaoh of Egypt decreed that because of the increasing numbers of Israelites, all first-born boys were to be drowned in the River Nile? Are these the half-choked heads? Is this the wail of Israelite women and children as they cry and 'roar' like the beasts in the fair, aware of their fate? Or is it a reference to the subordination of women as they work?

In the poem's concluding section, the girl meets her father in a much more hospitable setting with 'whiskey poured in two glasses', 'His clothes all finely

293 |

laundered'. Within these domestic interiors of the poet's imagination lies the remote **possibility of utopia**. The 'square of white linen', redolent of the survivor's suffering, shrunk and stained by the body's signifiers of hurt, becomes a relic of love and loss. Ní Chuilleanáin has commented, 'A relic is something you enclose, and then you enclose the reliquary in something else. In the *The Book of Kells* exhibition, the book satchel is in leather, which is meant to protect, and there is a shrine which in turn is meant to protect the book.' A relic is associated with people seeking comfort in difficult times. The past is beautifully evoked in the phrase 'The smooth foxed leaf has been hidden', with its haunting image of time-stained pages. Inside the book are 'crushed flowers', reminders that love was violated, yet something of it remains.

These memories have tremendous power; they 'crack' and push apart as if being reborn. Living and dead touch each other through such memories. The dust and noise of the cattle market, the cold starry bog have all evaporated to be replaced by this interior where the 'light is clean', making it easy to see. Comfort and hope are being offered as the poem suggests that the past is not dead.

⬛ Writing About the Poem

'Ní Chuilleanáin's poems explore how the most basic legends – family stories – fragment and alter in each individual's memory.' Discuss this statement with particular reference to the poem 'Following'.

Sample Paragraph

Ní Chuilleanáin's poem, 'Following', dredges up Irish family stories (the fair day, a wake, women sewing) and rearranges them, as cards are moved in 'shufflings'. This reconstructs and transforms the past so that we can see and understand from a new perspective. We are brought as followers, just like the girl in the fair, on a journey to discover that the past is not dead, but resonates through the present by means of relics, 'The square of white linen'. The title suggests that we are all following one another through life, like the girl and the father in the fair. In the masculine world of the fair, 'beasts packed solid as books' the girl found it hard to negotiate her way. The poet has identified the difficult role women have in life, 'dragging needles', employed in domestic drudgery. These women are unable to express their concerns, 'Half-choked'. The legends become 'crushed flowers' yet the poet suggests

EXAMINER'S COMMENT

This is a very impressive response which deserves the highest grade. The focus throughout is firmly placed on addressing the various parts of the question. Quotations are integrated effectively and the answer ranges widely from the title to the individual stories and the imagery used in conveying the narratives. Language is carefully controlled to express points clearly, e.g. 'This reconstructs and transforms the past so that we can see and understand from a new perspective'.

that they can 'crack' open the book in which they are enclosed. I felt that she was communicating the message of hope that the past does not stay in the past. Our memories do not remain 'shelved' but live again in the present.

📝 Class/Homework Exercises

1. 'The mysterious writing style of Ní Chuilleanáin allows the reader to explore the poems on many levels, each tracking a different aspect of the cycle of life.' Discuss this statement in relation to the prescribed poems of this poet on your course.

2. 'Ní Chuilleanáin's unsettling poetic voice can often seem deceptively simple.' Discuss this statement with particular reference to the poem 'Following'. Support your answer with reference to the text.

⊙ Points to Consider

- The poet assumes a familiar story-telling role in this mystery tale.

- Themes include Irish identity and the power of memory.

- Effective use of commas, dashes and run-on lines.

- Prominent sound effects (alliteration and assonance) add emphasis.

🔊 Kilcash

Title: Eiléan Ní Chuilleanáin's translation of the early 19th-century ballad *Caoine Cill Chais* (The Lament for Kilcash), an anonymous lament that the castle of Cill Chais stood empty, its woods cut down and all its old grandeur disappeared. Kilcash was one of the great houses of a branch of the Butler family near Clonmel, Co. Tipperary, until well into the 18th century. Ní Chuilleanáin's poem encompasses several generations of the Butler family, but the presiding spirit is that of Margaret Butler, Viscountess Iveagh (who died in 1744).

From the Irish, c. 1800

What will we do now for timber
With the last of the woods laid low —
No word of Kilcash nor its household,
Their bell is silenced now,
Where the lady lived with such honour,   5
No woman so heaped with praise,
Earls came across oceans to see her
And heard the sweet words of Mass.

It's the cause of my long affliction
To see your neat gates knocked down,   10
The long walks affording no shade now
And the avenue overgrown,
The fine house that kept out the weather,
Its people depressed and tamed;
And their names with the faithful departed,   15
The Bishop and Lady Iveagh!

The geese and the ducks' commotion,
The eagle's shout, are no more,
The roar of the bees gone silent,
Their wax and their honey store   20
Deserted. Now at evening
The musical birds are stilled
And the cuckoo is dumb in the treetops
That sang lullaby to the world.

Even the deer and the hunters   25
That follow the mountain way
Look down upon us with pity,
The house that was famed in its day;
The smooth wide lawn is all broken,
No shelter from wind and rain;   30
The paddock has turned to a dairy
Where the fine creatures grazed.

the last of the woods: a reference to the mass clearance of native Irish forests by plantation settlers to create agricultural land and to fuel the colonial economy. The woodlands belonging to the Butlers of Kilcash were sold in 1797 and 1801.

the lady: Margaret Butler, Viscountess Iveagh, a staunch Catholic (d. 1744).

The Bishop: Catholic clergy – including Lady Iveagh's brother-in-law – were often given shelter in Kilcash.

commotion: noise, clamour.

lullaby: soothing song.

paddock: enclosure.

Mist hangs low on the branches
No sunlight can sweep aside,
Darkness falls among daylight   35
And the streams are all run dry;
No hazel, no holly or berry,
Bare naked rocks and cold;
The forest park is leafless
And all the game gone wild.   40

And now the worst of our troubles:
She has followed the prince of the Gaels —
He has borne off the gentle maiden,
Summoned to France and to Spain.
Her company laments her   45
That she fed with silver and gold:
One who never preyed on the people
But was the poor souls' friend.

My prayer to Mary and Jesus
She may come safe home to us here   50
To dancing and rejoicing
To fiddling and bonfire
That our ancestors' house will rise up,
Kilcash built up anew
And from now to the end of the story   55
May it never again be laid low.

prince of the Gaels: probably a reference to the 18th Earl of Ormonde.

the gentle maiden: Countess of Ormonde, wife of the 18th Earl.

preyed: harmed, took advantage of.

'affording no shade now'

297 |

Personal Response

1. From your reading of the poem, what is your impression of Lady Iveagh? Refer to the text in your answer.
2. Choose one interesting image from 'Kilcash' that you consider particularly effective. Give reasons to explain why this image appealed to you.
3. Write your own individual response to the poem, referring closely to the text in your answer.

Critical Literacy

'Kilcash' comes from Eiléan Ní Chuilleanáin's *The Girl Who Married the Reindeer* (2001). Many of the poems in this collection deal with outsiders and the dispossessed. Kilcash was the great house of one of the branches of the Butler family near Clonmel, Co. Tipperary, until the 18th century. The Butlers were Catholic landed gentry who had come to Ireland as part of an Anglo-Norman invasion during the 12th century and had taken over vast amounts of land. Over time, the family became absorbed into Irish ways. Ní Chuilleanáin's version of the traditional Irish elegy, *Caoine Cill Chais*, mourns the death of Margaret Butler, Viscountess Iveagh.

Stanza one opens with a plaintive voice lamenting 'What will we do now for timber'. The ballad was originally composed in the early 1800s following the demise of the Butlers of Kilcash and the eventual clearing of the family's extensive woodlands, which had supplied timber for local people. **The early tone typifies the entire poem's sense of hopelessness now that the woods are 'laid low'.** The systematic felling of trees is symbolic of the decline of this aristocratic Catholic family. Following colonisation, the Irish were consigned to nature as a symbol of their barbarity. In some British circles, they were referred to as the 'natural wild Irish' because the country's remote boglands and forests offered shelter to Irish rebels. The poem emphasises the uneasy silence around Kilcash and the speaker pays extravagant tribute to 'the lady' of the house, who is immediately associated with Ireland's Catholic resistance: 'Earls came across oceans to see her.'

As always, Ní Chuilleanáin's approach is layered, recognising the genuine feelings of loss while suggesting a misplaced dependence on all those who exploited the native population. For the most part, however, the poem's anonymous narrator appears to express the desolation ('long affliction') felt by the impoverished and leaderless Irish of the time. There is no shortage of evidence to illustrate what has happened to the 'fine house'. Throughout stanzas two and three, broad assonant sounds add to the maudlin sentiments. The **'neat gates knocked down' and the 'avenue overgrown' reflect the dramatic turnaround in fortunes**. But is Ní Chuilleanáin's translation of the old song also unearthing an underlying sense of delight in the sudden fall of the mighty? There is 'no shade now' for the once-powerful gentry or for the impoverished community. Many of the references to the

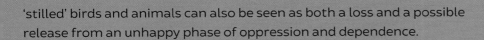

'stilled' birds and animals can also be seen as both a loss and a possible release from an unhappy phase of oppression and dependence.

Images of hardship taken from nature dominate stanzas four and five. The abandoned peasants are depicted as pitiable. The atmosphere becomes increasingly disturbing as the natural world order is transformed: 'Darkness falls among daylight/And the streams are all run dry.' **As in so many other Irish legends, the landscape reflects the terms of the Butlers' exile: 'The forest park is leafless.'** Negative language patterns – 'No sunlight', 'No hazel, no holly' – highlight the sense of mordant despondency resulting from abandonment. Relentlessly, the regular lines and ponderous rhythm work together to create a monotonous trance-like effect. The extravagant praise for 'the gentle maiden' (probably a reference to the wife of the 18th Earl) dominates stanza six. As a representative of the Butler dynasty, her absence is seen as 'the worst of our troubles' and she is glorified as someone 'who never preyed on the people' despite her privileged lifestyle.

The prayer-like tone of the final stanza is in keeping with the deep yearning for a return to the old ways in Kilcash. The Catholic allusion also reinforces the central importance of religion in expressing political and cultural identity. In wishing to restore the former Gaelic order, the speaker imagines lively scenes of communal celebration: 'fiddling and bonfire.' **The aspiration that the castle will be 'built up anew' offers a clear symbol of recovery.** This rallying call is in keeping with traditional laments and is characteristic of the poet's sympathies for the oppressed. Ní Chuilleanáin has retained the rhetorical style of Gaelic poetry throughout, revealing the experience of isolated communities through numerous images of restless desolation and uncomfortable silences.

'Kilcash' marks a significant transition in Irish history. As the old native aristocracy suffered military and political defeat and, in many cases, exile, the world order that had supported the bardic poets disappeared. In these circumstances, it is hardly surprising that much Irish poetry of this period laments these changes and the poet's plight. However, **Ní Chuilleanáin's translation of the old ballad differs from other versions in being more ambivalent towards Viscountess Iveagh and what she represented**. Is the poem a poignant expression of loss and a genuine tribute to those landlords who were seen as humane? Does the poet satirise the subservient native Irish who had been conditioned to accept some convenient generosity from the Catholic gentry? To what extent did the original lament present a romantic distortion of Ireland's history? Readers are left to decide for themselves.

✒ Writing About the Poem

'Eiléan Ní Chuilleanáin's poems retain the power to connect past and present in ways that never cease to fascinate.' Discuss this statement, with particular reference to 'Kilcash'.

Sample Paragraph

On a first reading, I thought that 'Kilcash' was a simple version of the old ballad, *Caoine Cill Chais*. After studying the poem, however, I feel that Ní Chuilleanáin has raised many interesting questions about Irish history. The opening lament of the peasants seems self-pitying – 'What will we do now for timber'. The compliments paid to Lady Iveagh focus on her Catholic faith and support for Gaelic culture – 'Earls came across oceans to see her'. As a young person looking back on this period of upheaval, I could appreciate the way impoverished Irish people had become dependent on the Catholic gentry as symbols of freedom. The poem repeatedly places 'the lady' as the embodiment of hope – 'the poor souls' friend'. The main insight I gained from the poem was that colonisation – whether by Catholic or Protestant landlords – had broken the Irish spirit. Ní Chuilleanáin manages to link past and present, broadening our view of the complex relationships between powerful interests and a conquered population.

EXAMINER'S COMMENT

An assured personal response, focused throughout and well illustrated with suitable quotations. The paragraph carefully highlights Ní Chuilleanáin's exploration of the plight of the native Irish community in various ways: 'impoverished Irish people had become dependent on the Catholic gentry'. Points are clearly expressed throughout in this excellent, top-grade answer.

✒ Class/Homework Exercises

1. 'Ní Chuilleanáin's distinctive poetic world provides an accessible platform for marginalised voices.' Discuss this view, with particular reference to 'Kilcash'.
2. 'While Eiléan Ní Chuilleanáin's poems often deal with complex themes, they have an enigmatic quality that engages readers.' To what extent is this true of 'Kilcash'? Support your answer with close reference to the poem.

⊙ Points to Consider

- **Traditional lament for Catholic aristocracy raises questions about Ireland's past.**

- **Desolate landscape and negative language reflect the mood of hopelessness.**

- **Regular rhythm; the prayer-like tone and stark images emphasise the atmosphere.**

- **Ambivalent ending intrigues readers about the poet's own viewpoint.**

9 🔊 Translation

for the reburial of the Magdalenes

The soil frayed and sifted evens the score —
There are women here from every county,
Just as there were in the laundry.

White light blinded and bleached out
The high relief of a glance, where steam danced   5
Around stone drains and giggled and slipped across water.

Assist them now, ridges under the veil, shifting,
Searching for their parents, their names,
The edges of words grinding against nature,

As if, when water sank between the rotten teeth   10
Of soap, and every grasp seemed melted, one voice
Had begun, rising above the shuffle and hum

Until every pocket in her skull blared with the note —
Allow us now to hear it, sharp as an infant's cry
While the grass takes root, while the steam rises: 15

> Washed clean of idiom · the baked crust
> Of words that made my temporary name ·
> A parasite that grew in me · that spell
> Lifted · I lie in earth sifted to dust ·
> Let the bunched keys I bore slacken and fall ·   20
> I rise and forget · a cloud over my time.

Subtitle: The Magdalenes refers to Irish women, particularly unmarried mothers, who were separated from their children and forced to work in convent laundries. Inmates were required to undertake hard physical labour, including washing and needlework. They also endured a daily regime that included long periods of prayer and enforced silence. In Ireland, such institutions were known as Magdalene laundries. It has been estimated that up to 30,000 women passed through such laundries in Ireland, the last one of which (in Waterford) closed on 25 September 1996.
frayed: ragged.
sifted: sorted, examined.
the laundry: clothes-washing area.

blared: rang out, resounded.

idiom: language, misinterpretation.

parasite: bloodsucker.

👤 Personal Response

1. Comment on the effectiveness of the poem's title, 'Translation', in relation to the themes that Ní Chuilleanáin addresses in the poem.
2. Choose one image from the poem that you found particularly interesting. Briefly explain your choice.
3. How does the poem make you feel? Give reasons for your response, supporting the points you make with reference to the text.

'Washed clean of idiom'

◉ Critical Literacy

During the early 1990s, the remains of more than 150 women were discovered at several Dublin religious institutions as the properties were being excavated. The bones, from women buried over a very long period, were cremated and reburied in Glasnevin Cemetery. Eiléan Ní Chuilleanáin's poem was read at the reburial ceremony to commemorate Magdalene laundry women from all over Ireland. 'Translation' links the writer's work with the belated acknowledgement, in the late 20th century, of the stolen lives and hidden deaths of generations of Irishwomen incarcerated in Magdalene convents.

The poem begins with a macabre description of the Glasnevin grave where the reburial is taking place: 'The soil frayed and sifted evens the score.' Ní Chuilleanáin expresses the feelings of the mourners ('here from every county') who are **united by a shared sense of injustice**. This dramatic ceremony represents a formal acknowledgement of a dark period in Ireland's social history. Line 4 takes readers back in time behind convent walls and imagines the grim laundry rooms in which the Magdelene women worked: 'White light blinded and bleached out/The high relief of a glance.'

The poet's delicate and precise language contrasts the grinding oppression of routine manual labour with the young women's natural playfulness. **Their stolen youth and lost gaiety are poignantly conveyed through familiar images of the laundry**, 'where steam danced/Around stone drains and giggled and slipped across water' (line 6). Vigorous verbs and a jaunty rhythm add emphasis to the sad irony of their broken lives. The relentless scrubbing was intended to wash away the women's sins. However, no matter how much the women washed, they were considered dirty and sinful throughout their lives.

All through the poem, Ní Chuilleanáin focuses on the importance of words and naming as though she herself is aiming to make sense of the shocking Magdalene story. But how is she to respond to the women who have come to the graveyard, 'Searching for their parents, their names'? Typically, the language is dense and multi-layered. In death, these former laundry workers are mere 'ridges under the veil' of the anonymous earth. The metaphor in line 7 also evokes images of the stern Magdalene nuns. **Ní Chuilleanáin sees all these women as victims of less enlightened times**, ironically recalled in the prayer-like note of invocation: 'Assist them now.'

The poem's title becomes clear as we recognise **Ní Chuilleanáin's intention to communicate ('translate') decades of silence into meaningful expression on behalf of the Magdalene laundry inmates**. Their relentless efforts to eventually become a 'voice' is compared to the almost impossible challenge of 'rising above the shuffle and hum' within the noisy laundry itself. In line 9, Ní Chuilleanáin visualises the women setting 'The edges of words grinding against nature' until their misrepresentation is overcome as it is turned to dust along with their bodies.

From line 13, much of the **focus is placed on exploring the experience of one of the nuns who managed the laundries**. As the true history emerges, she is also being cleansed of 'the baked crust/Of words that made my temporary name'. The 'temporary name' is her name in religion; that is, the saint's name she chose on entering strict convent life, which, as Ní Chuilleanáin notes, involved relinquishing her previous identity as an individual. She too has been exploited and the poet's generous tone reflects an understanding of this woman, who is caught between conflicting influences of duty, care, indoctrination and doubt, 'Until every pocket in her skull blared'. The evocative reference to the 'infant's cry' echoes the enduring sense of loss felt by young mothers who were forced to give up their babies shortly after birth.

In the poem's final lines, we hear the voice of a convent reverend mother, whose role is defined by 'the bunched keys I bore'. The reburial ceremony has also cleansed her from 'that spell' which maintained the cruel system she once served. Almost overwhelmed, she now recognises the 'parasite' power 'that grew in me' and only now can the keys she carries, an obvious symbol of her role as gaoler, 'slacken and fall'. **Bleak, disturbing images and broken**

rhythms have an unnerving, timeless effect. This woman's punitive authority over others has haunted her beyond the grave.

In the end, Ní Chuilleanáin's measured and balanced approach shows genuine compassion for all institutionalised victims, drawing together the countless young women and those in charge in their common confinement. In addition to their time spent in convents, they are now reunited, sifting the earth that they have all become. **The tragic legacy of these institutions involves women at many levels.** Nevertheless, the poem itself is a faithful translation, as these victims have been raised from their graves by the poet's response to their collective dead voice. Ní Chuilleanáin relates their compelling story to 'Allow us now to hear it'. She also tenderly acknowledges the complete silencing of the Irish Magdalenes as they did their enforced and, in some cases, lifelong penance.

Although Eiléan Ní Chuilleanáin's mournful 'translation' reveals glimpses of their true history, **none of these Magdalene women can ever be given back the lives they had before they entered the laundries**. The poem stops short of pretending to even the score in terms of power between those in authority and the totally subservient and permanently disgraced women under their control. At best, their small voices rise up together like 'steam' and form a 'cloud over my time' (**line 21**). This metaphor of the cloud can be construed as a shadow of shame over Irish society, but it can also be seen as a warning that the cycle of abuse is likely to be repeated.

⌨ Writing About the Poem

'Ní Chuilleanáin's poems address important aspects of women's experiences in an insightful fashion.' Discuss this view, with particular reference to 'Translation'.

Sample Paragraph

I would agree that 'Translation' deals with an issue which is important to Irish women. The scandal of the unfortunate girls in Magdalene convents deserves to be publicised. Ní Chuilleanáin's poem gave me a deeper understanding of their story. The reburial service was attended by relatives 'from every county', suggesting the scale of the mistreatment. The details of the cold laundries – where 'White light blinded' seemed a subtle way of symbolising the misguided actions of those religious orders who punished young girls. I admired the poet's fair treatment of those nuns who are also presented as being imprisoned. The last stanza was revealing as it envisaged one cruel nun who was still confused by her part in the cruelty. The poet makes it clear that she was a product of an oppressive Catholic Ireland. 'Translation' succeeds in explaining the true story of the Magdalene women. It is powerful because Ní Chuilleanáin avoids being over-emotional. Her quiet tone conveys sadness for this dreadful period which still lingers like 'a cloud over my time'.

EILÉAN NÍ CHUILLEANÁIN

✒ Class/Homework Exercises

1. 'Eiléan Ní Chuilleanáin's poetry offers a variety of interesting perspectives that vividly convey themes of universal relevance.' Discuss this statement with particular reference to 'Translation'.

2. 'In her poem "Translation", Ní Chuilleanáin's poetic voice is both critical and compassionate.' Discuss this statement with particular reference to the text.

⊙ Points to Consider

- The poet addresses aspects of the Magdalene laundries scandal.

- Several changes and translations are explored in the poem.

- Sensuous imagery evokes the harsh atmosphere in the laundry.

- Effective use of sound, contrast, mood and viewpoint throughout.

10 🔊 The Bend in the Road

This is the place where the child
Felt sick in the car and they pulled over
And waited in the shadow of a house.
A tall tree like a cat's tail waited too.
They opened the windows and breathed   5
Easily, while nothing moved. Then he was better.

Over twelve years it has become the place
Where you were sick one day on the way to the lake.
You are taller now than us.
The tree is taller, the house is quite covered in   10
With green creeper, and the bend   **creeper:** climbing plant.
In the road is as silent as ever it was on that day.

Piled high, wrapped lightly, like the one cumulus cloud   **cumulus:** rounded, fluffy.
In a perfect sky, softly packed like the air,
Is all that went on in those years, the absences,   15
The faces never long absent from thought,
The bodies alive then and the airy space they took up
When we saw them wrapped and sealed by sickness
Guessing the piled weight of sleep
We knew they could not carry for long;   20
This is the place of their presence: in the tree, in the air.

'This is the place'

👤 Personal Response

1. 'The importance of memory is a key theme in many of Ní Chuilleanáin's poems.' To what extent is this true of 'The Bend in the Road'? Briefly explain your answer.
2. Choose one image from 'The Bend in the Road' that you consider effective. Give reasons why this image appealed to you.
3. How would you describe the poem's conclusion? Is it mysterious? Hopeful? Comforting? Bitter? Briefly explain your response.

👁 Critical Literacy

'The Bend in the Road' is part of Eiléan Ní Chuilleanáin's poetry collection *The Girl Who Married the Reindeer.* **In many of these poems, the autobiographical becomes transformed as Ní Chuilleanáin takes a moment in time and fills it with arresting images, exact description, stillness and secrecy, linking together selected memories from various times and places. This poem's title suggests that the road will go on even though it is not visible at the moment.**

Stanza one opens with Ní Chuilleanáin pointing to the exact place where 'the child/Felt sick in the car and they pulled over'. The memory of such a familiar occurrence is given significance by the use of the demonstrative pronoun, 'This'. Run-on lines catch the flurry of activity as concerned adults attend to the sick child. Everything is still as they 'waited' for the sickness to pass. This suspended moment resonates as they linger 'in the shadow of a house'. **For a split second, an ominous – almost surreal – atmosphere begins to develop.** The poet introduces a slightly sinister simile, 'A tall tree like a cat's tail', peeking in from the world of fairy tale. Then the tree is personified: it 'waited too' as people and landscape merge in the moment of hush. Suddenly, a simple action ('They opened the windows') relieves the tension and everyone 'breathed/Easily'. The position of the adverb at the beginning of the line captures the relief at the recovery of the child. Yet the stationary atmosphere remained: 'while nothing moved.' However, the routine narrative of everyday life quickly resumes: 'Then he was better.'

In the second stanza, this roadside location takes on the shared resonance of memory: 'Over twelve years.' Readers are left imagining how the adults and child, when passing 'the place', would point it out as 'Where you were sick one day on the way to the lake'. The length of the line mirrors the long car journey. There is a sense of time being concentrated. Ní Chuilleanáin marvels at how the child has grown to adulthood: 'You are taller now than us.' The place has also changed – and even the tree is 'taller'. Assonance pinpoints how the nearby house is becoming yet more mysterious, 'quite covered in/With green creeper'. The insidious 'ee' sound mimics the silent takeover of the house by nature, as it recedes more and more into the shadows. Nature is alive. Creepings and rustlings stir, dispersing solidity and sureness. The poet cleverly places the line as if on a bend at the turn of a line: 'the bend/In the road is as silent as ever it was on that day.' Everything seems focused on the serenity of the place. **A bend in a road prevents us seeing what is coming next. Is this an obvious symbol of the human experience?** No one knows what lies ahead. The tone of this reflective stanza is introspective as Ní Chuilleanáin considers the undeniable passing of time and the human condition.

In the **final stanza**, memory and place interplay with other recollections. The poet's attention turns towards the sky, which she imagines 'Piled high' with past experiences. A lifetime's memories now tower 'like the one cumulus cloud/In a perfect sky'. The alliteration of the hard 'c' successfully captures the billowing cloud as it sails through the sky. **Similarly, the recollections of 'all that went on in those years' heave and surge as they drift through the poet's consciousness.** Naturally, they flow from the exact description of 'the bend/In the road'. They are now visible as feelings of loss expand into the present: 'The faces never long absent from thought.' Ní Chuilleanáin had lost not only her father and mother, but also her sister. But she remembers them **similarly** as they were, 'bodies alive then and the airy space they took up', just as the cloud in the sky. Poignantly, the poet also recalls them in their final sickness, 'wrapped and sealed by sickness', as if they had been parcelled for dispatch away from the ordinary routine of life by the ordeal of suffering.

However, the harsh reality of sickness and old age is also recognised: 'We knew they could not carry for long.' Just as the cloud grows bigger as it absorbs moisture, finally dissolving into rain, so did the poet's loved ones buckle beneath the weight of their illness, under the 'piled weight of sleep'. **Ní Chuilleanáin finds constant reminders of her family's past in the natural world.** She uses a simple image of cloud-like shapes of pillows and bed-covers as they surrender to sickness. Characteristically, the thinking within the poem has progressed considerably. The poet has widened its scope, its spatial dimension, to include those external experiences to which she so eloquently pays witness. Indeed, the poem now stands as a monument to silence and time, absence and presence, past and present. The moment of stillness is evoked. This roadside location takes on a special importance. It marks the place where lost family members now reside. Ní Chuilleanáin's alliterative language is emphatic: 'This is the place of their presence.' They belong 'in the tree, in the air'. As in so many of her poems, Ní Chuilleanáin honours the invisible, unseen presence of other thoughts and feelings that – just like the bend in the road – lie waiting in silence to be discovered and brought to life again.

✒ Writing About the Poem

'Eiléan Ní Chuilleanáin's poetry illuminates moments of perception in exact description.' Discuss this view in relation to 'The Bend in the Road'. Use suitable reference and quotation to support the points you make.

Sample Paragraph

'The Bend in the Road' is filled with accurate description. The opening lines pinpoint the exact place where 'the child/Felt sick in the car'. The conversational language, 'They opened the windows', 'Then he was better', brings me into this precise moment. I experience the tree, as if a child, through the almost cartoon-like simile, 'A tall tree like a cat's tail'. Yet, an otherworldly experience is present as personification transforms the tree into a living being; it 'waited too'. The place has become a metaphor for the reality of being human. The poet suddenly realises that the child has now grown into a man, 'You are taller than us now'. Another layer is added with the perception that the place has become filled with the 'presence' of those 'faces never long absent from thought'. I now began to understand that in a single moment, the distinctions between life and death, being and memory,

EXAMINER'S COMMENT

This is a top-grade personal response that addresses the poet's interest in transience and memory. Apt, accurate quotes provide good support for developed discussion points which range effectively through the poem. There is some highly impressive focus on aspects of the poet's distinctive style. Expression is also excellent throughout, e.g. 'The place has become a metaphor for the reality of being human'.

all become blurred. Through precise description, this poet transports readers into an understanding that many experiences, 'all that went on in those years', can be savoured in various forms, 'softly packed like the air'.

✒ Class/Homework Exercises

1. 'Space in Ní Chuilleanáin's poetry is used as an expression of one's experience of the world and is a metaphor for the linking together of self and the world.' Discuss this statement, with particular reference to 'The Bend in the Road'.

2. 'The evocative power of a specific location is central to Ní Chuilleanáin's "The Bend in the Road".' Discuss this view, supporting your answer with reference to the poem.

◎ Points to Consider

• **Key themes include memory, family, transience, loss and grief.**

• **Symbolism used throughout the poem to suggest meaning.**

• **Effective use of assonance and alliteration to create atmosphere.**

• **Recurring references to sickness add unity to the poem.**

11 🔊 On Lacking the Killer Instinct

EILÉAN NÍ CHUILLEANÁIN

One hare, absorbed, sitting still,
Right in the grassy middle of the track,
I met when I fled up into the hills, that time
My father was dying in a hospital —
I see her suddenly again, borne back   5
By the morning paper's prize photograph:
Two greyhounds tumbling over, absurdly gross,
While the hare shoots off to the left, her bright eye
Full not only of speed and fear
But surely in the moment a glad power,   10

Like my father's, running from a lorry-load of soldiers
In nineteen twenty-one, nineteen years old,
Such gladness, he said, cornering in the narrow road
Between high hedges, in summer dusk.
                       The hare   15
Like him should never have been coursed,
But, clever, she gets off; another day
She'll fool the stupid dogs, double back
On her own scent, downhill, and choose her time
To spring away out of the frame, all while   20
The pack is labouring up.
                   The lorry was growling
And he was clever, he saw a house
And risked an open kitchen door. The soldiers
Found six people in a country kitchen, one   25
Drying his face, dazed-looking, the towel
Half covering his face. The lorry left,
The people let him sleep there, he came out
Into a blissful dawn. Should he have chanced that door?
If the sheltering house had been burned down, what good   30
Could all his bright running have done
For those that harboured him?
                  And I should not
Have run away, but I went back to the city
Next morning, washed in brown bog water, and   35
I thought about the hare, in her hour of ease.

hare: mammal resembling a large rabbit.
absorbed: engrossed, immersed, preoccupied.

absurdly: ridiculously, nonsensically.
gross: disgusting, outrageous.

coursed: hunted with greyhounds.

frame: picture, enclosure.
labouring: moving with difficulty.

👤 Personal Response

1. Who, in your opinion, lacked the killer instinct in this poem? Was it the hare, the soldiers, the greyhounds, the father, the poet? Refer closely to the text in your response.
2. The poet alters time and place frequently in this poem. With the aid of quotations, trace these changes as the poem develops.
3. Did you find the poem's conclusion satisfying or mystifying? Give reasons for your response, referring closely to the text.

👁 Critical Literacy

'On Lacking the Killer Instinct' is part of Eiléan Ní Chuilleanáin's *The Sun-fish* collection. A sunfish is so-called due to its habit of basking on the water's surface. Ní Chuilleanáin often presents daily life with a sense of mystery and otherworldliness as the poems move between various realms of experience. Each scene lies open to another version of the narrative. She blurs the distance between past and present in this three-part poem. History, which is something of an Irish obsession, always informs the present. This poet discovers and remembers. As she herself has said, 'In order for the poem to get written, something has to happen.'

The title of the poem immediately intrigues and unsettles. The opening lines focus on a stationary hare, silent, engrossed, 'absorbed', at rest. It is a vivid picture. Why is this hare preoccupied? The sibilant alliterative phrase, 'sitting still', captures the motionless animal in 'the middle of the track'. This **naturalistic setting** and image is brought into high resolution as the poet recounts that her own journey 'up into the hills' caused her to meet this creature. Ní Chuilleanáin juxtaposes the stillness of the wild hare with her own headlong flight from the awful reality, 'that time/My father was dying in a hospital'. In describing this terrible experience, her tone is remarkably controlled – detached, yet compassionate.

Another narrative thread is introduced in line 6 when the poet recalls the 'morning paper's prize photograph'. Here the predators are presented as ungainly, almost comical characters incapable of purposeful action: 'Two greyhounds tumbling over, absurdly gross.' The broad vowels and repetition

'While the hare shoots off to the left'

of 'r' highlight the hounds' unattractively large appearance. Irish coursing is a competitive sport where dogs are tested on their ability to run and overtake the hare, turning it without capturing it. It is often regarded as a cruel activity that causes pain and suffering to the pursued creature. From the start of the poem, **readers are left wondering who exactly lacks the killer instinct**. Do the dogs not have the urge to pounce and kill? Has the hare got the killer instinct, running for its life, showing the strong will to survive against all odds? The rapid run-on lines mimic the speed and agility of the hare exulting in 'glad power'.

In line 11, the **reader is taken into another realm** – a common feature of Ní Chuilleanáin's interconnected narratives. In this case, she recalls another pursuit. Her father was a combatant in the Irish Civil War in 1922 and was on the run. Like the hare, he fled, 'cornering in the narrow road/Between high hedges, in summer dusk'. Both are linked through 'gladness' as they exult in their capacity to outrun their pursuers. For her father, this was a 'lorry-load of soldiers' – the compound word emphasising the unequal odds against which the poet's father struggled. This is similar to the hare's predicament against the 'Two greyhounds'. The precise placing of 'The hare' tucked away at the end of line 15 suggests the animal's escape. Ní Chuilleanáin comments that neither the hare nor her father should ever have 'been coursed'. She is happy to think that on some other occasion, the hare is likely to outwit the 'stupid dogs' and will 'spring away out of the frame', nimbly escaping her pursuers. In Irish coursing, the hare is not run on open land but in a secure enclosure over a set distance. The heavy, panting exertions of the pursuing dogs is illustrated in the run-through line, 'all while/The pack is labouring up'.

Ní Chuilleanáin returns to her father's story in line 22, imagining a moment of danger from his time as a fugitive. The scene is dominated by the threatening sound of a lorry, 'growling' like a pursuing hound. The repetition of the adjective 'clever' links her father and the hare as he too made his escape. Intent on surviving, 'he saw a house/And risked an open kitchen door'. **The enemy soldiers go through the motions of pursuit cursorily, seemingly lacking the killer instinct** when they 'Found six people in a country kitchen'. Ní Chuilleanáin is characteristically ambivalent about why the rebels were not challenged, reminding us of the contradictory attitudes among the various combatants of the Civil War.

For whatever reason, the fugitives ('one/Drying his face, dazed-looking') were not arrested and their deception worked. The poet's father is allowed refuge: 'The people let him sleep there.' Throughout Ireland's troubled history, 'safe houses' existed that sheltered those on the run. In her mind's eye, the poet pictures her father emerging in triumph the next day 'Into a blissful dawn' (line 29). In a **series of questions**, she considers his crucial decision to stand his ground and feign innocence. In retrospect, anything might have happened to affect the outcome at 'the sheltering house'.

Ní Chuilleanáin emphasises how chance has played such a significant role – not just in her father's life, but in Ireland's history.

The poet concludes by returning to the opening scene. Having observed the hare and remembered her father's encounter during the Civil War, she now realises that she should never have run away from her dying father. Her decision to return is seen as a mature one – almost like a religious ritual in which the poet cleanses herself, 'washed in brown bog water'. Is this a form of absolution to remove her guilt for running away? Typically, she uses this unifying symbol to gently draw the poem's three narratives together. After the common experience of the turbulence of the run, all three (the hare, the father and the poet herself) have entered a new state of being – calm composure. Ní Chuilleanáin reflects on 'the hare, in her hour of ease', the soft monosyllabic final word gently conveying a sense of peace and reconciliation. The poem closes as it began, with the **beautiful silent image of the hare**, self-possessed and serene after all the turmoil of the chase.

☐ Writing About the Poem

'Eiléan Ní Chuilleanáin is a quiet, introspective, enigmatic poet.' Discuss this statement with particular reference to 'On Lacking the Killer Instinct'.

Sample Paragraph

EXAMINER'S COMMENT

This insightful paragraph offers a very clear and focused response to a testing question. Interesting critical discussion – aptly illustrated by accurate quotations – ranges widely, tracing the subtle development of the poem's various narrative threads. Impressive use of language throughout adds clarity to the key points. The questions posed towards the end round off the discussion effectively in this excellent top-grade answer.

'On Lacking the Killer Instinct' moved effortlessly, mysteriously weaving three different narratives: the story of the hare, the history of Ní Chuilleanáin's father's escape in 1921 and her own flight from the city. She celebrates resilience, the hare's 'bright eye' is full of 'a glad power'. Similarly, her father exulted in his cleverness, as he out-manoeuvred the 'lorry-load of soldiers'. The poet also faced up to death and 'went back to the city'. Her impressionistic style is similar to watching a photograph as it slowly develops before our eyes. The reader is effortlessly guided through different times and places as the focus of the poet's gaze shifts from the hunt of the hare in coursing to the hunt of her father in the Civil War. She then quietly reflects on her own flight and concludes that running does not solve problems, 'what good/Could all his bright running have done'. In the end, this poet poses questions that resonate. Does she too lack the killer instinct? The word 'ease' suggests that staying calm is more effective than running. Is the killer instinct worth having? This introspective poet leaves us with an image of stillness to think about.

EILÉAN NÍ CHUILLEANÁIN

Class/Homework Exercises

1. 'Eiléan Ní Chuilleanáin's poems elude categories and invite and challenge the reader in equal measure.' Discuss this statement with particular reference to 'On Lacking the Killer Instinct'.

2. 'Ní Chuilleanáin is capable of blending multiple narratives with great skill in her poetry.' To what extent is this the case in 'On Lacking the Killer Instinct'? Support your answer with reference to the poem.

Points to Consider

- Interwoven stories: hunting the hare, her father's death and Ireland's Civil War.

- Effective use of rhythm and contrast – movement and stillness.

- Subtle blending of past and present, time and place.

- Alliterative and sibilant sound effects echo related ideas throughout.

12 🔊 To Niall Woods and Xenya Ostrovskaia, married in Dublin on 9 September 2009

Title: An epithalamium is a poem (or song) in celebration of a wedding. Eiléan Ní Chuilleanáin has included this poem (to her son Niall and his bride, Xenya) as the introductory dedication in her poetry collection *The Sun-fish*.

When you look out across the fields
And you both see the same star
Pitching its tent on the point of the steeple —
That is the time to set out on your journey,
With half a loaf and your mother's blessing.   5

Leave behind the places that you knew:
All that you leave behind you will find once more,
You will find it in the stories;
The sleeping beauty in her high tower
With her talking cat asleep   10
Solid beside her feet — you will see her again.

sleeping beauty: European fairy tale from 'La Belle au bois dormant' (Beauty of the sleeping wood) by Charles Perrault and 'Dornröschen' (Little Briar Rose) by the Brothers Grimm.

When the cat wakes up he will speak in Irish and Russian
And every night he will tell you a different tale
About the firebird that stole the golden apples,
Gone every morning out of the emperor's garden,   15
And about the King of Ireland's Son and the Enchanter's Daughter.

the firebird: Russian fairy tale; 'Tsarevitch Ivan, the Fire Bird and the Gray Wolf' by Alexander Afanasyev.
the King of Ireland's Son: Irish fairy tale; 'The King of Ireland's Son' by Padraic Colum.
Book of Ruth: religious story from the Old Testament.

The story the cat does not know is the Book of Ruth
And I have no time to tell you how she fared
When she went out at night and she was afraid,
In the beginning of the barley harvest,   20
Or how she trusted to strangers and stood by her word:

You will have to trust me, she lived happily ever after.

Or how she trusted to strangers: In the Bible story, Boaz owned the field Ruth harvested. He was a relative of the family and by law could 'redeem' her if he married her now that she was a widow. He wished to do so because he admired how she had stood by her mother-in-law, 'For wherever you go, I will go'.

'the firebird that stole the golden apples'

👤 Personal Response

1. Do you think the references to fairy tales are appropriate on the occasion of Eiléan Ní Chuilleanáin's son's marriage? Give one reason for your answer.

2. In your opinion, what is the dominant tone of voice in the poem? Is it one of warning, reassurance, hope, consolation? Briefly explain your response with reference to the poem.

3. Write your own short personal response to the poem, highlighting the impact it made on you.

👁 Critical Literacy

'I write poems that mean a lot to me' (Eiléan Ní Chuilleanáin). This particular poem is dedicated to her son, Niall, and his new bride, Xenya, on the happy occasion of their marriage. Folklore is central to this poet's work. Her mother, Eilís Dillon, was a famous writer of children's stories. Fairy tales allow Ní Chuilleanáin the opportunity to approach a subject from an oblique, non-confessional perspective. It gives distance. Story-tellers rarely comment on or explain what happens. They simply tell the tale. In this poem, Ní Chuilleanáin refers to folklore and a well-known Bible story as she addresses the young couple.

The first stanza opens with **warm advice** from a loving mother as she gives the young man leave to set out on his own journey through life with his new partner. Run-on lines contain a beautiful, romantic image of a harmonious vision: 'you both see the same star.' Personification and alliteration bring this natural image to radiant life, 'Pitching its tent on the point of the steeple', suggesting the new home which the young couple are about to set up for themselves. **Ní Chuilleanáin's gaze is one of relentless clarity and attentiveness.** She illuminates details. She also counsels that it is the right time to go, 'to set out on your journey' when you are prepared ('With half a loaf') and with good wishes ('and your mother's blessing'). She combines colloquial and fairy tale language. The tone is warm, but also pragmatic – offering practical advice to the newlyweds to make the most of whatever they have to start with: 'half a loaf is better than none.'

Stanza two begins with the imperative warning: 'Leave behind.' The mother is advising the couple to forget 'the places that you knew'. Is 'places' a metaphor for their actual homes or their cultural environments? Or does it refer to values the young people hold sacred? She consoles them that past experiences can still be found 'in the stories'. Ní Chuilleanáin now weaves an intricate web of such stories from many different sources. The first tale is that of 'sleeping beauty in her high tower'. This classic folk story involves a beautiful princess, enchantment, and a handsome prince who has to brave the obstacles of tall trees that surround the castle and its sleeping princess.

Is Ní Chuilleanáin illustrating that the path to true love is filled with difficulties and that only the brave will be successful? The extended run-on lines suggest the hundred years' sleep of the spellbound princess, who can only be awakened by a kiss. The poet also makes use of another familiar element of fairy tales – talking animals. In this case, the 'talking cat' probably refers to Irish folklore, and the King of Cats, a renowned teller of tales. Ní Chuilleanáin is able to link the basic characteristics of the animal with human behaviour. The cat slumbers with the princess, 'Solid', stable and dependable, beside her feet. Despite the poet's realism, however, this fairy tale allusion is primarily optimistic.

In stanza three, Ní Chuilleanáin imagines the cat awakening and telling stories in both 'Irish and Russian', a likely reference to the young couple's **two cultural backgrounds**. The poet has said that in her work she is trying 'to suggest, to phrase, to find a way to make it possible for somebody to pick up certain suggestions ... They might not be seeing what I am seeing.' The poet continues to set her personal wishes for Niall and Xenya within the context of folktales, turning to the Russian tradition: 'Tsarevitch, the Fire Bird and the Gray Wolf.' Again, the hero of this story is on a challenging mission, as he attempts to catch the 'firebird that stole the golden apples ... out of the emperor's garden'. The assonance of the broad vowel 'o' emphasises the exasperation of the repeated theft. As always in folklore, courage and determination are required before the hero can overcome many ordeals and find true happiness.

Ní Chuilleanáin introduces the Irish tradition with the story of the King of Ireland's son, who must pluck three hairs from the Enchanter's beard in order to save his own life. On his quest, he gains the hand of Fedelma, the Enchanter's youngest daughter. But he falls asleep and loses her to the King of the Land of Mist. **Is the poet simply advising her son and daughter-in-law that love must be cherished and never taken for granted?** Throughout the poem, she draws heavily on stories where heroes have to fight for what they believe in. All of these tales convey the same central meaning – that lasting love has to be won through daring, determination and sacrifice.

In the playful link into stanza four, Ní Chuilleanáin remarks that 'the story the cat does not know is the Book of Ruth'. This final story is not from the world of folklore, but from the Bible (although the poet has commented that 'a lot of religious narrative is very folkloric'). The Book of Ruth teaches that **genuine love can require uncompromising sacrifice**, and that such unselfish love will be well rewarded. This particular tale of inclusivity shows two different cultures coming together. The Israelites (sons of Naomi) marry women from the Moab tribe, one of whom is Ruth. She embraces Naomi's people, land, culture and God. This is very pertinent to the newly married couple, as they are also from different lands and cultures. Not surprisingly, the biblical tale is one of loving kindness – but it also includes a realistic message. After her husband's death, Ruth chooses to stay with her mother-in-law and undertakes the backbreaking farm work of gleaning to support the family. This involves lifting the grain and stalks left behind after the harvesting of barley. The metaphor of the harvest is another reminder that married couples will reap what they sow, depending on the effort and commitment made to their relationship.

The poem's last line is placed apart to emphasise its significance. Ní Chuilleanáin tells the newlyweds that they 'will have to trust me' – presumably just as Ruth trusted her mother-in-law, Naomi. For doing this, she was rewarded with living 'happily ever after', as in the best tales. The poet's quietly light-hearted approach, however, does not lessen her own deeply felt hopes for Niall and Xenya. **All the stories she has used are concerned with the essential qualities of a loving relationship** – and share a common thread of courage, faithfulness and honesty as the couple journey to a happy future. Tales and dreams are the shadow-truths that will endure. Ní Chuilleanáin's final tone is clearly sincere, upbeat and forward-looking.

✒ Writing About the Poem

**'The imagination is not the refuge but the true site of authority.'
Comment on this statement in relation to the poem 'To Niall Woods and Xenya Ostrovskaia, married in Dublin on 9 September 2009'.**

Sample Paragraph

I feel that Ní Chuilleanáin's poem has subtle messages which only become clear after several readings. I think the poet is counselling her son and his new bride, Xenya, that stories, 'the imagination' are where truth, 'the true site of authority' lies. The stories she chooses, 'sleeping beauty in her high tower', 'the firebird that stole the golden apples' and the 'King of Ireland's Son and the Enchanter's Daughter' all suggest that perseverance and sincerity win the day. Nothing worthwhile is won easily. I thought the inclusion of the story of Ruth was very apt as it involved two cultures which is relevant to the couple's Irish and Russian origins. People in this new era will have to 'trust' strangers. I understood that Ní Chuilleanáin is showing that no matter where these imaginative tales come from, Europe, Russia, Ireland or the Bible, obstacles have to be overcome in life through determination. I thought the poet was clever because by putting this insight into the realm of a fairy story, it does not sound like preaching which the young couple might resent, yet the message rings true through time from this 'site of authority', the kingdom of storytelling.

EXAMINER'S COMMENT

A sustained personal response showing genuine engagement with the poem. The focused opening tackles the discussion question directly. This is followed by several clear points, e.g. 'perseverance and sincerity win the day', 'Nothing worthwhile is won easily', 'obstacles have to be overcome', tracing the development of thought throughout the poem. Accurate quotations and clear expression ensure the highest grade.

✒ Class/Homework Exercises

1. What impression of Ní Chuilleanáin do you get from reading 'To Niall Woods and Xenya Ostrovskaia, married in Dublin on 9 September 2009'? Write at least one paragraph in response, illustrating your views with reference to the text of the poem.

2. 'Ní Chuilleanáin's poems are often seen as challenging, but ultimately rewarding.' To what extent is this true of 'To Niall Woods and Xenia Ostrovskaia, married in Dublin on 9 September 2009'? Support your answer with reference to the poem.

⊙ Points to Consider

- The advice to the young couple is couched in the language of a fairy tale.

- Recurring references to Bible stories and legends.

- Effective use of personification, alliteration and sibilance.

- Ending is sincere, sympathetic and optimistic.

Sample Leaving Cert Questions on Ní Chuilleanáin's Poetry

1. 'Eiléan Ní Chuilleanáin's captivating stories explore significant issues for modern-day Ireland, in an intriguing and attractive style.' Discuss this statement, developing your response with reference to the themes and language evident in the poems by Ní Chuilleanáin on your course.

2. 'Ní Chuilleanáin's multi-layered poems invite readers into a variety of settings and enhance our understanding of the world around us.' Discuss this view, developing your response with reference to the poems by Eiléan Ní Chuilleanáin on your course.

3. 'Eiléan Ní Chuilleanáin's thought-provoking subject matter and distinctive poetic style can sometimes prove challenging.' Discuss this statement, developing your response with reference to the themes and language evident in the poems by Ní Chuilleanáin on your course.

How do I organise my answer?

(Sample question 2)

'Ní Chuilleanáin's multi-layered poems invite readers into a variety of settings and enhance our understanding of the world around us.' Discuss this view, developing your response with reference to the poems by Eiléan Ní Chuilleanáin on your course.

Sample Plan 1

Intro: *(Stance: agree with viewpoint in the question)* Ní Chuilleanáin's innovative poetry challenges with a vast canvas of people, places, voices, times and images. Weaving fragmentary narratives, she propels readers into a greater awareness of the world. She focuses on death, communication, memory, sacrifice and salvation.

Point 1: *(Blended stories – memory and death)* 'Deaths and Engines' uses surreal tactile imagery to link two stories, a plane crash and her father's death. Both share the nightmarish event of losing control ('too late to stop'). Acceptance of powerlessness of individual in difficult times.

Understanding the Prescribed Poetry Question

Marks are awarded using the PCLM Marking Scheme: P = 15; C = 15; L = 15; M = 5 Total = 50

- **P** (Purpose = 15 marks) refers to the set question and is the launch pad for the answer. This involves engaging with all aspects of the question. Both theme and language must be addressed, although not necessarily equally.
- **C** (Coherence = 15 marks) refers to the organisation of the developed response and the use of accurate, relevant quotation. Paragraphing is essential.
- **L** (Language = 15 marks) refers to the student's skill in controlling language throughout the answer.
- **M** (Mechanics = 5 marks) refers to spelling and grammar.
- Although no specific number of poems is required, students usually discuss at least 3 or 4 in their written responses.
- Aim for at least 800 words, to be completed within 45–50 minutes.

Point 2: *(Ambivalent detailed scenario – lack of communication/comprehension)* 'Street' entices reader and would-be lover into an altered world. Cinematic close-up ('white trousers/Dangling a knife on a ring at her belt') reveals uncertain atmosphere. Dreamlike encounter draws attention to gaps in communication and comprehension.

Point 3: *(Altered landscapes – power of memory)* 'Following' details changing settings; dust and noise of cattle mart ('beasts packed solid'), cold bog ('shivering bog by starlight'). Memory does not remain 'shelved' but will 'crack' so dead and living can reconnect through relics ('crushed flowers').

Point 4: *(Complex themes – sacrifice/reward)* 'All for You' reveals tremendous sacrifice of nun's celibate religious life through personification of architectural detail, staircase ('Sprawling') and orderly provision store ('tins shining in ranks'). Submission to God's will 'key' to salvation.

Conclusion: Ní Chuilleanáin's poems offer elusive visions and subtle messages. Breaking down barriers between shifting realms, fragmented narratives open doors into multiple worlds and experiences. Challenging perspectives from which to view our own world.

Sample Paragraph: Point 4

Strange hypnotic images from convent life appear in Ní Chuilleanáin's poem 'All for You'. The writhing 'staircase of the hall', described as 'Sprawling', seems both welcoming and threatening. The poet refers to the bible story of the serpent that Moses constructed to gain salvation from God for his people. The harsh staircase of life must also be climbed to gain salvation. The nun's choice of a confined celibate life is suggested by slender assonant sounds, 'The tins shine in ranks … Rich with shrivelled fruit'. A violent image, 'rage of brushwood', reveals the intensity of the nun's vocation and also echoes another bible story – about the burning bush. The 'key' representing both confinement and freedom shows the paradox of Christian faith. Redemption can only be achieved through submission to God's will. This complex and challenging poem moves through various settings, focusing mainly on the Christian belief of salvation through surrender to God.

EXAMINER'S COMMENT

As part of a full essay, this is a strong, top-grade paragraph showing clear engagement with the poem. The discussion points relating to Ní Chuilleanáin's dense imagery and sound effects are particularly impressive. Accurate supportive quotations are effectively worked into the critical analysis. Language use is also excellent throughout.

(Sample question 3)

'Eiléan Ní Chuilleanáin's thought-provoking subject matter and distinctive poetic style can sometimes prove challenging.' Discuss this statement, developing your response with reference to the themes and language evident in the poems by Ní Chuilleanáin on your course.

Sample Plan 2

Intro: *(Stance: agree with viewpoint in the question)* Ní Chuilleanáin addresses universal concerns of exploiter and exploited and disturbing contrasts between the past and present. Poems challenge the reader to wonder and reflect. Unique style interweaves narratives, using layered fragments of powerful visual and aural imagery.

Point 1: *(Exploiter/exploited – dramatic contrasts)* 'Lucina Schynning in Silence of the Nicht' suggests material and cultural deprivation ('without roast meat or music'). Repulsive imagery traces the devastation left by Cromwell ('plague'). Contrasting positive sense of resilience expressed in animal imagery ('chirp of the stream running').

Point 2: *(Landlord/tenant – translation of traditional Irish lament)* 'Kilcash' explores impact of change on Irish society past and present ('What will we do now'). Only solution offered is the restoration of the big house 'Kilcash'. Ambivalent attitude of poet – is this a genuine tribute to humane landlords or a satire on subservience of Irish?

Point 3: *(Past/present – sardonic humour)* 'The Second Voyage' describes mythic tale of the Greek hero, Odysseus, battling with the treacherous ocean ('simmering sea'). Mockery of inflated sense of masculine power ('rammed/The oar'). Enigmatic poem poses the question whether recollected memory captivates more than routine present experience.

Point 4: *(Offender/victim – detailed imagery)* 'Translation' offers perceptive account of wrongs inflicted on Irish women in Magdalene laundries. Sensuous imagery captures the harsh atmosphere in the laundry. Inclusion of authority figure as victim challenges modern readers' perceptions.

Conclusion: Ní Chuilleanáin investigates universal themes of oppressor and oppressed, using Irish history's troubled backstory. Mythic references explore man's frustration with what he possesses and challenge us to re-examine our own views.

Sample Paragraph: Point 4

'Translation' offers an intriguing account of a very dark period in Irish history. Ní Chuilleanáin focuses on the terrible oppression of the laundry's young women – something that should never be repeated or forgotten. The poem made me think about their loss of youth and happiness. The bleak atmosphere – 'light blinded' – is poignantly contrasted with their natural playfulness, suggested by the lively image, 'steam danced/Around stone drains and giggled'. The poet also notes the nun's loss of identity, 'my temporary name'. Both the girls' lives and hers have been 'bleached out'. Fortunately, her rule over the girls is now gone, 'the bunched keys I bore slacken'. I found it interesting that a shame still hangs over the nun, 'a cloud over my time'. The inclusion of Magdalene victims and authority figures, such as the nun, as equal victims of a less tolerant time is likely to be challenged by many people today.

EXAMINER'S COMMENT

Good personal response demonstrating close engagement with the poem. As part of a full essay, it shows an appreciation of Ní Chuilleanáin's thought-provoking presentation of victims. Critical commentary is well supported by suitable quotation and some awareness of poetic techniques, including evocative imagery and atmosphere. Expression is assured throughout this successful high-grade paragraph.

EXAM FOCUS

- As you may not be familiar with some of the poems referred to in the sample plans, substitute poems that you have studied closely.
- Key points about a particular poem can be developed over more than one paragraph.
- Paragraphs may also include cross-referencing and discussion of more than one poem.
- Remember that there is no single 'correct' answer to poetry questions, so always be confident in expressing your own considered response.

Leaving Cert Sample Essay

'Eiléan Ní Chuilleanáin's captivating stories explore significant issues for modern-day Ireland, in an intriguing and attractive style.' Discuss this statement, developing your response with reference to the themes and language evident in the poems by Ní Chuilleanáin on your course.

Sample Essay

1. Eiléan Ní Chuilleanáin's poems engage readers with stories, in a variety of settings. These intimate narratives are often blended to include universal issues that are relevant to today's Ireland. Her vibrant imagery and range of interesting references produce fascinating and mysterious poems.

2. 'The Bend in the Road' takes a familiar family event, a child who once 'felt sick in the car' on a quiet country road. The poem involves readers through the use of personification from the slightly sinister world of fairy tales, 'A tall tree like a cat's tail'. Ní Chuilleanáin reminds us of the universal truth that life does not permit us to see into the future. This is important for everyone in modern Ireland – we cannot take anything for granted as everything can change in an instant. By combining different narratives, the poet shows how the past can sometimes be found in the present. 'Piled high' clouds remind her of lost loved ones. In their final days they were 'wrapped and sealed by sickness', like parcels about to be dispatched. In this compelling poem, an ordinary family story is transformed into an engaging reflection on love and memory through layers of vivid imagery.

3. Another harsh truth, the death of the poet's mother, is addressed in 'Fireman's Lift'. The poem is set inside Parma Cathedral in northern Italy. The close relationship between mother and daughter is vividly captured, 'I was standing beside you looking up'. Strong verbs, such as 'spiralling' and 'heaving', describe what is depicted in the religious artwork – the huge effort of the angels lifting Mary into the glory of heaven. The image of the angels acting as 'A crane and a cradle' for Mary reminds the poet of the nurses, 'heads bowed', who looked after her mother during her illness. It is time for her mother, like the Virgin, to go 'spiralling to heaven'. For Ní Chuilleanáin, this represents an acceptance of loss. The poem is a powerful lesson for modern Ireland to accept what cannot be changed.

4. The relevance of history is a theme in 'On Lacking the Killer Instinct'. Ní Chuilleanáin recalls her father's escape from the Black and Tans. This is when in 1921 British military soldiers hunted down her father. But he escaped by hiding in a safe house. Sibilant sounds show his relief as he escaped 'into a blissful dawn'. The poet also tries escaping when she 'fled up into the hills' at a tough time in her own past when her father was dying in hospital. There she met 'one hare' which also like her father had been hunted, 'coursed'. Through these interwoven stories, Ní Chuilleanáin teaches us a valuable lesson for life. We can't always 'run away' from difficulties but must stand our ground like her father and the hare experienced in an 'hour of ease'.

INDICATIVE MATERIAL

- **Ní Chuilleanáin's captivating stories** (engaging recollections from her past, family relationships, stories about Ireland's complex history, compelling accounts of women's experience, universal folktales and myths, spiritual life, etc.)

... explore:

- **significant issues for modern-day Ireland** (relevance of myth and history, the enduring need for compassion, importance of the feminine perspective, universal themes, e.g. love, loss, memory, death, afterlife, etc.)
- **intriguing and attractive style** (vivid imagery, layered quality of the work, reference/allusions, choice of settings and moods: surreal/suggestive/evocative/obscure/mysterious, etc.)...

5. 'To Niall Woods and Xenya Ostrovskaia' closely links two folktales. The Russian 'firebird' story and the Irish tale of 'the Enchanter's Daughter' are used to honour the two distinct cultures of the newly-married couple. Ní Chuilleanáin engages readers with the frustration felt by the hero on his mission to capture the thieving firebird. This is done through broad assonance sounds, 'stole the golden apples'. She is reminding the young couple that courage and determination are required if true happiness is to be achieved. The Irish tale recounts how love must never be taken for granted. The King of Ireland's son lost the Enchanter's Daughter because he fell asleep. Once again, these stories emphasise the importance of determination and sacrifice, making them relevant to qualities that Irish people now need more than ever.

6. 'Translation' is based on the Magdalene convents' scandal. The poem addresses an issue that is important to every Irish person. Without becoming angry or over-emotional, Ní Chuilleanáin makes the point that abuse of any individual is wrong. The dramatic description of the infamous laundries – places where 'white light blinded' the unfortunate victims – sums up the tragic events of a once shameful Ireland and teaches the lesson that such cruelty should ever happen again. Ní Chuilleanáin is respectful towards those nuns who were also victims of an oppressive religious system that was supported by the state. Like the young girls who were so mistreated, some of these nuns were also imprisoned, even losing their own names and identities by taking the names of saints.

7. Ní Chuilleanáin's poetry isn't always easy to understand, but memory and reflection are central to many of the poems on our course. There is often a dream-like quality which allows readers to take their own meaning – particularly from the open-ended poems that leave us asking questions. I enjoyed Ní Chuilleanáin's lyrical poetry which included stories from her family life. These were thought-provoking and often illustrated important issues about love, loss and endurance.

(800 words)

EXAMINER'S COMMENT

This solid top-grade response addresses the question's three key elements (the poet's stories, issues and style), although a little more focus on relevancy to today's Ireland would have been welcome. The short introductory paragraph gives a clear overview that shows good engagement with Ní Chuilleanáin's poems. Effective use is made of reference to support perceptive discussion. The importance of interwoven narratives and sound effects is illustrated – particularly in paragraphs 3 and 5. Apart from some awkwardness in paragraph 4, expression is generally well controlled throughout this impressive essay.

GRADE: H1
P = 15/15
C = 13/15
L = 13/15
M = 5/5
Total = 46/50

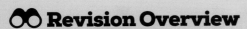 Revision Overview

'Lucina Schynning in Silence of the Nicht'
Powerful monologue addresses themes of exploitation, loss and resistance.

'The Second Voyage'
Dramatic presentation of theme of transience. Innovative use of mythical Greek hero's love/hate relationship with sea.

'Deaths and Engines'
Themes of memory, loss and death. Blending of two narratives (plane and father's death).

'Street'
Intriguing oblique narrative of falling in love. Central puzzling enigma.

'Fireman's Lift'
Vivid memory poem explores themes of death, regeneration and love.

'All for You'
Intricately layered broken narrative depicts theme of transience through analysis of the challenges and rewards of religious life.

'Following'
Themes of power, of memory and unjust balance of power through metaphor of journey.

'Kilcash'
Translation of Irish lament addresses theme of impact of change on Irish society, past and present.

'Translation'
Belated acknowledgment of wrongs perpetrated on Irish women in Magdalene laundries.

'The Bend in the Road'
Blended autobiographical events express transience and loss. The continuing existence of memory is acknowledged and honoured.

'On Lacking the Killer Instinct'
Interwoven introspective narratives bridge past and present. Enigmatic examination of theme of powerful and powerless, through illustrations of hunter and hunted.

'To Niall Woods and Xenya Ostrovskaia, married in Dublin 9 September 2009'
Celebratory epithalamium blends folk tales and biblical stories. Theme of sacrifice needed for success.

Last Words

'There is something second-sighted about Eiléan Ní Chuilleanáin's work. Her poems see things anew, in a rinsed and dreamstruck light.'
Seamus Heaney

'Ní Chuilleanáin's eccentric poems uncover hidden dramas in many guises, and she continually holds us captive by her luminous voice.'
Molly Bendall

'Inspiration comes from everywhere, from the places I go and the things I do. I never write unless I have an idea that seems really interesting to me.'
Eiléan Ní Chuilleanáin

 SUFFERING   HISTORY/ MEMORY   TIME   DEATH   LOVE   RELATIONSHIPS   RELIGION/ SPIRITUALITY   STRENGTH

Sylvia Plath
1932–1963

'Out of the ash
I rise with my red hair
And I eat men like air.'

Born in Boston, Massachusetts in 1932, Sylvia Plath is a writer whose best-known poems are noted for their intense focus and vibrant, personal imagery. Her writing talent – and ambition to succeed – was evident from an early age. She kept a journal during childhood and published her early poems in literary magazines and newspapers. After studying Art and English at college, Plath moved to Cambridge, England in the mid-1950s. Here she met and later married the poet Ted Hughes. The couple had two children, Frieda and Nicholas, but the marriage was not to last. Plath continued to write through the late 1950s and early 1960s. During the final years of her life, she produced numerous confessional poems of stark revelation, channelling her long-standing anxiety and doubt into poetic verses of great power and pathos. At her creative peak, Sylvia Plath took her own life on 11 February 1963.

Investigate Further

To find out more about Sylvia Plath, or to hear readings of her poems, you could search some useful websites, such as YouTube, BBC poetry, poetryfoundation.org and poetryarchive.org, or access additional material on this page of your eBook.

Prescribed Poems

Note that Plath uses American spellings and punctuation in her work.

(OL) indicates poems that are also prescribed for the Ordinary Level course.

1 Black Rook in Rainy Weather

On the stiff twig up there
Hunches a wet black rook
Arranging and rearranging its feathers in the rain.
I do not expect a miracle
Or an accident   5

To set the sight on fire
In my eye, nor seek
Any more in the desultory weather some design,   **desultory:** unexceptional, oppressive.
But let spotted leaves fall as they fall,
Without ceremony, or portent.   10   **portent:** omen.

Although, I admit, I desire,
Occasionally, some backtalk
From the mute sky, I can't honestly complain:
A certain minor light may still
Lean incandescent   15   **incandescent:** glowing.

Out of kitchen table or chair
As if a celestial burning took
Possession of the most obtuse objects now and then –
Thus hallowing an interval   **hallowing:** making holy.
Otherwise inconsequent   20   **inconsequent:** of no importance.

By bestowing largesse, honor,   **largesse:** generous, giving.
One might say love. At any rate, I now walk
Wary (for it could happen
Even in this dull ruinous landscape); skeptical,   **skeptical:** wary, suspicious.
Yet politic; ignorant   25   **politic:** wise and likely to prove advantageous.

Of whatever angel may choose to flare
Suddenly at my elbow. I only know that a rook
Ordering its black feathers can so shine
As to seize my senses, haul
My eyelids up, and grant   30

A brief respite from fear
Of total neutrality. With luck,
Trekking stubborn through this season
Of fatigue, I shall
Patch together a content   35

Of sorts. Miracles occur,
If you care to call those spasmodic
Tricks of radiance miracles. The wait's begun again,
The long wait for the angel,
For that rare, random descent.   40

spasmodic: occurring in bursts.

'Hunches a wet black rook'

👤 Personal Response

1. What is the mood of the poet? How does the weather described in the poem reflect this mood?
2. Select one image from the poem that you find particularly striking or dramatic. Briefly explain your choice.
3. What do you think the final stanza means? Consider the phrase 'The wait's begun again'. What is the poet waiting for?

👁 Critical Literacy

'Black Rook in Rainy Weather' was written while Plath was studying in Cambridge in 1956. It contains many of her trademarks, including the exploration of emotions, the use of weather, colour and natural objects as symbols, and the dreamlike world. She explores a number of themes: fear of the future, lack of identity and poetic inspiration.

Stanza one begins with the straightforward description of a bird grooming itself, which the poet observes on a rainy day. But on closer inspection, the mood of the poem is set with the words 'stiff' and 'Hunches'. The bird is at the mercy of the elements ('wet') and there is no easy movement. **This atmospheric opening is dull and low key.** The black rook is a bird of ill omen. But the bird is presenting its best image to the world as it sits 'Arranging and rearranging its feathers'. Plath longed to excel in both life and art. If she were inspired by poetry, the rook would take on a new light as if on fire. Yet she doesn't see this happening. Even the weather is 'desultory' in the fading season of autumn. Poetic inspiration is miraculous; it is not ordinary. The world is experienced in a heightened way. Notice the long line, which seems out of proportion with the rest as she declares that she doesn't expect any order or 'design' in the haphazard weather. The decaying leaves will fall with no ritual, without any organisation. **This is a chaotic world**, a random place with no design, just as poetic inspiration happens by chance. It is also accidental, like the falling leaves.

After this low-key opening, the poem starts to take flight in stanzas three and four when the poet states: 'I desire'. Plath employs a witty metaphor as she looks for 'some backtalk' from the 'mute sky'. **She would like to connect with it.** It could happen on her walk, or even at home if she were to experience a 'certain minor light' shining from an ordinary, everyday object like a chair. The association of fire and light makes an ordinary moment special. It is 'hallowing'; it is giving generously ('largesse'). She is hoping against hope. Plath may be sceptical, but she is going forward carefully in case she misses the magic moment. **She must stay alert and watchful.** She must also be 'politic', wise.

Stanzas six, seven and eight explore poetic inspiration. Plath doesn't know if it will happen to her or how it will happen. Two contrasting attitudes are at loggerheads: hope and despair. The rook might inspire her: '**Miracles occur**'. If she were motivated, it would relieve 'total neutrality', this nothingness she feels when living uninspired. Although she is tired, she is insistent, 'stubborn'. The poet will have to 'Patch' something together. She shows human vulnerability, but she is trying. This new-found determination is a very different tone from the negative one at the beginning.

Literature was as important to Plath as friends and family. What she can't live without, therefore, is inspiration – her life would be a dark, passionless existence. **Depression** is an empty state with no feeling or direction, yet her view of creativity is romantic. It is miraculous, available only to a chosen few. 'The long wait for the angel' has begun. Notice the constant use of the personal pronoun 'I'. This is a poet who is very aware of self and her own personal responses to events and feelings. The outside world becomes a metaphor for her own interior world.

Plath uses both archaic language and slang, as if reinforcing the randomness of the world. This is also mirrored in the run-on lines. All is haphazard, but carefully arranged, so even the extended final sentence stretches out as it waits for the 'random descent' of inspiration. Throughout the poem's **carefully arranged disorder**, two worlds are seen. One is negative: 'desultory', 'mute', 'dull', 'stubborn', 'fatigue'. This is indicative of Plath's own bleak mood. The other world is positive: 'light', 'celestial', 'largesse', 'love', 'shine'. This offers the possibility of radiance.

✒ Writing About the Poem

'Plath's poems are carefully composed and beautifully phrased.' Write a paragraph in response to this statement, illustrating your answer with close reference to the poem 'Black Rook in Rainy Weather'.

Sample Paragraph

Just like the rook in 'Black Rook in Rainy Weather', Plath 'arranges and rearranges' her words with precision and care to communicate the dull life of 'total neutrality' which occurs when she is not inspired, when nothing sets 'the sight on fire'. I particularly admire how she arranges disorder in the poem. This mirrors the chance of poetic inspiration. Long lines poke untidily out of the first three stanzas, seeking the 'minor light' to 'Lean incandescent' upon them. I also like how the lines run in a seemingly untidy way into each other, as do some stanzas. Stanza three goes into four, as it describes the chance of a light coming from an ordinary object, such as a kitchen chair, which is seen only if the poet is inspired. The alliteration of 'rare, random' in the last line echoes the gift of poetic technique which will be given to the poet if she can receive the blessing of poetic inspiration: 'Miracles occur'.

EXAMINER'S COMMENT
Close reading of the poem is evident in this top-grade original response to Plath's poetic technique. Quotations are very well used here to highlight the poet's ability to create anarchic order.

✐ Class/Homework Exercises

1. Plath criticised the poem, 'Black Rook in Rainy Weather' for its 'glassy brittleness'. In your opinion, what does she mean? Refer to both the content and style of the poem, supporting your answer with reference to the text.
2. In your opinion, has the poet given up hope of being inspired? Use reference to the poem in your answer.

⊙ Points to Consider

- **Waiting for poetic inspiration, the hope for something better.**
- **Despondency – negative adjectives, harsh verbs.**
- **Miracle of inspiration, contrasting imagery of fire and light.**
- **Careful rhyme patterns echo design of the rook's plumage.**
- **Language – colloquial and formal, slang and religious terminology.**

POETRY FOCUS

2 The Times Are Tidy

Unlucky the hero born
In this province of the stuck record
Where the most watchful cooks go jobless
And the mayor's rôtisserie turns
Round of its own accord.   5

There's no career in the venture
Of riding against the lizard,
Himself withered these latter-days
To leaf-size from lack of action:
History's beaten the hazard.   10

The last crone got burnt up
More than eight decades back
With the love-hot herb, the talking cat,
But the children are better for it,
The cow milks cream an inch thick.   15

province: a remote place.
stuck record: the needle would sometimes get jammed on a vinyl music album.

rôtisserie: meat on a rotating skewer.

lizard: dragon.

crone: old witch.

'riding against the lizard'

👤 Personal Response

1. What is suggested by the poem's title? Is Plath being cynical about modern life? Develop your response in a short paragraph.
2. Select one image from the poem which suggests that the past was much more dangerous and exciting than the present. Comment on its effectiveness.
3. Do you agree or disagree with the speaker's view of modern life? Give reasons for your answer.

◉ Critical Literacy

'The Times Are Tidy' was written in 1958. In this short poem, Plath casts a cold eye on contemporary life and culture, which she sees as bland and unadventurous. The poem's ironic title clearly suggests Plath's dissatisfaction with the over-regulated society of her day. Do you think you are living in a heroic age or do you believe that most people have lost their sense of wonder? Is there anyone in public life whom you really admire?

Stanza one is dominated by hard-hitting images reflecting how the world of fairytale excitement has disappeared. From the outset, **the tone is scornful and dismissive**. Plath believes that any hero would be totally out of place amid the mediocrity of our times. True talent ('the most watchful cooks') is largely unrewarded. The unexpected imagery of the 'stuck record' and the mayor's rotating spit symbolise complacent monotony and lack of progress, particularly during the late 1950s, when Plath wrote the poem. Both images convey a sense of purposeless circling, of people going nowhere. It seems as though the poet is seething with frustration at the inertia and conformity of her own times.

Plath's **darkly embittered sense of humour** becomes evident in stanza two. She laments the current lack of honour and courage – something which once existed in the world of fairytales. Unlike the past, contemporary society is compromised. There are no idealistic dragon-slayers any more. The worker who dares to stand up and criticise ('riding against the lizard') is risking demotion. The modern dragon – a metaphor for the challenges we face – has even been reduced to a mere lizard. Despite this, we are afraid of confrontation and prefer to retreat. The verb 'withered' suggests the weakness and decay of our safe, modern world. The poet openly complains that 'History's beaten the hazard'. Over time, we have somehow defeated all sense of adventure and daring. These qualities belong in the distant past.

In stanza three, Plath continues to contrast past and present. Witches are no longer burned at the stake. This might well suggest that superstition has disappeared, and with it, all imagination. The last two lines are ironic in tone, reflecting the poet's deep **disenchantment with the excesses of our consumer society**. The final image – 'the cow milks cream an inch thick' – signifies overindulgence.

The poet clearly accepts that **society has changed for the worse**. Children may have everything they want nowadays, but they have lost their sense of wonder and excitement. Plath laments the loss of legendary heroism. Medieval dragons and wicked witches (complete with magic potions and talking cats) no longer exist. Her conclusion is that life today is unquestionably less interesting than it used to be. Unlike so much of Plath's work, the personal pronoun 'I' is not used in this poem. However, the highly

contemptuous views and weary, frustrated tone clearly suggest that Plath feels unfulfilled.

✒ Writing About the Poem

Write a paragraph in which you comment on Plath's critical tone in 'The Times Are Tidy'.

Sample Paragraph

The tone of voice in 'The Times Are Tidy' is extremely critical of modern life. Plath has nothing good to say about today's world as she sees it. The poem's title is self-satisfied, just like the neatly organised society that Plath seems to despise. The opening comment – 'Unlucky the hero born/In this province' – emphasises this negative tone. The poet's mocking attitude becomes increasingly disparaging as she rages against the unproductive images of easy living – 'the stuck record' and 'the mayor's rôtisserie'. Plath goes on to contrast today's apathetic society with the medieval era, when knights in armour existed. The poet omits all the positive aspects of modern life and chooses to give a very one-sided view. Plath ends on a sarcastic note, sneering at the advances of our world of plenty – 'cream an inch thick'. The voice here is both critical and superior.

EXAMINER'S COMMENT

This top-grade paragraph demonstrates strong analytical skills and is firmly focused on Plath's judgmental tone. The supporting references range widely and effectively illustrate the poet's critical attitude. Quotations are particularly well integrated and the management of language is assured throughout.

✒ Class/Homework Exercises

1. Outline the main theme in 'The Times Are Tidy'. In your answer, trace the way the poet develops her ideas during the course of the poem.
2. Trace the changing tones in the poem 'The Times Are Tidy'. Support your answer with close reference to the text.

⊙ Points to Consider

- **Poet's distaste for pursuit of materialism prevalent in 1950s American society.**

- **Collapse of moral standards in public life.**

- **Death of the spirit of adventure, no challenge to society's smugness.**

- **Humour and irony, derisive tone, entertaining images and sound effects.**

- **Contrast between modern 'tidy' times and 'untidy' times of legend.**

3 Morning Song

Love set you going like a fat gold watch.
The midwife slapped your footsoles, and your bald cry
Took its place among the elements.

midwife: a person trained to assist at childbirth.
elements: primitive, natural, atmospheric forces.

Our voices echo, magnifying your arrival. New statue.
In a drafty museum, your nakedness   5
Shadows our safety. We stand round blankly as walls.

I'm no more your mother
Than the cloud that distils a mirror to reflect its own slow
Effacement at the wind's hand.

Effacement: gradual disappearance.

All night your moth-breath   10
Flickers among the flat pink roses. I wake to listen:
A far sea moves in my ear.

pink roses: images on the wallpaper.

One cry, and I stumble from bed, cow-heavy and floral
In my Victorian nightgown.
Your mouth opens clean as a cat's. The window square   15

Whitens and swallows its dull stars. And now you try
Your handful of notes;
The clear vowels rise like balloons.

vowels: speech sounds made without stopping the flow of the breath.

'clear vowels rise'

👤 Personal Response

1. Comment on the suitability and effectiveness of the simile in line 1.
2. What is the attitude of the mother to the new arrival? Does her attitude change in the course of the poem? Refer to the text in your answer.
3. A metaphor links two things so that one idea explains or gives a new viewpoint about the other. Choose one interesting metaphor from the poem and comment on its effectiveness.

👁 Critical Literacy

'Morning Song' was written in 1961. Plath explores the complex issues of the relationship between a mother and her child, celebrating the birth of the infant but also touching on deep feelings of loss and separation.

Do all mothers immediately welcome and fall in love with a new baby? Are some of them overwhelmed or even depressed after giving birth? Are parents often anxious about the new responsibilities a baby brings? Plath wrote this poem after two intensely personal experiences, celebrating the birth of her daughter, Frieda, who was 10 months old, and shortly after a miscarriage. The poem is realistic and never strays into sentimentality or cliché. The title 'Morning' suggests a new beginning and 'Song' a celebration.

Stanza one describes the arrival of the child into the world in a confident, rhythmic sentence announcing the act of creation: 'Love set you going'. The simile comparing the child to a 'fat gold watch' suggests a plump baby, a rich and precious object. Broad vowel effects emphasise the physical presence of the infant. The 'ticking' sound conveys action and dynamism, but also the passage of time. Plath's child is now part of the mortal world where change and death are inevitable. At this moment of birth, the baby is the centre of attention as the midwife and parents surround her. But this is a cruel world, as we see from the words 'slapped' and 'bald'. The infant is part of the universe as she takes her place among the 'elements'. The verbs in this stanza are in the past tense – **the mother is looking back at the event**. The rest of the poem is written in the present tense, which adds to the immediacy of the experience.

Stanza two has a feeling of disorientation, as if the mother feels separated from the child now that she has left the womb. There is a nightmarish, surreal quality to the lines 'Our voices echo, magnifying your arrival'. Plath sees the child as a new exhibit ('New statue') in a museum. Commas and full stops break up the flow of the lines and **the tone becomes more stilted and detached**. The child as a work of art is special and unique, but the museum is 'drafty', again a reference to the harshness of the world. The baby's vulnerability is stressed by its 'nakedness'. The midwife's and parents' frozen response is caught in the phrase 'blankly as walls'. They anxiously observe, unsure about their ability to protect. This baby also represents a threat to

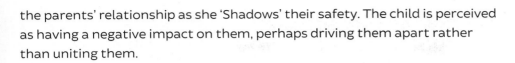

the parents' relationship as she 'Shadows' their safety. The child is perceived as having a negative impact on them, perhaps driving them apart rather than uniting them.

Stanza three focuses on the **complex relationship between child and mother**. Plath feels she can't be maternal ('no more your mother'). This is vividly shown in the image of the cloud that rains, creating a puddle. **But in the act of creation, it destroys itself and its destruction is reflected in the pool of water.** Throughout her life, the poet was haunted by a fear of her own personal failure. Does she see a conflict between becoming a mother and remaining a writer? She also realises that as the child grows and matures she will age, moving closer to death, and this will be reflected in the child's gaze. The mood of this stanza is one of estrangement and powerlessness. Notice how the three lines of the stanza run into each other as the cloud disappears.

In stanza four, the tone changes to one of intimate, maternal love as the caring mother becomes alert to her child's needs. The situation described is warm and homely – the 'flat pink roses' are very different from the chill 'museum' of a previous stanza. The fragile breathing of the little child is beautifully described as 'your moth-breath/Flickers'. **Onomatopoeia in 'Flickers' mimics the tiny breathing noises of the child.** The mother is anticipating her baby's needs as she wakes ('listen'). The breathing child evokes happy memories of Plath's seaside childhood ('A far sea moves in my ear').

The infant cries and the attentive mother springs into action. She laughs at herself as she describes the comical figure she makes, 'cow-heavy and floral' in stanza five. She feels awkward as she 'stumble[s]' to tend her child, whose eager mouth is shown by a startling image ('clean as a cat's') when it opens wide to receive the night feed of milk. **The stanza flows smoothly** over into stanza six, just as nature flows to its own rhythm and does not obey clocks or any other man-made rules. Night becomes morning as the child swallows the milk and the window swallows the stars.

Children demand a parent's time and energy. **This child now defines herself** with her unique collection of sounds ('Your handful of notes'). This poem opened with the instinctive, elemental 'bald' cry of a newborn, but closes on a lovely, happy image of music and colour, as the baby's song's notes 'rise like balloons'.

✒ Writing About the Poem

'Morning Song' begins with the word 'Love'. How does Plath treat the theme of love over the course of the poem? Support your answer with reference to the text.

Sample Paragraph

'Morning Song' treats the theme of love by addressing both the joy of parental love and also the shock new parents experience. It opens with a tender statement that the poet's daughter was conceived in love – 'Love set you going'. This warm tone changes, however, to the curiously disengaged voice of the second stanza where the parents 'stand round blankly as walls'. The enormity of the event of the birth of their child into a harsh world, 'drafty museum', seems to overwhelm them. In the third stanza, the sense of separation deepens and Plath admits that she does not really feel like the child's mother at all. Instead, she explores her feelings of worthlessness through the complex image of the disintegrating cloud, which creates only to be destroyed in the act of creation. The poem ends on a more affectionate note as the attentive mother feeds her child while listening to her baby's song 'rise like balloons'. For me, the gentle effect of this image suggests the innocence of the infant.

EXAMINER'S COMMENT

A succinct, focused and well-supported response showing good personal engagement with the poem. The central point about Plath's conflicting emotions is clearly stated and the development of thought is traced throughout the poem. Excellent language control and impressive vocabulary (e.g. 'curiously disengaged voice', 'complex image of the disintegrating cloud') are in keeping with the top-grade standard.

Class/Homework Exercises

1. 'The sense of alienation is often agonisingly evoked in Plath's poetry.' To what extent is this true of 'Morning Song'? Support your answer with reference to the poem.
2. 'Sylvia Plath makes effective use of unusual and startling imagery to explore deeply personal themes.' Discuss this view with particular reference to the poem, 'Morning Song'.

Points to Consider

- Poet's ambivalent attitude to motherhood: loss of individual identity conflicting with deep love.

- Striking, unexpected imagery: contrasts between the child's delicacy and the mother's clumsiness.

- Development from inanimate objects (the watch, statue, mirror, cloud) to animate objects (moth, cow, cat, singer).

- Varying tones: tender, anxious, alienated, reflective, caring, fulfilled.

- Intense feelings of dislocation replaced by increasing sense of inter-connectedness.

4 Finisterre

This was the land's end: the last fingers, knuckled and rheumatic,
Cramped on nothing. Black
Admonitory cliffs, and the sea exploding
With no bottom, or anything on the other side of it,
Whitened by the faces of the drowned.   5
Now it is only gloomy, a dump of rocks –
Leftover soldiers from old, messy wars.
The sea cannons into their ear, but they don't budge.
Other rocks hide their grudges under the water.

The cliffs are edged with trefoils, stars and bells   10
Such as fingers might embroider, close to death,
Almost too small for the mists to bother with.
The mists are part of the ancient paraphernalia –
Souls, rolled in the doom-noise of the sea.
They bruise the rocks out of existence, then resurrect them.   15
They go up without hope, like sighs.
I walk among them, and they stuff my mouth with cotton.
When they free me, I am beaded with tears.

Our Lady of the Shipwrecked is striding toward the horizon,
Her marble skirts blown back in two pink wings.   20
A marble sailor kneels at her foot distractedly, and at his foot
A peasant woman in black
Is praying to the monument of the sailor praying.
Our Lady of the Shipwrecked is three times life size,
Her lips sweet with divinity.   25
She does not hear what the sailor or the peasant is saying –
She is in love with the beautiful formlessness of the sea.

Gull-colored laces flap in the sea drafts
Beside the postcard stalls.
The peasants anchor them with conches. One is told: 30
'These are the pretty trinkets the sea hides,
Little shells made up into necklaces and toy ladies.
They do not come from the Bay of the Dead down there,
But from another place, tropical and blue,
We have never been to.   35
These are our crêpes. Eat them before they blow cold.'

land's end: literally 'Finisterre'; the western tip of Brittany.

Admonitory: warning.

trefoils: three-leaved plants.

paraphernalia: discarded items.
doom-noise: hopeless sounds.

Our Lady of the Shipwrecked: the mother of Christ prayed for sailors.

conches: shells.

trinkets: cheap jewellery.

crêpes: light pancakes.

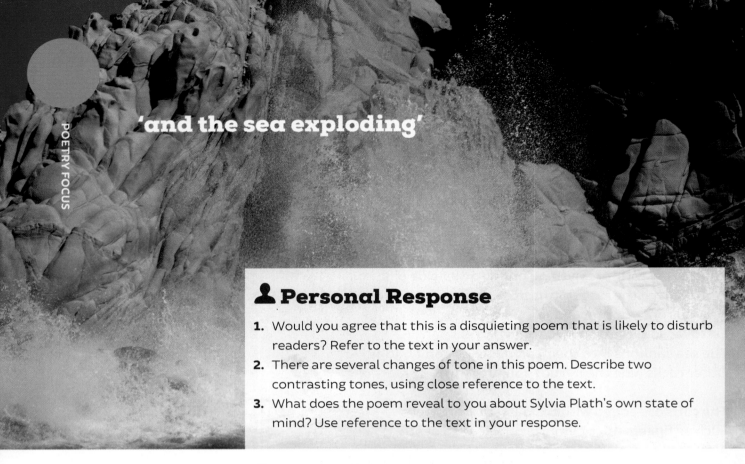

'and the sea exploding'

👤 Personal Response

1. Would you agree that this is a disquieting poem that is likely to disturb readers? Refer to the text in your answer.
2. There are several changes of tone in this poem. Describe two contrasting tones, using close reference to the text.
3. What does the poem reveal to you about Sylvia Plath's own state of mind? Use reference to the text in your response.

👁 Critical Literacy

'Finisterre' was written in 1960 following Plath's visit to Brittany, France. As with many of her poems, the description of the place can be interpreted both literally and metaphorically.

The sea has always inspired poets and artists. It is at times welcoming, menacing, beautiful, peaceful and mysterious. Throughout her short life, Sylvia Plath loved the ocean. She spent her childhood years on the Atlantic coast just north of Boston. This setting provides a source for many of her poetic ideas. Terror and death loom large in her descriptive poem 'Finisterre', in which the pounding rhythm of storm waves off the Breton coast represents **Plath's inner turmoil**.

Stanza one opens dramatically and immediately creates a disturbing atmosphere. Plath describes the rocky headland as being 'knuckled and rheumatic'. In a series of powerful images ('Black/Admonitory cliffs', 'the sea exploding'), the poet recreates the uproar and commotion of the scene. The **grisly personification** is startling, linking the shoreline with suffering and decay. There is a real sense of conflict between sea and land. Both are closely associated with death ('the faces of the drowned'). The jagged rocks are compared to 'Leftover soldiers' who 'hide their grudges under the water'. There is a noticeable tone of regret and protest against the futility of conflict, which is denounced as 'old, messy wars'.

Plath's **negative imagery** is relentless, with harsh consonant sounds ('knuckled', 'Cramped') emphasising the force of raging storm waves. The use of contrasting colours intensifies the imagery. As the 'sea cannons' against the headland, the atmosphere is 'only gloomy'. It is hard not to see the bleak seascape as a reflection of Plath's own unhappy state of mind.

In stanza two, the poet turns away from the cruel sea and focuses momentarily on the small plants clinging to the cliff edge. However, these 'trefoils, stars and bells' are also 'close to death'. If anything, they reinforce the **unsettling mood** and draw the poet back to the ocean mists, which she thinks of as symbolising the souls of the dead, lost in 'the doom-noise of the sea'. Plath imagines the heavy mists transforming the rocks, destroying them 'out of existence' before managing to 'resurrect them' again. In a **surreal sequence**, the poet enters the water ('I walk among them') and joins the wretched souls who lie there. Her growing sense of panic is suggested by the stark admission: 'they stuff my mouth with cotton'. The experience is agonising and leaves her 'beaded with tears'.

Plath's thoughts turn to a marble statue of 'Our Lady of the Shipwrecked' in stanza three. Once again, in her imagination, she creates a **dramatic narrative** around the religious figure. This monument to the patron saint of the ocean should offer some consolation to the kneeling sailor and a grieving peasant woman who pray to the mother of God. Ironically, their pleas are completely ignored – 'She does not hear' their prayers because 'She is in love with the beautiful formlessness of the sea'. Is the poet expressing her own **feelings of failure and despondency here**? Or is she also attacking the ineffectiveness of religion? The description of the statue is certainly unflattering. The figure is flighty and self-centred: 'Her marble skirts blown back in two pink wings'. In contrast, the powerful ocean remains fascinating.

In the fourth stanza, Plath turns her attention to the local Bretons who sell souvenirs to tourists. Unlike the previous three stanzas, **the mood appears to be much lighter** as the poet describes the friendly stall-keepers going about their business. It is another irony that their livelihood (selling 'pretty trinkets') is dependent on the sea and its beauty. Like the statue, the locals seem unconcerned by the tragic history of the ocean. Indeed, they are keen to play down 'the Bay of the Dead' and explain that what they sell is imported 'from another place, tropical and blue'. In the final line, a stall-holder advises the poet to enjoy the pancakes she has bought: 'Eat them before they blow cold'. Although the immediate mood is untroubled, the final phrase brings us back to the earlier – and more disturbing – parts of the poem where Plath described the raging storms and the nameless lost souls who have perished at sea.

✒ Writing About the Poem

Write a paragraph commenting on Sylvia Plath's use of detailed description in 'Finisterre'.

Sample Paragraph

In 'Finisterre', the opening images of the rocks – 'the last fingers, knuckled and rheumatic' – are of decrepit old age. The strong visual impact is a feature of Plath's writing. The first half of the poem is filled with memorable details of the windswept coastline. Plath uses broad vowels to evoke a pervading feeling of dejection. Words such as 'drowned' and 'doom' help to create this dismal effect. The dramatic aural image, 'The sea cannons', echoes the roar of turbulent waves crashing onto the rocks. Plath's close observation is also seen in her portrait of the holy statue – 'Her lips sweet with divinity'. The poem ends with a painstaking sketch of the traders selling postcards and 'Little shells made up into necklaces and toy ladies'. Overall, the use of details throughout the poem leaves readers with a strong sense of place and community.

EXAMINER'S COMMENT

Quotations are very well used here to highlight Plath's ability to create specific scenes and moods through precise description. The examples range over much of the poem and the writing is both varied and controlled throughout. A top-grade response.

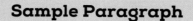 Class/Homework Exercises

1. It has been said that vivid, startling imagery gives a surreal quality to 'Finisterre'. Using reference to the poem, write a paragraph responding to this statement.
2. 'Plath's unique imagination addresses unhappiness and hopelessness.' To what extent do you agree with this statement? Support your answer with suitable reference to 'Finisterre', referring to the poem's content and style.

⊙ Points to Consider

- **Fearful, ominous description of ordinary place.**
- **Disquieting tone of Our Lady of the Shipwrecked as aloof and self-absorbed.**
- **Ironic contrast between sweet appearance of statue and grim reality of shipwrecks in bay.**
- **Formal structure of poem contrasts with terror of situation.**
- **Striking images and sounds, personification, rich symbolism.**

5   **Mirror**

I am silver and exact. I have no preconceptions.
Whatever I see I swallow immediately
Just as it is, unmisted by love or dislike.
I am not cruel, only truthful –
The eye of a little god, four-cornered.   5
Most of the time I meditate on the opposite wall.
It is pink, with speckles. I have looked at it so long
I think it is part of my heart. But it flickers.
Faces and darkness separate us over and over.

Now I am a lake. A woman bends over me,   10
Searching my reaches for what she really is.
Then she turns to those liars, the candles or the moon.
I see her back, and reflect it faithfully.
She rewards me with tears and an agitation of hands.
I am important to her. She comes and goes.   15
Each morning it is her face that replaces the darkness.
In me she has drowned a young girl, and in me an old woman
Rises toward her day after day, like a terrible fish.

exact: accurate, giving all details; to insist on payment.
preconceptions: thoughts already formed.

reaches: range of distance or depth.

agitation: shaking, trembling.

'The eye of a little god, four-cornered

👤 Personal Response

1. Select two images that suggest the dark, sinister side of the mirror. Comment briefly on your two choices.
2. What, in your opinion, is the main theme or message of this poem?
3. Write your own personal response to this poem, referring closely to the text in your answer.

👁 Critical Literacy

'Mirror' was written in 1961 as Sylvia Plath approached her twenty-ninth birthday. In this dark poem, Plath views the inevitability of old age and death, our preoccupation with image and our search for an identity.

Do you think everyone looks at themselves in a mirror? Would you consider that people are fascinated, disappointed or even obsessed by what they see? Does a mirror accurately reflect the truth? Do people actually see what is reflected or is it distorted by notions and ideals which they or society have? Consider the use of mirrors in fairytales: 'Mirror, mirror on the wall, who's the fairest of them all?' Mirrors are also used in myths – like the story of Narcissus, who drowned having fallen in love with his reflection – and in children's books such as *Through the Looking Glass*. Mirrors are also used in horror films as the dividing line between fantasy and reality.

In this poem, Plath gives us a startling new angle on an everyday object. The function of a mirror is to reflect whatever is put in front of it. Stanza one opens with a ringing declaration by the mirror: 'I am silver and exact'. This **personification has a sinister effect** as the mirror describes an almost claustrophobic relationship with a particular woman. The dramatic voice of the mirror is clear and precise. It announces that it reports exactly what there is without any alteration. We have to decide if the mirror is telling the truth, as it says it has no bias ('no preconceptions'). It does not judge; it reflects the image received. The mirror adopts the position of an impartial observer, but it is active, almost ruthless ('I swallow').

Yet how truthful is a mirror image, as it flattens a three-dimensional object into two dimensions? The image sent out has no depth. The voice of the mirror becomes smug as it sees itself as the ruler of those reflected ('The eye of a little god'). Our obsession with ourselves causes us to worship at the mirror that reflects our image. In the modern world, people are often disappointed with their reflection, wishing they were thinner, younger, better looking. But **the mirror insists it tells the truth**; it doesn't flatter or hurt. The mirror explains how it spends its day gazing at the opposite wall, which is carefully described as 'pink, with speckles'. It feels as if the wall is part of itself. This reflection is disturbed by the faces of people and the dying light. The passage of time is evoked in the phrase 'over and over'.

In stanza two, the tension increases and the mirror announces that it is 'a lake'. Both are flat surfaces that reflect. However, a lake is another dimension, it has depth. **There is danger.** The image is now drawn into its murky depths. The woman is looking in and down, not just at. It is as if she is struggling to find who she really is, what her true path in life is. Plath frequently questioned who she was. Expectations for young women in the 1950s were limiting. Appearance was important, as were the roles of wife, mother and homemaker. But Plath also wanted to write: 'Will I submerge my embarrassing desires and aspirations, refuse to face myself?' The mirror becomes irritated and jealous of the woman as she turns to the deceptive soft light of 'those liars, the candles or the moon'. **The woman is dissatisfied with her image.** In her insecurity, she weeps and wrings her hands. Plath always tried to do her best, to be a model student, almost desperate to excel and be affirmed. Is there a danger in seeking perfection? Do we need to love ourselves as we are? Again, the mirror pompously announces 'I am important to her'.

The march of time passing is emphasised by 'comes and goes', 'Each morning' and 'day after day'. The woman keeps coming back. The mirror's sense of its significance is shown by the frequent use of 'I' and the repetition of 'in me'. As time passes, the woman is facing the truth of her human condition as her reflection changes and ages in the mirror. Her youth is 'drowned', to be replaced by a monstrous vision of an old woman 'like a terrible fish'. **The lonely drama of living and dying is recorded with a nightmarish quality**. There is no comforting rhyme in the poem, only the controlled rhythm of time. The mirror does not give what a human being desires: comfort and warmth. Instead, it impersonally reminds us of our mortality.

✒ Writing About the Poem

What is your personal response to the relationship between the mirror and the woman? Support your views with reference to the poem.

Sample Paragraph

I feel the mirror is like an alter ego, which is coolly appraising the woman in an unforgiving way. The mirror is 'silver'. Although the mirror repeatedly states that it does not judge, 'I have no preconceptions', the woman feels judged and inadequate: 'She rewards me with tears and an agitation of hands.' I think the relationship between the woman and the mirror is dangerous. She does indeed 'drown' in the mirror, as she never feels good enough. The complacent mirror rules her like a 'little god, four-cornered'. This relationship shows a troubled self, a lack of self-love.

Who is saying that the older woman is 'like a terrible fish'? I think the mirror has become the voice of a society which values women only for their looks and youth, rather than what they are capable of achieving.

✒ Class/Homework Exercises

1. 'Plath's use of dramatic monologue is an unsettling experience for readers.' Discuss this statement with reference to 'Mirror'.
2. 'All who share the human condition have a bright and dark side.' Discuss Plath's exploration of this theme in her poem 'Mirror'. In your response, pay particular attention to her use of imagery.

⊙ Points to Consider

- Key themes include transience and mortality.
- Chilling personification of the mirror.
- Exploration of identity, duality of being.
- Startlingly shocking imagery and drama convey frightening tone.

6 Pheasant

You said you would kill it this morning.
Do not kill it. It startles me still,
The jut of that odd, dark head, pacing

Through the uncut grass on the elm's hill.
It is something to own a pheasant,   5
Or just to be visited at all.

I am not mystical: it isn't
As if I thought it had a spirit.
It is simply in its element.

That gives it a kingliness, a right.   10
The print of its big foot last winter,
The tail-track, on the snow in our court –

The wonder of it, in that pallor,
Through crosshatch of sparrow and starling.
Is it its rareness, then? It is rare.   15

But a dozen would be worth having,
A hundred, on that hill – green and red,
Crossing and recrossing: a fine thing!

It is such a good shape, so vivid.
It's a little cornucopia.   20
It unclaps, brown as a leaf, and loud,

Settles in the elm, and is easy.
It was sunning in the narcissi.
I trespass stupidly. Let be, let be.

You: probably addressed to Plath's husband.

jut: extending outwards.

mystical: spiritual, supernatural.

pallor: pale colour.

crosshatch: criss-cross trail.

cornucopia: unexpected treasure.

narcissi: bright spring flowers.

'in its element'

👤 Personal Response

1. Comment on Sylvia Plath's attitude to nature based on your reading of 'Pheasant'.
2. Compile a list of the poet's arguments for not killing the pheasant.
3. Write a paragraph on the effectiveness of Plath's imagery in the poem.

👁 Critical Literacy

'Pheasant' was written in 1962 and reflects Plath's deep appreciation of the natural world. Its enthusiastic mood contrasts with much of her more disturbing work. The poem is structured in eight tercets (three-line stanzas) with a subtle, interlocking rhyming pattern (known as terza rima).

The poem opens with an urgent plea by Plath to spare the pheasant's life: 'Do not kill it'. In the first two stanzas, the tone is tense as the poet offers a variety of reasons for sparing this impressive game bird. She is both shocked and excited by the pheasant: 'It startles me still'. Plath admits to feeling honoured in the presence of the bird: 'It is something to own a pheasant'. The broken rhythm of the early lines adds an abruptness that heightens the sense of urgency. **Plath seems spellbound by the bird's beauty** ('The jut of that odd, dark head') now that it is under threat.

But the poet is also keen to play down any sentimentality in her attitude to the pheasant. Stanza three begins with a straightforward explanation of her attitude: 'it isn't/As if I thought it had a spirit'. Instead, **she values the bird for its graceful beauty and naturalness**: 'It is simply in its element.' Plath is keen to show her recognition of the pheasant's right to exist because it possesses a certain majestic quality, 'a kingliness'.

In stanza four, the poet recalls an earlier winter scene when she marvelled at the pheasant's distinctive footprint in the snow. The bird has made an even greater impression on Plath, summed up in the key phrase 'The wonder of it', at the start of stanza five. She remembers **the colourful pheasant's distinguishing marks against the pale snow**, so unlike the 'crosshatch' pattern of smaller birds, such as the sparrow and starling. This makes the pheasant particularly 'rare' and valuable in Plath's eyes.

The poet can hardly contain her regard for the pheasant and her tone becomes increasingly enthusiastic in stanza six as she dreams of having first a 'dozen' and then a 'hundred' of the birds. In a few **well-chosen details**, she highlights their colour and energy ('green and red,/Crossing and recrossing') before adding an emphatic compliment: 'a fine thing!' Her delight continues into stanza seven, where Plath proclaims her ceaseless admiration for the pheasant: 'It's a little cornucopia', an inspirational source of joy and surprise.

Throughout the poem, the poet has emphasised that the pheasant rightly belongs in its natural surroundings, and this is also true of the final lines. Stanza eight is considered and assured. From the poet's point of view, **the pheasant's right to live is beyond dispute**. While the bird is 'sunning in the narcissi', she herself has become the unwelcome intruder: 'I trespass stupidly'. Plath ends by echoing the opening appeal to spare the pheasant's life: 'Let be, let be.' The quietly insistent repetition and the underlying tone of unease are a final reminder of the need to respect nature.

It has been suggested that the pheasant symbolises Plath's insecure relationship with Ted Hughes. For various reasons, their marriage was under severe strain in 1962 and Plath feared that Hughes was intent on ending it. This interpretation adds a greater poignancy to the poem.

✒ Writing About the Poem

There are several mood changes in 'Pheasant'. What do you consider to be the dominant mood in the poem? Refer to the text in your answer.

Sample Paragraph

The mood at the beginning of 'Pheasant' is nervous and really uptight. Plath seems to have given up hope about the pheasant. It is facing death. She repeats the word 'kill' and admits to being shocked at the very thought of what the bird is facing. But she herself seems desperate and fearful. This is shown by the sentence, 'Do not kill it'. But the outlook soon changes. Plath describes the pheasant 'pacing' and 'in its element'. But she seems less stressed as she describes the 'kingliness' of the pheasant. But the mood soon settles down as Plath celebrates the life of this really beautiful bird. The mood becomes calmer and ends in almost a whisper, 'Let be, let be'.

EXAMINER'S COMMENT

This is a reasonable middle-grade answer to the question, pointing out the change of mood following the first stanza. Some worthwhile references are used to show the poem's principal mood. The expression, however, is flawed in places (e.g. repeatedly using 'But' to start sentences). This response requires more critical analysis and development to raise the standard.

✒ Class/Homework Exercises

1. Plath sets out to convince the reader of the pheasant's right to life in this poem. Does she succeed in her aim? Give reasons for your answer.
2. 'Sylvia Plath's deep appreciation of the harmonious order of the natural world is expressed through vivid imagery.' To what extent is this true of her poem 'Pheasant'? Support your answer with reference to the text.

⊙ Points to Consider

- Heartfelt plea on behalf of the rights of wild creatures.
- Graphic description of beauty of bird.
- Tension, poet as intruder.
- Imperatives (verbal commands) inject urgency.
- Subtle music, casual flow of the rhythm of normal speech.

7 Elm

Title: the wych elm is a large deciduous tree, with a massive straight trunk and tangled branches. It was once a favourite timber of coffin makers. Plath dedicated the poem to a close friend, Ruth Fainlight, another American poet.

For Ruth Fainlight

I know the bottom, she says. I know it with my great tap root:
It is what you fear.
I do not fear it: I have been there.

Is it the sea you hear in me,
Its dissatisfactions?   5
Or the voice of nothing, that was your madness?

Love is a shadow.
How you lie and cry after it
Listen: these are its hooves: it has gone off, like a horse.

All night I shall gallop thus, impetuously,   10
Till your head is a stone, your pillow a little turf,
Echoing, echoing.

Or shall I bring you the sound of poisons?
This is rain now, this big hush.
And this is the fruit of it: tin-white, like arsenic.   15

I have suffered the atrocity of sunsets.
Scorched to the root
My red filaments burn and stand, a hand of wires.

Now I break up in pieces that fly about like clubs.
A wind of such violence   20
Will tolerate no bystanding: I must shriek.

The moon, also, is merciless: she would drag me
Cruelly, being barren.
Her radiance scathes me. Or perhaps I have caught her.

I let her go. I let her go   25
Diminished and flat, as after radical surgery.
How your bad dreams possess and endow me.

the bottom: lowest depths.
tap root: the main root.

arsenic: poison.

atrocity: massacre, carnage

filaments: fibres, nerves.

scathes: injures, scalds.

I am inhabited by a cry.
Nightly it flaps out
Looking, with its hooks, for something to love.   30

I am terrified by this dark thing
That sleeps in me;
All day I feel its soft, feathery turnings, its malignity.   **malignity:** evil.

Clouds pass and disperse.   **disperse:** scatter widely.
Are those the faces of love, those pale irretrievables?   35   **irretrievables:** things lost
Is it for such I agitate my heart?   for ever.

I am incapable of more knowledge.
What is this, this face
So murderous in its strangle of branches? –

Its snaky acids hiss.   40   **snaky acids:** deceptive
It petrifies the will. These are the isolate, slow faults   poisons.
That kill, that kill, that kill.   **petrifies:** terrifies.

'I am terrified by this dark thing'

👤 Personal Response

1. There are many sinister nature images in this poem. Select two that you find particularly unsettling and comment on their effectiveness.
2. Trace and examine how love is presented and viewed by the poet. Support the points you make with reference to the text.
3. Write your own individual response to this poem, referring closely to the text in your answer.

◉ Critical Literacy

Written in April 1962, 'Elm' is one of Sylvia Plath's most intensely dramatic poems. Plath personifies the elm tree to create a surreal scene. It 'speaks' in a traumatic voice to someone else, the 'you' of line 2, the poet herself – or the reader, perhaps. The two voices interact throughout the poem, almost always expressing pain and anguish. Critics often associate these powerful emotions with the poet's own personal problems – Plath had experienced electric shock treatment for depression. However, this may well limit our understanding of what is a complex exploration of many emotions.

The opening stanza is unnerving. The poet appears to be dramatising an exchange between herself and the elm by imagining what the tree might say to her. The immediate effect is eerily surreal. From the start, **the narrative voice is obsessed with instability and despair**: 'I know the bottom'. The tree is described in both physical terms ('my great tap root' penetrating far into the ground) and also as a state of mind ('I do not fear it'). The depth of depression imagined is reinforced by the repetition of 'I know' and the stark simplicity of the chilling comment 'It is what you fear'.

The bizarre exchange between the two 'speakers' continues in stanza two. The elm questions the poet about the nature of her **mental state**. Does the wind blowing through its branches remind her of the haunting sound of the sea? Or even 'the voice of nothing' – the numbing experience of madness?

Stanzas three and four focus on the dangers and disappointments of love – 'a shadow'. The tone is fearful, emphasised by the comparison of a wild horse that has 'gone off'. The relentless sounds of the wind in the elm will be a bitter reminder, 'echoing' this loss of love 'Till your head is a stone'. **Assonance** is effectively used here to heighten the sense of hurt and abandonment. For much of the middle section of the poem (stanzas five to nine), the elm's intimidating voice continues to dramatise a series of horrifying experiences associated with insanity. The tree has endured extreme elements – rain ('the sound of poisons'), sunshine ('Scorched to the root'), wind ('of such violence') and also the moon ('Her radiance scathes me'). **The harsh imagery and frenzied language** ('burn', 'shriek', 'merciless') combine to create a sense of shocking destructiveness.

Stanzas ten and eleven mark a turning point where the voices of the tree and the poet become indistinguishable. This is achieved by the seemingly harmless image of an owl inhabiting the branches, searching for 'something to love'. The speaker is haunted by 'this dark thing'. The **poet's vulnerability** is particularly evident in her stark admission: 'I feel its soft, feathery turnings, its malignity'. Plath has come to relate her unknown demons to a deadly tumour.

In the last three stanzas, the poet's voice seems more distant and calm before the final storm. The image of the passing clouds ('the faces of love') highlight the notion of rejection as the root cause of Plath's depression. The poem ends on a visionary note when she imagines being confronted by a 'murderous' snake that appears in the branches: 'It petrifies the will'. The scene of **growing terror builds to a hideous climax** until her own mental and emotional states (her 'slow faults') end up destroying her. The intensity of the final line, 'That kill, that kill, that kill', leaves readers with a harrowing understanding of Plath's paralysis of despair.

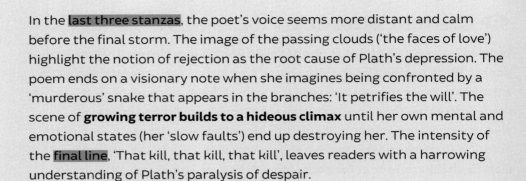

✒ Writing About the Poem

Do you think that 'Elm' has a surreal, nightmarish quality? In your response, refer to the text to support your views.

Sample Paragraph

I agree that Plath created a disturbing mood in 'Elm'. Giving the tree a voice of its own is like something from a child's fairy story. Plath compares love to a galloping horse. The poem is mainly about depression and madness. So it's bound to be out of the ordinary. The speaker is confused and asks weird questions, such as 'Is it the sea you hear in me?' She is obsessive and totally paranoid. Everything is against her, as far as she imagines it. The weather is an enemy even, the rain is 'tin-white like arsenic'. The end is as if she is having a dream and imagines a fierce snake in the tree coming after her. This represents Plath's deepest nightmare, the fear of loneliness. Violent images – 'a hand of wires', 'snaky acids hiss' – create a surreal atmosphere. The poem is confusing – especially the images.

EXAMINER'S COMMENT

This short mid-grade paragraph includes some worthwhile references to the poem's disturbing aspects. The points are note-like, however, and the writing style lacks control in places. Effective use of apt quotations.

✎ Class/Homework Exercises

1. What evidence of Plath's deep depression and hypersensitivity is revealed in the poem 'Elm'? Refer closely to the text in your answer.
2. Plath said of her later poetry, 'I speak them to myself ... aloud'. In your opinion, how effective are the sound effects and use of direct speech in the poem 'Elm'? Support your views with accurate quotation.

⊙ Points to Consider

- **Inner torment, awful fear of being oneself.**
- **Terrifying personification of elm.**
- **Rich symbolism and imagery, effective sounds.**
- **Nightmare world, surreal mood, paralysis of fear, threat of madness.**
- **Simple unvarnished style, poem overflows with poet's feelings of lost love.**

Poppies in July

SYLVIA PLATH

Little poppies, little hell flames,
Do you do no harm?

hell flames: most poppies are red, flame-like.

You flicker. I cannot touch you.
I put my hands among the flames. Nothing burns.

And it exhausts me to watch you   5
Flickering like that, wrinkly and clear red, like the skin of a mouth.

A mouth just bloodied.
Little bloody skirts!

There are fumes that I cannot touch.
Where are your opiates, your nauseous capsules?   10

fumes: the effects of drugs.

opiates: sleep-inducing narcotics.
nauseous: causing sickness.

If I could bleed, or sleep! –
If my mouth could marry a hurt like that!

Or your liquors seep to me, in this glass capsule,
Dulling and stilling.

liquors: drug vapours.
capsule: small container.

But colorless. Colorless.   15

colorless: drained, lifeless.

'You flicker. I cannot touch you'.

👤 Personal Response

1. Comment on the title, 'Poppies in July'. Is the title misleading? Give a reason for your response.
2. What evidence can you find in 'Poppies in July' that the speaker is yearning to escape?
3. Colour imagery plays a significant role in the poem. Comment on how effectively colour is used.

👁 Critical Literacy

Like most confessional writers, Sylvia Plath's work reflects her own personal experiences, without filtering any of the painful emotions. She wrote 'Poppies in July' in the summer of 1962, during the break-up of her marriage.

The first stanza is marked by a sense of unease and foreboding. The speaker (almost certainly Plath herself) compares the blazing red poppies to 'little hell flames' before directly confronting them: 'Do you do no harm?' **Her distress is obvious** from the start. The poem's title may well have led readers to expect a more conventional nature poem. Instead, the flowers are presented as being highly treacherous, and all the more deceptive because they are 'little'.

Plath develops the fire image in lines 3–6. However, even though she places her hands 'among the flames', she finds that 'Nothing burns' and she is forced to watch them 'Flickering'. It almost seems as though she is so tired and numb that **she has transcended pain** and can experience nothing: 'it exhausts me to watch you'. Ironically, the more vivid the poppies are, the more lethargic she feels.

The uncomfortable and disturbed mood increases in the fourth stanza with two **startling images**, both personifying the flowers. Comparing the poppy to 'A mouth just bloodied' suggests recent violence and physical suffering. The 'bloody skirts' metaphor is equally harrowing. There is further evidence of the poet's overpowering weariness in the prominent use of broad vowel sounds, for example in 'exhausts', 'mouth' and 'bloodied'.

In the fifth stanza, Plath's disorientated state turns to a distracted longing for escape. Having failed to use the vibrancy of the poppies to distract her from her pain, she now craves the feeling of oblivion or unconsciousness. But although she desires the dulling effects of drugs derived from the poppies, her **tone reflects her feelings of helplessness** as she describes the 'fumes that I cannot touch'.

The mood becomes even more distraught in lines 11–12, with the poet begging for any alternative to her anguished state. 'If I could bleed, or sleep!'

is an emphatic plea for release. It is her final attempt to retain some control of her life in the face of an overwhelming sense of powerlessness. Plath's **growing alienation** seems so unbearably intense at this point that it directly draws the reader's sympathy.

The last three lines record the poet's surrender, perhaps a kind of death wish. Worn down by her inner demons and the bright colours of the poppies, Plath lets herself become resigned to a 'colorless' world of nothingness. Her **complete passivity** and vulnerability are emphasised by the dreamlike quality of the phrase 'Dulling and stilling'. As she drifts into a death-like 'colorless' private hell, there remains a terrible sense of betrayal, as if she is still being haunted by the bright red flowers. The ending of 'Poppies in July' is so dark and joyless that it is easy to understand why the poem is often seen as a desperate cry for help.

✒ Writing About the Poem

'Poppies in July' is one of Plath's most disturbing poems. What aspects of the poem affected you most?

Sample Paragraph

'Poppies in July' was written when Plath was struggling with the fact that her husband had deserted her. This affected her deeply and it is clear that the poppies are a symbol of this difficult time. Everything about the poem is negative. The images of the poppies are nearly all associated with fire and blood. Plath's language is alarming when she compares the poppies to 'little hell flames' and also 'the skin of a mouth'. The most disturbing aspect is Plath's own unstable mind. She seems to be in a kind of trance, obsessed by the red colours of the poppies, which remind her of blood. She seems suicidal – 'If I could bleed'. For me, this is the most disturbing moment in the poem. The poet cannot stand reality and seeks a way out through drugs or death. The last image is of Plath sinking into a dull state of drowsiness, unable to cope with the world around her.

EXAMINER'S COMMENT

Overall, a solid high-grade response which responds personally to the question. While some focus is placed on the disturbing thought in the poem, there could have been a more thorough exploration of Plath's style and how it enhances her theme of depression.

✒ Class/Homework Exercises

1. Would you agree that loneliness and pain are the central themes of 'Poppies in July'? Refer to the text of the poem when writing your response.

2. Discuss how the poet uses vivid description in this poem to explore her negative feelings. Support your answer with reference to the text.

⊙ Points to Consider

- Desire to escape into oblivion.

- Personal aspect, engaged in inner conflict.

- Compelling drama, upsetting imagery, intense mood of despair.

- Despairing mood conveyed in downward motion of poem.

- Contrast between dynamic, vivid flowers, a symbol of vibrancy of life, and longed-for dullness of oblivion.

The Arrival of
the Bee Box

I ordered this, this clean wood box
Square as a chair and almost too heavy to lift.
I would say it was the coffin of a midget
Or a square baby
Were there not such a din in it.   5

The box is locked, it is dangerous.
I have to live with it overnight
And I can't keep away from it.
There are no windows, so I can't see what is in there.
There is only a little grid, no exit.   10

grid: wire network.

I put my eye to the grid.
It is dark, dark,
With the swarmy feeling of African hands
Minute and shrunk for export,
Black on black, angrily clambering.   15

swarmy: like a large group of bees.

How can I let them out?
It is the noise that appalls me most of all,
The unintelligible syllables.
It is like a Roman mob,
Small, taken one by one, but my god, together!   20

I lay my ear to furious Latin.
I am not a Caesar.
I have simply ordered a box of maniacs.
They can be sent back.
They can die, I need feed them nothing, I am the owner.   25

Caesar: famous Roman ruler.

I wonder how hungry they are.
I wonder if they would forget me
If I just undid the locks and stood back and turned into a tree.
There is the laburnum, its blond colonnades,
And the petticoats of the cherry.   30

laburnum: tree with yellow hanging flowers.
colonnades: long groups of flowers arranged in a row of columns.

They might ignore me immediately
In my moon suit and funeral veil.
I am no source of honey
So why should they turn on me?
Tomorrow I will be sweet God, I will set them free.   35

The box is only temporary.

moon suit: protective clothing worn by beekeepers; all-in-one suit.

'It is the noise
that appalls me'

👤 Personal Response

1. How would you describe the poet's reaction to the bee box – fear or fascination, or a mixture of both? Refer to the text in your response.
2. Select two surreal images from the poem and comment on the effectiveness of each.
3. Would you describe this poem as exploring and overcoming one's fears and anxieties? Is the ending optimistic or pessimistic, in your opinion?

👁 Critical Literacy

'The Arrival of the Bee Box' was written in 1962, shortly after Plath's separation from her husband. Her father, who died when she was a child, had been a bee expert and Plath had recently taken up beekeeping. She explores order, power, control, confinement and freedom in this deeply personal poem.

The poem opens with a simple statement: 'I ordered this'. Straightaway, the emphasis is on order and control. The poet's tone in stanza one seems both matter-of-fact and surprised, as if thinking: 'Yes, I was the one who ordered this' and also 'Did I really order this?' **This drama has only one character, Plath herself.** We observe her responses and reactions to the arrival of the bee box. Notice the extensive use of the personal pronoun 'I'. We both see and hear the event.

The box is described as being made of 'clean wood' and given a homely quality through the simile 'Square as a chair'. But then a surreal, dreamlike metaphor, 'the coffin of a midget/Or a square baby', brings us into a **nightmare world**. The abnormal is suggested by the use of 'midget' and 'square baby'. The coffin conveys not only death, but also entrapment and confinement, preoccupations of the poet. The box has now become a sinister object. A witty sound effect closes the first stanza, as 'din in it' mimics the sound of the bees. The noisy insects are like badly behaved children.

Stanza two explores the **poet's ambivalent attitude to the box**. She is curious to see inside ('I can't keep away from it'). Yet she is also frightened by it, as she describes the box as 'dangerous'. She peers in. The third stanza becomes claustrophobic with the repetition of 'dark' and the grotesque image of 'the swarmy feeling of African hands/Minute and shrunk for export'. The milling of the bees/slaves is vividly captured as they heave around in the heat amid an atmosphere of menace and oppression, hopelessly desperate.

We hear the bees in stanza four. The metaphor of a Roman mob is used to show how they will create **chaos and danger if they are let loose**. The assonance of 'appalls' and 'all' underlines the poet's terror. The phrase 'unintelligible syllables', with its onomatopoeia and its difficult pronunciation, lets us hear the angry buzzing. Plath is awestruck at their collective force and energy: 'but my god, together!'

In stanza five the poet tries to listen, but only hears 'furious Latin' she does not understand. She doubts her capacity to control them, stating that she is 'not a Caesar', the powerful ruler of the Romans. She regards them as 'maniacs'. Then she suddenly realises that if she has ordered them, she can return them: 'They can be sent back'. **She has some control of this situation.** Plath can even decide their fate, whether they live or die: 'I need feed them nothing'. She has now redefined the situation as she remembers that she is 'the owner'. They belong to her.

The poet's feminine, nurturing side now emerges as she wonders 'how hungry they are'. The stereotype of the pretty woman surfaces in the description of the bees' natural habitat of trees in stanza six. Plath thinks that if she releases them, they would go back to the trees, 'laburnum' and 'cherry'. She herself would then merge into the landscape and become a tree. This is a reference to a Greek myth where Daphne was being pursued by Apollo. When she begged the gods to save her, they turned her into a tree.

The poet refers to herself in her beekeeping outfit of veil and boiler suit in stanza seven. She rhetorically asks why the bees would attack her, as she can offer no sustenance ('I am no source of honey'). **She decides to be compassionate**: 'Tomorrow I will be sweet God, I will set them free'. She realises that they are imprisoned for the time being: 'The box is only temporary'.

This poem can also be read on more than one level. The box could represent the poet's attempt to be what others expect, the typical 1950s woman – pretty, compliant, nurturing. The bees could symbolise the unstable side of her personality, which both fascinated and terrified Plath. **The box is like Pandora's box**: safe when locked, but full of danger when opened. Although she finds this disturbing, she also feels she must explore it in the interests of developing as a poet. The references to the doomed character of Daphne and the 'funeral veil' echo chillingly. Would these dark thoughts, if given their freedom, drive her to suicide? The form of this poem is seven stanzas of five lines. One final line stands alone, free like the bees or her dark thoughts. If the box represents Plath's outside appearance or body, it is mortal, it is temporary.

✒ Writing About the Poem

How does this poem address and explore the themes of order and power? Write a paragraph in response. Support your views with reference to the text.

Sample Paragraph

'The Arrival of the Bee Box' opens with a reference to order, 'I ordered this'. It is an assertion of power. Throughout the poem the repetition of 'I' suggests a person who consciously chooses to act in a certain way. 'I put my eye to the grid'. It is as if the poet wishes to confront and control her fears over the contents of the box. This box contains live bees, whose well-being lies in the hands of the poet. 'I need feed them nothing'. The box metaphor suggests claustrophobic control. Although she realises that she is not 'Caesar', the mighty Roman ruler, she can choose to be 'sweet God'. She alone has the power to release the bees, 'The box is only temporary'. This poem can also be read as referring to the control a person exercises when confronting their innermost fears and desires. The person can choose to contain them or confront them.

EXAMINER'S COMMENT

This is an assured top-grade response which focuses well on the central themes of order and power. Apt and accurate quotations are used effectively. The opening point on Plath's use of the personal pronoun is particularly impressive.

✒ Class/Homework Exercises

1. How does Plath create a dramatic atmosphere in 'The Arrival of the Bee Box'?
2. Plath examines repression in 'The Arrival of the Bee Box'. Why do you think she fears a loss of control? In your response, refer to both the subject matter and style.

⊙ Points to Consider

- **Central themes include power, control, freedom, self-expression.**
- **Innovative use of metaphor, contrasting moods.**
- **Unusual personification, startling images and drama.**
- **Clever word-play, witty sound effects, internal rhyme.**
- **Disconcerting ending emphasised by single stand-alone line.**

10 **Child**

Your clear eye is the one absolutely beautiful thing.
I want to fill it with color and ducks,
The zoo of the new

Whose name you meditate –   5
April snowdrop, Indian pipe,
Little

Stalk without wrinkle,
Pool in which images
Should be grand and classical

Not this troublous   10
Wringing of hands, this dark
Ceiling without a star.

meditate: reflect.

Indian pipe: American woodland flower.

Stalk: plant stem.

classical: impressive, enduring.

troublous: disturbed.

👤 **Personal Response**

1. What was your own immediate reaction after reading 'Child'? Refer to the poem in your answer.
2. Which images in the poem are most effective in contrasting the world of the child and the world of the adult?
3. Plath uses various sound effects to enhance her themes in 'Child'. Comment briefly on two interesting examples.

'The zoo of the new'

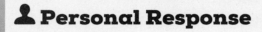

👁 Critical Literacy

Sylvia Plath's son was born in January 1962. A year later, not long before the poet's own death, she wrote 'Child', a short poem that reflects her intense feelings about motherhood.

The opening line of stanza one shows the **poet's emphatic appreciation of childhood innocence**: 'Your clear eye is the one absolutely beautiful thing'. The tone at first is hopeful. Her love for the new child is generous and unconditional: 'I want to fill it with color'. The childlike language is lively and playful. Plath plans to give her child the happiest of times, filled with 'color and ducks'. The vigorous rhythm and animated internal rhyme in the phrase 'The zoo of the new' are imaginative, capturing the sense of **youthful wonder**.

In stanza two, the poet continues to associate her child with all that is best about the natural world. The baby is like the most fragile of flowers, the 'April snowdrop'. The soothing broad vowel assonance in this phrase has a musical effect, like a soft lullaby. Yet her own fascination appears to mask a deeper concern. Plath feels that such a perfect childhood experience is unlikely to last very long. Despite all her positive sentiments, what she wants for **the vulnerable child** seems directly at odds with what is possible in a **flawed world**.

Run-on lines are a recurring feature of the poem and these add to the feeling of freedom and innocent intensity. Stanza three includes two **effective comparisons**, again taken from nature. Plath sees the child as an unblemished 'Stalk' that should grow perfectly. A second quality of childhood's pure innocence is found in the 'Pool' metaphor. We are reminded of the opening image – the child's 'clear eye', always trusting and sincere.

The poet would love to provide a magical future for her young child, so that the pool would reflect 'grand and classical' images. However, as a loving mother, she is trapped between her **idealism** – the joy she wants for her child – and a **distressing reality** – an awareness that the child's life will not be perfectly happy. This shocking realisation becomes clear in stanza four and overshadows her hopes completely. The final images are stark and powerful – the pathetic 'Wringing of hands' giving emphasis to her helplessness. The last line poignantly portrays the paradox of the tension between Plath's dreams for the child in the face of the despair she feels about the oppressive world: this 'Ceiling without a star'. The intensely dark mood is in sharp contrast with the rest of the poem. The early celebration has been replaced by anguish and an overwhelming sense of failure.

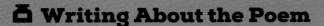

✒ Writing About the Poem

Do you think 'Child' is a positive or negative poem? Refer to the text in explaining your response.

Sample Paragraph

'Child' is about inadequacy. The poet wants the best for her son. Although the first half of the poem focuses on her wishes to protect him, this changes. Plath starts off by wanting to fill the boy's life with happy experiences (bright colours and toys). There are references to nature right through the poem and Plath compares her son to an 'April snowdrop'. This tender image gave me a positive feeling. Everything about the child is wonderful at first. This changes at the end. The mood turns negative. Plath talks of being confined in a darkened room that has a 'Ceiling without a star'. This is in total contrast with the images early on which were of the outdoors. The ending is 'troublous' because Plath fears her child will grow up and experience pain just as she has.

EXAMINER'S COMMENT

This paragraph addresses the question well and offers a clear response. There is some good personal engagement which effectively illustrates the changing mood from optimism to pessimism and uses apt quotations in support. The style of writing is a little note-like and pedestrian. Fresher expression and more development of points would have raised the standard from its present good solid middle grade.

✐ Class/Homework Exercises

1. Write a paragraph comparing 'Child' with 'Morning Song'. Refer to theme and style in both poems.
2. 'Plath explores the changing nature of parental love in her poem 'Child'. How does she reveal her sense of inadequacy in providing for her child? Support your response by reference to the poem.

⊙ Points to Consider

- One of several poems about children, moving from tenderness to anxiety.
- Lullaby, easy flowing movement, images of light and darkness.
- Contrast between love of child and poet's own depression.
- Appropriate style, clear, simple language.
- Juxtaposition of joyful, colourful world of child and dark despair of poet.

Sample Leaving Cert Questions on Plath's Poetry

1. 'Sylvia Plath makes effective use of various stylistic features to express a range of intense and compelling feelings.' Discuss this view, developing your response with reference to both the themes and poetic style of Sylvia Plath on your course.
2. 'Plath's powerful portrayal of the world of nature is conveyed through verbal energy and strikingly vivid symbolism.' To what extent do you agree or disagree with this view? Develop your response with reference to poems by Sylvia Plath on your course.
3. 'Sylvia Plath makes creative use of language and imagery to add layers of meaning to her work.' Discuss this statement, developing your response with reference to the language and themes found in the poetry of Plath on your course.

How do I organise my answer?

(Sample question 1)

'Sylvia Plath makes effective use of various stylistic features to express a range of intense and compelling feelings.' Discuss this view, developing your response with reference to both the themes and poetic style of Sylvia Plath on your course.

Sample Plan 1

Intro: *(Stance: agree with viewpoint in the question)* Plath's gripping emotional experiences are often painfully revealed through her use of startling imagery, careful choice of language.

Point 1: *(Conflicting feelings – startling imagery)* 'Morning Song' explores the conflicting emotions of new parents. Vibrant similes capture affection and pride ('Love set you going like a fat gold watch') and anxiety ('We stand round blankly as walls'). Precisely drawn images ('One cry, and I stumble from bed') show the mother embracing her new role.

Point 2: *(Mixed feelings – ranging imagery and moods)* 'Child' recreates the wonder of the simple world of a child through imaginative internal rhyme ('The zoo of the new'). Contrasting images of tenderness ('April snowdrop') and failure ('Ceiling without a star').

Understanding the Prescribed Poetry Question

Marks are awarded using the PCLM Marking Scheme:
P = 15; C = 15; L = 15; M = 5
Total = 50

- **P** (Purpose = 15 marks) refers to the set question and is the launch pad for the answer. This involves engaging with all aspects of the question. Both theme and language must be addressed, although not necessarily equally.
- **C** (Coherence = 15 marks) refers to the organisation of the developed response and the use of accurate, relevant quotation. Paragraphing is essential.
- **L** (Language = 15 marks) refers to the student's skill in controlling language throughout the answer.
- **M** (Mechanics = 5 marks) refers to spelling and grammar.
- Although no specific number of poems is required, students usually discuss at least 3 or 4 in their written responses.
- Aim for at least 800 words, to be completed within 45–50 minutes.

NOTE

In keeping with the PCLM approach, the student has to take a stance by agreeing, disagreeing or partially agreeing that Plath makes effective use of:

– **various stylistic features** (vivid visual imagery, rich symbolism, lively personification, careful rhyme, dramatic settings, evocative moods and tones, etc.)

... to express:

– **a range of intense and compelling feelings** (powerful search for personal identity, troubling attitudes, deep desire for inspiration/escape, awareness of nature, transience, etc.)

Point 3: *(Desire for inspiration – precise language structure)* 'Black Rook in Rainy Weather' shows both bird and poet carefully 'Arranging and rearranging' feathers and words. The randomness of life is created by lines and stanzas running untidily into each other.

Point 4: *(Distress – startling comparative language)* 'Poppies in July' records the poet's distress through the unlikely comparison of colourful summer flowers to 'little hell flames'. She longs to escape reality. Soft 'l' sounds ('Dulling', 'colorless') suggest her descent into nothingness.

Conclusion: Plath's inner turmoil is successfully revealed in her use of shocking imagery, telling contrasts and disturbing tones. Various poetic techniques highlight her extreme emotional struggles.

Sample Paragraph: Point 1

'Morning Song' reveals the mixed feelings a new mother can experience after the birth of a baby. Plath uses a very unexpected image to show the natural feelings of joy, 'Love set you going like a fat gold watch'. This suggests the regular sound of the little baby's ticking heartbeat. Another surprising image reveals how anxious parents feel, 'We stand around blankly as walls'. The mother seems strangely alienated from her child. Weather images of transience, such as 'cloud' and 'wind', suggest she is worried about losing her identity as an individual. Her own personality is being gradually destroyed, 'slow effacement', by her newfound identity as a mother. But Plath also introduces precise, tender images of her little baby, e.g. 'moth-breath flickers', to show the mother beginning to settle in to embracing her new role. Her pride in the baby is clearly seen in the colourful concluding simile of her baby's cries which she imagines rising 'like balloons'.

EXAMINER'S COMMENT

Succinct and successful commentary that engages well with the poem. Focused well on how contrasting images emphasise the poet's conflicted feelings about her child. Some reference to sound effects or tone would have been welcome. Relevant supportive quotes are well integrated into the critical analysis. Expression is also controlled throughout this top-grade response.

(Sample question 2)

'Plath's powerful portrayal of the world of nature is conveyed through verbal energy and strikingly vivid symbolism.' To what extent do you agree or disagree with this view? Develop your response with reference to poems by Sylvia Plath on your course.

NOTE

In keeping with the PCLM approach, the student has to take a stance by agreeing, disagreeing or partially agreeing with the statement that:

– **Plath's powerful portrayal of the world of nature** (keen appreciation of nature's vitality, close observation of the impact of physical environment, deep sense of people's complex relationship with natural world, etc.)

... is conveyed through:

– **verbal energy and strikingly vivid symbolism** (rich imagery/ metaphors/ symbols, thought-provoking contrasts, startling personification, sinister dramatic language, etc.)

Sample Plan 2

Intro: *(Stance: agree with viewpoint in the question)* Plath's awareness of nature's wonders reflected in closely observed details. Poems convey her own troubled state of mind and people's complex relationship with the natural world. Vigorous language describes landscape, flora and wildlife.

Point 1: *(Description of place – personification)* 'Finisterre' uses vivid personification to dramatise the struggle between land ('Admonitory cliffs') and water ('sea exploding'). Turbulent seascape scene contrasts between the 'sweet' appearance of Our Lady's statue and the tragic reality of drowned victims ('in the doom-noise of the sea').

Point 2: *(Close observation – repetition, dramatic language)* 'Elm' is also physically and metaphorically described ('strangle of branches'). Frantic verbs ('burn', 'drag',) establish a destructive mood. Emphatic repetition suggests the paralysis of despair ('That kill, that kill').

Point 3: *(Vitality of natural world – disturbing aural and visual imagery)* 'Poppies in July' shocks by presenting flowers associated with happiness as symbols of evil ('little hell flames', 'Little bloody skirts'). Energetic onomatopoeia ('Flickering', 'wrinkly') suggests the sensitive interior of a mouth ('just bloodied').

Point 4: *(Man's relationship with nature –varied tones)* 'Pheasant' explores poet's appreciation of the bird in its natural habitat ('pacing/ Through the uncut grass'). A firm verbal command ('Do not kill it') shows Plath's activism on behalf of the wild bird. Admiring tone ('kingliness', 'such a good shape') replaced by shame at human intrusion ('I trespass stupidly').

Conclusion: Plath's acute observations of nature expose a beautiful yet brutal world onto which she projects her personal feelings of doubt and obsession. Stunning visual and aural techniques leave a lasting impression on readers.

Sample Paragraph: Point 4

In her poem, 'Pheasant', Plath describes the world of nature very effectively using detailed description of a 'rare' bird 'in its element'. She is clearly fascinated by the bird's beauty, 'such a good shape'. To her, it is a symbol of perfection. The poet becomes its protector, begging for its life, 'Do not kill it'. Plath shows her concern by repeating her call, 'Let be, let be', and this shows the urgency of her plea to respect nature. It's obvious that she really admires this bird which is so richly coloured, 'green and red'. The use of soft sibilant sound effects create a wonderful picture of feeling at ease while she watches the pheasant 'sunning in the narcissi'. But the poet suddenly realises she is intruding on nature's scene and she becomes ashamed. The phrase, 'I trespass stupidly', reveals her awareness that she should not be there.

EXAMINER'S COMMENT

As part of a full essay answer, this short high-grade paragraph shows a close understanding of the poem. Discussion points deal with both aspects of the question (the portrayal of nature as a symbol of perfection and Plath's poetic style). There is some good engagement with the text, particularly in addressing how Plath's concerns are conveyed through sounds and repetition. Supportive quotations are carefully integrated into the commentary throughout.

EXAM FOCUS

- As you may not be familiar with some of the poems referred to in the sample plans, substitute other prescribed poems that you have studied closely.
- Key points about a particular poem can be developed over more than one paragraph.
- Paragraphs may also include cross-referencing and discussion of more than one poem.
- Remember that there is no single 'correct' answer to poetry questions, so always be confident in expressing your own considered response.

Leaving Cert Sample Essay

'Sylvia Plath makes creative use of language and imagery to add layers of meaning to her work.' Discuss this statement, developing your response with reference to the language and themes found in the poetry of Plath on your course.

Sample Essay

1. Plath's personal poems explore her intense feelings about many themes, such as control and oppression in 1950's American society. Her poetry is filled with thought-provoking ideas. These range from the negative impact society has on the individual to reflections on her own mental state. Throughout her poetry, striking visual imagery, personification and strong sound effects are cleverly used to express her views.

2. Plath presents an interesting picture of the monotonous world of 1950's America in 'The Times are Tidy'. It's clear that she herself felt unfulfilled there – especially with its bland, highly organised society. This is suggested in the carefully ordered rhymes she uses – 'record'/'accord', 'lizard'/'hazard'. Plath also makes use of subtle images which suggest the dreary routine of everyday life, 'the stuck record', 'the mayor's rôtisserie'. She savagely mocks American materialism and the excesses of this consumer society, 'cream an inch thick'. The poet sees personality being crushed, 'withered'. She regrets the loss of individual heroism, 'Unlucky the hero born/In this province'.

3. Her tone is highly ironical throughout the poem. For Plath, the 1950s was a disappointing period of time which she believed was dull and uninspiring. I get the impression she was thinking back to the Second World War when Americans did have some sense of heroism. The poem ends on a negative tone. Plath believes that the joy and excitement have gone. American children might be growing up in well-off families – 'are better for it', but their sense of adventure has been lost.

4. The dramatic experience of a woman confronting the reality of her reflected image is the main subject of 'Mirror'. Society can sometimes view women as worthless when they are no longer young. Plath takes on the cold, critical voice of the mirror, 'the eye of a little god'. She describes the damaging relationship between the controlling mirror and the dependent woman. Totally dissatisfied with what is reflected back to her, she stands 'with tears and an agitation of hands'. A highly disturbing metaphor, 'I am a lake', suggests the woman's dangerous situation. The 'truthful' mirror reflects the reality that every day she is getting older, 'like a terrible fish'. Plath's inventive personification is used to question the pressure society puts on women to maintain a youthful appearance of prettiness.

5. 'Elm' also uses terrifying personification to show how life's pressures can push a person close to insanity. In this dramatic poem, a surreal conversation takes place between the poet and the elm. The tree questions the poet about her mental wellbeing. Is she longing for love which has disappeared? This is skilfully compared to a runaway animal, 'gone off, like a horse'. The use of intense language ('burn', 'shriek') adds to the destructive mood. Unsettling images and harsh sound effects explore the theme of loss of control and madness. The poet confesses that her feelings of deep-rooted despair resemble a cancer that is silently increasing in size, 'All day I feel its soft, feathery turnings'.

6. Ironically, while Plath criticised American society for its control and order in 'The Times are Tidy', she herself now takes up this very same role in her poem, 'The Arrival of the Bee Box'. She 'ordered this', so now she is in charge of what happens to the bees. There are numerous dream-like

scenes linked to history and power struggles. In referring to 'the swarmy feeling of African hands … angrily clambering', Plath makes readers consider the history of slavery and the abuse of power. Onomatopoeia and repetition suggest their captivity in the shocking image of imprisoned people. The noise of the imprisoned bees is conveyed in the phrase, 'unintelligible syllables' of the 'Roman mob'.

7. The poem raises many subtle questions. Would the escape of the bees lead to destruction? Do they represent Plath's own dark thoughts of rebellion against the repressive society of her time? Once again, the poem could represent her effort to be what is expected. The perfect American stereotype. Images, such as, 'petticoats of the cherry' and 'stood back' suggest a submissive pretty woman. One who knows her place.

8. At one point, she refers to the bees as 'a box of maniacs'. This metaphor could possibly be linked to the poet's own fears. Mainly about her own repressed emotions and her general mental state. In the end, she decides to be kind, 'I will set them free'. The line, 'The box is only temporary', shows that the poet has chosen freedom for the bees and herself.

9. Plath's effective use of language highlights her wide-ranging thoughts on the theme of power. She opposed the social expectations where girls are thought of as inferior to males. I thought the ideas in her poetry were subtle and had many possible meanings.

(780 words)

EXAMINER'S COMMENT

A good personal response to the question, exploring interesting ideas in Plath's poetry. Focused well on the use of imagery, personification and mood, with impressive analysis of these stylistic features in paragraphs 2, 4 and 5. The critical commentary is supported by suitable quotation ranging across several key poems. Points are coherent and generally well-developed – although there is some disjointed note-like commentary in paragraphs 7 and 8. Overall, expression is clear throughout this solid top-grade essay.

GRADE: H1
P = 15/15
C = 14/15
L = 14/15
M = 5/5
Total = 48/50

∞ Revision Overview

'Black Rook in Rainy Weather'
Life-affirming poem in which Plath explores the mystery of poetic inspiration and the importance of appreciating everyday life as it is.

'The Times Are Tidy'
Focuses on political themes and the poet's personal dissatisfaction with the materialistic and unheroic era she lived in.

'Morning Song'
Feeling estranged from her own child, the poet addresses themes of motherhood, alienation and human frailty.

'Finisterre'
Dramatic seascape depicting a turbulent scene that reflects the poet's troubled state of mind and her thoughts on the futility of conflict.

'Mirror'
In this chilling poem, the personified mirror reflects Plath's own thoughts about identity and people's fixation with their inevitable mortality.

'Pheasant'
The poet is embarrassed by her unwitting intrusion into a natural scene, yet she enjoys and appreciates the beauty of the pheasant in its element.

'Elm'
Plath invents a demon in her subconscious that gives her a self-destructive vision. Shocked by this powerful, violent and uncontrolled experience, she surrenders to mental exhaustion.

'Poppies in July' (OL)
Expresses the longing to escape from deep depression. The poet is so emotionally drained that she struggles to find any feeling that connects her to reality.

'The Arrival of the Bee Box'
Plath explores various feelings of power and powerlessness associated with bee-keeping. The poet's indecisiveness seems to reflect her own chaotic state of mind.

'Child' (OL)
This dark yet beautiful poem captures Plath's personal insecurity concerning her marriage and her conflicted feelings as a mother.

💬 Last Words

'Her poems have that heart-breaking quality about them.'
Joyce Carol Oates

'Artists are a special breed. They are passionate and temperamental. Their feelings flow into the work they create.'
J. Timothy King

'I am a genius of a writer. I have it in me. I am writing the best poems of my life.'
Sylvia Plath

 CREATIVITY   REGRET   NATURE   WONDER   LOVE   AGEING   IDENTITY   ESCAPE   CHILDHOOD   FREEDOM

W. B. Yeats
1865–1939

'I have spread my dreams under your feet …'

William Butler Yeats was born in Dublin in 1865. The son of a well-known Irish painter, John Butler Yeats, he spent much of his childhood in Co. Sligo. As a young writer, Yeats became involved with the Celtic Revival, a movement against the cultural influences of English rule in Ireland that sought to promote the spirit of our native heritage. His writing drew extensively from Irish mythology and folklore. Another great influence was the Irish revolutionary Maud Gonne, a woman as famous for her passionate nationalist politics as for her beauty. She rejected Yeats, who eventually married another woman, Georgie Hyde Lees. However, Maud Gonne remained a powerful figure in Yeats's writing. Over the years, Yeats became deeply involved in Irish politics and despite Ireland's independence from England, his work reflected a pessimism about the political situation here. He also had a lifelong interest in mysticism and the occult. Appointed a senator of the Irish Free State in 1922, he is remembered as an important cultural leader, as a major playwright (he was one of the founders of Dublin's Abbey Theatre) and as one of the greatest 20th-century poets. Yeats was awarded the Nobel Prize in 1923 and died in 1939 at the age of 73.

Investigate Further

To find out more about W. B. Yeats, or to hear readings of his poems, you could do a search of some of the useful websites available such as YouTube, BBC Poetry, poetryfoundation.org and poetryarchive.org, or access additional material on this page of your eBook.

Prescribed Poems

(OL) indicates poems that are also prescribed for the Ordinary Level course.

1

The Lake Isle of Innisfree

I will arise and go now, and go to Innisfree,
And a small cabin build there, of clay and wattles made:
Nine bean-rows will I have there, a hive for the honey-bee,
And live alone in the bee-loud glade.

And I shall have some peace there, for peace comes dropping slow,   5
Dropping from the veils of the morning to where the cricket sings;
There midnight's all a glimmer, and noon a purple glow,
And evening full of the linnet's wings.

I will arise and go now, for always night and day
I hear lake water lapping with low sounds by the shore;   10
While I stand on the roadway, or on the pavements grey,
I hear it in the deep heart's core.

Innisfree: island of heather.
clay and wattles: rods and mud were used to build small houses.

midnight's all a glimmer: stars are shining very brightly in the countryside.
linnet: songbird.

lapping: gentle sounds made by water at the edge of a shore.
heart's core: essential part; the centre of the poet's being.

'lake water lapping'

👤 Personal Response

1. This appealing poem explores the dream of escaping to find a peaceful paradise. Comment on Yeats's use of imagery to describe this ideal place.
2. What does the poem reveal to you about Yeats's own state of mind? Use reference to the text in your response.
3. The third stanza uses stirring sound effects (alliteration, broad vowel sounds, regular rhyme and rhythm) to conjure up Innisfree. Comment on one aural effect which you found interesting.

👁 Critical Literacy

'The Lake Isle of Innisfree' was written in 1890. Yeats was in London, looking in a shop window at a little toy fountain. He was feeling very homesick. He said the sound of the 'tinkle of water' reminded him of 'lake water'. He was longing to escape from the grind of everyday life and he wrote an 'old daydream of mine'.

This timeless poem has long been a favourite with exiles everywhere, as it **expresses a longing for a place of deep peace**. The poet's decision to go is unannounced in solemn biblical language, suggesting a carefully thought-out choice. Then the poet describes the idyllic life of self-sufficiency: 'Nine bean-rows' and 'a hive for the honey-bee'. These details give the poem a timeless quality as the poet lives 'alone in the bee-loud glade'.

Stanza two describes Innisfree so vividly that the future tense of 'I will arise' slips gently into the present tense: 'There midnight's all a glimmer'. Repetition ('peace', 'dropping') lulls readers into this tranquil place. Beautiful imagery brings us through the day, from the gentle white mists of the morning that lie like carelessly thrown veils over the lake to the blazing purple of the heather under the midday sun. The starry night, which can only be seen in the clear skies of the countryside, is vividly described as 'midnight's all a glimmer', with slender vowel sounds suggesting the sharp light of the stars. The soft 'l', 'm' and 'p' sounds in this stanza create a gentle and magical mood.

The third stanza repeats the opening, giving the air of a solemn ritual taking place. The **verbal music** in this stanza is striking, as the broad vowel sounds slow down the line 'I hear lake water lapping with low sounds by the shore', emphasising peace and tranquility. Notice how the alliteration of 'l' and assonance of 'o' recreate the serenity of the scene. The only **contemporary detail** in the poem is 'pavements grey', suggesting the relentless concrete of the city. The exile's awareness of what he loves is eloquently expressed as he declares he hears the sound 'in the deep heart's core'. The monosyllabic ending drums home his deep longing for this place. The harmony of this peaceful

island is reinforced by the regularity of the end rhyme (a, b, a, b) and the four even beats in every fourth line.

✒ Writing About the Poem

'W. B. Yeats writes dramatic poetry that addresses the human desire for harmony and fulfilment.' Discuss this statement with reference to 'The Lake Isle of Innisfree'.

Sample Paragraph

'The Lake Isle of Innisfree', depicts a tranquil refuge from modern living. A dramatic opening, 'I will arise and go now, and go to Innisfree', declares his intention in a tone heightened by the repetition of the single syllable verb. In this idyllic place, time stands still. The steady end-rhyme ('Innisfree', 'honey-bee') and broad vowel sounds ('alone in the bee-loud glade') convey an alluring vision of tranquillity. The hypnotic description suggests quietness. The alliteration and assonance ('lake water lapping with low sounds by the shore') enables us to experience this calm atmosphere, even though Yeats is stranded on the 'pavements grey'. The poet's dream is universal, because we all long for peace. In the end, Yeats succeeds in instilling this vision 'in the deep heart's core'.

✒ Class/Homework Exercises

1. 'Yeats is a perceptive and subtle poet, both in terms of his universal themes and his lyrical style'. Discuss this view with reference to 'The Lake Isle of Innisfree'.
2. 'Yeats's poems are often defined by a tension between the real world in which the poet lives and an ideal world that he imagines.' Discuss this view with reference to 'The Lake Isle of Innisfree'.

⊙ Points to Consider

- Poetic vision of longing and desire for utopian escape.
- Formal opening and repetition give the sense of a solemn ritual.
- Romantic details and sensual images place the poem out of time while concrete description produces a realistic experience for the reader.
- Verbal music (assonance, alliteration, onomatopoeia) heighten the reader's involvement.
- Traditional rhyming structure and the steady beats of the concluding line of each quatrain add a sense of stability and security.

2 September 1913

What need you, being come to sense,
But fumble in a greasy till
And add the halfpence to the pence
And prayer to shivering prayer, until
You have dried the marrow from the bone?   5
For men were born to pray and save:
Romantic Ireland's dead and gone,
It's with O'Leary in the grave.

Yet they were of a different kind,
The names that stilled your childish play,   10
They have gone about the world like wind,
But little time had they to pray
For whom the hangman's rope was spun,
And what, God help us, could they save?
Romantic Ireland's dead and gone,   15
It's with O'Leary in the grave.

Was it for this the wild geese spread
The grey wing upon every tide;
For this that all that blood was shed,
For this Edward Fitzgerald died,   20
And Robert Emmet and Wolfe Tone,
All that delirium of the brave?
Romantic Ireland's dead and gone,
It's with O'Leary in the grave.

Yet could we turn the years again,   25
And call those exiles as they were
In all their loneliness and pain,
You'd cry, 'Some woman's yellow hair
Has maddened every mother's son':
They weighed so lightly what they gave.   30
But let them be, they're dead and gone,
They're with O'Leary in the grave.

you: merchants and business people.

O'Leary: John O'Leary, Fenian leader, one of Yeats's heroes.

they: the selfless Irish patriots.

the wild geese: Irish independence soldiers forced into exile in Europe after 1690.

Edward Fitzgerald: 18th-century Irish aristocrat and revolutionary.
Robert Emmet and Wolfe Tone: Irish rebel leaders. Emmet was hanged in 1803. Tone died by suicide in prison after being sentenced to death in 1798.

'Romantic Ireland's dead and gone'

👤 Personal Response

1. Comment on the effectiveness of the images used in the first five lines of the poem.
2. How would you describe the tone of this poem? Is it bitter, sad, ironic, angry, etc.? Refer closely to the text in your answer.
3. In the final stanza, Yeats changes the refrain, cautioning the middle class not to judge the heroes. Why, in your opinion, does Yeats offer this warning? Support your views with reference to the poem.

👁 Critical Literacy

'September 1913' is typical of Yeats's hard-hitting political poems. Both the content and tone are harsh as the poet airs his views on public issues, contrasting the idealism of Ireland's heroic past with a materialistic, uncultured present.

This poem is set against two events which **exposed anti-culturalism** and grasping commercialism in contemporary Ireland. Dublin Corporation refused to house paintings donated by Hugh Lane to the Irish people; and 1913 was the year of a general strike and lockout of the workers in Dublin who mostly lived in poverty in run-down tenements.

The first stanza begins with a derisive **attack on a materialistic society** that Yeats sees as being both greedy and hypocritical. Ireland's middle classes are preoccupied with making money and with slavish religious devotion. The rhetorical opening is sharply sarcastic, as the poet depicts the petty, penny-pinching shopkeepers who 'fumble in a greasy till'. Yeats's tone is as angry as it is ironic: 'For men were born to pray and save'. Images of the dried bone and 'shivering prayer' are equally forceful – the poor are exploited by ruthless employers and a domineering Church. This disturbing picture leads the poet to regret the loss of 'Romantic Ireland' in the concluding refrain.

Stanza two develops the contrast between past and present as Yeats considers the **heroism and generosity of an earlier era**. Ireland's patriots – 'names that stilled' earlier generations of children – could hardly have been more unlike the present middle class. Yeats clearly relates to the self-sacrifice of idealistic Irish freedom fighters: 'And what, God help us, could they save?' These contemptuous words echo the fearful prayers referred to at the start of the poem. The heroes of the past were so selfless that they did not even concern themselves with saving their own lives.

The wistful and nostalgic tone of stanza three is evident in the rhetorical question about all those Irish soldiers who had been exiled in the late 17th century. Yeats's high regard for these men is evoked by comparing them to 'wild geese', a wistful metaphor reflecting their nobility. Yet the poet's admiration for past idealism is diminished by the fact that **such heroic dedication was all for nothing**. The repetition of 'for this' hammers home Yeats's contempt for the pious materialists of his own imperfect age. In listing a roll of honour, he singles out the most impressive patriots of his own class, the Anglo-Irish Ascendancy. For the poet, Fitzgerald, Emmet and Tone are among the most admirable Irishmen. In using the phrase 'All that delirium of the brave', Yeats suggests that their passionate dedication to Irish freedom bordered on a frenzied or misplaced sense of daring in the eyes of the materialists.

This romanticised appreciation continues into the final stanza, where the poet imagines the 'loneliness and pain' of the heroic dead. His empathy towards them is underpinned by an **even more vicious portrayal of the new middle class**. He argues that the establishment figures of his own time would be unable to comprehend anything about the passionate values and dreams of 'Romantic Ireland'. At best, they would be confused by the ludicrous self-sacrifice of the past. At worst, the present generation would accuse the patriots of being insane or of trying to impress friends or lovers. Perhaps Yeats is illustrating the cynical thinking of his time, when many politicians courted national popularity. 'Some woman's yellow hair' might well refer to the traditional symbol of Ireland as a beautiful woman.

The poet's disgust on behalf of the patriots is rounded off in the last two lines: 'But let them be, they're dead and gone'. The refrain has been changed slightly, adding further emphasis and a **sense of finality**. After reading this savage satire, we are left with a deep sense of Yeats's bitter disillusionment towards his contemporaries. The extreme feelings expressed in the poem offer a dispirited vision of an unworthy country. Some critics have accused Yeats of over-romanticising the past. Whether or not this is true, the poem challenges us to examine the present values of modern Ireland, our understanding of Irish history and the meaning of heroism.

✒ Writing About the Poem

'W. B. Yeats often makes uses of contrasting images of self-interest and selflessness to communicate powerful feelings.' Discuss this statement in relation to 'September 1913'.

Sample Paragraph

Contrast plays a central role in 'September 1913'. The poem's angry opening lines are aimed at the merchants who 'fumble in a greasy till'. Their behaviour is reflected by vivid imagery. These individuals exploit ordinary people and could not be more unlike the Irish patriots –

POETRY FOCUS

'names that stilled your childish play'. Yeats also uses the beautiful image of the wild geese spreading 'the grey wing upon every tide' to describe the flight of Irish soldiers who refused to accept colonial rule. The imagery is taken from the world of nature and makes us aware of Yeats's high opinion of those heroes. The poet's feeling is evident in his violent description of the materialistic society of his own time – especially those who have 'dried the marrow from the bone'. Stark contrasts carry the argument throughout the poem and leave a deep impression on readers.

EXAMINER'S COMMENT

Well-focused on how the poet's imagery patterns convey deeply felt views. This top-grade response is also effectively supported by suitable reference and accurate quotation. Informed discussion covers a range of contrasting images (such as greed, natural beauty and violence). There is evidence throughout of close interaction with the poem. Expression is controlled, and the paragraph is rounded off with a succinct concluding sentence.

✒ Class/Homework Exercises

1. 'W. B. Yeats manages to create a series of powerfully compelling moods throughout "September 1913".' Discuss this statement with reference to both the subject matter and style of the poem.
2. 'Yeats frequently addresses political themes in poems that are filled with tension and drama.' Discuss this view with reference to 'September 1913'.

⊙ Points to Consider

- **Central contrast between the materialistic present and the romanticised past.**
- **The heroic patriots were idealistic, unlike the self-serving middle classes of 1913.**
- **Various tones: disillusionment, irony, admiration, resignation.**
- **Effective use of repetition, vivid imagery, colloquial language.**
- **Refrain emphasises Yeats's deep sense of disenchantment with Ireland's cynical establishment.**

3 The Wild Swans at Coole

The trees are in their autumn beauty,
The woodland paths are dry,
Under the October twilight the water
Mirrors a still sky;
Upon the brimming water among the stones   5
Are nine-and-fifty swans.

brimming: filled to the very top or edge.

The nineteenth autumn has come upon me
Since I first made my count;
I saw, before I had well finished,
All suddenly mount   10
And scatter wheeling in great broken rings
Upon their clamorous wings.

clamorous: loud, confused noise.

I have looked upon those brilliant creatures,
And now my heart is sore.
All's changed since I, hearing at twilight,   15
The first time on this shore,
The bell-beat of their wings above my head,
Trod with a lighter tread.

Trod ... tread: walked lightly; carefree.

Unwearied still, lover by lover,
They paddle in the cold   20
Companionable streams or climb the air;
Their hearts have not grown old;
Passion or conquest, wander where they will,
Attend upon them still.

lover by lover: swans mate for life; this highlights Yeats's loneliness.

Companionable: friendly.

Attend upon them still: waits on them yet.

But now they drift on the still water,   25
Mysterious, beautiful;
Among what rushes will they build,
By what lake's edge or pool
Delight men's eyes when I awake some day
To find they have flown away?   30

'The bell-beat of their wings'

👤 Personal Response

1. Why do you think the poet chose the season of autumn as his setting? What changes occur at this time of year? Where are these referred to in the poem?
2. In your opinion, what are the main contrasts between the swans and the poet? Describe two, using close reference to the text.
3. What do you think the final stanza means? Consider the phrase 'I awake'. What does the poet awake from?

👁 Critical Literacy

'The Wild Swans at Coole' was written in 1916. Yeats loved spending time in the West of Ireland, especially at Coole, the home of Lady Gregory, his friend and patron. He was 51 when he wrote this poem, which contrasts the swans' beauty and apparent immortality with Yeats's ageing, mortal self.

The poem opens with a tranquil, serene scene of **autumnal beauty** in the park of Lady Gregory's home in Galway. This romantic image is described in great detail: the 'woodland paths are dry'. It is evening, 'October twilight'. The water is 'brimming'. The swans are carefully counted, 'nine-and-fifty'. The use of the soft letters 'l', 'm' and 's' emphasise the calm of the scene in stanza one.

In stanza two, the poem moves to the personal as he recalls that it is nineteen years since he first counted the swans. The word 'count' links the two stanzas. The poet's counting is interrupted as these mysterious creatures all suddenly rise into the sky. Run-through lines suggest the flowing movement of the rising swans. Strong verbs ('mount', 'scatter') reinforce this natural action. The great beating wings of the swans are captured in the onomatopoeic 'clamorous wings'. They are independent and refuse to be restrained. The ring is a symbol of eternity. The swans are making the same patterns as they have always made; they are unchanging.

Stanza two is linked to stanza three by the phrases 'I saw' and 'I have looked'. Now the poet tells us his 'heart is sore'. He has taken stock and is **dissatisfied with his emotional situation**. He is fifty-one, alone and unmarried and concerned that his poetic powers are lessening: '**All's changed**'. All humans want things to remain as they are, but life is full of change. He has lost the great love of his life, the beautiful Irish activist Maud Gonne. He also laments the loss of his youth, when he 'Trod with a lighter tread'. Nineteen years earlier, he was much more carefree. The noise of the beating wings of the swans is effectively captured in the compound word 'bell-beat'. The alliterative 'b' reinforces the steady, flapping sound. The poet is using his intense personal experiences to express universal truths.

The swans in stanza four are **symbols of eternity**, ageless, 'Unwearied still'. They are united, 'lover by lover'. They experience life together ('Companionable streams'), not on their own, like the poet. He envies them their defiance of time: 'Their hearts have not grown old'. They do what they want, when they want. They are full of 'Passion or conquest'. By contrast, he is indirectly telling us, he feels old and worn out. The **spiral imagery** of the 'great broken rings' is reminiscent of the spirals seen in ancient carvings representing eternity. Yeats believed there was a cyclical pattern behind all things. The swans can live in two elements, water and air, thus linking these elements together. They are living, vital, immortal, unlike their surroundings. The trees are yellowing ('autumn beauty') and the dry 'woodland paths' suggest the lack of creative force which the poet is experiencing. Yeats is heartbroken and weary. Only the swans transcend time.

Stanza five explores a **philosophy of life**, linked to the previous stanza by the repetition of 'still'. The swans have returned to the water, 'Mysterious, beautiful'. The poem ends on a speculative note as the poet asks where they will 'Delight men's eyes'. Is he referring to the fact that **they will continue to be a source of pleasure to someone else** long after he is dead? The swans appear immortal, a continuing source of happiness as they practise their patterns, whereas the poet is not able to continue improving his own writing, as he is mortal. The poet is slipping into the cruel season of winter while the swans infinitely 'drift on the still water'.

✒ Writing About the Poem

'W. B. Yeats makes effective use of rich, dramatic symbols to address themes of transience and mortality.' Discuss this view with reference to 'The Wild Swans at Coole'.

Sample Paragraph

Two contrasting symbols are used in 'The Wild Swans at Coole'. The swans represent youthful passion while autumn symbolises the sadness of ageing. Yeats is presenting the view that life is fragile. The swans epitomise unchanging nature. The poet's confession, 'my heart is sore', engages the reader in accepting the profound truth that humanity cannot conquer time. Unlike the poet, the swans 'drift on the still water', but they are not subject to time's powers. Yeats is connected to the decay of autumn, 'October twilight' where 'woodland paths are dry', all of which signify advancing age. In considering these symbols, Yeats is led to ask a penetrating question about the transience of beauty and creative energy, 'when I awake some day/ To find

EXAMINER'S COMMENT

A perceptive top-grade response to the question. Informed discussion based on the poet's awareness of key symbols (the swans and the natural world). Effective supporting reference and accurate quotations throughout. Expression is also very good ('accepting the profound truth', 'penetrating question') and the paragraph is rounded off with an impressive personal comment.

they have flown away? 'I particularly liked the final rhyme which trails off into the distance – just like the 'brilliant creatures'.

✒ Class/Homework Exercises

1. 'W. B. Yeats frequently uses personal aspects of his own life to evocatively explore universal truths.' Discuss this view with reference to 'The Wild Swans at Coole'.
2. 'Yeats often draws on the beauty and stillness of the natural world to convey a deep sense of loss.' Discuss this statement with reference to 'The Wild Swans at Coole'.

⊙ Points to Consider

- Intense personal meditation on the search for lasting beauty in a transient world.

- Sad tone reflects concerns about ageing, romantic rejection, political upheaval, fading creativity.

- Slow rhythm conveys the poet's meditative mood.

- Vivid visual descriptive details portray places and creatures.

- Dynamic verbs, compound words and onomatopoeia capture the energy of the swans.

- Use of contrast highlights the gap between mortality and eternity.

- Poem ends on an optimistic note.

4 An Irish Airman Foresees His Death

Title: The Irish airman in this poem is Major Robert Gregory (1881–1918), son of Yeats's close friend Lady Gregory. He was shot down and killed while on service in northern Italy.

I know that I shall meet my fate
Somewhere among the clouds above;
Those that I fight I do not hate,
Those that I guard I do not love;
My country is Kiltartan Cross,   5
My countrymen Kiltartan's poor,
No likely end could bring them loss
Or leave them happier than before.
Nor law, nor duty bade me fight,
Nor public men, nor cheering crowds,   10
A lonely impulse of delight
Drove to this tumult in the clouds;
I balanced all, brought all to mind,
The years to come seemed waste of breath,
A waste of breath the years behind   15
In balance with this life, this death.

Those that I fight: the Germans.
Those that I guard: Allied countries, such as England and France.
Kiltartan: townland near the Gregory estate in Co. Galway.
likely end: outcome.

tumult: turmoil; confusion.

'I balanced all'

👤 Personal Response

1. 'This poem is not just an elegy or lament in memory of the dead airman. It is also an insight into the excitement of warfare.' Write your response to this statement, using close reference to the text.

2. Repetition is used throughout the poem. Does it suggest Gregory's boredom with everyday life? Or his unstoppable drive for adventure? Refer closely to the poem in your response.

3. In your opinion, what is the central or dominant mood in the poem? Refer to the text in your answer.

👁 Critical Literacy

Thousands of Irishmen fought and died in the British armed forces during World War I. Robert Gregory was killed in Italy at the age of 37. The airman's death had a lasting effect on Yeats, who wrote several poems about him.

Is it right to assume anything about young men who fight for their country? Why do they enlist? Do they always know what they are fighting for? In this poem, Yeats expresses what he believes is the airman's viewpoint as he comes face to face with death. This **fatalistic attitude** is established in the emphatic opening line. The poem's title also leads us to believe that the speaker has an intuitive sense that his death is about to happen. But despite this premonition, he seems strangely resigned to risking his life.

In lines 3–4, he makes it clear that he neither hates his German enemies nor loves the British and their allies. His thoughts are with the people he knows best back in Kiltartan, Co. Galway. Major Gregory recognises the irony of their detachment from the war. The ordinary people of his homeland are unlikely to be affected at all by whatever happens on the killing fields of mainland Europe. Does he feel that he is abandoning his fellow countrymen? What is the dominant tone of lines 7–8? Is there an underlying bitterness?

In line 9, the speaker takes time to reflect on why he joined the air force and immediately dismisses the obvious reasons of conscription ('law') or patriotism ('duty'). As a volunteer, Gregory is more openly cynical of the 'public men' and 'cheering crowds' he mentions in line 10. Like many in the military who have experienced the realities of warfare, **he is suspicious of hollow patriotism** and has no time for political leaders and popular adulation. So why did Robert Gregory choose to endanger his life by going to war? The answer lies in the key comments 'A lonely impulse of delight' (line 11) and 'I balanced all' (line 13). The first phrase is paradoxical. The airman experiences not just the excitement, but also the isolation of flying. At the same time, his 'impulse' to enlist as a fighter pilot reflects both his **desire for adventure** as well as his regret.

The last four lines explain the real reason behind his decision. It was neither rash nor emotional, but simply a question of balance. Having examined his life closely, Gregory has chosen the heroism of a self-sacrificing death. It is as though he only feels truly alive during the 'tumult' of battle. Yeats's language is particularly evocative at this point. Awesome air battles are effectively echoed in such dynamic phrasing as 'impulse of delight' and 'tumult in the clouds'. This **sense of freedom and power** is repeatedly contrasted with the dreary and predictable security of life away from the war – dismissed out of hand as a 'waste of breath'. From the airman's perspective, as a man of action, dying in battle is in keeping with 'this life' that he has chosen. Such a death would be his final adventurous exploit.

Some commentators have criticised Yeats's poem for glorifying war and pointless risk-taking. Others have suggested that the poet successfully highlights Anglo-Irish attitudes, neither exclusively Irish nor English. The poet certainly raises interesting questions about national identity and ways of thinking about war. However, in writing an elegy for Robert Gregory, he emphasises the **airman's daring solitude**. Perhaps this same thrill lies at the heart of other important choices in life, including the creative activity of artists. Is there a sense that the poet and the pilot are alike, both of them taking calculated risks in what they do?

✒ Writing About the Poem

'Some of Yeats's most poignant poems have a tragic vision, a sense that life is meaningless and has to be endured.' Discuss this view, with particular reference to 'An Irish Airman Foresees His Death'.

Sample Paragraph

The title suggests tragedy. However, the 'Irish Airman' is courageous in the face of danger. Although the word 'fate' suggests an inevitable destiny, the poem is dominated by a mood of resignation. The calm tone – 'I know that I shall meet my fate' – and slow rhythm is like a chant or a prayer. While the pilot is realistic about his chances in war, he seems to have distanced himself from everything. He admits the truth about his passion for adventure – 'A lonely impulse of delight' – and this might signify that he views life as beyond his control. The ending is pessimistic, and he repeats the phrase 'waste of breath' to emphasise the absurdity of life. Overall, the speaker is caught between realism and pessimism. The subtle concluding line sums this up – 'In balance with this life, this death' – and leaves a sense of his tragic dilemma.

> **EXAMINER'S COMMENT**
>
> An insightful, focused response to the question. Perceptive discussion engages with the airman's fatalistic attitude. Apt, accurate quotations are integrated effectively into the commentary. Expression is well controlled and vocabulary is also impressive ('inevitable destiny', 'sheer absurdity of life', 'subtle concluding line'). A solid, top-grade standard.

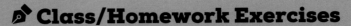

🖊 Class/Homework Exercises

1. 'W. B. Yeats's evocative poems can raise interesting questions about national identity.' Discuss this statement with reference to 'An Irish Airman Foresees His Death'.
2. 'Yeats's most compelling poetry often explores fatalistic themes.' Discuss this view with reference to 'An Irish Airman Foresees His Death'.

◉ Points to Consider

- Yeats adopts the persona of Major Robert Gregory, who died in 1918.
- Dramatic monologue form engages the sympathy of readers.
- Contrasting attitudes and tones: passion, detachment, resignation, courage, joy, loneliness.
- Effective use of repetition, rhyme and contrast.

5 Easter 1916

I have met them at close of day
Coming with vivid faces
From counter or desk among grey
Eighteenth-century houses.
I have passed with a nod of the head   5
Or polite meaningless words,
Or have lingered awhile and said
Polite meaningless words,
And thought before I had done
Of a mocking tale or a gibe   10
To please a companion
Around the fire at the club,
Being certain that they and I
But lived where motley is worn:
All changed, changed utterly: 15
A terrible beauty is born.

That woman's days were spent
In ignorant good-will,
Her nights in argument
Until her voice grew shrill.   20
What voice more sweet than hers
When, young and beautiful,
She rode to harriers?
This man had kept a school
And rode our wingèd horse;   25
This other his helper and friend
Was coming into his force;
He might have won fame in the end,
So sensitive his nature seemed,
So daring and sweet his thought.   30
This other man I had dreamed
A drunken, vainglorious lout.
He had done most bitter wrong
To some who are near my heart,
Yet I number him in the song;   35
He, too, has resigned his part
In the casual comedy;
He, too, has been changed in his turn,
Transformed utterly:
A terrible beauty is born.   40

Title: On 24 April 1916, Easter Monday, about 700 Irish Republicans took over several key buildings in Dublin. These included the Four Courts, Bolands Mills, the Royal College of Surgeons and the General Post Office. The rebellion lasted six days and was followed by the execution of its leaders. The Rising was a pivotal event in modern Irish history.
them: the rebels involved in the Rising.

motley: ridiculous clothing.

That woman: Countess Markievicz, friend of Yeats and a committed nationalist.

This man: Padraig Pearse, poet and teacher, was shot as a leader of the Rising.
wingèd horse: Pegasus, the mythical white horse that flies across the sky, was a symbol of poetic inspiration.
This other: Thomas MacDonagh, writer and teacher, executed in 1916.

This other man: Major John MacBride was also executed for his part in the rebellion. He was the husband of Maud Gonne.
most bitter wrong: there were recurring rumours that MacBride had mistreated Maud Gonne.

Hearts with one purpose alone
Through summer and winter seem
Enchanted to a stone
To trouble the living stream.
The horse that comes from the road,   45
The rider, the birds that range
From cloud to tumbling cloud,
Minute by minute they change;
A shadow of cloud on the stream
Changes minute by minute;   50
A horse-hoof slides on the brim,
And a horse plashes within it;
The long-legged moor-hens dive,
And hens to moor-cocks call;
Minute by minute they live: 55
The stone's in the midst of all.

Too long a sacrifice
Can make a stone of the heart.
O when may it suffice?
That is Heaven's part, our part   60
To murmur name upon name,
As a mother names her child
When sleep at last has come
On limbs that had run wild.
What is it but nightfall?   65
No, no, not night but death;
Was it needless death after all?
For England may keep faith
For all that is done and said.
We know their dream; enough   70
To know they dreamed and are dead;
And what if excess of love
Bewildered them till they died?
I write it out in a verse –
MacDonagh and MacBride   75
And Connolly and Pearse
Now and in time to be,
Wherever green is worn,
Are changed, changed utterly:
A terrible beauty is born.   80

needless death: Yeats asks
if the Rising was a waste
of life, since the British
were already considering
independence for Ireland.

Connolly: Trade union
leader and revolutionary,
executed in 1916.

👤 Personal Response

1. Describe the atmosphere in the opening stanza of the poem. Refer closely to the text in your answer.
2. 'Easter 1916' has many striking images. Choose two that you find particularly interesting and briefly explain their effectiveness.
3. On balance, does Yeats approve or disapprove of the Easter Rising? Refer to the text in your answer.

👁 Critical Literacy

Yeats, who was in London at the time of the Rising, had mixed feelings about what had happened. He was clearly fascinated but also troubled by this heroic and yet in some ways pointless sacrifice. He did not publish the poem until 1920.

In the opening stanza, Yeats recalls how he used to meet some of the people who were later involved in the Easter Rising. He was unimpressed by their 'vivid faces' and he remembers routinely dismissing them with 'Polite meaningless words'. His admission that he **misjudged these insignificant Republicans** as subjects for 'a mocking tale or a gibe' among his clever friends is a reminder of his derisive attitude in 'September 1913'. Before 1916, Yeats had considered Ireland a ridiculous place, a circus 'where motley is worn'. But the poet confesses that the Rising transformed everything – including his own condescending apathy. In the stanza's final lines, Yeats introduces what becomes an ambivalent refrain ending in 'A terrible beauty is born'.

This sense of shock and the need to completely re-evaluate his views is developed in stanza two. The poet singles out individual martyrs killed or imprisoned for their activities, among them his close friend Countess Markievicz. He also mentions Major John MacBride, husband of Maud Gonne, who had refused Yeats's proposal of marriage. Although he had always considered MacBride as little more

'changed utterly'

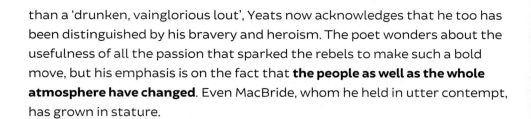

than a 'drunken, vainglorious lout', Yeats now acknowledges that he too has been distinguished by his bravery and heroism. The poet wonders about the usefulness of all the passion that sparked the rebels to make such a bold move, but his emphasis is on the fact that **the people as well as the whole atmosphere have changed**. Even MacBride, whom he held in utter contempt, has grown in stature.

In stanza three, Yeats takes powerful images from nature and uses them to explore the meaning of Irish heroism. The metaphor of the stubborn stone in the stream might represent the defiance of the revolutionaries towards all the forces around them. **The poet evokes the constant energy and dynamism of the natural world**, focusing on the changes that happen 'minute by minute'. Image after dazzling image conjure up a vivid picture of unpredictable movement and seasonal regeneration (as 'hens to moor-cocks call') and skies change 'From cloud to tumbling cloud'. For the poet, the Rising presented many contradictions, as he weighs the success of the revolt against the shocking costs. In contrasting the inflexibility of the revolutionaries with the 'living stream', he **indicates a reluctant admiration for the rebels' dedication**. Does Yeats suggest that the rebels risked the loss of their own humanity, allowing their hearts to harden to stone? Or is he also thinking of Maud Gonne and blaming her cold-hearted rejection of him on her fanatical political views?

In the final stanza, the poet returns to the metaphor of the unmoving stone in a flowing stream to warn of the dangers of fanaticism. The rhetorical questions about the significance of the rebellion reveal his **continuing struggle to understand** what happened. Then he asks the single most important question about the Rising: 'Was it needless death after all', particularly as 'England may keep faith' and allow Ireland its independence, all of which would prompt a more disturbing conclusion, i.e. that the insurgents died in vain.

Yeats quickly abandons essentially unanswerable questions about the value of the Irish struggle for freedom. Instead, he simply pays tribute to the fallen patriots by naming them tenderly, 'As a mother names her child'. The final assertive lines commemorate the 1916 leaders in dramatic style. Setting aside his earlier ambivalence, Yeats acknowledges that these patriots died for their dreams. The hushed tone is reverential, almost sacred. The rebels have been transformed into martyrs who will be remembered for their selfless heroism 'Wherever green is worn'. The insistent final refrain has a stirring and increasingly disquieting quality. The poem's central paradox, 'A terrible beauty is born', concludes that **all the heroic achievements of the 1916 Rising were at the tragic expense of human life**.

✒ Writing About the Poem

'W. B. Yeats's public poetry responds to particular situations in terms that can often seem unclear and contradictory.' Discuss this view with reference to both the subject matter and style of 'Easter 1916'.

Sample Paragraph

Yeats admired, yet was troubled by the 1916 Rising. The sound of the resonating refrain, 'All changed, changed utterly', adds a solemn note. Yet Yeats also honestly debates the wisdom of the uprising, asking 'Was it needless death after all?' The image of the heart as a stone reflects the poet's own torn emotions because it not only suggests the fierce determination of those rebels involved, but also underlines the inflexibility of their thinking. The poem concludes with a list of the rebel leaders and the realisation that the implacable stone in the midst of the 'living stream' does change the flow. These famous Irish names had changed history. The paradoxical statement, 'A terrible beauty is born', reflects the poet's admiration of the rebels' sacrifice and also his shocked reaction to the events they unleashed.

EXAMINER'S COMMENT

A focused, top-grade response that addresses the question directly. The commentary throughout shows a very good understanding of Yeats's divided views. Points are aptly supported with accurate quotation. Some perceptive discussion regarding the poet's use of the stone symbol to illustrate his appreciation of how the 1916 Rising had changed Irish history. Expression ('resonating', 'inflexibility', 'implacable') is also impressive.

✎ Class/Homework Exercises

1. 'W. B. Yeats explores complex political themes in richly energetic language.' Discuss this statement with reference to 'Easter 1916'.
2. 'Yeats honestly reflects on change and immortality in his dynamic, lyrical poetry.' Discuss this view with reference to 'Easter 1916'.

⊙ Points to Consider

- **Deeply felt elegy commemorating a controversial historical event.**
- **Effective contrast of formal structure with colloquial language.**
- **Ambivalent attitudes of admiration and shock.**
- **Formal rhyme scheme, rhythmic phrases, economy of language.**
- **Symbolism, repetition, antithesis and paradox all convey the poet's contradictory views.**
- **Thrilling refrain resonates with the consequence of change.**

6 The Second Coming

Turning and turning in the widening gyre
The falcon cannot hear the falconer;
Things fall apart; the centre cannot hold;
Mere anarchy is loosed upon the world,
The blood-dimmed tide is loosed, and everywhere   5
The ceremony of innocence is drowned;
The best lack all conviction, while the worst
Are full of passionate intensity.

Surely some revelation is at hand;
Surely the Second Coming is at hand.   10
The Second Coming! Hardly are those words out
When a vast image out of Spiritus Mundi
Troubles my sight: somewhere in sands of the desert
A shape with lion body and the head of a man,
A gaze blank and pitiless as the sun,   15
Is moving its slow thighs, while all about it
Reel shadows of the indignant desert birds.
The darkness drops again; but now I know
That twenty centuries of stony sleep
Were vexed to nightmare by a rocking cradle,   20
And what rough beast, its hour come round at last,
Slouches towards Bethlehem to be born?

Title: a reference to the Bible. It is from Matthew and speaks of Christ's return to reward the good.

in the widening gyre: Yeats regarded a cycle of history as a gyre. He visualised these cycles as interconnecting cones that moved in a circular motion, widening outwards until they could not widen any further, then a new gyre or cone formed from the centre of the circle created. This spun in the opposite direction to the original cone. The Christian era was coming to a close and a new, disturbed time was coming into view. In summary, the gyre is a symbol of constant change.
falcon: a bird of prey, trained to hunt by the aristocracy.
falconer: the trainer of the falcon. If the bird flies too far away, it cannot be directed.
Mere: nothing more than; only.
anarchy: lack of government or order. Yeats believed that bloodshed and a worship of bloodshed were the end of an historical era.
blood-dimmed: made dark with blood.
Spiritus Mundi: Spirit of the World, the collective soul of the world.
lion body and the head of a man: famous statue in Egypt; an enigmatic person.
desert birds: birds of prey.
twenty centuries: Yeats believed that two thousand years was the length of a period in history.
vexed: annoyed; distressed.
rocking cradle: coming of the infant Jesus.
rough beast: the Antichrist.
Bethlehem: birthplace of Christ. It is usually associated with peace and innocence, and it is terrifying that the beast is going to be born there. The spiral has reversed its spinning. A savage god is coming.

'lion body and the head of a man'

👤 Personal Response

1. In your opinion, what is the central mood in the opening stanza? Anxiety? Confusion? Fear? Support your views with reference to the text.

2. Yeats uses symbols to express some of his most profound ideas. What symbols in this poem appeal to you? Use reference to the text in your response.

3. 'Yeats is yearning for order, and fearing anarchy.' Discuss two ways in which the poem illustrates this statement. Support your answer with reference to the text.

👁 Critical Literacy

'The Second Coming' is a terrifying, apocalyptic poem written in January 1919 against a background of the disintegration of three great European empires at the end of World War I and the catastrophic War of Independence in Ireland. These were bloody times. Yeats yearned for order and feared anarchy.

Sparked off by both disgust at what was happening in Europe as well as his interest in the occult, Yeats explores, in stanza one, what he perceives to be the failure at the heart of society: 'Things fall apart'. In his opinion, **the whole world was disintegrating** into a bloody, chaotic mess. This break-up of civilisation is described in metaphorical language. For Yeats, the 'gyre' is a symbol representing an era. He believed that contrary expanding and contracting forces influence people and cultures and that the Christian era was nearing its end. The failure of the old world order is conveyed through hunting imagery, 'The falcon cannot hear the falconer'. We have lost touch with Christ, just as the falcon loses touch with the falconer as he swings into ever-increasing circles. This bird was trained to fly in circles to catch its prey. The circular imagery, with the repetitive '-ing', describes the continuous, swirling movement. Civilisation is also 'Turning and turning in the widening gyre' as it buckles and fragments.

The **tension** is reflected in a list of contrasts: 'centre' and 'fall apart', 'falcon' and 'falconer', 'lack all conviction' and 'intensity', 'innocence' and 'anarchy'. The strain is too much: 'the centre cannot hold'. The verbs also graphically describe this chaotic world: 'Turning and turning', 'loosed', 'drowned', 'fall apart'. Humans are changing amidst the chaos: 'innocence is drowned'. **Anarchy** is described in terms of a great tidal wave, 'the blood-dimmed tide', which sweeps everything before it. The compound word reinforces the overwhelming nature of the water. Yeats feels that the 'best', the leaders and thinkers, have no energy; they are indifferent and 'lack all conviction'. On the other hand, the 'worst', the cynics and fanatics, are consumed with hatred and violence, 'full of passionate intensity'.

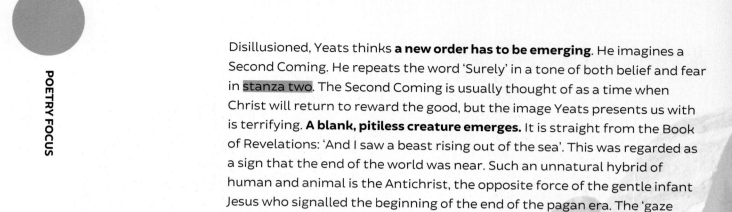

Disillusioned, Yeats thinks **a new order has to be emerging**. He imagines a Second Coming. He repeats the word 'Surely' in a tone of both belief and fear in stanza two. The Second Coming is usually thought of as a time when Christ will return to reward the good, but the image Yeats presents us with is terrifying. **A blank, pitiless creature emerges.** It is straight from the Book of Revelations: 'And I saw a beast rising out of the sea'. This was regarded as a sign that the end of the world was near. Such an unnatural hybrid of human and animal is the Antichrist, the opposite force of the gentle infant Jesus who signalled the beginning of the end of the pagan era. The 'gaze blank' suggests its lack of intelligence. The phrase 'pitiless as the sun' tells us the creature has no empathy or compassion. It 'Slouches'. It is a brutish, graceless monstrosity.

The **hostile environment** is a nightmare scenario of blazing desert sun, shifting sands and circling predatory birds. The verbs suggest everything is out of focus: 'Reel', 'rocking', 'Slouches'. 'The darkness drops again' shows how disorder, disconnectedness and the 'widening gyre' have brought us to nihilism. This seems to be a prophetic statement, as fascism was to sweep the world in the mid-20th century. Then Yeats has a moment of epiphany: 'but now I know'. Other eras have been destroyed before. The baby in the 'rocking cradle' created an upheaval that resulted in the end of 'twenty centuries of stony sleep'.

Yeats believed that a **cycle of history** lasted two thousand years in a single evolution of birth, growth, decline and death. All change causes upheaval. The Christian era, with its qualities of innocence, order, maternal love and goodness, is at an end. The new era of the 'rough beast' is about to start. It is pitiless, destructive, violent and murderous. This new era has already begun: 'its hour come round at last'. It is a savage god who is coming, uninvited. The spiral has reversed its motion and is now spinning in the opposite direction. The lack of end rhyme mirrors a world of chaos. Yeats looks back over thousands of years. We are given a thrilling and terrifying prospect from a vast perspective of millennia.

✒ Writing About the Poem

'Yeats frequently uses powerful and disturbing imagery to express a dark vision of the future.' Discuss this view with reference to 'The Second Coming'.

Sample Paragraph

The themes of stability and chaos are central to 'The Second Coming'. From the opening line, 'Turning and turning in the widening gyre', Yeats presents the disturbing image of the falcon spinning out of control. The sense of disintegration continues and the language becomes more violent – 'The blood-dimmed tide is loosed'. Dramatic details create a dark vision of life – 'anarchy is loosed'. There is irony in the poet's prophecy of a new saviour ('The Second Coming'). Unlike the first Christian Messiah, the next one will be a 'rough beast' bringing unknown horrors – 'A shape with lion body'. Yeats believed that Christianity was about to be replaced by a world where evil would triumph. The image of the sinister beast, with its 'gaze blank and pitiless as the sun' was particularly chilling.

EXAMINER'S COMMENT

A clear, insightful response to the question. Informed points focused directly on how Yeats's imagery conveyed his pessimistic prophecy. Good choice of accurate quotations provide support throughout. Expression is impressive also: varied sentence length, wide-ranging vocabulary ('sense of disintegration') and good control of syntax. A top-grade standard.

✒ Class/Homework Exercises

1. 'W. B. Yeats's political poems are remarkable for their forceful language and sensuous imagery.' Discuss this statement with reference to 'The Second Coming'.
2. 'Yeats often presents a dramatic tension between order and disorder.' Discuss this view with reference to 'The Second Coming'.

◉ Points to Consider

- The poem's title has obvious biblical associations.
- Scenes of anarchy and disorder lead to an apocalyptical vision of the future.
- Variety of tones/moods: foreboding, disillusionment, fear, despair.
- Effective use of contrast, dramatic imagery, symbols, striking comparisons.

7 Sailing to Byzantium

Title: for Yeats, this voyage would be one taken to find perfection. This country only exists in the mind. It is an ideal. The original old city of Byzantium was famous as a centre of religion, art and architecture.

I

That is no country for old men. The young
In one another's arms, birds in the trees
– Those dying generations – at their song,
The salmon-falls, the mackerel-crowded seas,
Fish, flesh, or fowl, commend all summer long   5
Whatever is begotten, born, and dies.
Caught in that sensual music all neglect
Monuments of unageing intellect.

That: Ireland – all who live there are subject to ageing, decay and death.

dying generations: opposites are linked to show that in the midst of life is death.

sensual music: the young are living life to the full through their senses and are neglecting the inner spiritual life of the soul.

II

An aged man is but a paltry thing,
A tattered coat upon a stick, unless   10
Soul clap its hands and sing, and louder sing
For every tatter in its mortal dress,
Nor is there singing school but studying
Monuments of its own magnificence;
And therefore I have sailed the seas and come   15
To the holy city of Byzantium.

paltry thing: worthless, of no importance. Old age is not valued in Ireland.
tattered coat: an old man is as worthless as a scarecrow.
unless/Soul clap its hands and sing: man can only break free if he allows his spirit the freedom to express itself.
Nor is there ... own magnificence: all schools of art should study the discipline they teach, while the soul should study the immortal art of previous generations.

III

O sages standing in God's holy fire
As in the gold mosaic of a wall,
Come from the holy fire, perne in a gyre,
And be the singing-masters of my soul.   20
Consume my heart away; sick with desire
And fastened to a dying animal
It knows not what it is; and gather me
Into the artifice of eternity.

O sages: wise men, cleansed by the holy fire of God.
Come ... artifice of eternity: Yeats asks the sages to teach him the wonders of Byzantium and gather his soul into the perfection of art.
perne in a gyre: spinning; turning very fast.
fastened to a dying animal: the soul trapped in a decaying body.

IV

Once out of nature I shall never take   25
My bodily form from any natural thing,
But such a form as Grecian goldsmiths make
Of hammered gold and gold enamelling
To keep a drowsy Emperor awake;
Or set upon a golden bough to sing   30
To lords and ladies of Byzantium
Of what is past, or passing, or to come.

past, or passing, or to come: in eternity, the golden bird sings of transience (passing time).

'the holy city of Byzantium'

👤 Personal Response

1. This poem tries to offer a form of escape from old age. Does it succeed? Write a paragraph in response, with support from the text.
2. Why are the 'Monuments of unageing intellect' of such importance to the poet? What does this imply about Yeats's Ireland?
3. The poem is defiant in its exploration of eternity. Discuss, using reference or quotation.

👁 Critical Literacy

'Sailing to Byzantium' confronts the universal issue of old age. There is no easy solution to this problem. Yeats found the idea of advancing age repulsive and he longed to escape. Here he imagines an ideal place, Byzantium, which allowed all to enjoy eternal works of art. He celebrates what humanity can create and he bitterly condemns the mortality to which man is subject.

Yeats wrote, 'When Irishmen were illuminating the Book of Kells … Byzantium was the centre of European civilization … so I symbolise the search for the spiritual life by a journey to that city.'

The poet declares the theme in the first stanza as he confidently declaims that the world of the senses is not for the old – they must seek another way which is timeless, **a life of the spirit and intellect**. The word 'That' tells us he is looking back, as he has already started his journey. But he is looking back wistfully at the world of the lovers ('The young/In one another's arms') and the world of teeming nature ('The salmon-falls, the mackerel-crowded seas'). The compound words emphasise the dynamism and fertility of the life of the senses, even though he admits the flaw in this wonderful life of plenty is mortality ('Those dying generations'). The life of the senses and nature is governed by the harsh cycle of procreation, life and death.

The poet asserts in the second stanza that **what gives meaning to a person is the soul**, 'unless/Soul clap its hands and sing'. Otherwise an elderly man is worthless, 'a paltry thing'. We are given a chilling image of the thin, wasting frame of an old man as a scarecrow in tattered clothes. In contrast, we are shown the wonders of the intellect as the poet tells us that all schools of art study what they compose, what they produce – 'Monuments of unageing intellect'. These works of art are timeless; unlike the body, they are not subject to decay. Thus, music schools study great music and art schools study great paintings. The life of the intellect and spirit must take priority over the life of the senses. Yeats will no longer listen to the 'sensual music' that is appropriate only for the young, but will study the carefully composed 'music' of classic art.

In Byzantium, the buildings had beautiful mosaics, pictures made with little tiles and inlaid with gold. One of these had a picture of martyrs being burned. Yeats addresses these wise men ('sages') in stanza three. He wants them to whirl through time ('perne in a gyre') and come to **teach his soul how to 'sing'**, how to live the life of the spirit. His soul craves this ('sick with desire'), **but it is trapped in the decaying, mortal body** ('fastened to a dying animal'). This is a horrendous image of old age. The soul has lost its identity: 'It knows not what it is'.

He pleads to be saved from this using two interesting verbs, 'Consume' and 'gather'. Both suggest a desire to be taken away. A fire consumes what is put into it and changes the form of the substance. Yeats wants a new body. He pleads to be embraced like a child coming home: 'gather me'. But where will he go? He will journey into the cold world of art, 'the artifice of eternity'. 'Artifice' refers to the skill of those who have created the greatest works of art, but it also means artificial, not real. Is the poet suggesting that eternity also has a flaw?

The fourth stanza starts confidently as Yeats declares that 'Once out of nature', he will be transformed into the ageless perfect work of art, the **golden bird**. This is the new body for his soul. Now he will sing to the court. But is the court listening? The word 'drowsy' suggests not. Isn't he singing about transience, the passing of time: 'what is past, or passing, or to come'? Has this any relevance in eternity? Is there a perfect solution to the dilemma of old age?

Yeats raises these questions for our consideration. He has explored this problem by contrasting the abundant life of the young with the 'tattered coat' of old age. He has shown us the golden bird of immortality in opposition to the 'dying animal' of the decaying body. The poet has lulled us with end-rhymes and half-rhymes. He has used groups of threes – 'Fish, flesh, or fowl', 'begotten, born, and dies', 'past, or passing, or to come' – to argue his case. At the end of the poem, do we feel that Yeats genuinely longs for the warm, teeming life of the senses with all its imperfections, rather than the cold, disinterested world of the 'artifice of eternity'?

✍ Writing About the Poem

'W. B. Yeats frequently uses vigorous language to denounce transience and old age.' Discuss this view with reference to 'Sailing to Byzantium'.

Sample Paragraph

In 'Sailing to Byzantium', Yeats confronts old age. A grotesque image of an old man as a scarecrow, 'A tattered coat upon a stick', is presented. The figure is unable to move, graphically illustrating age. The vivid adjective 'tattered' suggests the physical wear and tear elderly people endure. Yeats longed to escape this fate, through a passionate appeal to the 'sages' to 'Consume my heart away'. Thinking of time's decay, he is 'sick with desire' just as in his poem, 'The Wild Swans at Coole' – 'And now my heart is sore'. So Yeats decides to shed the 'dying animal' of his ageing body and change into a golden bird, a precious, immortal work of art. Ironically, the bird's function is reduced to keeping a 'drowsy Emperor awake' while, like the scarecrow, it is 'set upon a golden bough'. I feel that it is the allure of 'The young/In one another's arms' that Yeats really craves. His rich dynamic description of youth is achieved through compound words ('salmon-falls') and alliteration, 'Fish, flesh, fowl'. He longs to be young again.

EXAMINER'S COMMENT

A successful top-grade response that focuses on both aspects of the question. Points are developed and aptly illustrated with accurate quotation. Impressive discussion regarding the poet's robust, vigorous style ('graphically illustrating', 'passionate appeal', 'rich dynamic description'). Some insightful personal response and cross-referencing show close engagement with Yeats's poems. Expression throughout is very well controlled.

Class/Homework Exercises

1. 'Yeats's search for truth serves to highlight the intense fury and disillusionment expressed in his poetry.' Discuss this view with reference to 'Sailing to Byzantium'.

2. 'W. B. Yeats makes effective use of imagery and symbolism to communicate thought-provoking insights about life.' Discuss this statement with reference to 'Sailing to Byzantium'.

⊙ Points to Consider

- Central themes include transience, old age and the timeless world of art.

- Rich symbols, metaphors, imagery and similes communicate the complexity of humans' struggle with transience and decay.

- Balance, contrast and paradox reveal the complexity of the problem of old age.

- Compound words, onomatopoeia, intriguing use of verbs lend energy and passion to the argument.

8 *from* Meditations in Time of Civil War: The Stare's Nest By My Window

W. B. YEATS

The bees build in the crevices
Of loosening masonry, and there
The mother birds bring grubs and flies.
My wall is loosening; honey-bees,
Come build in the empty house of the stare.   5

We are closed in, and the key is turned
On our uncertainty; somewhere
A man is killed, or a house burned,
Yet no clear fact to be discerned:
Come build in the empty house of the stare.   10

A barricade of stone or of wood;
Some fourteen days of civil war;
Last night they trundled down the road
That dead young soldier in his blood:
Come build in the empty house of the stare.   15

We had fed the heart on fantasies,
The heart's grown brutal from the fare;
More substance in our enmities
Than in our love; O honey-bees,
Come build in the empty house of the stare.   20

Title: Stare is another name for the starling, a bird with distinctive dark brown or greenish-black feathers.

grubs: larvae of insects.

civil war: the Irish Civil War (1922–23) between Republicans, who fought for full independence, and supporters of the Anglo-Irish Treaty.
trundled: rolled.

fare: diet (of dreams).

enmities: disputes; hatred.

'days of civil war'

👤 Personal Response

1. Comment on how Yeats creates an atmosphere of concern and insecurity in stanzas two and three.
2. In your opinion, how effective is the symbol of the bees as a civilising force amid all the destruction of war? Support your answer with close reference to the poem.
3. How would you describe the dominant mood of the poem? Is it positive or negative? Refer closely to the text in your answer.

👁 Critical Literacy

The Irish Civil War prompted Yeats to consider the brutality and insecurity caused by conflict. It also made him reflect on his own identity as part of the Anglo-Irish Ascendancy. The poet wrote elsewhere that he had been shocked and depressed by the fighting during the first months of hostilities, yet he was determined not to grow bitter or to lose sight of the beauty of nature. He wrote this poem after seeing a stare building its nest in a hole beside his window.

Much of the poem is dominated by the images of building and collapse. Stanza one introduces this tension between creativity ('bees build') and disintegration ('loosening'). In responding to the bitter civil war, Yeats finds suitable **symbols in the nurturing natural world** to express his own hopes. Addressing the bees, he asks that they 'build in the empty house of the stare'. He is desperately conscious of the political vacuum presently being filled by bloodshed. His desperate cry for help seems heartfelt in tone. There is also a possibility that the poet is addressing himself – he will have to revise his own attitudes to the changing political realities caused by the war.

In stanza two, Yeats expresses a sense of being **threatened by the conflict** around him: 'We are closed in'. The use of the plural pronoun suggests a community under siege. He is fearful of the future: 'our uncertainty'. Is the poet reflecting on the threat to his own immediate household or to the once-powerful Anglo-Irish ruling class? The constant rumours of everyday violence are highlighted in the stark descriptions: 'A man is killed, or a house burned'. Such occurrences seem almost routine in the grim reality of war.

Stanza three opens with a **haunting image**, the 'barricade of stone', an enduring symbol of division and hostility. The vehemence and inhumanity of the times is driven home by the stark report of soldiers who 'trundled down the road' and left one 'dead young soldier in his blood'. Such atrocities add greater depth to the plaintive refrain for regeneration: 'Come build in the empty house of the stare'.

In the final stanza, Yeats faces up to the root causes of war: 'We had fed the heart on fantasies'. Dreams of achieving independence have led to even greater hatred ('enmities') and intransigence than could have been imagined. It is a tragic irony that the Irish nation has become more divided than ever before. The poet seems despairing as he accepts the failure represented by civil conflict: 'The heart's grown brutal'. It is as though he is reprimanding himself for daring to imagine a brave new world. His **final plea for healing** and reconstruction is strengthened by an emphatic 'O' to show Yeats's depth of feeling: 'O honey-bees,/Come build in the empty house of the stare'.

✒ Writing About the Poem

'Yeats's poetic vision is one of darkness and disappointment, balanced by moments of insight and optimism.' Discuss this view with reference to 'The Stare's Nest By My Window' *from* 'Meditations In Time Of Civil War'.

Sample Paragraph

In 'The Stare's Nest By My Window', Yeats reveals his views on the Irish Civil War. Throughout the poem, there are recurring images of destruction. Observing the bees outside his window, he is surprised to see something purposeful going on within the 'loosening masonry'. Although the crumbling building suggests the break-up of the Irish nation, there is also an ironic recognition of something new happening. This is typical of the poet's ambivalent attitude – similar to his view of Easter 1916 as a 'terrible beauty'. The positive image of the bees is symbolic of recovery from the conflict. The poet's use of symbolism contrasts the two forces of devastation and regeneration when he urges the bees to 'build in the empty house'. However, there are several dark images that show the poet's realism, e.g. the 'house burned' and the tragic life of the 'young soldier in his blood'. These are stark reminders of human loss – the reality of conflict. But in the end, Yeats seems to argue that we can learn from nature. He hopes that just as the birds take care of their young, Ireland will recover from warfare.

EXAMINER'S COMMENT

A well-written top-grade response. Informed discussion focused throughout on the balance between Yeats's positive and negative attitudes. Accurate quotations provided good support. Cross-referencing shows engagement with the poet's complex views. Expression throughout is very well controlled ('recurring images', 'ironic recognition', 'stark reminders of human loss').

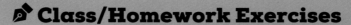 Class/Homework Exercises

1. 'W. B. Yeats often uses startling language and imagery to raise key questions about Irish nationalism.' Discuss this statement, referring both to the subject matter and style of 'The Stare's Nest By My Window'.

2. 'Yeats's poems frequently address serious issues in a fresh and accessible style.' Discuss this view with reference to 'The Stare's Nest By My Window'.

⊙ Points to Consider

- Another of Yeats's political poems expressing his personal views on Irish history.

- Central themes: Civil War violence and destruction; the natural world.

- Effective use of repetition, varying tones (dismay, hopelessness, acceptance, yearning).

- Contrasting images of destruction ('loosening masonry') and renewal ('bees build').

9 In Memory of Eva Gore-Booth and Con Markiewicz

W. B. YEATS

The light of evening, Lissadell,		**Lissadell:** the Gore-Booth family home in Co. Sligo.
Great windows open to the south,		
Two girls in silk kimonos, both		**kimonos:** traditional Japanese robes.
Beautiful, one a gazelle.		**gazelle:** graceful antelope.
But a raving autumn shears	5	**shears:** cuts.
Blossom from the summer's wreath;		
The older is condemned to death,		
Pardoned, drags out lonely years		
Conspiring among the ignorant.		**Conspiring:** plotting; scheming.
I know not what the younger dreams –	10	
Some vague Utopia – and she seems,		**Utopia:** a perfect world.
When withered old and skeleton-gaunt,		
An image of such politics.		
Many a time I think to seek		
One or the other out and speak	15	
Of that old Georgian mansion, mix		
Pictures of the mind, recall		
That table and the talk of youth,		
Two girls in silk kimonos, both		
Beautiful, one a gazelle.	20	
Dear shadows, now you know it all,		
All the folly of a fight		**folly:** foolishness.
With a common wrong or right.		
The innocent and the beautiful		
Have no enemy but time;	25	
Arise and bid me strike a match		
And strike another till time catch;		
Should the conflagration climb,		**conflagration:** blazing inferno.
Run till all the sages know.		**sages:** philosophers.
We the great gazebo built,	30	**gazebo:** ornamental summer house, sometimes seen as a sign of extravagance.
They convicted us of guilt;		
Bid me strike a match and blow.		

'that old Georgian mansion'

👤 Personal Response

1. What mood does Yeats create in the first four lines of the poem? Explain how he achieves this mood.
2. Would you agree that this is a poem of contrasts? How does Yeats use contrasts to express his thoughts and feelings? Support your points with relevant reference.
3. What picture of Yeats himself emerges from this poem? Use close reference to the text to support the points you make.

👁 Critical Literacy

Yeats wrote this poem about the two Gore-Booth sisters shortly after their deaths. He was 62 at the time. Eva was a noted campaigner for women's rights and Constance was a revolutionary who took part in the 1916 Rising. She later became the first woman elected to the British House of Commons at Westminster. The poet had once been fascinated by their youthful grace and beauty, but he became increasingly opposed to their political activism. Although the poem is a memorial to the two women, it also reveals Yeats's own views about the changes that had occurred in Ireland over his lifetime.

Stanza one begins on a nostalgic note, with Yeats recalling a magical summer's evening in the company of the Gore-Booth sisters. The details he remembers suggest a **world of elegance and privilege** in the girls' family home, Lissadell House, overlooking Sligo Bay. 'Great windows' are a reminder of the grandeur to be found in the Anglo-Irish 'Big House'. Eva and Constance are portrayed as being delicately beautiful, their elusive femininity indicated by the exotic 'silk kimonos' they wear. The poet compares one of the girls to 'a gazelle', stylishly poised and graceful.

The abrupt contrast of mood in line 5 disrupts the tranquil scene. Yeats considers the harsh effects of time and how it changes everything. He describes autumn (personified as an overenthusiastic gardener) as 'raving' and uncontrollable. The metaphor illustrates the way **time destroys** ('shears') the simple perfection of youth ('Blossom'). Typically, Yeats chooses images from the natural world to express his own retrospective outlook.

In lines 7–13, the poet shows his **deep contempt** for the involvement of both the Gore-Booth sisters in revolutionary politics. As far as Yeats is concerned, their activism 'among the ignorant' was a great mistake. These beautiful young women wasted their lives for a 'vague Utopia'. The graphic image of one of the girls growing 'withered old and skeleton-gaunt' is also used to symbolise the unattractive political developments of the era. Repulsed by the idea, Yeats retreats into the more sophisticated world of Lissadell's 'old Georgian mansion'.

The second stanza is in marked contrast to the first. Yeats addresses the spirits ('shadows') of Eva and Constance. The tone of voice is unclear. It appears to be compassionate, but there is an undertone of weariness as well. He goes on to scold the two women for wasting their lives on 'folly'. Yeats seems angry that their innocence and beauty have been sacrificed for nothing. It is as though he feels **they have betrayed both their own femininity and their social class**. If they had only known it, their one and only enemy was time.

In the final lines of the poem, Yeats dramatises his feelings by turning all his **resentment against time** itself. He associates the failed lives of the women with the decay of the Anglo-Irish Ascendancy. The energetic rhythm and repetition reflect his fury as he imagines striking match after match ('And strike another till time catch') and is consumed in a great 'conflagration'. The poet imagines that the significance of this inferno will eventually be understood by those who are wise, the 'sages'. In the last sentence, Yeats considers how 'They' (the enemies of the Anglo-Irish Ascendancy) hastened the end of a grand cultural era in Ireland. The 'great gazebo' is a symbol of the fine houses and gracious living that were slowly disappearing. The poem ends on a defiant note ('Bid me strike a match and blow'), with Yeats inviting the ghosts of Eva and Constance to help him resist the devastating effects of time.

✒ Writing About the Poem

'Many of Yeats's most evocative poems lament the loss of youth and beauty.' Discuss this view with reference to 'In Memory of Eva Gore-Booth and Con Markiewicz'.

Sample Paragraph

'In Memory of Eva Gore-Booth and Con Markiewicz' is largely focused on time as a destructive force. Yeats begins by describing the aristocratic sisters as 'Two girls in silk kimonos', the gentle sibilant sounds suggesting their elegance. The poem is really an elegy for the past and Yeats's nostalgic portrayal of the time he shared with the young women at Lissadell is filled with regret. The tone becomes more wistful as he remembers summer evenings 'and the talk of youth'. Yeats illustrates the effects of age when he contrasts the girls in their graceful refinement in their later years – 'withered old and skeleton-gaunt'. The image is startling, evidence of how he views the ravages of time. It is all the more shocking when compared with the delicate kimonos – symbols of lost beauty.

> **EXAMINER'S COMMENT**
>
> *A well-focused top-grade standard which directly addresses the question. Good discussion of the poem's mood of regret ('nostalgic portrayal', 'tone becomes more wistful'). Excellent use of contrasting images to illustrate the poet's theme. The references and quotes are carefully chosen and show clear engagement with the poem. Expression is also impressive.*

✒ Class/Homework Exercises

1. 'W. B. Yeats makes effective use of contrasting moods and atmospheres to express his strongly held ideas and heartfelt feelings.' Discuss this statement with reference to 'In Memory of Eva Gore-Booth and Con Markiewicz'.
2. 'Yeats frequently combines both a sensitive romantic nature and a fiercely critical voice.' Discuss this view with reference to both to the subject matter and style of 'In Memory of Eva Gore-Booth and Con Markiewicz'.

⊙ Points to Consider

- Elegy for a lost world of great beauty, style and sophistication.
- The poem reveals Yeats's own attitudes to the two sisters.
- Life's transience sharply contrasted with the longevity of art.
- Various tones: nostalgic, reflective, scornful, critical.
- Striking imagery of light and shade and seasonal change.

10 Swift's Epitaph

Title: Jonathan Swift, satirist and clergyman, author of *Gulliver's Travels* and dean of St Patrick's Cathedral. The original inscription in Latin is on his memorial in the cathedral. Yeats liked to spend time there.
Epitaph: inscription for a tomb or memorial.

Swift has sailed into his rest;
Savage indignation there
Cannot lacerate his breast.
Imitate him if you dare,
World-besotted traveller; he   5
Served human liberty.

his rest: suggestion of afterlife; death is not an end.
Savage indignation: the driving force of Swift's satirical work. He believed in a society where wrong was punished and good rewarded.
lacerate: cut; tear.
World-besotted: obsessed with travelling or with material concerns rather than spiritual matters.
he/Served human liberty: Yeats believed Swift served the liberty of the intellect, not liberty for the common people. Yeats associated democracy with organised mobs of ignorant people.

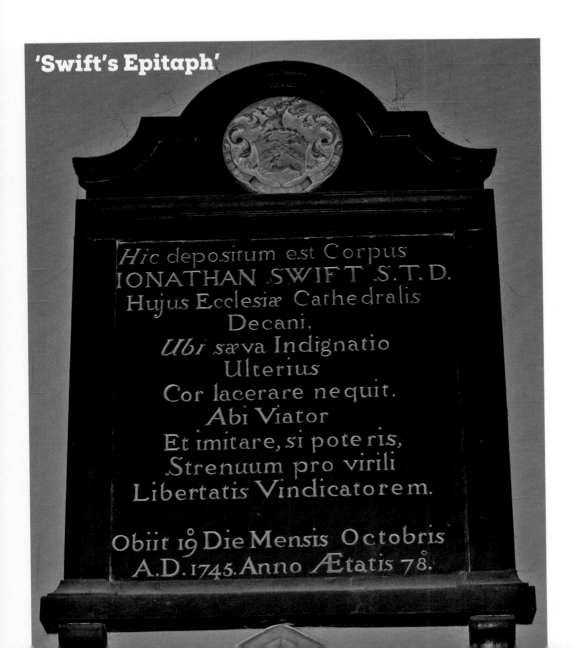

'Swift's Epitaph'

👤 Personal Response

1. How would you describe the tone of this poem?
2. Comment on the poet's use of the verb 'lacerate'. What do you think Yeats is trying to convey?

👁 Critical Literacy

'Swift's Epitaph' is a translation from the original Latin epitaph composed by Swift for himself. Yeats adds a new first line to the original. He regarded this epitaph as the 'greatest ... in history'.

W. B. Yeats admired Swift, who was proud and solitary and belonged to the Anglo-Irish tradition, as did Yeats himself. He regarded the Anglo-Irish as superior. He once said, 'We have created most of the modern literature of this country. We have created the best of its political intelligence.' Yeats's additional first line to the epitaph conveys a dignified sailing into the spiritual afterlife by the deceased Swift. The rest of the poem is a **translation** from the Latin original. Swift is now free from all the negative reactions he was subjected to when alive: 'Savage indignation there/Cannot lacerate his breast.' Swift's self-portrait conveys the impression of a man of fierce **independence and pride**. 'Imitate him if you dare' is the challenge thrown down like a gauntlet to the reader to try to be like him. 'World-besotted traveller' can be read as a man who has travelled extensively in his imagination as well as in reality. His contribution to humanity is summed up in the final sentence: 'he/Served human liberty'. **He freed the artist** from the masses so that the artist could 'make liberty visible'. The tone of this short, compressed poem is proud and defiant, like Swift.

🖋 Writing About the Poem

'W. B. Yeats frequently confronts the painful reality of death in fierce, challenging poetry.' Discuss this view with particular reference to 'Swift's Epitaph'.

Sample Paragraph

Yeats wrote two epitaphs – his own in 'Under Ben Bulben' and this translation of Swift's. Both show a disregard for life as a permanent end in itself. Yeats reveals a fearless, confident Swift departing this life for the next in the sibilant line, 'Swift has sailed into his rest'. The metaphor highlights the natural progression of the soul returning to its eternal rest. Death is a reality of life's circle. Swift's 'Savage indignation' was directed at the two great evils of society, starvation and emigration. But 'there', in paradise, he is able to leave aside his life's work and all the criticism he received. The verb 'lacerate' suggests the public backlash he suffered as a result. Yeats challenges readers, asking if we are brave enough to stand up (like Swift) for what is right, 'Imitate him if you dare'.

EXAMINER'S COMMENT

A top-grade response that shows good engagement with Yeats's poetry. This focused paragraph examines the poet's philosophy in some detail – and particularly his belief that what matters is the legacy an individual leaves behind after death. Several excellent discussion points are effectively supported with suitable quotation and there is fluent control of language throughout.

✒ Class/Homework Exercises

1. 'Yeats uses dramatic and forceful language to express his passionate views on ageing and the passing of time.' Discuss this statement with reference to 'Swift's Epitaph'.
2. 'W. B. Yeats often chooses confrontation when exploring universal themes in thought-provoking poetry.' Discuss this view with reference to 'Swift's Epitaph'.

⊙ Points to Consider

- **The satirist Jonathan Swift made a strong impact on Yeats's imagination.**

- **Sibilant metaphor of sailing suggests the ease of passage from this life to the next.**

- **Emphatic language highlights Swift's efforts to improve the human condition and the resulting response.**

- **Poem offers a direct provocative challenge to readers.**

11 An Acre of Grass

Picture and book remain,
An acre of green grass
For air and exercise,
Now strength and body goes;
Midnight, an old house   5
Where nothing stirs but a mouse.

My temptation is quiet.
Here at life's end
Neither loose imagination,
Nor the mill of the mind   10
Consuming its rag and bone,
Can make the truth known.

Grant me an old man's frenzy,
Myself must I remake
Till I am Timon and Lear   15
Or that William Blake
Who beat upon the wall
Till Truth obeyed his call;

A mind Michael Angelo knew
That can pierce the clouds,   20
Or inspired by frenzy
Shake the dead in their shrouds;
Forgotten else by mankind,
An old man's eagle mind.

acre: the secluded garden of Yeats's home, where he spent his final years.

an old house: the house was in Rathfarnham, Co. Dublin.

loose imagination: vague, unfocused ideas.

frenzy: wildly excited state.

Timon and Lear: two of Shakespeare's elderly tragic heroes, both of whom raged against the world.
William Blake: English visionary poet and painter (1757–1827).

Michael Angelo: Michelangelo, Italian Renaissance artist (1475–1564).

shrouds: burial garments.

'An acre of green grass'

👤 Personal Response

1. How does Yeats create a mood of calm and serenity in the opening stanza?
2. Briefly explain the change of tone in stanza three.

👁 Critical Literacy

Written in 1936 when Yeats was 71, the poet expresses his resentment towards ageing gracefully. Instead, he will dedicate himself to seeking wisdom through frenzied creativity. People sometimes take a narrow view of the elderly and consider them completely redundant. In Yeats's case, he is determined not to let old age crush his spirit.

Stanza one paints a picture of retirement as a surrender to death. Yeats's life has been reduced to suit his basic needs. 'Picture and book' might refer to the poet's memories. Physically weak, he feels like a prisoner whose enclosed garden area is for 'air and exercise'. There is an underlying **feeling of alienation and inactivity**: 'nothing stirs'.

In stanza two, the poet says that it would be easy to give in to the stereotypical image of placid contentment: 'My temptation is quiet', especially since old age ('life's end') has weakened his creative powers. **Yeats admits that his 'loose imagination' is not as sharp as it was when he was in his prime.** He no longer finds immediate inspiration ('truth') in everyday experiences, which he compares to life's 'rag and bone'.

The third stanza opens on a much more dramatic and forceful note as the poet confronts his fears: 'Grant me an old man's frenzy'. Yeats's personal prayer is totally lacking in meekness. Instead, he urges himself to focus enthusiastically on his own creative purpose – 'frenzy'. **He pledges to 'remake' himself** in the image of such heroic figures as Timon, Lear and William Blake. The passionate tone and run-on lines add to his sense of commitment to his art.

In stanza four, Yeats develops **his spirited pursuit of meaningful old age** by reflecting on 'A mind Michael Angelo knew'. The poet is stimulated and encouraged to follow the great artist's example and 'pierce the clouds'. The image suggests the daring power of imagination to lift the spirit in the search for truth and beauty. The final lines build to a climax as Yeats imagines the joys of 'An old man's eagle mind'. Such intense creativity can 'Shake the dead' and allow the poet to continue experiencing life to its fullest.

✒ Writing About the Poem

'W. B. Yeats uses powerful language and imagery to express his personal views.' Discuss this statement with reference to 'An Acre of Grass'.

Sample Paragraph

Yeats takes a highly unusual approach to ageing in 'An Acre of Grass'. To begin with, his subdued tone suggests that he is happy in his quiet 'acre of green grass'. Everything seems organised, yet a little too organised for his liking. In the first few lines, we see someone close to second childhood, engrossed in his 'Picture and book'. Acutely aware of his years, he resents being at 'life's end'. Clearly, he yearns for renewed energy and inspiration. His forceful language emerges in the second half of the poem when he demands 'an old man's frenzy'. His need to be creative again is illustrated by the references to Lear (the tragic king in Shakespeare's play who fought to the bitter end) and to William Blake and Michelangelo. Like them, Yeats wants to live a productive life – with an 'eagle mind'. The dramatic metaphor typifies his startling imagery. In these final lines, his tone is defiant.

EXAMINER'S COMMENT

There is some good discussion in this paragraph and a clear sense of engagement. Informed points focused on the subdued tone and irony in the early stanzas. Accurate quotations are integrated effectively into the commentary. Expression is impressive also: varied sentence length, ranging vocabulary ('yearns for renewed energy and inspiration', 'dramatic metaphor typifies his startling imagery') and good control of syntax. A top-grade standard.

Class/Homework Exercises

1. 'Some of Yeats's most thought-provoking poems combine his personal concerns with public issues.' Discuss this view with reference to 'An Acre of Grass'.
2. 'Yeats uses simple and direct language in exploring his concerns about ageing and death.' Discuss this statement with reference to 'An Acre of Grass'.

Points to Consider

- Confessional poem addresses familiar themes of old age and artistic revitalisation.

- Striking contrast between his initial acceptance of age and his final determination to renew himself.

- Effective use of imagery to show that the house has also been engulfed by old age.

- References to Blake, Timon of Athens and King Lear focus on Yeats's desired poetic-frenzy.

12 *from* Under Ben Bulben

V

Irish poets, learn your trade,
Sing whatever is well made,
Scorn the sort now growing up
All out of shape from toe to top,
Their unremembering hearts and heads   5
Base-born products of base beds.
Sing the peasantry, and then
Hard-riding country gentlemen,
The holiness of monks, and after
Porter-drinkers' randy laughter;   10
Sing the lords and ladies gay
That were beaten into the clay
Through seven heroic centuries;
Cast your mind on other days
That we in coming days may be   15
Still the indomitable Irishry.

VI

Under bare Ben Bulben's head
In Drumcliff churchyard Yeats is laid,
An ancestor was rector there
Long years ago, a church stands near,   20
By the road an ancient cross.
No marble, no conventional phrase;
On limestone quarried near the spot
By his command these words are cut:
    Cast a cold eye   25
    On life, on death.
    Horseman, pass by!

whatever is well made: great art.

base: low; unworthy.

indomitable: invincible; unbeatable.

Under bare Ben Bulben's head: defiant symbol of the famous mountain.

ancestor: the poet's great-grandfather.

Horseman: possibly a symbolic figure from local folklore; or possibly any passer-by.

'Under bare Ben Bulben's head'

👤 Personal Response

1. Comment on the tone used by Yeats in giving advice to other writers. Refer to the text in your answer.
2. From your reading of the poem, explain the kind of 'Irishry' that Yeats wishes to see celebrated in poetry. Support the points you make with reference or quotation.
3. Describe the mood of Drumcliff churchyard as visualised by the poet. Use close reference to the text to show how Yeats uses language to create this mood.

👁 Critical Literacy

This was one of Yeats's last poems. Sections V and VI of the elegy sum up his personal views on the future of Irish poetry and also include the enigmatic epitaph he composed for his own gravestone. Using art as a gateway to spiritual fulfilment is characteristic of the poet.

Section V is a hard-hitting address by Yeats to his contemporaries and all the poets who will come after him. He encourages them to set the highest 'well-made' standards for their work. His uncompromisingly negative view of contemporary writing ('out of shape from toe to top') is quickly clarified. The reason why modern literature is in such a state of confusion is that the poets' 'unremembering hearts and heads' **have lost touch with tradition**. The formality and discipline of great classic poetry have been replaced by unstructured writing and free verse. The authoritative tone becomes even more scathing as Yeats rebukes the inferiority of his peers as 'Base-born products'.

It is not only intellectual artistic tradition that the poet admires; he finds another valuable tradition in the legends and myths of old Ireland. Yeats urges his fellow writers to 'Sing the peasantry'. But he also advises them to **absorb other cultural traditions**. Here he includes the 'Hard-riding country gentlemen' of his own Anglo-Irish class and the 'holiness of monks' – those who seek truth through ascetic or spiritual means. Even the more sensuous 'randy laughter' of 'Porter-drinkers' can be inspirational. For Yeats, the peasant and aristocratic traditions are equally worth celebrating. Irish history is marked by a combination of joy, heroism, defeat and resilience. Yet despite (or perhaps because of) his harsh criticism of the present generation, there is little doubt about the poet's passionate desire to encourage new writing that would reflect the true greatness of 'indomitable Irishry'.

Section VI is a great deal less confident. Writing in the third person, Yeats describes his final resting place in Drumcliff. The voice is **detached and dignified**. Using a series of unadorned images, he takes us to the simple churchyard at the foot of Ben Bulben. The mountain stands as a proud symbol of how our unchanging silent origins outlive human tragedy. It is to

W. B. YEATS

his Irish roots that the poet ultimately wants to return. His wishes are modest but curt – 'No marble'. Keen to avoid the well-worn headstone inscriptions, Yeats provides his own incisive epitaph. The three short lines are enigmatic and balance opposing views, typical of so much of his poetry. The poet's last warning ('Cast a cold eye') reminds us to live measured lives based on a realistic understanding of the cycle of life and death. The beautiful Christian setting, subdued tone and measured rhythm all contribute to the quiet dignity of Yeats's final farewell.

✒ Writing About the Poem

'W. B. Yeats's inspired poetry gives expression to the spirit of a whole nation through his distinctive style.' Discuss this view with reference to 'Under Ben Bulben'.

Sample Paragraph

'Under Ben Bulben' addresses themes close to Yeats's heart – the perfection of art, Irish nationalism and the reality of death. The poet's views are expressed in an imperative voice: 'Irish poets, learn your trade'. Yeats believed in traditional verse, spending hours shaping a poem. He is bitterly opposed to the free verse of contemporary poets, 'Scorn the sort now growing up/All out of shape from toe to top'. His use of enjambed lines and the inverted phrase ('toe to top') mimics the ugliness of modern poetry. He also makes being Irish something to be desired, a race, undefeated after years of oppression, 'Still the indomitable Irishry', even inventing a new word to express our unique culture. The modern poets he is addressing are urged to remember this, 'Cast your minds on other days'. Yeats's poetry practises what he preaches, presenting a 'well-made' poem with a vision of what it means to be Irish.

EXAMINER'S COMMENT

A top-grade response that explores Yeats's writing style alongside the central theme of Irishness. Points are aptly illustrated with accurate quotation. Some impressive discussion regarding the poet's critical tone in mocking aspects of contemporary poetry. Expression throughout is clear and well controlled.

✎ Class/Homework Exercises

1. 'W. B. Yeats has remarked that his poetry is generally written out of despair.' Discuss this statement, referring to both the subject matter and style of 'Under Ben Bulben'.
2. 'Yeats's forceful language and vivid imagery convey his intense vision of life and death.' Discuss this view with reference to 'Under Ben Bulben'.

⊙ Points to Consider

- Self-epitaph achieving his aim 'to hammer my thoughts into unity'.

- Formal vision of integrated spiritual reality, natural cycle of life and death.

- Revitalised use of traditional rhyme scheme and metered poetry (strict four-beat rhythm).

- Use of colloquial language. Short lines give a modern quality to the poem.

- Distinctive poetic voice, authoritative, compelling, direct and exhilarating.

13 Politics

W. B. YEATS

Title: winning and using power to govern society.

'In our time the destiny of man presents its meanings in political terms.'
Thomas Mann

How can I, that girl standing there,
My attention fix
On Roman or on Russian
Or on Spanish politics?
Yet here's a travelled man that knows   5
What he talks about,
And there's a politician
That has read and thought,
And maybe what they say is true
Of war and war's alarms,   10
But O that I were young again
And held her in my arms.

Thomas Mann was a German novelist who argued that the future of humanity is determined by states and governments.

On Roman or on Russian/ Or on Spanish politics: a reference to the political upheavals of Europe in the 1930s.

'O that I were young again'

👤 Personal Response

1. This poem suggests that politics is not important. Does the poet convince you? Write a paragraph in response, with reference to the text.
2. Where does the language used in the poem convey a sense of deep longing? Comment briefly on the effectiveness of this.

👁 Critical Literacy

'Politics' is a satire written in 1939, when Yeats was 73, in response to a magazine article. He said it was based on 'a moment of meditation'.

A **satire** uses ridicule to expose foolishness. A magazine article praised Yeats for his 'public' work. The poet was delighted with this word, as one of his aims had always been to 'move the common people'. However, the article went on to say that Yeats should have used this 'public' voice to address public issues such as politics. Yeats disagreed, as he had always regarded politics as dishonest and superficial. He thought professional politicians manipulated through 'false news'. This is evident from the ironic comment, 'And maybe what they say is true'. Here we see the poet's indifference to these matters.

This poem addresses **real truths**, the proper material for poems, the universal experience of **human relationships**, not the infinite abstractions that occupied politicians ('war and war's alarms'). Big public events, Yeats is suggesting, are not as important as love. The girl in the poem is more important than all the politics in the world: 'How can I … My attention fix/ On Roman or on Russian/Or on Spanish politics'? So Yeats is overthrowing the epigraph at the beginning of the poem, in which the novelist Thomas Mann states that people should be concerned with political matters. Politics is the winning and using of power to govern the state. Yeats is adopting the persona of the distracted lover who is unable to focus on the tangled web of European politics in the 1930s. This poem was to be placed in his last poetry collection, almost like a farewell, as he states again that what he desires is youth and love.

But this poem can also give another view. Is the 'she' in the poem Ireland? Yeats had addressed public issues in poems such as 'Easter 1916' and 'September 1913' and he was already a senator in the Irish government. As usual, he leaves us with questions as he draws us through this deceptively simple poem with its **ever-changing tones** that range from the questioning opening to mockery, doubt and finally longing. The **steady rhyme** (the second line rhymes with the fourth and so on) drives the poem forward to its emphatic **closing wish**, the cry of an old man who wishes to recapture his youth and lost love.

✒ Writing About the Poem

'Yeats's final poems are particularly poignant because all that matters to him is youth and love.' Discuss this view with reference to 'Politics'.

Sample Paragraph

It's thought that 'Politics' is Yeats's last poem – and it expresses his belief in the importance of emotions over everything else. Although written in 1938 when Europe was edging towards war, the poet is unable to focus on public affairs – 'Roman or on Russian/Or on Spanish politics'. Instead, he is more interested in a beautiful girl who is nearby. His tone is tender – 'O that I were young again/ And held her in my arms'. As in 'Sailing to Byzantium', he is well aware of the impossibility of reversing time – and that is what makes the poem so moving. The exclamation 'O' is all the more touching because the poet understands how hopeless his desires are. For me, this bittersweet realisation makes 'Politics' one of Yeats's most poignant poems.

✒ Class/Homework Exercises

1. 'W. B. Yeats frequently writes simple but beautiful poems that have universal significance.' Discuss this statement with reference to 'Politics'.
2. 'Despite his intense disappointment with reality, Yeats can often find hope in his imagination.' Discuss this view with reference to 'Politics'.

◎ Points to Consider

- Central focus on the poet's nostalgia for his younger days.
- Yeats is preoccupied with private human interaction rather than public or political situations.
- The poet expresses little optimism or even interest in the future.
- Various tones: reflective, sceptical, ironic, nostalgic, resigned.
- Effective use of contrasts: intellect and emotion, age and youth, male and female.

Understanding the Prescribed Poetry Question

Marks are awarded using the PCLM Marking Scheme: P = 15; C = 15; L = 15; M = 5 Total = 50

- **P** (Purpose = 15 marks) refers to the set question and is the launch pad for the answer. This involves engaging with all aspects of the question. Both theme and language must be addressed, although not necessarily equally.

- **C** (Coherence = 15 marks) refers to the organisation of the developed response and the use of accurate, relevant quotation. Paragraphing is essential.

- **L** (Language = 15 marks) refers to the student's skill in controlling language throughout the answer.

- **M** (Mechanics = 5 marks) refers to spelling and grammar.

- Although no specific number of poems is required, students usually discuss at least 3 or 4 in their written responses.

- Aim for at least 800 words, to be completed within 45–50 minutes.

NOTE

In keeping with the PCLM approach, the student has to take a stance by agreeing, disagreeing or partially agreeing with the statement:

– **Yeats's reflective poetry** (conflict, disappointment, loss, mortality, ageing, escape, perfection of art, immortality, eternity, etc.)

... is defined through:

– **the tension between idealism and reality** (contrasting imagery, compelling symbols, dramatic language, powerful rhetoric, intense paradoxes, conflicting moods and tones, etc.)

Sample Leaving Cert Questions on Yeats's Poetry

1. 'W. B. Yeats's reflective poetry is defined largely by the tension between his search for an ideal world and the failure to escape reality.' To what extent do you agree or disagree with this statement? In developing your answer, discuss both the themes and poetic language of the poetry of W. B. Yeats on your course.

2. 'Yeats's poetry can sometimes seem obscure and challenging, but his powerful language has enduring appeal.' Discuss this view, developing your answer with reference to both the themes and poetic style of the poetry of W. B. Yeats on your course.

3. From your study of the poetry of W. B. Yeats on your course, select the poems that, in your opinion, best demonstrate his effective use of rich symbolism and vivid imagery to explore a range of poetic themes. Justify your response, developing your answer with reference to the poetry of W. B. Yeats on your course.

How do I organise my answer?

(Sample question 1)

'W. B. Yeats's reflective poetry is defined largely by the tension between his search for an ideal world and the failure to escape reality.' To what extent do you agree or disagree with this statement? In developing your answer, discuss both the themes and poetic language of the poetry of W. B. Yeats on your course.

Sample Plan 1

Intro: (*Stance: agree with viewpoint in the question*) Yeats's poetry is distinguished by a powerful strain between his pursuit of an ideal state and the inability to flee the harsh reality of everyday life. Effective use of forceful imagery, dramatic language and a variety of compelling tones.

Point 1: (*Elegy – world of beauty and grace/ugly reality – contrast*) 'In Memory of Eva Gore-Booth and Con Markiewicz' nostalgically recalls an elegant world, juxtaposing it against the ravages of time. Contemptuous tone conveys Yeats's resentment at real life choices made by Gore-Booth sisters ('gazelle' transforms into 'skeleton-gaunt').

Point 2: (*Confession – ageing/renewal – vivid imagery, allusions*) 'An Acre of Grass' presents Yeats's resentful attitude to the reality of ageing ('Now strength and body goes'). He yearns for the artistic world ('an old man's frenzy'). Startling imagery captures the poet's intense desire for artistic activity and productivity ('Shake the dead in their shrouds').

Point 3: (*Self-epitaph – inferior modern literature/perfection of classical literature – imperative, contrast*) *from* 'Under Ben Bulben' contrasts ugliness of modern verse ('Base-born products') with perfection of heroic couplets ('learn your trade,/Sing whatever is well made').

Point 4: (*Satire – ageing/renewal – contrasts*) 'Politics' ironically comments on reality of politicians' false promises ('And maybe what they say is true') with his deeply held belief in the power of the emotions ('O that I were young again/And held her in my arms').

Conclusion: Yeats frequently reveals his inner struggle in confronting human realities. He creates poetry bringing his ideal world to life to enable us to see beyond what meets the eye while acknowledging but never fully accepting the harsh truths of everyday experience.

Sample Paragraph: Point 2

'An Acre of Grass' is Yeats's confession that he refuses to grow old gracefully. While he acknowledges the reality that he is 'Here at life's end', he despises old age's inactivity, 'nothing stirs'. Instead, he desires 'an old man's frenzy'. Yeats's internal struggle with the reality of ageing causes him to turn to his great role models. These include characters from Shakespeare, 'Timon and Lear', who challenged this unjust world. His desperate tone is evident in his prayer for help, 'Grant me'. But the poet is determined to continue with his artistic pursuits, despite his acknowledgement that his 'loose imagination' no longer finds inspiration in the dull 'rag and bone' of 'everyday routine. Dramatic verbs ('pierce', 'inspired') describe the creative vigour of this 'old man's eagle mind'. His tone reflects his inner conflict.

EXAMINER'S COMMENT
Sustained top-grade response that addresses the question. Analytical points show a clear understanding of the poem. There is close engagement with the text, particularly in the discussion of how the poet's turmoil is conveyed through vivid imagery, intense tones and contrasts. Impressive expression throughout and excellent use of supportive quotes.

(Sample question 2)

'Yeats's poetry can sometimes seem obscure and challenging, but his powerful language has enduring appeal.' Discuss this view, developing your answer with reference to both the themes and poetic style of the poetry of W.B. Yeats on your course.

Sample Plan 2

Intro: (*Stance: partially agree with viewpoint in the question*) Yeats forces readers to consider challenging concepts – transience, creativity, the

429 |

NOTE

In keeping with the PCLM approach, the student has to take a stance by agreeing and/or disagreeing that Yeats's poetry can sometimes seem

- **obscure and challenging** (complex philosophical themes – materialism/idealism, ageing/regeneration, nature/mysticism, art/beauty, political conflict/patriotism, unclear references/allusions, etc.)

... but there is enduring appeal in:

- **powerful language** (evocative imagery, startling sound effects, dramatic verbs, striking comparisons, engaging tones, compelling rhythms, etc.)

breakdown of civilisation, political change, heroism, the immortality of art. His powerful language has enduring appeal – forceful metaphors, vivid images and symbols, dramatic quality, repetition.

Point 1: (*Apocalyptic vision – chilling imagery, foreboding tone*) 'The Second Coming' presents compelling imagery – a falcon spiralling out of control ('turning and turning'). Interesting biblical imagery ('rough beast') lends authority and dramatic verbs emphasise the turbulent mood.

Point 2: (*Transience/eternity – absorbing symbols, compound words*) 'Sailing to Byzantium' tackles the eternal problem of mortality/immortality. Vigorous phrases ('salmon-falls', 'mackerel-crowded') evoke fertility. Poet regards ageing man as worthless ('paltry thing') presenting a haunting image of frailty and decay ('dying animal'). Using emphatic language, Yeats addresses this stimulating theme.

Point 3: (*Destruction/nurturing – rich metaphor, repetition, contrasts*) 'The Stare's Nest By My Window' *from* 'Meditations in Time of Civil War', introduces nature's regenerative power ('bees build') to expose the horrific damage wreaked by conflict ('A man is killed, or a house burned'). Repetitive image of political vacuum ('empty house of the stare') contrasted with maternal nurturing ('mother birds bring grubs and flies').

Point 4: (*Provocative challenge – sibilant language, defiant tone*) 'Swift's Epitaph' opens with an evocative metaphor describing Swift's death ('sailed into his rest'). This serene image contrasts with reality of hostile reaction ('Savage indignation') to Swift's efforts for improving humanity.

Conclusion: Yeats defiantly confronts his readers with challenging, but clearly defined themes, including the future, transience and conflict. Attractive writing style, inspiring visual and aural effects, innovative language and a rich variety of tones all excite the reader.

Sample Paragraph: Point 1

'The Second Coming' presents another challenging idea – the apocalyptic vision of society's collapse. This is seen in the image of the falcon spiralling out of control, 'Turning and turning and in the widening gyre'. Yeats believes that fanatics are taking control, 'the worst/Are full of passionate intensity'. Although he presents us with a disturbing image of humanity's spirit rising in a shocking 'Second Coming', he vividly describes it – 'blank and pitiless as the sun'. As always, the poet's alliteration, 'darkness drops', strikes a foreboding note. Vigorous visual imagery, 'blood-dimmed tide', reinforces the hectic scene. For Yeats, the era of innocence and order symbolised by the 'rocking cradle' in Bethlehem is disappearing. In its place, is a new era where a savage god will be 'moving its slow thighs'. A difficult subject is brought to life by the power of the poet's language.

Leaving Cert Sample Essay

'W. B. Yeats makes effective use of rich symbolism and vivid imagery to explore a range of poetic themes.' Discuss this statement, developing your answer with reference to both the themes and poetic style of the poetry of W. B. Yeats on your course.

Sample Essay

1. The passing of time, political change and the search for spiritual meaning are recurring themes in Yeats's poetry. He is often angry about ageing and the limits of human existence. He offers his personal opinions on public and universal themes in poems such as 'The Lake Isle of Innisfree', 'September 1913', 'The Wild Swans at Coole' and 'Easter 1916'. Yeats communicates his views in a powerful display of vibrant symbolism and vivid imagery.

2. In 'The Lake Isle of Innisfree', Yeats addresses a personal yet public theme, the longing of exiled emigrants to return to the peace of their homeland. Beautiful images describe the idyllic existence on Innisfree. The intensity of noonday heat on the heather is suggested by the broad-vowelled phrase 'purple glow'. The serenity of this magical place is evoked through slow broad vowels, alliterative 'l' sounds and onomatopoeia, 'I hear lake water lapping with low sounds by the shore'. This hypnotic vision – and Yeats's deep sense of longing – is interrupted by the startling reality of impersonal urban life, 'I stand on the roadway, or on the pavements grey'. Insistent monosyllable sounds emphasise the poet's deep desire to escape, 'I hear it in the deep heart's core'.

3. 'The Wild Swans at Coole' uses equally contrasting images. The swans are a powerful symbol of youthful vigour. Alliteration and onomatopoeia convey the dynamism of the noisy swans 'wheeling in great broken rings'. The swans' strong relationship, 'Lover by lover', is noted. Swans usually mate for life. This serene image is interrupted, as in the previous poem, with the bitter reality of Yeats's personal anguish. Unlike these 'brilliant creatures', he is ageing. He has been disappointed in life, 'now my heart is sore'. Yet, it is the dream which lingers in the reader's mind due to the poet's technical brilliance. The swans 'still drift on the still water,/ Mysterious, beautiful'. Yeats, again has combined personal and universal concerns, lost love and transience in haunting language.

4. In contrast to such lyrical beauty, the political poem, 'September 1913', attacks Irish citizens who focus on materialistic gain. Their attitude to religion is also mocked – they count 'prayer to shivering prayer'. Yeats was furious at the Dublin merchant classes of early 20th century Dublin who refused to fund the Hugh Lane Gallery and who were partly

INDICATIVE MATERIAL

• **Yeats's effective use of rich symbolism and vivid imagery** (powerful metaphors, colourful similes, vibrant descriptive details, striking references and allusions, lively aural imagery, etc.)

... that explore:

• **a range of poetic themes** (public and private, reality/ escape, transience/ immortality, exhilaration/ tragedy of conflict, materialistic present/ romanticised past, creativity, culture, etc.)

responsible for the trade union lockout. In contrast, Yeats communicates the idealistic dream which these merchants do not understand. He reminds them that there were once patriotic heroes who 'stilled your childish play'. The price they paid was the 'hangman's rope' or exile from their homeland, 'The grey wing upon every tide'. Yeats has taken a local conflict and given it a global application through powerful visual and aural imagery.

5. 'Easter 1916' is another political poem highlighting Yeats's feelings. He is condescending towards those who fought for Irish freedom. He is barely civil, exchanging 'polite meaningless words' with them. The poet thought of Ireland as a land of fools who wore the clothes of clowns, 'where motley is worn'. Yet another paradox, 'A terrible beauty', acknowledges the pain and suffering of the rebels of 1916. Their devotion to a cause made their hearts 'Enchanted to a stone'. Yeats believed that dedication to an ideal resulted in men losing their humanity. This is indeed 'terrible'. However, their devotion also made it 'beautiful'.

6. Yeats addresses the conflict between mortality and immortality in 'Sailing to Byzantium'. The poet belittles an old man through the use of the telling symbol, 'at tattered coat upon a stick'. Alienated from a youthful Ireland, described in dynamic images, 'salmon-falls', 'mackerel-crowded seas', he lists the inescapable cycle of life, 'begotten, born, and dies'. He will fight against old age through art. Yeats rejects the decaying mortal body, 'A dying animal', and decides to become a golden bird 'set upon a golden bough' to continue his trade as poet, singing of 'what is past or passing or to come'. But this time the dream does not work. The Emperor is 'drowsy', inattentive. Byzantium, this mythical symbol of 'artifice' does not satisfy. Instead, it is the realistic image of the 'young/in one another's arms' which lingers in the reader's mind. The poet poses the problem of mortality and immortality and leaves it to the reader to consider.

7. Yeats repeatedly considers public and private themes, including escape, transience, conflict and death. These are carefully shaped, resulting in poems that echo 'like a ringing bell' due to forceful symbolism and compelling imagery.

(760 words)

W. B. YEATS

👓 Revision Overview

'The Lake Isle of Innisfree' (OL)
In this beautiful poem, filled with sensual images, Yeats dreams of escaping the modern world to find peace in the countryside.

'September 1913'
Disenchanted with materialism, Yeats contrasts Ireland's past with the self-serving values of modern society.

'The Wild Swans at Coole' (OL)
A persistent sense of failure and regret underlies this poem in which Yeats explores the transience of human life.

'An Irish Airman Foresees His Death' (OL)
In this presentation of the power of the human spirit, Yeats addresses Irish national identity.

'Easter 1916'
The force of political passion is central to this poem in which Yeats expresses his conflicted emotions regarding the Easter Rising.

'The Second Coming'
Yeats's longing for order leads him to envision some sort of Second Coming. This was traditionally associated with the return of Christ to Earth.

'Sailing to Byzantium'
Yeats yearns for meaning in this complex poem which addresses the reality of ageing.

'The Stare's Nest By My Window'
Yeats returns to the subject of moral and social collapse, and the search for renewal. The desire for freedom is central to the poem.

'In Memory of Eva Gore-Booth and Con Markiewicz'
Yeats laments time's effects on beauty and youthful idealism. The poem also considers the contribution that artists make to society.

'Swift's Epitaph'
Yeats's high regard for Swift can be seen as part of his commitment to Anglo-Irish cultural politics.

'An Acre of Grass'
Another confessional poem. The loss of poetic vision makes Yeats long for insight into the mystery of life and death.

from 'Under Ben Bulben'
Facing death, Yeats embraces the spiritual world of eternity. He urges Irish poets to share his vision for fulfilment through art.

'Politics'
In this nostalgic poem, Yeats acknowledges human weakness. He believed love is more important than politics in shaping destiny.

💬 Last Words

'Yeats's poetry is simple and eloquent to the heart.'
Robert Louis Stevenson

'He had this marvellous gift of beating the scrap metal of the day-to-day life into a ringing bell.'
Seamus Heaney

'All that is beautiful in art is laboured over.'
W. B. Yeats

 CREATIVITY   TRANSIENCE   MEANING OF LIFE   LOVE   IRELAND   NATURE   HISTORY/ MEMORY   LONGING   ART   HEROISM

The Unseen Poem

'Students should be able ... to read poetry conscious of its specific mode of using language as an artistic medium.'
(DES English Syllabus, 4.5.1)

Note that responding to the unseen poem is an exercise in aesthetic reading. It is especially important, in assessing the responses of the candidates, to guard against the temptation to assume a 'correct' reading of the poem.

Reward the candidates' awareness of the patterned nature of the language of poetry, its imagery, its sensuous qualities, and its suggestiveness.

SEC Marking Scheme

In the Unseen Poem 20-mark question, you will have 20 minutes to read and respond to a short poem that you are unlikely to have already studied. Targeted reading is essential. **Read over the questions** first to focus your thoughts and feelings.

In your **first reading** of the poem:
- Aim to get an initial sense of what the poet is saying and think about why the poet is writing about that particular subject.
- What is happening? Who is involved? Is there a sense of place and atmosphere?
- Underline interesting words or phrases that catch your attention. Avoid wasting time worrying about any words that you don't understand. Instead, **focus on what makes sense** to you.

Read through the poem **a second time:**
- Who is speaking in the poem? Is it the poet or another character?
- Is the poet describing a scene?
- Or remembering an experience?
- What point is the poet making?
- What do you notice about the poet's language use?
- How does the poem make you feel?
- Did it make you wonder? Trust your own reaction.

Check the **'Glossary of Common Literary Terms'** on GillExplore.ie

- **Theme** (the central idea or message in a poem. There may be more than one theme)
- **Imagery** (includes similes, metaphors, symbols and personification)
- **Sound (aural) effects** – often referred to as onomatopoeia (includes alliteration, assonance, sibilance, rhyme and repetition)
- **Tone** (nostalgic, happy, sad, reflective, angry, optimistic, etc.)
- **Mood** (atmosphere can be relaxed, mysterious, poignant, uneasy, etc.)
- **Rhythm** (the pace or movement of lines, similar to the musical 'beat' of a song. Rhythm often reflects mood and can be slow, regular, rapid, uneven, etc.)
- **Language** (the poet's choice and order of words, including imagery and poetic devices)
- **Style** (the use of language. Poets choose various techniques, such as imagery, tone, etc. to convey meaning and emotion)
- **Lyric** (poem that expresses the poet's thoughts and feelings. Lyric poems are often short and sometimes resemble a song in form or style)
- **Rhyme** (the occurrence of the same or similar sounds – usually at the end of a line. Rhyme often adds emphasis)
- **Stanza** (two or more lines of poetry that together form a section of a poem)
- **Persona** (the speaker or 'voice' in the poem … This may or may not be the poet)
- **Personification** (where a thing is treated as a living being. In 'Mirror', Sylvia Plath gives an everyday household object human qualities, allowing it to speak – 'I am exact')
- **Enjambment** (when a line doesn't have punctuation at the end. The resulting run-on lines usually add emphasis)
- **Irony** (when there is a different meaning from what is stated, e.g. the title of Plath's poem, 'The Times Are Tidy')
- **Emotive language** (language that affects the reader's feelings, e.g. 'The streets that couldn't shelter them' in Paula Meehan's 'Prayer for the Children of Longing')
- **Contrasts** (contrasting themes, tones and images highlight differences and similarities, e.g. Seamus Heaney contrasts two violent settings in 'The Tollund Man')
- **Structure and layout** (a poem's form can be identified by analysing its structure or shape. Hopkins's sonnets are fourteen lines only and divided into two parts. The first eight lines are called the octave and often describe a problem, idea or situation. The next six lines are called the sestet and present a response to the octave)

> **REMEMBER!**
> *'This section [Unseen Poetry] was often not answered, resulting in a loss of 20 marks. Omitting questions or parts of questions has a deleterious effect and is often due to poor time management.'*
> **Chief Examiner's Report**

Unseen Poem – Practice 1

Read the following poem by Alan Bold and answer **either** Question 1 **or** Question 2 which follow.

1 Autumn

Autumn arrives
Like an experienced robber
Grabbing the green stuff
Then cunningly covering his tracks
With a deep multitude
Of colourful distractions.
And the wind,
The wind is his accomplice
Putting an air of chaos
Into the careful diversions
So branches shake
And dead leaves are suddenly blown
In the faces of inquisitive strangers.
The theft chills the world,
Changes the temper of the earth
Till the normally placid sky
Glows red with a quiet rage.

Alan Bold

---

1. (a) What do you learn about the poet's attitude to autumn in the above poem? Support your answer with reference to the poem. (10)

(b) Identify two images from the poem that make an impact on you and give reasons for your choice. (10)

OR

2. Discuss the appeal of this poem, commenting on its theme, tone and the poet's use of language and imagery. Support your answer with reference to the poem. (20)

Sample Answer 1

Q1. (a) (Poet's attitude to autumn)
(Basic response)

The poet's attitude to autumn is not good at all because he calls autumn an experienced robber which is a negative thing. Alan does not compare the beauty in which nature is full of descriptive scenery of leaves falling in countryside areas. I think he's wrong about autumn to call it a theif in the night because this is not the whole picture at all and he only sees the negative side like storms and trees shaking. There is another story to the beauty of autumn's nature other than the dead leaves which are a reminder of death which is a totally negative side. Alan has a pesimmistic attitude and this is too narrow to be true to life.

EXAMINER'S COMMENT

- Makes one valid point about negativity.
- Little development or use of reference.
- No focus on the varied aspects of autumn.
- Expression is awkward and repetitive.
- Incorrect spellings ('theif', 'pesimmistic').
  Marks awarded: 3/10

Sample Answer 2

Q1. (a) (Poet's attitude to autumn)
(Top-grade response)

Alan Bold has a very playful outlook towards the season of autumn. In comparing it to a cunning 'experienced' robber who sneaks in every year to steal 'the green stuff' that grows in summer, he seems fascinated by the way nature changes so secretively. Bold develops the metaphor throughout the poem, closely observing how the wind (autumn's 'accomplice') creates chaos, tossing colourful leaves across the ground. Autumn is depicted as a powerful natural force which not only changes the landscape, but also affects how people feel. This is evident in the poem's final lines where he suggests that autumn marks the transition into winter and is a reminder that nature can be destructive – and even something to be feared. The poet's overall attitude is that the season of autumn warns human beings about our fragile relationship with the natural world.

EXAMINER'S COMMENT

- Insightful answer that engages closely with the poem.
- Interesting final point about nature's destructive power.
- Good use made of supportive quotations throughout.
- Varied sentence length, fluent expression.
- Grammar and spellings are excellent.
  Marks awarded: 10/10

Sample Answer 3

Q1. (b) (Two images that make an impact)
(Basic response)

'the faces of inquisitive strangers' This is the first image that makes an impact on me and my reasons for my choice is that it is just as it would happen in reality when people are in parks. This when we see the leaves are blown around into your face during October. If people have young children with them they never stop asking questions about the weather and everything.

'normally placid sky' The second image from the poem that made an impact on me and my reason for my choice is because this is that it is pure Irish weather in which the clouds are grey. It is usually about to rain in Ireland just like the calm before the storm. It does not exactly stay placid for long in this country. This image is detailed and true to life.

EXAMINER'S COMMENT

- *Little engagement with the poem's language.*
- *Limited point about the realism of both images.*
- *Needs more developed discussion.*
- *Drifted into general commentary.*
- *Repetitive, flawed expression throughout.*

Marks awarded: 4/10

Sample Answer 4

Q1. (b) (Two images that make an impact)
(Top-grade response)

I thought the 'experienced robber' image was powerful. The simile suggests that autumn is sly – disturbing the peace of summer. Bold cleverly develops the comparison, emphasising the criminal image of the season, with associated words, such as 'covering his tracks' and 'cunningly'. The effect is playful – autumn is fooling everyone into a false sense of security by disguising the changes that are happening to the climate. This lively colourful season is not to be fully trusted.

In a second striking image, the poet personifies the wind, describing it as autumn's 'accomplice' in creating widespread havoc. It creates an air of chaos – literally. This gives nature a human characteristic, which only strengthens its awesome power. The wind shows autumn to be even more terrifying because something so strong is merely its accomplice.

EXAMINER'S COMMENT

- *Perceptive analysis of the poet's inventive language.*
- *Good understanding of the extended metaphor.*
- *Effective use of apt textual reference.*
- *Excellent expression throughout.*

Marks awarded: 9/10

Unseen Poem – Practice 2

Read the following poem by Grace Nichols and answer **either** Question 1 **or** Question 2 which follow.

Roller-Skaters

Flying by
on the winged-wheels
of their heels

Two teenage earthbirds
zig-zagging
down the street

Rising
unfeathered –
in sudden air-leap

Defying law
death and gravity
as they do a wheely

Landing back
in the smooth swoop
of youth

And faces gaping
gawking, impressed
and unimpressed

Only mother watches – heartbeat in her mouth

Grace Nichols

1. (a) What do you think the poet is saying about the relationships between parents and their children in 'Roller-Skaters'? Support your answer with reference to the poem. (10)

   (b) Identify two images from the poem that make an impact on you and give reasons for your choice. (10)

OR

2. Discuss the language, including the imagery, used by the poet throughout this poem. Make detailed reference to the poem in support of your answer. (20)

Sample Answer 1

Q2. (Poet's language use)
(Basic response)

The poet's language including the imagry used by the poet is very detailed. It shows a street where roller skaters are taking place. The details show they are brave doing the wheely and zig zags as they are actually risking their lives for the sport they love. I myself have mixed feelings about the imagry because it shows how they jump in amazing tricks. Like leaps but on the other hand their mother is afraid that he will be hurt. The language describes the danger.

People out in the street are looking at the image of these skaters. This is an image of risking life or just to show off to attract attention. The images make me think of the danger involved behind the first impressions of an exciting sport that attracts kids in every city. At the start it is very exciting because no one is injured so far but as Grace protrays the skaters more in a detailed way the language becomes more dangerous for example when she says there is a risk of death during the wheely. No wonder the mother watching has an image of her heart in her mouth because it is a dangerous situation and she is not too impressed.

EXAMINER'S COMMENT
- *Makes some points about detailed description.*
- *Little development or use of close reference to language.*
- *Minimal focus on the effectiveness of imagery.*
- *Expression is awkward and repetitive at times.*
- *Mechanical errors ('imagry', 'protrays').*
Marks awarded: 6/20

Sample Answer 2

Q2. (Poet's language use)
(Top-grade response)

Vivid imagery and energetic language are key features in this poem. Nichols describes the roller skaters 'Flying by' and having 'winged-wheels'. Both descriptions are metaphors as the skaters are not actually 'flying' nor do they have real 'wings'. The poem can be seen as one developed metaphor that suggests the breakneck actions of the skaters. Short lines and dynamic verbs, such as 'zig-zagging' suggest their speed.

The skaters are compared to 'earthbirds' which is very effective. I can imagine that they will take off into the air at any minute. Later on, they are described as 'unfeathered', which links back to the same idea that they are defying 'death and gravity'. Towards the end, the poet mentions the 'smooth sweep of youth' and suggests that the skaters are enjoying their freedom.

The poem's rhythm is lively throughout and not interrupted by punctuation. This highlights the reckless moves the skaters make. Run-on lines create a sense of continuous movement. Sound effects play a huge part. There is a pattern of slender vowels – e.g. 'winged-wheels' – in the opening lines which increases the pace. The alliteration suggests the repeated actions of the skaters.

The layout is arranged in a series of short lines and this highlights the skaters' lively movement. The final separate line cleverly suggests how the mother is outside of the action and can only watch from a distance as her child takes risks.

EXAMINER'S COMMENT
- *Focused on the effectiveness of language throughout.*
- *Ranges over various aspects, including imagery and sound.*
- *Well-developed discussion of the bird metaphor.*
- *Insightful comments on rhythm and structure.*
- *Good expression (although 'suggests' is overused). Marks awarded: 18/20*

REMEMBER!
There is no single 'correct' reading of the poem. Respond to the poem honestly. How does it make you feel? Trust your own reaction.

Unseen Poem – Practice 3

Read the following poem by David Harmer and answer **either** Question 1
or Question 2 which follow.

3 At Cider Mill Farm

I remember my uncle's farm
Still in mid-summer
Heat hazing the air above the red roof tops
Some cattle sheds, a couple of stables
Clustered round a small yard
Lying under the hills that stretched their long back
Through three counties.

I rolled with the dogs
Among the hay bales
Stacked high in the barn he built himself
During a storm one autumn evening
Tunnelled for treasure or jumped with a scream
From a pirate ship's mast into the straw
Burrowed for gold and found he'd buried
Three battered Ford cars deep in the hay.

He drove an old tractor that sweated oil
In long black streaks down the rusty orange
It chugged and whirred, coughed into life
Each day as he clattered across the cattle grids
I remember one night my cousin and I
Dragging back cows from over the common
We prodded them homeward through the rain
And then drank tea from huge tin mugs
Feeling like farmers.

He's gone now, he sold it
But I have been back for one last look
To the twist in the lane that borders the stream
Where Mary, Ruth and I once waded
Water sloshing over our wellies
And I showed my own children my uncle's farm
The barn still leaning over the straw
With for all I know three battered Ford cars
Still buried beneath it.

David Harmer

1. **(a)** What is your impression of the poet's experiences on the farm in 'At Cider Hill Farm'? Support your answer with reference to the poem. (10)

    (b) Select two images from the poem that appeal to you and give reasons for your choice. (10)

    OR

2. Discuss the language used by the poet, commenting on imagery, tone and sound effects. Support your answer with reference to the poem. (20)

Sample Answer 1

Q1. (a) (Poet's experiences on the farm)
(Basic response)

My impression of David Harmer is he remembers spending happy times on his holidays in cider mill farm. It belonged to his uncle who was the farm owner during his childhood, so he would have been there in the holidays. He had happy experiences splashing in the river and messing with the dogs but his best experience is of the one time he drank tea from the mugs belonging to the proper farmers after working with the cattle one evening. But the boy was dissapointed after the farm was sold, any child would naturally suffer from dissapointment by loosing their freedom. Up to then the farm life was very appealing, a good break away from school during the holidays.

> **EXAMINER'S COMMENT**
> • Some references to the poet's happy experiences.
> • These could have been more effectively supported by quotes.
> • Lacks discussion on stylistic features, e.g. nostalgic tone.
> • Capital letter errors and misspellings ('dissapointed', 'loosing').
> Marks awarded: 4/10

Sample Answer 2

Q1. (a) (Poet's experiences on the farm)
(Top-grade response)

Harmer's reminiscences are of exciting childhood days on his uncle's farm. From the start, his tone is nostalgic, 'Heat hazing the air above the red roof tops'. The vowel sounds and gentle alliteration emphasise the poet's happy memories of far-off times. The images of rural scenes show the impact that the countryside 'under the hills' had on him. I think it's almost as if the changing seasons matched the change in the poet's life as he grew up. The mood is enthusiastic, however. The boy's sense of adventure is seen when exploring new sensations among the farm animals, 'We prodded them homeward through the rain'. He seems fascinated by the 'rusty orange' tractor – 'It chugged and whirred'. As a child, he delighted in creating his own world. It's clear that the time on the farm was important, so much so that he wants to pass on his memories to his own children.

> **EXAMINER'S COMMENT**
> • Intuitive response focusing on the poet's idyllic childhood.
> • Good range of discussion points.
> • Well-supported by suitable quotations.
> • Effective reference to imagery, tone and sound effects.
> • Confident expression and excellent mechanics.
> Marks awarded: 10/10

Sample Answer 3

Q1. (b) (Two appealing images)
(Basic response)

The first appealing image is of 'one night dragging cows' because this shows cows don't hurry and have to be prodded with sticks. They nearly have to get dragged along as the image says, so this is the reason why this is a good image as it really shows farmers totally have their hands full trying to get animals to go anywhere.

The next image is 'three battered Ford cars'. This is the second appealing image of cars rusting in a field. This can be seen in parts of the country where cars are dumped and they are a complete and total eyesore to the public who have to look at them. So in one way this is not appealing as an image because some people just dump rubbish anywhere.

EXAMINER'S COMMENT
- *Slight points that need to be much more developed.*
- *Drifts into irrelevant general commentary.*
- *No attempt to examine the effectiveness of the language.*
- *Repetitive expression lacks fluency.*
Marks awarded: 3/10

Sample Answer 4

Q1. (b) (Two appealing images)
(Top-grade response)

There are many appealing images in this poem. I liked the ones that focused on the poet's carefree childhood, such as 'Heat hazing the air above the red roof tops'. The summer setting has strong associations with warmth and happiness. The poet remembers the haze of bright sunlight and the vivid red colours of the farm buildings. This vibrant imagery suggests an exaggerated childlike memory which is reinforced by the 'h' and 'r' alliteration. The line has a dreamlike quality, suggesting the wonder of the experience.

Some of the feelings the poet recalls are reinforced by sound images, for example, 'Water sloshing over our wellies'. The onomatopoeic effect of 'sloshing' echoes the squelching noises made by the children as they splashed through the water. This all contributes to the upbeat mood of the poem. Harmer is re-living a moment when he was totally happy-go-lucky on his uncle's farm.

EXAMINER'S COMMENT
- *Perceptive analysis of visual and aural imagery.*
- *Well-developed discussion examining language closely.*
- *Points supported by relevant textual reference.*
- *Excellent expression and varied vocabulary throughout.*
Marks awarded: 10/10

THE UNSEEN POEM

Unseen Poem – Practice 4

Read the following poem by Rosita Boland and answer **either** Question 1 **or** Question 2 which follow.

Lipstick

Home from work one evening,
I switched the radio on as usual,
chose a knife and started to slice
red peppers, scallions, wild mushrooms.

I started listening to a programme about Iran.
After the Shah fled, Revolutionary Guards
patrolled the streets of Teheran
looking for stray hairs, exposed ankles
and other signs of female disrespect.

The programme ended.
I was left standing in my kitchen
looking at the chopped vegetables on the table;
the scarlet circles of the peppers
delicate mouths, scattered at random.

When they discovered a woman wearing lipstick
they razor-bladed it off:
replaced one red gash with another.

Rosita Boland

445 |

1. (a) What do you learn about the kind of person the poet is from reading this poem? Explain your answer with reference to the poem. (10)

(b) Identify a mood or feeling evoked in 'Lipstick' and explain how the poet creates this mood or feeling. Support your answer with reference to the poem. (10)

OR

2. What impact did this poem make on you? Refer closely to the text in discussing its theme, tone and the poet's use of language and imagery. (20)

Sample Answer 1

Q2. (Impact of the poem)
(Basic response)

This was a hard to understand poem about a worker who comes home to make a meal. But she starts to listen to the news about what is happening in the war. I think she imagines the soilders running wild attacking people. One soilder uses a knife and attacks an innocent woman who is just dressed up and wearing lipstick which is her basic human right and just out for the evening. This guard should of known better. This is the part of the poem that made the most impact on me personally.

This is the theme of war and the tone of this poem is showing what happens on the back streets in some parts of the world. If your not doing harm you should be left in peace. There is a big difference between the image of the innocent woman out to enjoy herself on a night out as she is intitled and the angry language of the soilder who attacks her for no reason. Unfortunately it is not a state of peace everywhere else which is the main impact of the poem.

EXAMINER'S COMMENT

- *Makes one reasonable point about the impact of violence.*
- *Only slight engagement with the poem.*
- *No convincing analysis of the poet's language use.*
- *Expression could have been much more controlled.*
- *Mechanical errors ('soilder', 'intitled', 'should of', 'your').*
Marks awarded: 6/20

Sample Answer 2

Q2. (Impact of the poem)
(Top-grade response)

Although the language is simple in this poem, it actually makes the point that routine violence against women is still common in some societies. This makes a greater impact as the poem develops because the poet's tone is almost relaxed in the first stanza – 'I switched the radio on as usual'. The programme is truly shocking. Boland points out the stark difference between what we take for granted as normality here at home and the grotesque reality of life in conflict areas, such as the Middle East.

The vivid image of the attack on the civilian is horrific. The poet creates a dramatic effect by contrasting the girl's beauty and the brutal violence she experiences. The guard's vicious action is foreshadowed by the earlier image of the poet herself using a kitchen knife to slice vegetables. I can relate to her sense of revulsion as she imagines the Iranian policeman's use of a razor blade to replace 'one red gash with another'.

The quiet tone of the final stanza reflects her sense of failure, 'left standing there in my kitchen'. Vivid images of the half-chopped vegetables, particularly the 'scarlet circles of the peppers', are closely associated with the 'Delicate mouths' of vulnerable women who suffer vicious abuse and injustice.

EXAMINER'S COMMENT

- *Convincing personal response to the question.*
- *Points are clear, incisive and aptly supported.*
- *Links theme and stylistic features very well.*
- *Perceptive analysis of tone, imagery and contrast.*
- *Excellent expression, fluent and varied.*
- *Marks awarded: 20/20*

REMEMBER!

Avoid wasting time worrying about any words in an Unseen Poem that you don't understand. Instead, focus on what makes sense to you.

Unseen Poem Revision Points

- **Study the wording of questions** to identify the task that you have to do.

- Express your **key points** clearly.

- Include **supportive reference or quotation** (correctly punctuated).

- Refer to both the poet's **style** (how the poem is written) as well as the **themes** (what the poet is writing about).

- **Select interesting phrases** that give you an opportunity to discuss subject matter and use of language.

- **Avoid summaries** that simply repeat the text of the poem.

- **Engage with the poem** by responding genuinely to what the poet has written.

Unseen Poem – Practice 5

Read the following poem by Pat Boran and answer **either** Question 1
or Question 2 which follow. (Allow 20 minutes to complete the answer.)

5 Stalled Train

In the listening carriage, someone's
phone
cries out for help. A student frisks
himself,
a woman weighs her handbag
then stares into space. Our train
is going nowhere. We've stood here
so long now the cattle in this field
have dared come right up close
to chew and gaze. We tell ourselves
that somewhere down the line
things we cannot understand
are surely taking place — the future
almost within reach — and into each
small telephone that rings
or shudders now, like doubt,
we commit (if still in whispers)
our hopes and fears, our last known
whereabouts.

Pat Boran

1. (a) In your opinion, is the dominant mood in the poem positive or
negative? Explain your answer with reference to the poem. (10)

(b) Identify two images from the poem that you find interesting
and give reasons for your choice. (10)

OR

2. Discuss the impact of this poem, with reference to
its theme and the poet's use of language and
imagery. Refer closely to the text in support
of your answer. (20)

PROMPT!

• *Think about the poet's
attitude to modern life.*
• *Imagery is vivid, graphic,
cinematic.*
• *Surreal, mysterious, dream-like
atmosphere.*
• *Effective use of personification and
symbols.*
• *Final lines are disturbing.*
• *Poem raises many
interesting questions.*

Acknowledgements

The authors and publisher are grateful to the following for permission to reproduce copyrighted material:

'Lipstick' by Rosita Boland, from *Dissecting the Heart*, 2003. Copyright © Rosita Boland, reproduced by kind permission of the author and The Gallery Press, Loughcrew, Oldcastle, County Meath, Ireland;

'Autumn' by Alan Bold. Copyright © Alan Bold, reprinted with permission of Alice Bold;

'Stalled Train' by Pat Boran, from *Then Again*, 2019. Copyright © Pat Boran, reproduced by kind permission of Dedalus Press;

'There's a certain Slant of light', 'I felt a Funeral, in my Brain', 'A Bird came down the Walk', 'I Heard a fly buzz – when I died', 'The Soul has Bandaged moments', 'I could bring You Jewels – had I a mind to', 'A narrow Fellow in the Grass', 'I taste a liquor never brewed', 'After great pain, a formal feeling comes' by Emily Dickinson. *The Poems of Emily Dickinson: Reading Edition*, edited by Ralph W. Franklin, Cambridge, Mass.: The Belknap Press of Harvard University Press, Copyright © 1998, 1999 by the President and Fellows of Harvard College. Copyright © 1951, 1955 by the President and Fellows of Harvard College. Copyright © renewed 1979, 1983 by the President and Fellows of Harvard College. Copyright © 1914, 1918, 1919, 1924, 1929, 1930, 1932, 1935, 1937, 1942 by Martha Dickinson Bianchi. Copyright © 1952, 1957, 1958, 1963, 1965 by Mary L. Hampson;

'At Cider Mill Farm' by David Harmer, from *The Works 3* chosen by Paul Cookson, published by Macmillan Children's Books, 2004. Copyright © David Harmer, used by permission of the author;

'The Forge', 'Bogland', 'The Tollund Man', 'Sunlight', 'A Constable Calls', 'The Skunk', 'The Harvest Bow', 'The Underground', 'Postscript', 'A Call', 'Tate's Avenue', 'The Pitchfork', 'Lightenings viii' by Seamus Heaney, from *100 Poems*, published by Faber and Faber Ltd, 2018;

'Cora, Auntie', 'Hearth Lesson', 'Prayer for the Children of Longing', 'Death of a Field', 'Them Ducks Died for Ireland', 'The Exact Moment I Became a Poet' by Paula Meehan, reprinted by kind permission of Carcanet Press, Manchester, UK. 'Buying Winkles', 'The Pattern', 'The Statue of the Virgin at Granard Speaks', 'My Father Perceived as a Vision of St. Francis' by Paula Meehan, reprinted by kind permission of Dedalus Press. All poems from *As If By Magic: Selected Poems*, published by Dedalus Press, 2020;

'Roller-Skaters' by Grace Nichols, from *Give Yourself a Hug*, 1994. Copyright © Grace Nichols, reproduced with permission of Curtis Brown Group Limited, London on behalf of Grace Nichols;

'Lucina Schynning in Silence of the Nicht', 'The Second Voyage', 'Deaths and Engines', 'Street', 'Fireman's Lift', 'All for You', 'Following', 'Kilcash', 'Translation', 'The Bend in the Road', 'On Lacking the Killer Instinct', 'To Niall Woods and Xenya Ostrovskaia, married in Dublin on 9 September 2009' by Eiléan Ní Chuilleanáin, from *Collected Poems*, 2020. All poems reproduced by kind permission of the author and The Gallery Press, Loughcrew, Oldcastle, County Meath, Ireland;

'Black Rook in Rainy Weather', 'The Times are Tidy', 'Morning Song', 'Finisterre', 'Mirror', 'Pheasant', 'Elm', 'Poppies in July', 'The Arrival of the Bee Box', 'Child' by Sylvia Plath, from *Collected Poems*, published by Faber and Faber Ltd, 2002.